CONFORM TO DEFORM

THE WEIRD &
WONDERFUL WORLD OF
SOME BIZZARE

WESLEY DOYLE

JAW
BONE

CONFORM TO DEFORM
THE WEIRD & WONDERFUL
WORLD OF SOME BIZZARE
WESLEY DOYLE

A Jawbone book
First edition 2023
Published in the UK and the USA by
Jawbone Press
Office G1
141–157 Acre Lane
London SW2 5UA
England
www.jawbonepress.com

ISBN 978-1-911036-95-1

Printed by Short Run Press, Exeter, Devon

1 2 3 4 5 27 26 25 24 23

TABLE OF CONTENTS

INTRODUCTION

ON JULY 15, 1983, the electronic duo Soft Cell appeared on the Channel 4 music show *Switch*. The pair—Marc Almond and Dave Ball—had scored a massive global hit two years previously with their cover of Gloria Jones's 'Tainted Love', but since that initial success they seemed unconcerned about maintaining a career as pop stars, and their music had become darker and consciously less commercial. For their *Switch* appearance, they appeared as they always had done: Almond up front with Ball on keys at the back. They rattled through a ramshackle version of forthcoming single 'Soul Inside' before Almond introduced saxophonist Gary Barnacle and guest vocalist Clint Ruin. Sat in front of the TV, my fourteen-year-old self was unaware that his life was about to take a turn.

Ruin—resplendent in leather jacket, aviator shades, and gravity-defying quiff—emitted a blood-curdling scream before the drum machine kicked in and he and Almond began trading lines. Ball abandoned his keyboard for some heavily distorted guitar, and Barnacle seemed to be playing a different song entirely. The reverb on the vocals soon made whatever words were being sung indecipherable, and Almond and Ruin ended up in a heap on the floor, entangled in microphone leads, screaming into each other's faces. Five minutes in and, with the cacophony showing no sign of an end, the producers ran the credits and the screen faded to black. It was the most incredible thing I'd ever seen.

I was already a big fan of Soft Cell. I'd liked 'Tainted Love', but I didn't properly fall for their seedy synth-pop until the follow-up single, 'Bedsitter'. I was given their debut album, *Non Stop Erotic Cabaret*, for Christmas in 1981 and eagerly followed their exploits in the pages of *Smash Hits* and occasionally *Sounds* or *Record Mirror*. As much as I loved Soft Cell, though, it was the 1983 album *Untitled* by Almond's side project Marc & The Mambas that really expanded my musical horizons. It wasn't just the other artists' songs he covered—Lou Reed, Scott Walker, Syd Barrett; all new to me—it was the people he worked with: Anni Hogan, the preternaturally talented pianist who would be at Almond's side for much of his 80s solo work; and Matt Johnson, who co-wrote and played on several tracks. Johnson also recorded as

THE THE, and when his 'Uncertain Smile' single was released a few months later, I bought it on spec. It remains one of my favourite records. Soon, I started to notice all this new music had the same two words on the sleeves: Some Bizzare.

They also had cryptic messages, signed by the mysterious 'Ø'. 'You can only have 100% trust in yourself.' 'Destruction is not negative, you must destroy to build.' 'With every kick in the face and every hurdle you pass the rewards get greater.' Through the music press I discovered 'Ø' was in fact Some Bizzare boss Stevo, who, despite only being a teenager, was managing these artists and brokering deals with major record labels on their behalf. The more I read about Stevo, it became apparent that he was as much a focus for the press as his artists, and he was heavily involved in how they were presented to the world.

Part of that presentation was the artwork that adorned the records—all Some Bizzare releases had the most incredible sleeves. Whether the vivid images captured by photographer Peter Ashworth, the evocative design and brush work of Huw Feather, the beautifully grotesque paintings of Val Denham, or the twisted and disturbing art of Andy 'Dog' Johnson, the visual side of Some Bizzare was as striking as the music.

The uncredited song Soft Cell played on that *Switch* performance was 'Ghostrider' by Suicide. I also discovered that 'Clint Ruin' was an Australian called J.G. Thirlwell, who recorded under the name Scraping Foetus Off The Wheel—you can imagine how that went down in my local Our Price. I set about seeking out not only the music of other Some Bizzare artists but the bands they aligned with: Nick Cave, The Cure, Siouxsie & The Banshees, Danielle Dax, Sex Gang Children. I also caught the Batcave tour when it came to the neighbouring town of St Albans. I'd found my tribe.

When Marc & The Mambas' second album, *Torment And Toreros,* arrived later in the year, it shocked and elated me in equal measure. It was dark, passionate, vicious, tortured, beautiful, and damned. Johnson wasn't on it this time, but the name Frank Want was. That name also featured on THE THE's debut album, *Soul Mining*. Frank, it transpired, was another pseudonym for J.G. Thirlwell. The pieces were falling into place.

Nostalgia was a notable absence in the early-to-mid 80s; there was no looking back, the momentum was always forward. I never bought a record from a previous decade—why would I? There was so much going on right in front of me. Everything about Some Bizzare was new—the artists, the attitude. It was transgressive but courted the mainstream, it was oblique but wanted to communicate, it was niche but didn't see why it couldn't be incredibly successful. I made many a blind purchase during this time. As a teenager, this was a great financial risk: £5.49 was a lot of money, so you had to commit to your purchases. Not that I ever had any problem with a Foetus or Cabaret Voltaire record, but I'd be lying if I said there weren't some worrying moments when Psychic TV and Einstürzende Neubauten first hit the turntable. And as for Swans . . . But I persevered, and through Some Bizzare my ideas of what popular music could be kept expanding.

So who were the people who brought these new sounds to us? I was endlessly fascinated by Stevo and the Some Bizzare family. On record-buying trips to London, I would wander through St Anne's Court, past the Some Bizzare offices at Trident Studios, and look up at the windows. *What is going on up there?* I'd wonder. Plenty, as I've since found out.

Much has been written about maverick record label bosses from the 1980s, including Creation's Alan McGee, Factory's Tony Wilson, and Postcard's Alan Horne, all of whom were, to varying degrees, headline-makers in their own right. Stevo and Some Bizzare had a roster to rival them all, yet his tale remained untold. His label released music that was challenging and credible yet still capable of serious commercial success. Both as record label and management company, Some Bizzare not only brought the world Soft Cell and THE THE but also gave left-field acts such as Cabaret Voltaire, Psychic TV, and Einstürzende Neubauten a decent crack at mainstream success. Yet for all the incredible music Some Bizzare produced, the impact these releases had on popular culture, and the cast of colourful characters—not least of all Stevo himself—no one had been prepared to get that story down. I couldn't understand why. So my reason for writing this book is simple: I wanted to read it, and it seemed no one else was going to do it.

Once a publishing deal was in place, it was a case of tracking the relevant people down and convincing them to contribute. It became apparent that Stevo's complex business relationships with the artists and major labels he licensed them to might just be the reason this book hadn't been written before. It would surely take a lawyer, not a music writer, to unravel all the contractual disputes and labyrinthine legal wrangles that plague the label to this day. But that would have made for a very dull book indeed. Instead, I channelled my fourteen-year-old self and wrote the Some Bizzare book he would have wanted to read: light on litigation, heavy on the music and the mavericks who made it.

The process of writing this oral history has given me the opportunity to talk with those mavericks. It's been a labour of love, and I hope I've done them and their work justice. A few key artists are sadly no longer with us, and a couple didn't want to be involved. But of the eighty or so individuals I interviewed, most had happy memories of the time when the Some Bizzare offices—wherever they happened to be—became not just a workplace but a home.

As for Stevo—who initially took a lot of convincing to be involved, then eventually tried to take over—he was everything I could have wanted and more. A complicated, contrary figure who feels shut out from the industry in which he made his name, he is the Peter Pan of post-punk. His desire to correct the record and right wrongs as he saw them left me with hours and hours of audio to work with. And despite the bluster and obfuscation—intentional and otherwise—he's still capable of creating sparks of genius. He is also a genuinely funny man. No matter how exasperating he can be—and believe me, he can—I could never truly feel aggrieved by Stevo. I sincerely hope his plans for a Some Bizzare relaunch come to fruition, and all the music he facilitated in the 80s and 90s and beyond will be remastered and available as shiny new reissues. I'll be the first person in the queue for them.

Just I was finishing off this book, Soft Cell headed out to play their first North American shows in twenty years. The five-date tour—sadly without Dave Ball for health reasons—arrived at New York's Beacon Theatre on August 30, 2022. After playing through a selection of new and back catalogue material, Marc Almond announced a special guest for the encore, and out strode J.G. Thirlwell, still stick thin, this time resplendent in a white suit. They tore through 'Ghostrider', just as they had on that TV show nearly four decades earlier. It was just as wild and chaotic, beautiful, and righteous—weird and wonderful. Still Bizzare after all these years.

WESLEY DOYLE, OCTOBER 2022

CAST OF CHARACTERS

In order of appearance . . .

STEVO (Stephen Pearce, founder of Some Bizzare, 1980–present)

J.G. THIRLWELL (Scraping Foetus Off The Wheel, You've Got Foetus On Your Breath, Foetus Art Terrorism, Foetus Uber Frisco, Foetus All-Nude Review, Foetus Interruptus, Wiseblood)

STEPHEN 'MAL' MALLINDER (Cabaret Voltaire)

DANIEL MILLER (The Normal; founder of Mute Records)

STEVE PARRY (Neu Electrikk)

DAVID KNIGHT (The Fast Set)

ROGER QUAIL (Clock DVA)

CHRIS BOHN (writer, *NME*)

TONY MAYO (Naked Lunch)

MATT JOHNSON (THE THE)

MARC ALMOND (Soft Cell, Marc & The Mambas, solo artist)

HUW FEATHER (illustrator, designer)

NICK CASH (Fad Gadget, Unmen)

VAL DENHAM (artist, painter)

JOSE WARDEN (Vicious Pink Phenomena)

BRIAN MOSS (Vicious Pink Phenomena)

DAVE BALL (Soft Cell, The Grid)

ANNI HOGAN (Marc & The Mambas, The Willing Sinners, La Magia, solo artist)

MARK CHUNG (Einstürzende Neubauten)

ROB COLLINS (Some Bizzare, 1983–86)

GAVIN FRIDAY (Virgin Prunes)

BEVERLEY GLICK (writer, *Sounds*, *Record Mirror*)

STEVE HOVINGTON (B-Movie)

MARTIN PATTON (Dead Good Records; Some Bizzare, 1980–82)

NEIL ARTHUR (Blancmange)

PETER ASHWORTH (photographer)

CHRIS ANDREWS (Blah Blah Blah)

RUSTY EGAN (Visage, Blitz Club DJ; Trident Studios co-owner)

JULIA ADAMSON (Illustration)

JANE ROLINK (Some Bizzare, 1982–87)

POLLY BIRKBECK (PR, Savage & Best)

MIKE THORNE (producer)

JOHN LUONGO (producer, president of Pavillion Records)

KARL O'CONNOR (Regis, British Murder Boys; founder of Downwards Records)

JESSAMY CALKIN (writer)

FLOOD (producer)

IAN TREGONING (producer, manager of Yello)

ZEKE MANYIKA (Orange Juice, solo artist)

STEVE SHERLOCK (Neu Electrikk, Marc & The Mambas)

ALAURA O'DELL (Paula P-Orridge, Psychic TV, Temple Ov Psychic Youth)

PAUL 'BEE' HAMPSHIRE (Into A Circle, Temple Ov Psychic Youth)

ANNE STEPHENSON (Venomettes, Marc & The Mambas)

GINI BALL (Venomettes, Marc & The Mambas)

ANDREAS McELLIGOTT (aka Andi Sex Gang of Sex Gang Children)

TEST DEPT

PAUL WHITE (designer)

CARLOS PERON (Yello, solo artist)

BRIAN POOLE (Renaldo & The Loaf)

MICHAEL GIRA (Swans)

JARBOE (Swans)

WARNE LIVESEY (producer)

JOHN GRANT (solo artist)

KEVIN FOAKES (DJ Food, Strictly Kev; designer)

DAVE BARTRAM (Showaddywaddy)

LEE KAVANAGH (Some Bizzare, 1988–92)

RICHARD NORRIS (The Grid)

MIKE HOLDSWORTH (Some Bizzare, 1990–92)

TIM HUTTON (solo artist)

PAUL SHEARSMITH (Echo City)

COLIN SCHAVERIEN (Some Bizzare, 1996–99)

ANDY WIGMORE (Some Bizzare PR, 1996)

CHRIS WILKIE (Dubstar)

BILLY REEVES (theaudience)

ANDY JONES (Koot)

ANDY PETTITT (Some Bizzare, 1999–2004)

KAI MOTTA (solo artist)

LARA PADDOCK (Some Bizzare, 2007–08)

HUW WILLIAMS (Risqué)

PEDRO GRANJA DE CARVALHO (Pedro INF, solo artist)

9

Pre-1980 Redefining the prologue

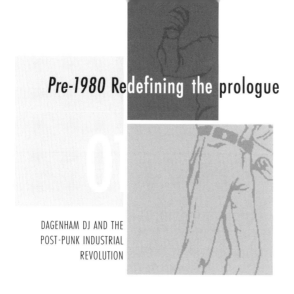

DAGENHAM DJ AND THE
POST-PUNK INDUSTRIAL
REVOLUTION

I was a very difficult child. I had a speech impediment until I was 14. I couldn't pronounce S, F, PH, C, CH, so I couldn't read and write. So they put me in the dunces' class. I did work experience schemes. I was on probation, never went to school. It was funny, I saw an advert on television: 'Truancy, they'll end up criminals,' it said. I said, 'Hold on, I never went to school.' I didn't know what the word 'patronising' meant, but you can feel it. My last school report said, 'Your son will never get further than the dole queue.' I came into this business with nothing and if I leave it with nothing, I've lost nothing.

STEVO to Paul Sexton, *Select*, February 1991

J.G. THIRLWELL I was lucky enough to live in London between 1978 and 1983, which was just such an incredible time for music. And the London that I experienced—still very much a post-war city in a lot of ways—is gone now. People like Matt Johnson grew up there and could tell a lot more stories, but when I arrived in 1978 it was a really crazy and wonderful time to be there. If you imagine punk rock as the Big Bang, then this was the aftershock and the expanding universe of post-punk. A lot of people who were liberated by the revolutionary and antisocial aspect of punk rock were also kind of bored by the traditional rock'n'roll form that music was rooted in, and they were the ones who ended up taking a radical and different approach to their instruments. That evolution happened so quickly; PIL were only a year on from the Sex Pistols, and the leap Wire made from *Pink Flag* to *154* was huge. Siouxsie & The Banshees, The Pop Group, Scritti Politti, This Heat, Throbbing Gristle; it was like this splintered universe that was enabled by the explosion of independent labels.

STEPHEN 'MAL' MALLINDER I feel it's perhaps one of the most significant times in terms of popular culture, in the sense that punk, for all its laudable intent, the bulk of it wasn't particularly innovative or creative. There were obviously good records, but it felt like the embers underneath were much more interesting—things like The Pop Group, A Certain Ratio, Orange Juice, the people who were in the slipstream of punk. That felt like something new, whereas punk was an energy, but in terms of the music, it just felt quite anachronistic to us. All the things that came in on the tailcoats of punk I thought was the more interesting, rather than stuff like The Damned. PIL were almost a case study in punk and what came after: they emerged out of what the Sex Pistols were doing and encapsulated how punk broke down into the new stuff.

DANIEL MILLER Punk was obviously a defining moment in music, and not just the music itself but the attitude and the DIY aesthetic that came out of it. So there was punk rock, which was the music, and then there was a punk ideology, and a lot of people who weren't really musicians saw things through this punk prism. And I think quite a lot of those were big fans of electronic music. It was a very exciting period—you could call it post-punk, but not as a genre.

STEVE PARRY There was so much going on in London at that time, independent wise. The Throbbing Gristle happenings, This Heat, it was incredibly creative, inventive, it was a really buoyant time. I think it may have been a reaction to some of the politics in the country.

The North was a pretty desperate place, the towns and cities seemed to be decaying, so people were drawn to London, I think. There were the remnants of the Sheffield scene, people like Vice Versa, and the likes of Thomas Leer had come down from Scotland.

DAVID KNIGHT After punk stirred things up, the live music scene in London was buzzing with great bands playing almost every night, and I was lucky enough to live there. Two gigs I saw in 1978 affected my musical direction deeply—Throbbing Gristle at the Filmmakers' Co-Op, and This Heat at the Basement Club, Covent Garden. Two very obscure bands at the time, in two tiny off-the-rock-circuit venues. Both grabbed my already inquisitive conceptions of music with both hands and squeezed them into new shapes. I'd just started work and managed to get my hands on an EMS VCS3 synthesizer—just like the one Eno had. I spent most evenings noodling away recording sound-on-sound cacophonies onto my Akai 4000DS reel-to-reel. Interestingly, while I was synthing away in my bedroom in my parents' Battersea council flat, just across Westbridge Road on the adjacent estate, Thomas Leer and Robert Rental were recording their fabulous *The Bridge* album. I'd seen the address on the back of Rental's single but was too shy to go across and knock.

STEPHEN 'MAL' MALLINDER The interesting thing with Sheffield was that it didn't really have a record label as such. Edinburgh had Fast, Manchester had Factory, Liverpool had Zoo, London had Rough Trade. Sheffield had bands, but it didn't have an aggregator that a label provided. There was a noticeable void in the sense Sheffield relied on other agencies to put its music out. I don't know why that was, there just wasn't a massive entrepreneurial streak. Steve Singleton had Neutron, which had really good releases, but it came as a response to what was happening rather than a catalyst—all the early movers, like ourselves, The Human League, and The Comsat Angels, had already gone with other labels. There was no media based in Sheffield either. So, even though things did become decentralised by punk, that was pushed more by people like Tony Wilson or Bill Drummond. Sheffield didn't quite experience it in the same way, which is why we had our records released by labels outside of the city.

ROGER QUAIL Sheffield was insular, but not in a bad way, and everyone was quite supportive of each other. Cabaret Voltaire were always very generous with their time in helping other young bands who were trying to get started. Maybe there is this image of the Cabs as being very dour and very Northern, and quite serious. My experience of Richard, Mal, and Chris is the opposite of that: they were really warm, friendly, funny, and affable people to spend time with, and also brilliantly creative people as well. As a band, Clock DVA were very lucky to fall in with people who would try to keep an eye out for us.

CHRIS BOHN You'd get some incredible double bills back then, like The Birthday Party and DAF at the Moonlight Club in West Hampstead, or Throbbing Gristle and Cabaret Voltaire at the Prince of Wales Conference Centre, below the YMCA on Tottenham Court Road. I'd try to get to gigs early to make sure I saw both bands, and there'd be four or five people in the queue ahead of me. There was always this character with a massive flop of red hair coming forward with really odd eye makeup and I'd think, *Who's that freak?* He probably looked at me and thought, *Who's that square?* After a while we were on nodding terms, and then one day I was walking up Tottenham Court Road with Wolfgang Spelmans from DAF and we bumped into 'the freak,' and it turned out his name was Jim and he worked in the singles department at Virgin, and we got chatting about all the great records coming out of Germany on the Zickzack label. He was also putting out his own music under a variety of names that incorporated the word Foetus on his own Self Immolation label.

J.G. THIRLWELL I would go to Rough Trade all the time, and then I worked in a record store, so I knew everything that was coming out. And at that time, it was possible to keep up with all the releases. You could see the bands too, as they played all the time. People like Monochrome Set, Joy Division, Swell Maps, and Essential Logic would play in London every couple of weeks, and it was, like, 50p to get in. Then there was Daniel Miller putting out his single as The Normal on his own label Mute, which showed not only had the way music was created been democratised, but so too had the way it was manufactured and distributed. There was just a flood of creativity and things seem to happen really fast.

STEVO At school, if you're not taking exams because you can't read the questions, and you've got a speech impediment, etc., then they just try and get you a job. So, for two days a week, you'd go to work, and then they'd up it to three days and then four, and by the time it comes to leave school you're already employed. The first job they got me doing was painting and decorating, then I started at Phonogram's manufacturing plant in Chadwell Heath, which led to working in their warehouse on the River Road Industrial Estate in Barking. I then moved onto delivering for them, so I was taking vinyl to all the shops in West End. We'd pull up in the van, and I'd jump out with four really big, heavy boxes, straight into the shop, signature, out, next shop. I wasn't working *for* Phonogram, just the

13

company that dealt with their distribution. I've never worked for any record label except my own.

TONY MAYO Naked Lunch formed in 1979 and came from punk, but we started using synths. The electronic music circles we moved in were more about having fun than punk was, more hedonistic than nihilistic. We were using old analogue synths, monophonic ones where we had to manually change patches between songs. At the same time, we were facing an audience who weren't used to electronic bands and were more interested in people with guitars leaping around and being abusive and spitting. Obviously we were aware of bands like The Human League and Fad Gadget, but everyone was very much in their own bubbles, getting on with their own stuff. Bands would cross paths, but they weren't really interacting.

DAVID KNIGHT A friend worked at Beggars Banquet's Earls Court shop, and I'd given them a cassette of my home recordings. One day he was listening to it in the shop, and the co-manager, Peter Kent, asked who it was. On being told, Peter said something along the lines of, 'Me and Ivo Watts-Russell are starting a label, tell your friend if he wants to do an electronic version of a glam rock song, we'll put it out.' The Human League had already covered a Gary Glitter song, so it felt a bit unoriginal, and I didn't really do 'songs', but I was being offered a deal without even trying. The three-note riff of T. Rex's 'Children Of The Revolution' was just about within the range of my keyboard skills, so I quickly recorded a version at home, which Peter and Ivo liked. I needed a B-side, so I knocked 'Junction One' together on the spot. For some reason it was decided that should be the A-Side. Peter and Ivo named their label Axis, and my single was one of the first releases.

MATT JOHNSON In the late 1970s I was working in Soho at Music de Wolfe's recording studio. I was out most nights at gigs. I got to know quite a lot of people in what's now referred to as the post-punk scene. I wasn't a fan of punk, but there was that wonderful couple of years immediately after, which I think was one of the most fertile times in British music. It was a small scene so I got to know a lot of the people involved quite well: Wire, This Heat, Throbbing Gristle, Thomas Leer, J.G. Thirlwell, Cabaret Voltaire, Daniel Miller, amongst many others. I also spent a lot of time hanging around the offices of various independent record labels, playing my early recordings—tracks from *See Without Being Seen* and the unreleased *Spirits* album—to the likes of Mike Alway at Cherry Red, Ivo at 4AD, Geoff Travis at Rough Trade and Rod Pearce at Fetish records.* I was a teenager, but I was very ambitious and anxious to get going. I'd been in bands since I was eleven, so I felt I should really start putting records out.

MARC ALMOND I started at Leeds Polytechnic Fine Art department in 1976, just at the time when the whole punk scene was starting to happen in a big way. In music, in the media, in fashion, it was all anyone was talking about, and it certainly influenced the work I was doing at the time. During my first few weeks at the college, the Anarchy tour came to the Poly, with the Sex Pistols, The Clash, and the Heartbreakers. And on the TV viewers were outraged by swearing on the *Today* show with Bill Grundy. Siouxsie Sioux was one of the Pistols followers at that time, before becoming a prominent figure on the punk scene herself. Siouxsie & The Banshees were hugely influential to me. Barely a week went by without two or three of the current bands playing at the college or at the University. And Leeds clubs such as F Club and the Warehouse showcased all the big names and the acts who were influenced by them. It was a musical feast to gorge on, you could go out every night and see a great—or sometimes not so great—band. But you went to see everybody.

HUW FEATHER Marc and I met at King George V gramma school in Southport, which was full of lovely, white middle-class Tory boys. He was new and I was asked by the headmaster to help him induct him into the school. I was a theatre geek, and I loved conjuring, stage craft and illusion, and wanted to be a magician. I was also in love with London, and because I had relations there, I was allowed to go on the train from an early age to see the magicians, musicals, and variety theatre. All these things seemed to be in Soho, so there was huge romance attached to the area for me. Marc and I hung out together and developed a passion for sleaze glamour, films, theatre, camp—all those kinds of things. We spent summers working in Southport together, including the Flora Hall & Theatre, so we were learning about things like stagecraft, stage handling, spotlighting; all the stuff that makes a show happen. Then we were both kicked out of school on the same day and both enrolled in the art college on the same day. We did projects together and had our

---

* No relation to Stevo.

tables next to each other in our own little corner, and it was there we developed our design relationship from the age of sixteen onward.

MARC ALMOND It's hard to underestimate the DIY, cut-and-paste, in-your-face, transgressive and political influence punk had on many of the art students at the college, me included. When I started there I had a bad Bolan-influenced perm, and within a week or two I'd cut it all off, spiked it up, and dyed it black or blonde, depending on my mood. I wore eye makeup every day and dressed in thrift store glam or the latest punk inspired clothes from X Clothes in Leeds. A couple of other art students, Tony and Michelle, made spattered T-shirts of punk imagery, and I wore them with drainpipes. My main performance works at the time were punk-inspired, dark, campy, transgressive performance art with Throbbing Gristle–inspired soundtracks. I sometimes performed outside of the relative safety of the art department under stupid pseudonyms like Peter Mayhem, shocking drama students by bursting blood capsules while wearing a wedding dress or smearing cat food all over my body, all set to a thrashed guitar soundtrack. A reviewer called it the most nihilistic and depressing thing he'd ever seen, and I was proud of that. A number of musicians started out at Leeds Fine Art Polytechnic, including Green Gartside from Scritti Politti and my good friend Frank Tovey aka Fad Gadget. Sheffield also had a burgeoning raw electronic scene—Human League, Cabaret Voltaire, and Vice Versa (who became ABC).

NICK CASH I met Frank Tovey at St Martins School of art on a foundation course in '74–75. Frank and I collaborated on some artwork and became friends. He went to Leeds Polytechnic to do performance, and when he came back to London he made his first single for Mute under the name Fad Gadget. I did some percussion on the album, *Fireside Favourites*, and he asked me to do some gigs, but I was playing with PragVEC at the time so couldn't.

DANIEL MILLER At Mute we didn't have a clue what we were doing, really—we didn't know how to make records, we didn't know how to release records, we just did it on instinct. And I think that was what was very exciting about it.

VAL DENHAM In the summer of 1979, an old college friend invited me to their final degree show presentation at the Leeds Polytechnic art department. It was a performance piece called *The Surreal Tea Room*. There was a piano, and the room was filled with art students all sipping tea from cups and saucers. A piano was being played and a mysterious little person kept walking in and out of the room, wearing a white waiter's jacket and too much makeup, asking if they needed more tea. I asked my friend who he was. 'Oh that's Marc,' he replied. 'You'll get on with him.'

JOSE WARDEN Marc and I hung out with the same crowd back in Leeds during the late 70s. We were the ones that didn't quite fit in with everyone else, and just gravitated toward each other. I was introduced to Dave Ball in 1979 when he teamed up with Marc to form Soft Cell.

BRIAN MOSS Jose and I got on really well with Marc and Dave—they were talented people but also had a great sense of humour, were easy going and into the same things as us.

DAVE BALL Marc had heard my strange electronic bleeps coming out of the college studio and popped in for a cup of tea. He said he was working on a new performance piece and wondered if I would be interested in creating some mad electronic music for him to use. I remember working on two of Marc's pieces, 'Glamour In Squalor' and 'Twilights & Lowlifes'. The titles have always stuck in my mind as they summed up the underlying themes of many of our future collaborations as Soft Cell, as well as Marc's solo work.

MARC ALMOND From this melting pot came Soft Cell—our sound and image was shaped by my performance art pieces and the songs Dave was writing about his consumerist nightmare dystopian world view. He had a Korg synthesizer, which was an exotic rare instrument at the time, and initially we were inspired by the US punk of Suicide and Devo, German electronica like Kraftwerk, UK industrial music, glam, punk, and northern soul. This was all shot through with our dark, sardonic sense of humour and a jaded sarcasm.

ANNI HOGAN I went to Leeds University in 1979 to do international history and politics, and it was quite an exclusive course, but as soon as I got there all I wanted to do was music. My freshers' week gig was Buzzcocks supported by Joy

17

Division. Buzzcocks was absolutely thrillingly amazing, but Joy Division blew my mind. After that it was A Certain Ratio, Siouxsie & The Banshees, Magazine, all amazing. Then I started going to the Faversham pub where the barman was a Bowie fanatic lookalike and the jukebox was packed with amazing alternative stuff, everything from post-punk to obscure electronic stuff. I started washing glasses at the Amnesia club, was asked to DJ and then ended up being the promotor on £7 a week. It was such a laugh, total amateur hour, but at the same time so amazing and transformative, the last great era of music probably.

STEVO There was a shop in Stratford that used to sell disco equipment, and my mum bought me a disco unit on hire purchase, through Provident Financial. I would use it to DJ, and then pay her back from the fees I was getting. That's how I started. The music I was buying as a consumer was jazz funk because I loved dance music, and soul. But I didn't want to play that when I was DJing, I wanted to play stuff that people hadn't heard before, the stranger bands that were around. My brother Joe used to listen to John Peel and he liked Cabaret Voltaire and Throbbing Gristle. I picked up on that music from my brother and would play it when I DJed. I was trying to make an atmosphere that was intensive.

MARK CHUNG Punk had arrived in Germany, as things did at that time, a couple of years late. There was quite a thriving independent scene in Germany for the first time, inspired by very much by the UK punk situation and the do-it-yourself ethos. Of course, there were some bands who were trying to be the UK Subs or Crass, but it quickly found its own flavour and became quite specific. Because Germany is a decentralised country, being a federal state and with the capital of West Berlin kind of out of the picture in many ways, you had all these subcentres—Dusseldorf, Cologne, Hamburg—that were all having their own music scenes. Many acts came from an anarchistic punk background, and it really was an alternative economy. I was in a Hamburg-based punk band called Abwärts, and we pressed up our own records and sold twenty thousand albums, which we thought was crazy.

ROB COLLINS I've never felt like I've ever had a real job. Record companies were very different back then compared to how they are now. It wasn't so structured and there weren't people turning up who had been to university to get a degree in music marketing. People would come up through the ranks, or like me start at the bottom. I left school, did some roadying, and then worked at Island Records in the post room. From there I went to Virgin and worked in A&R. It was a pretty raucous place, full of people who loved music and were very easy to get on with. So I was always going to shows or going to the pub and talking about music, and people were always having parties after work. There were the usual amount of substances going around, both in and out of the office, so it was a hell of a lot of fun. And the bands that Virgin were signing back then were bands that I was already really into, like Magazine, Simple Minds, and Japan.

GAVIN FRIDAY When you actually think of it, that post-punk period, from the late 70s to '83/'84, was such an extraordinary time. I'm not talking about the stuff that made the charts but the many great records and great bands that made up the alternative, and it's sort of ignored in many ways.

Virgin Prunes were never aligned with any goth movement or anything like that. We formed in Dublin in 1978 and how we looked was how we looked. I think a lot of the post-punk bands were really the bastard sons of Johnny Lydon and David Bowie. The latter was a big touchstone—the Berlin period opened up the synth and the alternative world even more. And then when the Sex Pistols broke up and PIL took on that Germanic, improvisational, DIY approach to music, they became another example of how to do it. There was a sort of unwritten rule that all majors were evil and bad, so there was a tendency to gravitate toward independent labels. The phrases 'rock'n'roll' and 'chart placing' were never on the agenda.

When you can see through people,
It may sometimes (hopefully not many) . . . hurt.
But when you can see, you know!
So your earnest altruistic attitude
Cannot be abused!!!

Ø, from the sleeve of THE THE's 'Perfect' twelve-inch (1983)

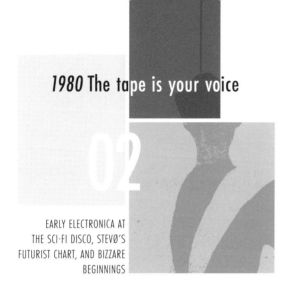

1980 The tape is your voice

EARLY ELECTRONICA AT
THE SCI-FI DISCO, STEVØ'S
FUTURIST CHART, AND BIZZARE
BEGINNINGS

STEVO Artist-and-repertoire is like a magnet. Artistically, if you produce something like Foetus, for example, it will inspire loads of young musicians. What I respected with Celluloid in France was that they were involved with Gong. And the same for Virgin, with Chrome; artists that sold very little, but inspired people, and brought other artists in. And that interested me. So, when I was DJing, bands heard about the music I was playing and wanted to be involved. I put on gigs in places like Retford and Canning Town, and bands approached me to play. That's what acquisition is.

DAVID KNIGHT The first four singles on the Axis label were released simultaneously on January 1, 1980: 'A new label for a new decade.' And also a label which wouldn't last longer than January, as they were immediately slapped with a lawyer's letter from an already-existent Axis label. All four singles were deleted once the initial pressings had sold out. I think around two thousand of each were pressed. Peter and Ivo renamed the label 4AD, and out of those initial bands just took Bauhaus with them.

MARC ALMOND I used to spend all my money on records and clothes. At lunchtimes I worked at Leeds Playhouse behind the bar and at night at the Warehouse in the cloakroom. I eventually worked my way up to DJing, along with fellow student

Chris Neat (who later designed the 'Tainted Love' sleeve). We used to play early electronic music and the artier side of punk, influenced by what London clubs like Blitz and St Moritz were playing. New Romantic grew out of Punk, but it was a posier, more flamboyant movement. Early Soft Cell got tagged with the New Romantic label, but we didn't mind at first. We thought it was a good bandwagon to get us noticed in London, and besides I loved the dressing up aspect.

TONY MAYO We'd seen a handmade flyer for night at the Chelsea Drugstore on the Kings Road. It was billed as a 'Sci-Fi Disco' with 'DJ Stevo playing the weirdest sounds ever heard this side of the universe.' So we went to see who this 'Stevo' was and what he was playing. What we found was a seventeen-year-old kid playing all the stuff we were into, to a half-empty room. But he was like an excited puppy with boundless drive and enthusiasm. And ideas, lots of ideas. We had a chat with him and decided to combine forces and start pushing electronic music. If we were going to be a band then we needed an audience, so we wanted to get a scene going.

DAVID KNIGHT I received a call from Stevo, who had tracked me down through 4AD, saying he liked the single and would I like to meet him at the Chelsea Drugstore one Monday night when he held his regular electronic disco. Being a Chelsea/Battersea boy, the Drugstore was one of my local haunts, and it was great to know something of interest was going on nearby. When I got there I was disappointed to find the place was virtually empty, but it did give me a chance to talk to Stevo, while he played a selection of the newer electronic singles from Cabaret Voltaire, Throbbing Gristle, The Normal, Fad Gadget, John Foxx, Thomas Leer, the ubiquitous Kraftwerk, and . . . me. It was great to hear my single being played in public, even though the singing would turn me bright red with embarrassment. Stevo said he was planning to put on gigs and asked if I was interested in playing.

TONY MAYO In March we played at Studio 21 near Tottenham Court Road tube station. It was like the Blitz, one of the New Romantic electronic clubs, run by Jock McDonald, who despite being in punk act The Bollock Brothers was a pretty popular DJ and promotor on the emerging scene. It was very androgynous there, blurring the lines between sexuality. London was a bit aggressive then, but there was no fighting at Studio 21—it was a more relaxed environment. Until you left and then you'd get abuse from people outside or cab drivers. The scene was also very small, there were probably only about two hundred people in it originally down in London.

STEVO It would be interesting to see when the term *New Romantic* was actually first published, because if you said it to someone in 1980, they wouldn't know what the hell you were talking about. At the beginning you had Futurist music, and the Blitz Kids was separate scene, just a very small scene in London of rich kids dressing up. So you had the Blitz Kids and the Futurists, that was it—there was no New Romantic. New Romantic is something that has been put together by the media. New Romantic in 1980 is a lie.

BEVERLEY GLICK The whole New Romantic thing was still in its infancy, and it wasn't called that then, the name came later. It was still Bowie and Roxy nights at Billy's in the late 70s.* But that was separate from what Stevo was doing. There was always a split between the New Romantic Blitz crowd that Spandau Ballet and Visage emerged from, and the Futurist crowd where Stevo was really the leading figure. And one didn't have much time for the other really. The Blitz crowd looked down their noses at people like Stevo and Soft Cell.

J.G. THIRLWELL I knew Stevo peripherally prior to him starting the label. I was the singles buyer at Virgin Records on Oxford Street, and I would get in every obscure European import and keep a pretty deep stock. Stevo was delivering records for Phonogram as his day job and would DJ in the evening. So he would deliver boxes of records and sometimes buy records from us for his DJ set. And I knew Matt Johnson because we were both published by Cherry Red and I'd met him at their Christmas party. Prior to that I'd seen THE THE a bunch of times, and he'd seen me around at concerts and stuff, and we ended up becoming really good friends and later collaborators.

MATT JOHNSON I had multiple projects going on at the time. I'd already put out 'Controversial Subject', THE THE's first single with Ivo at 4AD. During this period, THE THE was sort of on-off, in that it was a constantly changing—and

---

* Bowie Nights at Billy's were held every Tuesday at the subterranean Soho club. Many of the regulars would go on to define what became known as the New Romantic scene when the club moved to the more upmarket Blitz in Covent Garden in 1980.

I was never quite sure who was in and who was out. Then there was a studio-only group with Colin Lloyd Tucker called The Gadgets, and we'd done an album for Vinyl Solution. Plus, I was still working at De Wolfe, so there was a lot happening. My main memories are of a very creative time, full of decent, interesting people who were very encouraging. I soon left De Wolfe to concentrate full time on music and went on the dole. I had very little money, but that was secondary to me and didn't really matter. I considered the dole as a sort of arts grant because, unlike my older brother, Andrew, I didn't go to college.

STEVE PARRY I answered a little ad in *NME* or *Sounds* and the bloke who put it in there was Matt Johnson. I remember him being really inquisitive, looking to do his own thing, and having a curious tuning on his guitar. I didn't know what contribution I could make to his stuff, so didn't take it any further. I then formed Neu Electrikk with a couple of other guys, Derek Morris and Steve Sherlock.

STEVE HOVINGTON B-Movie had established a local following in Mansfield and the surrounding area. We used to play a venue in Lincoln called the Vaults, literally setting up next to the cigarette machine with skinheads skulking in the corner. It was slightly terrifying, to be honest with you. We were doing gigs supporting The Angelic Upstarts at the Sandpiper in Nottingham, and it was a bit of a baptism of fire. We came to the attention of Martin Patton and Andy Stephenson, who ran Dead Good records. They liked us, and we recorded a couple of tracks for their *East* compilation album that they put out in 1980. We were a three-piece at the time, but we had big ideas. We were into Tubeway Army, early Ultravox, Simple Minds, and Magazine, and our aspiration was to be like those bands. Synths were just becoming sort of affordable and that was the direction we were aiming for. Then Rick Holliday joined, and we had the keyboard player we wanted.

MARTIN PATTON My business partner in Dead Good Andy Stephenson and I were using a local studio—and I use the term 'studio' loosely—run by two lovely guys out in little town called Wragby, just north of Lincoln. Andy Dransfield from the studio (who now owns and runs Chapel Studios at South Thoresby in Lincolnshire) suggested we should put together a compilation of Lincoln bands, which became the *East* album, on our own Dead Good label. That was financed entirely by the studio—we didn't put any money into it. B-Movie had been using the studio too, and Andy recommended we take a look at them, so we did and they went on the album. We ended up signing them to Dead Good and put out the *Take Three* EP, and then they did a brilliant session for Radio Trent in Nottingham, which was a big leap in their songwriting (I think this was when we first heard 'Nowhere Girl' and 'Remembrance Day'). We decided to release 'Nowhere Girl' on twelve-inch—the 'genius' idea was to have a twelve-inch single on one side and an album on the other. It ended up being a bit of a manufacturing nightmare and we failed to sort it out properly. We were literally making it up as we went along—we did not have a clue. However, despite this, Dead Good was now starting to get some national press, and it was around this time that we noticed *Sounds* (along with the *NME* and *Melody Maker*, one of the big three weekly music papers at the time) was publishing a 'Futurist' chart compiled by somebody called Stevo, so we sent them some records, and B-Movie appeared in it the following week.

TONY MAYO The first joint thing we did with Stevo was a gig at the Retford Porterhouse in Nottinghamshire. Stevo called it 'the first Futurist fun night': Cabaret Voltaire headlined, preceded by us and THE THE. Matt lived about five miles away from me, so we gave him a lift up, and we developed a friendship.

MATT JOHNSON I was living above my parents' pub, the Crown in Loughton, Essex, at the time, and I got a phone call out of the blue from Stevo—I don't know how he got my number. My dad used to laugh, because I was getting calls from Theo at Cherry Red publishing, Ivo at 4AD, and now Stevo. He would say, 'Who are these bloody blokes called O phoning up all the time?' I think Tony Mayo from Naked Lunch had already warned me about Stevo, saying he was a madman or whatever, but I took the call, and he asked us to support Cabaret Voltaire up in Retford at the Porterhouse. I was a big fan of Cabaret Voltaire, but I'd already put some records out by this point and we were now playing our own shows, so doing a gig 150 miles away for a crate of beer wasn't that appealing. He must have upped the offer to two crates of beer because we ended up doing it! It was good fun and Cabaret Voltaire were gentlemen. After that we got more and more involved with him.

ROGER QUAIL I've actually got a recording of that gig—it's really good, the Cabs were terrific. There was this bloke there who was the epitome of a cockney geezer, there is no other way to describe him. And that was Stevo. He was every kind of Del Boy stereotype that you could ever wish for manifested in front of you, and we just didn't know what to make of him, this motormouth bigging himself and this Futurist scene of his up. It may be a Sheffield thing, but we all had this innate distrust of Southerners, especially mouthy, cockney ones. But my prevailing memory is that he was wearing a black shirt that had the red Throbbing Gristle flash embroidered on front of it, which he proudly said his mum had done for him, which I just thought it was quite sweet, really. But it did make him look like a Futurist John Bull toby jug.

STEPHEN 'MAL' MALLINDER My first memory of meeting Stevo was at the Retford Porterhouse with THE THE. He was wearing a collarless shirt, like a Ben Sherman, but he'd put a big red Throbbing Gristle flash on the front of it. Matt and I were laughing at it, calling it 'Stevo's Throbbing Sherman'. I can't remember anything about the gig, but I remember that shirt!

STEVE HOVINGTON I saw an advert in *Sounds* for a DJ at the Chelsea Drugstore in London called Stevø, with a line through the 'o' to make it look avant-garde, and he was looking for bands to play down there. As luck had it, he'd organised a Cabaret Voltaire gig with THE THE at the Retford Porterhouse, which was our local venue. I went along and at the end of the evening plucked up the courage to give him tape on my way out. I'd never met anybody from London before, and Stevo was like one of those cockneys us blokes from the North wake up worrying about in the middle of the night. But he seemed like a nice chap, even with his accent. I got a phone call the following morning, saying he really liked the tape but we sounded like Hawkwind and should wear silver suits and furry boots onstage. He did ask us to come down to play in London, though, and we suddenly found one of the tracks from the tape, 'Walking Dead', was in his Futurist chart in *Sounds*.

BEVERLEY GLICK *Sounds* was still a rock paper when I started there; certainly the heavy metal and hard-rock genres were highly valued. But Alan Lewis, who was the editor at the time, had an awareness of the different tribes in music and wanted to serve them all. So he made space for the early electronic music, and then afterward for the New Romantic bands that I started to interview. Stevo was only seventeen and still a DJ when I first met him. As the editor's secretary at the time, I was the one tasked with trying to decipher his handwriting when he was asked to compile a Futurist chart for *Sounds*. He DJed at Chelsea Drugstore on the Kings Road at same time as Rusty was DJing at Blitz, so they were kind of contemporaries.

MARC ALMOND *Sounds* latched on to the burgeoning scene with their Futurist chart, which was where we first heard if this young DJ entrepreneur called Stevo. The chart consisted of bands he either knew or had seen play, or ones he'd discovered from the tapes and self-financed records he'd been sent.

In the dim and distant early months of 1980, a lone figure entered the *Sounds* scenario. Self-styled electro entrepreneur Stevo, complete with his half a lank fringe, offered up a chart the like of which had never before been witnessed. Full of bands who didn't fit the alternative label, weren't smart enough to be on Rough Trade, who mostly favoured the use of synthesised music. After much furrowing of brows in the editorial orifice [sic], a voice came from the blue proclaiming 'Let's call it a Futurist Chart!' And so, a new cult was born. At first the embryonic electro scene was taken with a pinch of salt, but week by week it gained in credibility and other so-called music papers took to discussing it as if it were their own.

BEVERLY GLICK (writing as Betty Page), *Sounds*, January 31, 1981

STEVO *They* called it the Futurist chart, not me. I used to clear the dance floor. I would go out for the purpose of doing that. My attitude was complete assault on the audience.

J.G. THIRLWELL Futurist was a short-lived term that ran parallel with New Romantic and was basically an umbrella term for alienated electronic music.

BEVERLEY GLICK Stevo was passionate about the music and played it all the time. From the fairly vanilla stuff from like Ultravox all the way through to Throbbing Gristle and the darker electronic stuff, with The Human League somewhere in the middle. So all of that music was under this big umbrella called Futurist, but when the New Romantics came along it all started to be divided up a bit.

ROGER QUAIL The Futurists were much more closely allied to industrial music, Throbbing Gristle, Cabaret Voltaire, DAF, Fad Gadget, that end of the spectrum, whereas I would associate the New Romantic thing more with people like Visage,

26

Ultravox, and this hilarious band from Barnsley called Danse Society. The Futurist thing was less flamboyant, more serious, and more experimental. But in terms of in terms of levels of pretentiousness they were reasonably equal.

NEIL ARTHUR I'd written embryonic versions of songs like 'I've Seen The Word', 'I Can't Explain', and 'Waves', which were influenced by Young Marble Giants, who I adored. Of course, my songs were massively improved by Stephen [Luscombe, Arthur's partner in Blancmange], but the main difference between what was on our first EP, *Irene & Mavis*, and the new stuff was structure: the new songs had verses and choruses. So, by the time we met Stevo, we'd moved on from the experimentation, tape loops, noises, and God-knows-what we were doing before.

TONY MAYO Stevo's Futurist chart was a mixture of available releases and demos from unsigned bands that he'd been sent. He put our demos of 'Weekend Behaviour' and 'Rabies' in there.

NEIL ARTHUR I remember the Futurist chart because tracks from the *Irene & Mavis* EP started appearing in it. The sleeve had Stephen's address on it, and Stevo got in touch. I met him and took the tube up to Stephen's place in Kilburn. I just didn't know what to make of Stevo at all, because he was dressed in all this gear that Gary Numan might have worn. We were wearing dead man's suits and overcoats, and I had a flat-top—that was the look. Stevo didn't look like that, he looked like he'd just stepped off of *Star Trek*. And that wasn't our scene: we were into Cabaret Voltaire and This Heat, difficult music. Anyway, we had a meeting in Stephen's flat, and Stevo said he was going to bring all these bands together. He mentioned a few names and I'd not heard of any of them, except THE THE and Soft Cell. I'd not even heard of Depeche Mode at that point, but we decided to work with him, although it was really confusing because we'd never had a contract or anything. It all seemed a bit bizarre, really. We didn't know what to make of him and were a bit suspicious. Also, we couldn't make head nor tail of what he was talking about.

BEVERLEY GLICK Stevo did used to come out with some very cryptic, slightly nonsensical, stream-of-consciousness speeches, but they were always quite funny. Even though he wasn't well educated, he used to come up with these little gems. I believe he had an innate intelligence.

STEVO Whenever I used to hear a new word, I'd ask what it means. I still do. So many people, when they hear a phrase they don't understand, keep their mouths shut. They're the idiots, not me.

STEVE HOVINGTON I felt the word Futurist didn't really unite the bands musically, it was more about a willingness to experiment. Stevo was always about breaking the mould, there was no toeing the line whatsoever, and the music had to somehow stick two fingers up to the record companies in some way or other.

TONY MAYO We didn't have much to do with B-Movie, but I do remember they used to get freaked out by our track 'Golden Showers', which was quite funny.

NEIL ARTHUR Stevo started putting gigs together, which is where we met Depeche Mode, B-Movie, and THE THE, and got to know the guys out of Naked Lunch. We all became good mates, especially with Depeche and Daniel Miller, but we didn't feel an affinity with what everyone else was doing. It's easy to look back and think, well we were all using synths, but it wasn't like that when we were working. At that time, if I had to put Blancmange anywhere, it would have been with the bands we were going to see, like Pere Ubu and This Heat. I didn't know we were going to end up sounded the way we did, but you almost can't help it. What do we sound like this for? I dunno! I thought we were going to sound like Red Krayola or Captain Beefheart, but we just didn't.

STEVE HOVINGTON Stevo arranged for us to play at the Canning Town Bridge House in East London. That was our first London show, and I remember going down there and, with all due respect to the place, it was quite a rough. There were a bunch of East End types playing pool, getting upset that we were setting up for a gig. We were only eighteen and there was no one there to see us, but we did meet two very quiet individuals cowering in the corner clutching a copy of the EP they'd just had pressed up, and they turned out to be Blancmange.

NEIL ARTHUR We played it the Bridgehouse Canning Town with B-Movie. There were about twelve people there.

STEVE HOVINGTON Stevo organised two nights at the Hammersmith Clarendon

28

Hotel in June, with DAF and Fad Gadget headlining, so we started taking him a bit more seriously. He put us on the bill for the first night, along with Naked Lunch. It wasn't a full-on New Romantic crowd—there was still a punk element, but it was starting to change. I was very impressed because Siouxsie & The Banshees were there when we were playing and also, very excitingly, Billy Currie from Ultravox stood next to me at the urinal. It was my moment of absolute fame; here he is, my idol, and while we were standing there I turned to him and said, 'I'm a massive fan of yours!'

ROGER QUAIL It was a dressed-up audience at the Clarendon, everyone was looking good, people had made the effort. THE THE were on first, and I think it's fair to say Matt's vision hadn't fully coalesced yet, and they were a skeletal version of what they came to be. Then it was us, Vice Versa, and then Fad Gadget. We had requested strobe lights for our performance, and, in fairness to Stevo, he happily obliged and got two or three strobes for us. When we were setting up, he came over and said, 'Here you are lads. I got these from the local nut house and they're really fucking powerful!' A testament to the bloke's resourcefulness.

TONY MAYO The Clarendon gigs were packed out, it was amazing. You still had the leather jackets and punks there, but this time the vibe had changed a little bit and it wasn't quite so gobby and abusive. People seemed to be a bit more openminded, and most of the audience were into what everyone was doing.

ROGER QUAIL Clock DVA had played with Fad Gadget before, supporting Cabaret Voltaire at ULU back in May. The Fad Gadget at that gig felt like a band, but by the time we got to the Clarendon it felt like a personality. In the space of two months, Frank had become a front man and was quite brilliant at it, and he only got better as his confidence grew. They were playing away, and it was going great. Then Frank picked up this homemade syn-drum, a sort of drumhead with some wiring hanging off it, threw it up in the air, and, as it came down, he headed it like a football. Blood immediately started running down his face, but he just carried on. And then someone, I don't know if it was Stevo, stopped the show, because he was obviously in a bad way. So Frank was led off, and everything stopped for about fifteen minutes. When he returned to the stage he got a hero's welcome, shirt covered in blood and bandages piled on his head—he looked like The Mummy!

It was one of the most extraordinary pieces of rock theatre that I've ever seen, just brilliant, and of course he owned the night.

NICK CASH Frank was always quiet extreme in his performance and would jump into audience, which led to fights with people, sometimes even the PA crew. He wanted the audience to be fully involved, not just passive consumers—probably something he got from Leeds and watching Iggy and others.

ROGER QUAIL Afterward, with Frank on his way to Westminster Hospital for stitches, Stevo brought the two lads from DAF, Robert and Gabi, backstage to meet us. We were hugely impressed just because they were German: we were like, 'Do you know Kraftwerk?' When you're nineteen you just assume that everyone in Germany knows everyone else. And we actually got paid too.

TONY MAYO As there was an association with us and Stevo, we decided to put together a tour, which was called the Electronic Indoctrination Tour, because that's what we felt we were doing: indoctrinating people about electronic music.* It was an interesting tour. Some people would stand there in complete incredulity and other people would get really aggressive. The abuse was phenomenal, but being ex-punks, we took it, and we would actually rile them back. I think that helped, to be honest: it didn't matter what they did, we weren't intimidated, and we weren't going anywhere.

STEVE PARRY Neu Electrikk were based in Croydon, and we were playing gigs and releasing records on our own Synaesthesia label. You basically could press a couple of hundred copies, sell them at gigs or get a distribution deal with Pinnacle, so that's what we did. We were getting little mentions in *Sounds* and *NME*, and, unbeknown to us, Stevo had got in touch with Rough Trade looking for a contact number. No one had a phone at the time, so the only number they had was for my parents. So, the next time I went to visit them, my mother said,

---

* The press release states the promoter as Stevo Promotions, giving his parents' Rugby Gardens address in Dagenham as the contact, and states that Modern English will also be playing while Stevo would be DJing 'most dates.' The erratic dates for the tour spanned July, August, and September and took in venues such as F Club in Leedsop, Scamps in Oxford, the Bridge House in Canning Town, Caves in Hastings, London's Hope & Anchor, Pips in Manchester, Cromwells in Norwich, and the Moonlight in London.

'Oh, I had this strange guy on the phone, he's called Stereo. He's very keen to talk to you.' Turns out he was on the phone to my mum for about an hour, telling her about everything he planned to do! Anyway, I called him back and I got a very professional-sounding Stevo on the phone and he started giving me the sales talk, basically saying, 'I'm a promoter but I'm going to start a record label and it's going to be the greatest record label on earth, and it's going to cause a musical revolution.' It sounded like total claptrap, but Stevo could be very persuasive. I asked him who he was managing, as I knew a lot of the bands on the circuit, and he said, 'You won't have heard of them,' but I persisted, and one of the names he mentioned was THE THE. So after I put the phone down on Stevo, I called Matt to see what was going on, and he said Stevo had given him the same spiel and told him he was managing Neu Electrikk!

PETER ASHWORTH I took my first picture of THE THE while still an assistant photographer, shooting at my employer's studio in Cubitts Yard, Covent Garden. Even back then I saw Matt as an enigma. Keith Laws was in the band at the time, and around August 1980 Tom Johnston and I joined too. Matt was working at De Wolfe in Wardour Street, and I did go to his parents' pub in Loughton, where he had use of the enormous basement. There were two tape machines twenty foot apart with tape loops stretched between them. His brother, Andy Johnson (aka Andy Dog), was working on his art down there too. A creative hive of energy. Matt was obviously very intent on being a musician and I was very intent on being a photographer. I'd already started to shoot some interesting record sleeves with Alex McDowell at Rocking Russian, one of the really hip emerging record-sleeve design companies at that time. So I was doing that, playing with THE THE, and at some point along the line I met Stevo.

STEVE PARRY We did a gig with THE THE at the Bridgehouse, Canning Town, with Stevo DJing. Matt's dad, Eddie, had something to do with putting it on as he knew the landlord. Stevo turned up, and he looked like a shite Philip Oakey from The Human League with a terrible haircut. You can't take a man seriously with a bad hairdo. Matt and I were discussing who was going to headline, and I said, 'Well, really it should be us, as we've got two singles out and you've only got one.' And Matt replied, 'But ours is on 4AD, which is a proper label, so we should headline.' We relented, but we were a little bit pissed off. And, also, there was no fucker there.

PETER ASHWORTH Early THE THE was discordant, quite punk, pure experiment. We played quite a few pubs and we emptied them, but we were determined to carve out a style and had the self-belief to keep pushing it. We started linking up with bands who were already working with Stevo, and the whole scene got tighter and tighter.

CHRIS ANDREWS We were art students from Colchester, playing around with the idea of performing as a kind of Dadaist noise band. We recorded our improvisations on cassette and sent them out to labels as we thought someone might be interested in putting them out. Rabid Records from Manchester liked 'In The Army' and 'Why Diddle' and produced a batch of singles, which they released on their Absurd Records imprint.

When we moved to London, 'In The Army' got played by John Peel, and we were invited to appear at the Futurama 2 festival in Leeds. It was our first gig and we took the opportunity to dress in something inappropriate: Elizabethan costumes hired from the Theatre Royal Stratford East costume department. It was being filmed for BBC2 and the cameras loved it, but the audience were bemused and the music press were upset.

TONY MAYO As part of the Electronic Indoctrination tour, we appeared at the Futurama 2 festival in Leeds, which was organised by local promotor John Keenan. It was held in this cavernous former tram shed in the centre of the city. We played on the Sunday, and Gary Glitter was the headliner. Despite being only second on, a film crew captured part of our set, and it was shown on BBC2. Stevo didn't attend either day of the festival, which meant not only did he miss us but he also missed Soft Cell, who played on the Saturday.

MARC ALMOND I had begged John Keenan to put Soft Cell on the bill of Futurama 2. We were third on, playing early versions of 'Frustration', 'Persuasion', and a cover of Black Sabbath's 'Paranoid' in the late morning sunlight.

Soft Cell were onstage, an electric band I think, although it might have been a loud buzz in the PA. They limped through a version of 'Paranoid'. I went outside for a walk.

author unknown, *NME*, September 20, 1980

ANNI HOGAN I first saw Marc and Dave hanging out at the Faversham, but the first time I saw Soft Cell play was at the Futurama 2 festival. I'd had nine dodos, but I remember them being wild and just surging off the stage—I was hooked in an instant. Everybody played that Futurama, it was fantastic—Young Marble Giants, The Banshees, Echo & The Bunnymen—but it was Soft Cell I loved the best. They came on dressed all in black and pulsating with phenomenal electronic energy. I was hooked in an instant and knew things would never be the same again. Marc and Dave started coming to Amnesia, and I just got to know them through DJing there, so it was music that brought everybody together, for sure.

MARC ALMOND Our expectations weren't very high. We always thought we would be a nice arty cult indie band and have a little career for a while, maybe make it a bit bigger at some point, not that we knew how to do that. Dave's mum lent him £2,000 (a huge sum at the time), and so we could press up a seven-inch EP called *Mutant Moments* with four very scratchy tracks.[*] It came to Stevo's attention and he asked us if we had any more, so we sent him a cassette of demos, and it wasn't long before we were regularly featured in his chart. At the time it was a really big deal for us. We were enjoying ourselves and thought anything could happen. And why not? We were appearing in a mainstream music paper chart.

BEVERLEY GLICK Everyone thought Stevo was a joke and no one took him seriously. He tried to dress up a bit, but it just looked awful on him—he was like a bricklayer in New Romantic clothes. But he was a lot smarter than pretty much everybody gave him credit for. Because of the way he presented himself, and because he was dyslexic and spoke in this really weird way people just thought he was stupid, and he wasn't at all.

After I got over my initial, 'Oh, he looks like a joke' vibe, I actually became quite fond of him and I was one of the only people who would talk to him when he came into the *Sounds* office. And as a result of that chart and the DJing, people started sending in tapes, and that's how he started to think about this idea of a compilation album.

---

[*] The *Mutant Moments* EP was Soft Cell's first single. Self-financed and released on their own Big Frock Rekords, it featured four lo-fi, rudimentary electronic sketches that nonetheless set out the band's stall as purveyors of dark, sardonic electro-pop.

DANIEL MILLER Like a lot of people I first became aware of Stevo through his chart in *Sounds*. He was playing our records and other stuff that I really liked, and I had no idea who he was or how old he was or anything. I got in touch with him just to say, *Thanks for playing our music*, and he told me that he wanted to release a compilation album. We talked about what that album could be, and initially it was going to be the music he was playing out. I knew quite a few of those bands, like Cabaret Voltaire and Throbbing Gristle, but in the end, I think he made the right decision to go with new artists that people hadn't really heard of before.

STEVO I asked Cabaret Voltaire to be on the original Some Bizzare album and they declined. I also wanted Vice Versa to be on and they declined too. Must have been a Sheffield thing.

TONY MAYO It was around August/September time that Stevo and I started chatting about putting a compilation together. We were still trying to push electronic music and he was constantly being sent demo tapes, so it kind of made sense.

MARTIN PATTON Out of the blue, Stevo rings us up and says, 'You know how to make records, don't you?' So we said, 'Yes we do,' to which he replied, 'Good, I've got an idea, do you want to talk about it?' So he came up to Lincoln, we met him off the train, and we ended up at my parent's house which was bit weird. We realised, here was a guy who's a bit left of field and slightly nuts but was also very driven and very excited by what he wanted to do. So we agreed to start a label, literally, within a few hours of meeting.

STEVO The idea of the label was to be aware of people's expectations but do almost the opposite. Not deliberately though, there's nothing more irritating than artists trying to be different for the sake of it. The spelling has nothing to do with dyslexia, it's spelt B I Z Z A R E on purpose. I like ambiguities.

MARTIN PATTON By the time a decision was made to put together a compilation album, Some Bizarre was Stevo, Steve Taylor, and myself. Steve and I travelled down to London and went to Stevo's house in Dagenham to listen to some of the cassettes he'd been sent. I think he was already in contact with Soft Cell by that point, and we already had B-Movie, but in that one afternoon alone we pulled out tapes from Depeche Mode, Blancmange, and THE THE. Crazy, really.

RUSTY EGAN He was probably about five years younger than me, an enthusiastic young kid. I'd already been in punk bands, signed a record deal, made an album, done all the things you want to do when you're fifteen, and I knew it wasn't for me. I was at the point where I wanted to do it all on my own. And Stevo echoed that, as he'd already been told to fuck off by every record company.

BEVERLEY GLICK There wasn't necessarily bad blood between Stevo and Rusty because they were both DJs at the time, but there was definitely competition. The New Romantic bands and the Futurist bands were like night and day, honestly. I did the first interview with Spandau Ballet, and that was quite a coup, because they hated the music press and didn't think they needed them. But it was my first commission when I started as a staff writer for *Sounds* in June 1980. Alan said, 'I want you to get an interview with Spandau Ballet, here's [manager] Steve Dagger's number.' I had no idea that they didn't want to speak to music journalists, and I think the reason they said yes to me was because they could tell that I was naive and would just lap up whatever they said, which is pretty much what happened.

RUSTY EGAN My memory of first meeting Stevo would've been on the Kings Road in the daytime and him giving me a flyer for one of his Chelsea Drugstore nights and asking me to come. I went along and got chatting to him, and he told me about the album he was putting together of unsigned bands. I'd never heard of Blancmange or Depeche Mode or Soft Cell.

MARC ALMOND We were a bit taken back when we first met Stevo. We expected a skinny, London fashion trendy or a post-punk journo type, aloof, maybe a bit pretentious and posey. But he was nothing like that. Short and stocky, a bit on the large side, wearing a black jumper that had a glue mark stripe across it at an angle (probably where he'd stuck white tape to look like Gary Numan) and black baggy trousers with a grown-out Phil Oakey haircut and badly applied blusher. And he was young, only seventeen at the time, and he had the gift of the gab, like a cockney barrow-boy. Yet he was immensely impressive and likeable in a strange fascinating way. He had a laugh that reminded me of Mutley from *Wacky Races*, and, most impressive of all, he had ideas and ambitions. Not expressed in a posh, condescending way but in an enthusiastic, excitable way, and he seemed intelligent beyond his years. A chancer perhaps, a name dropper and manipulative certainly, but add all that up and it came out as a kind of charisma. Of course, Dave and I had a lot of reservations, but no one else was knocking down our door to talk to us—quite the opposite. So we decided, certainly naively, that we would join Stevo for the ride. He had a chart in a national music paper, he ran a club, he was starting his own record label, and he lived in London. He ticked a lot of boxes.

DAVE BALL We chose Stevo because no one else was interested. He came to meet us in our flat in Leeds, and he said, 'Well, the things is, I wanna manage yous.' I don't think he knew exactly what being a manager entailed, but then again neither did we. Without legal advice we signed the contract and hoped for the best. We thought that at least we had someone who was from London, had a chart in *Sounds*, and knew people in the music business. We thought that might give us a better chance of some kind of success. And it did.

JOSE WARDEN In the early days of managing Soft Cell, Stevo often came up to Leeds and stay in the spare room of the house that Brian and I lived in. As Brian was the only driver out of all of us he would often drive Stevo around when he was up there.

BRIAN MOSS Stevo was crazy and zany, an off-the-wall kind of character, but he was a good laugh.

ANNI HOGAN I first became aware of Stevo through his Futurist chart, as I'd play stuff from it, and I met him at Amnesia. I couldn't work him out—there're some people you just can't read, and I found no point of connection with him except that he loved fantastic music. On one side of the coin he was like a bricky, but at the same time he loved Throbbing Gristle and Soft Cell. It was an odd thing because I was gay, so he couldn't fuck me, so he was not comfortable with me and I wasn't comfortable with him. But at the same time, he did give me some DJ work, some private parties and stuff.

MARC ALMOND Early on, we played a gig with Depeche Mode at Crocs, their home turf, and we got pelted with coins by some other 80's artists who were there. Depeche had great equipment and good outfits; we were a mess, the poor northerners.

DAVE BALL I'd watched Depeche Mode soundcheck and they were so tight. They were the local boys and were fantastic; we were the out-of-town headliners and we were dreadful. People were chucking pennies and laughing at us. We had to get our act together after that, so we went back to the drawing board.

TONY MAYO I was at the Crocs gig Soft Cell did with Depeche. I'd gone down with Stevo to give moral support. There were a couple of Spandau Ballet, a couple of Ultravox and Visage, all standing at the back, and the audience were not nice to them at all. They were jeering and throwing coins—they were horrible. What made it all the stranger to me was that it was the same crowd who would go and see Depeche Mode and be really into it. Yet at the time Depeche were a light-hearted pop band with really nice tunes and vocal harmonies. Soft Cell were far more edgy, and the crowd couldn't seem to handle that.

NEIL ARTHUR We supported Nash The Slash at the Fulham Greyhound in November, and Stevo came down, and I think that's where I poured the pint over him. He must've said something that I didn't like, as I wouldn't have done it lightly. It's a waste of a good drink, isn't it?

STEVE PARRY We didn't sign with Stevo, he was just in the background. He'd play your records at Billy's and put you in his Futurist chart, but it was still very low key—he was building up his roster. It was only really when he had the idea for the compilation album that he started to be a bit more proactive. He said to us, 'Have Neu Electrikk got any stuff going spare, anything hanging about?' There was no budget for us, and I think it was the same for THE THE, so basically, if you sent Stevo a track, it went on the album.

CHRIS ANDREWS 'In The Army' reached the top of the Futurist chart and we were introduced to him through our manager. We went to his parent's house in Dagenham and there was much talk about releasing a Blah Blah Blah album on Polydor and a compilation album of Futurist bands, which seem to take a while materialise.

37

MARC ALMOND I didn't really know most of the artists on the *Some Bizzare Album* as Stevo had already compiled it when Soft Cell was added. We gave him 'The Girl With The Patent Leather Face', a scratchy, cheap-sounding track inspired by J.G. Ballad about a girl who is left disfigured after a car crash and hangs around fetish bars.

TONY MAYO We were still working very closely with Stevo and having discussions about the compilation and how it was going to work. It was still short of a couple of tracks, so I spoke to Matt and Neil about getting a track from each of them. I also spoke to Dave from The Fast Set about getting a track on there.

DAVID KNIGHT I'd been putting together backing tracks under the name Transition (everything had to end '-tion' back in those days) as part of a new pop project with singer Marc Sebastian Jones. We booked an eight-track studio in Pimlico and recorded our best track—also called 'Transition'—and offered it to 4AD, but they were headed in other directions by then, and I'm not the pushiest of people, so it languished. Marc and I recruited Pete Farrugia, a young and highly gifted guitarist, and it was around this time we also became friendly with Blancmange and Nash The Slash.

Stevo got in touch to say he was putting together a compilation album of all the new bands he had encountered, and did we want to contribute? Stevo was very young, about seventeen, and although he was obviously very ambitious and had the gift of the gab, we really didn't want to give him our best track for a compilation album. So we decided to knock out another T Rex cover, this time 'King Of The Rumbling Spires'. We recorded it in a four-hour session at a Pimlico eight-track studio for about thirty quid—it's not my best moment on tape. Of course, as we now know, *Some Bizzare Album* was picked up by Phonogram and more or less became a major label A&R's shopping list. It taught me a very good lesson early on in life: if a thing's worth doing, it's worth doing well, because it's all people have to judge you by.

MATT JOHNSON Stevo was very colourful, younger than me—and I was pretty young myself—and he was from East London too. He was a peculiar character but very persuasive and very passionate, incredibly enthusiastic—a mini hurricane. Wherever he would go, things would happen, good and bad. He was good fun too with a very naughty, twisted sense of humour, which appealed to me. So, Keith Laws—who was the other member of THE THE at the time—and I decided to license him a track for the *Some Bizarre Album*.

STEVE PARRY I'd recommended SGS Studio to Matt, and, as he didn't drive at the time, I drove him over there. It was a disastrous session because the engineer did not like Matt or Keith at all. He made it plain he thought they were a couple of wankers. Obviously, Matt and Keith picked up on this, which wasn't good for creativity, so I ended up at the mixing desk doing what the engineer should've been doing. I think I played a little bit of guitar, too, but I'm not credited. The track was originally called 'Strawberry Sunset', but when the tape reels came back the engineer had crossed that out and in its place written 'The Bollock Dance'.

Because nobody was particularly pleased with the session, the reel-to-reel tape ended up in my possession. And I had it for months—nobody wanted it. Then one day I get a call from Matt saying they needed something for the *Some Bizzare Album*, and did I still have that tape they did at SGS? The track ended up being called 'Untitled' and they deliberately didn't supply any information on it, especially not the engineer's name.

JULIA ADAMSON We were based in Stockport but rehearsed at TJ Davidsons in Manchester, which most of the punk bands used. Initially, Zoo Records in Liverpool showed an interest us and we toured with their bands, Pink Military, Echo & The Bunnymen, Richard Strange, and Teardrop Explodes.

TONY MAYO Stevo was also keen to get Illustration on the album, so we drove to all the way up to Manchester to pick up their tape.

NEIL ARTHUR Despite the pint incident, our working relationship with Stevo continued, and he asked us for a song for his compilation album. We decided it would be 'Sad Day', which was another new song that we'd recorded on a 4-track in Stephen's front room. We gave it to Stevo and said that's it, it's finished, and it went on the album like that.

DAVID KNIGHT Stevo asked me to meet him at Sloane Square tube station to sign the contract for the *Some Bizzare Album*. It was only when I got there I found out that, to save money, he'd only bought a ticket to the next station up from Dagenham, then travelled on to Chelsea, with the plan to sign the contract across the ticket barrier. This was duly done, and off he went home again.

STEVE HOVINGTON Despite what was going on with B-Movie I'd accepted a place at Coventry University to study one of the UK's first media communication courses. So not only was I picking up an interest in Marxism, which started to creep my new songs, but the burgeoning 2 Tone thing was going on. I was really into early Thompson Twins and The Sound, and they inspired our track for the *Some Bizzare Album*, 'Moles'. It was more of an indie sound than an electronic one, which was what I was aiming for at the time. It was recorded at Studio Playground in Wragby, Lincolnshire especially for the album. We couldn't pay for it, so Martin and Andy must have made some kind of points deal with Stevo.

CHRIS ANDREWS At the time, the other acts on the album weren't that well known and didn't really behave like they were either. Our contribution to the *Some Bizzare Album*, 'Central Park', was different from them as it was improvised with no song structure or fashionable rhythm. It wasn't a dance track or ballad, more of a walk in the park. Film music maybe?

DANIEL MILLER I first got to hear about Soft Cell through Frank Tovey. He knew Marc from college in Leeds, and Marc had sent Frank a tape of Soft Cell to give to me. This is late 70s, way before I met Depeche or anything like that. I liked the demo tape but I didn't quite connect with it in a way that I would have wanted to if I was to work with them, but I thought what they were doing was really interesting.

Not that long afterwards, Fad Gadget was playing at the Bridge House in Canning Town, and the support band was Depeche Mode. That's when I first saw them live, and it was there that I decided I really wanted to do something with him. I went backstage and said, *That was amazing, I'd love to work with you.* They were trying to playing it cool a bit, but they knew about Mute and they were definitely interested in the idea. They were playing the Bridge House again the following week, supporting Wasted Youth, so I went along to that to have a proper chat. And Stevo was at that gig, along with Matt Johnson. I think Stevo had seen them at Crocs in Rayleigh, and he really liked them as well.

VINCE CLARKE We did a gig with Fad Gadget and Stevo came backstage.* He said, 'Look, we're doing the Some Bizzare tour, are you interested in doing it? And are you interested in signing to Some Bizzare?' Then Daniel came backstage as well; we kind of knew him because of 'TVOD' [the B-side of The Normal's 'Warm Leatherette']. It was a case of [going with] either. Stevo said, 'Look, if you sign with Some Bizzare, I can get you a support slot with Ultravox.' So it was a real heavy-duty decision, you know! But we decided, for some reason, that we'd go with Daniel. And then Daniel said, 'We'll just do a single.' The next thing we know, [Stevo was] like, 'Can you do a track for this compilation album?' which was amazing!

TONY MAYO Stevo decided he wanted 'Le Femme' on the compilation album, so he arranged for us to go to a sixteen-track studio in Forest Gate in East London to record it. While we were there, Depeche Mode were recording 'Photographic' and Soft Cell were recording 'Memorabilia', both with Daniel Miller.

DANIEL MILLER I really liked Marc and Dave and thought the music was great. We had a short period of time in the studio, maybe only two days, and we reconstructed 'Memorabilia' together. They had the basic song, and the bass line, and I did some percussion and drum things. It was very quick and intuitive. I think Marc only did one vocal take. He was in the booth, and I said to Dave, 'Should we do another?' and he just said, 'No, that'll be the best one.' We worked with a really great engineer called Pete Maben, and I think we recorded it in one day, and mixed it the next.

DAVE BALL Daniel Miller was a hero of ours. The only electronic music we were familiar with were things like Kraftwerk and Georgia Moroder with Donna Summer—we didn't really know any homegrown electronic artists. Then we heard The Normal, Fad Gadget, and Silicon Teens, and we thought, *Who is this guy Larry Least?*, which was the pseudonym Daniel used on the Silicon Teens records.†

---

* At the Bridgehouse, Canning Town, on November 11, 1980.
† Silicon Teens were a fictional band and a vehicle for Daniel Miller to create electro-pop versions of 1950s and 60s rock'n'roll standards. Miller played all instruments and sang, although Frank Tovey appeared as lead singer 'Darryl' in the video for the single 'Memphis Tennessee'. Miller used the production pseudonym Larry Least on the records—a play on Mickie Most, the 1960s pop producer and owner of RAK Records.

41

I don't know how many people got that joke but I always thought that was very witty. But Daniel was brilliant and we loved 'Warm Leatherette', 'Back To Nature', 'Memphis Tennessee', all those early Mute singles. We got Stevo to convince him to work with us, and we were really happy with the sessions.

DANIEL MILLER It was Stevo's eighteenth birthday during the sessions and he'd been partying all night and came down to the studio very drunk. And basically he threw up in the studio. There was a snooker table in the lounge, and we plonked him on there to let him sleep it off. We were all a bit annoyed about it because he hadn't given us much studio time, and we didn't really want to waste any of it looking after him. But it meant we had to work quickly, so it became part of the process, I suppose.

STEVO Yes, I was sick in the studio and, yes, the session did come to an abrupt ending. But that's why 'Memorabilia' sounds so raw. If they'd had another few hours to work on it, they would have fucked it up.

>>

TONY MAYO In November 1980, *Record Mirror* put Steve Strange on the cover under the headline 'Brave New Face' and over a double-page spread interviewed us, Soft Cell, Spandau Ballet, and Shock as the vanguard of the new electronic scene.

STEVE PARRY We were all sort of frustrated in the sense that we were making music and wanted to be heard and wanted to be on the radio, but to do that you had to play the game. I wrote to numerous record companies pushing Neu Electrikk and I just hit brick wall after brick wall. It starts to eat at you and you lose confidence your music. You look at the people that are doing OK, and you think, *Why are they getting successful?* When Stevo came along he was a breath of fresh air, as here was a guy who was going to the majors and saying, 'Why are you signing all this crap on a daily basis? There's a movement happening out there and you're missing it.'

TONY MAYO We had all the tracks for the *Some Bizzare Album*, so we had to decide what to do with it. I thought we should licence it, but Stevo wasn't sure and wanted to get advice from Daniel Miller. So, we all met up in early December at an

Indian restaurant in Kings Cross. Daniel was very much into staying independent and pure, while I was advocating the opposite. I wanted to get this music out to as many people as possible and get a scene rolling and start something. And eventually it was decided that it should be licensed to Phonogram.

DANIEL MILLER At that time I wanted Mute to be independent, but Stevo wanted to work with the majors—that was his vision for Some Bizzare. But knowing Stevo and knowing the kind of music that he loved, I thought that it would probably all end in tears.

STEVE PARRY Stevo worked for Phonogram and was constantly telling A&R man David Bates about new bands, and Bates basically said, 'Well, send me some music then.'

MARTIN PATTON We were still in Lincoln but we were now spending a lot of time going up and down to London on the train, probably three times a week, because we were putting it all together in London. Mark Dean (who went on to co-found Innervison Records and sign Wham!) was the prime mover—he was the one who did all the running. I presume he was an A&R scout. He suddenly appeared and he said, 'I'd love to licence this,' and I had no idea what 'licensing' meant at the time. Fast-forward a few weeks, Mark took us in to see A&R manager Roger Aimes, he agreed to fund it, and the album was on its way. So, really, the *Some Bizzare Album* is a Phonogram record, because we never owned it. We got an override of a few points—I don't remember how many, but nothing to get excited about. Had the three of us been a bit smarter, we would have done a deal whereby we licenced it to them and got it back after a certain amount of time. But we were *still* making it up as we went along.

STEVE HOVINGTON We'd done two EPs with Dead Good and we wanted to do an album, and had we stayed with them that's what might have happened. It would have been on an indie label and might have picked up a couple of plays on John Peel and not gone much further than that. When Stevo started talking up the *Some Bizzare Album*, the music press picked up on it, and we were very aware of that. We were very eager at the time to for anything that might get us noticed. So, Stevo became our manager. We went down to his place in Dagenham, and he

43

produced this bit of A4 paper, and said, 'Sign it,' and we did. Martin and Andy still had an interest in the band and were still around as part of Some Bizarre, in the beginning at least.

The Bizzare philosophy is that nothing is going to sound the same. You can't categorise the bands on the LP. THE THE are unlike anything else. Comparing them to Naked Lunch is like comparing Beethoven to Motörhead. You can't call it Futurist—and that name doesn't appear anywhere on the sleeve—just because it's electronic. Electronic music isn't fashion—it's a style of music. No one said flutes or violins were going to go out of fashion. What Futurist bands have in common is the synthesizer, but so do all rock bands have guitars in common, yet they aren't called 'yet another guitar band'. They said punk would destroy but it was just rock'n'roll. I hate rock'n'roll.

STEVO to Betty Page, *Sounds*, February 14, 1981

RUSTY EGAN I loved all of the early Some Bizarre stuff, but nobody believed me when I told them it came from this little bloke from Dagenham with a silly haircut wearing an old man's jacket from a charity shop. People in the established music industry didn't want to know Stevo. He was dyslexic, he was scruffy, he was not a cool Blitz kid. But he saw Depeche Mode at the Canning Town pub and immediately recognised they had talent. He ran around finding everything that would eventually be in my playlist. He was incredible.

MARTIN PATTON We cut the *Some Bizarre Album* at CTS Mastering out in Wembley. I think Neil from Blancmange was there, and Dave Gahan and Vince Clarke. I'm pretty sure Daniel Miller was there too because I seem to remember he did not leave Vince's side. Stevo always maintained he didn't want to sign Depeche Mode, but Daniel had been in the background with them for a long time, and I got the impression he may already have had a verbal agreement, at least, with them.

STEVO I'd already told Depeche that they should sign with Daniel. I went backstage at the Bridge House and told them I've got Soft Cell and B-Movie, and Daniel had time on his hands. The band were completely taken aback. I walked out of the dressing room and said to Daniel, 'I've just told Depeche to sign with you, so make sure you look after them.'

DANIEL MILLER Firstly, Depeche Mode weren't Stevo's to give. And secondly, they wanted to sign to Mute, not Some Bizarre. Him giving me Depeche Mode while he took Soft Cell wasn't the way I saw it. Mute was a tiny one-person label at the time and even if I wanted to, there was no way I could sign both of them. I really wanted to work with Depeche and they wanted to work with me, and that was that. It wasn't like he *gave* them to me, that's kind of a ridiculous thing to say.

JANE ROLINK I was into music big time. Coming from Barnsley, I'd go to Sheffield when I could to watch bands, I used to go and see Throbbing Gristle, Clock DVA, Cabaret Voltaire, everyone. And when I moved to London I was out on the scene every night, it was a really good time. I met Stevo when he was putting Depeche Mode on in a pub at Canning Town. He just came up to me and poured some beer in my glass and we just hit it off straight away. Stevo invited me along for a drink after Soft Cell had a meeting at Phonogram, and that's where I first met Marc and Dave outside their offices. We got on great, which was the same with everybody. It was brilliant, like being with your family.

TONY MAYO Before the album came out, I'd met up with Stevo and Marc at the Pearce family home in Dagenham, then drove into Soho to Billy's, where we were meeting the rest of Naked Lunch. It was there that Stevo announced that he'd decided to manage Soft Cell and that he wouldn't be working with us anymore. We weren't overly amused—we'd spent nearly a year working with him to push electronic music, helping put the album together, ferrying people around, only to be dropped just as it was coming together. We just walked out, and there was a lot of bad feeling.

A naive person can open his eyes in life, but someone with his eyes open can never end up naive.

STEVØ, from the sleeve of Psychic TV's *Force The Hand Of Chance* LP (1982)

1981 Dancing, laughing, drinking, loving

03

THE *SOME BIZZARE ALBUM*
IS RELEASED, B-MOVIE ARE
TIPPED FOR THE TOP, AND
'TAINTED LOVE' TAKES OVER
THE WORLD

STEVO The two 'Zs' and one 'R' was pretty cool on a marketing level. The concept of the label was, 'If they're paranoid, keep them paranoid.' If paranoia is a spark, throw gasoline on it. If you've got a concept like that, you can wind people up, and then you rattle the cages of those who are administrating the actual finances.

RUSTY EGAN Stevo and I became really good friends, but he kept being a weirdo. He looked up to people like Salvador Dalí or Francis Bacon—people who tried to annihilate their own careers. Stevo would throw petrol on a fire that he shouldn't have lit in the first place.

TONY MAYO I'm not being disingenuous or arrogant when I say this, but people forget what Naked Lunch did. We worked our bollocks off with Stevo to create this scene. I think the awful thing is, because we'd helped create this facade of Stevo being a success, people looked up to him, and it allowed him to take advantage.

STEVE PARRY I suppose we were all a bit gullible, but Stevo was a great raconteur, he just made you laugh, and that covered up a lot of sins. He'd give you good copy; we were frustrated and starving musicians, and he'd come in and say, 'I'm gonna start a record label and we're gonna take over the world.' That's the stuff you want to hear when you're in that situation.

BEVERLEY GLICK Stevo asked me to interview some of the bands on the *Some Bizzare Album* and organised for them to come to *Sounds* for a round-table discussion. He said he'd be there as well, but on the day he didn't turn up. I was left with all these random people who didn't know each other or what they were there for. And the bands I really wanted to talk to—Depeche Mode and Soft Cell—weren't there either. 'The Girl With The Patent Leather Face' was my favourite track on the album, so Stevo brought Soft Cell down from Leeds to the *Sounds* office sometime later. They were like a breath of fresh air. The Blitz crowd were extremely cliquey, very insular, and thought they were more important than anyone else. If you weren't in with the in-crowd, then you were totally out. And Marc and Dave were so not like that. They were down-to-earth and funny, full of northern charm and wit, and really grateful that I was interested in them—unlike the other lot, who just had a sense of entitlement. We just hit it off. They were outsiders, Stevo was an outsider, and I felt like an outsider too, because I'd just started out as a music journalist and was trying to cover a scene full of people who thought they were better and more fashionable than me.

Some Bizzare are about keeping people alert and puzzled, but everything about it is down to the bands. I didn't do it for commercial potential, [I did it] so some kid in Blackburn or wherever can get hold of [the album] without having to go to Rough Trade. I don't care if it doesn't sell, but I think it will be the biggest independent label album of this year or last year.

STEVO to Betty Page, *Sounds*, February 14, 1981

As the album's compiler—DJ Stevo—has laudably shunned well-known names in favour of the new and untried, *Some Bizzare Album* will inevitably include a quota of the derivative along with the adventurous. The jokey irony aside, there's precious little of the genuinely unusual on this record and about half of it suggests a movement prepared to coast on the work of pioneering precedents like Eno, John Foxx, Human League, OMITD, and, of course, Gary Numan.

CHRIS BOHN (writing as Biba Kopf), *NME*, February 7, 1981

What we find here is electronic dance music/electronic experimental music as opposed to the more disco-oriented, sophisticated Visages and Ultravoxes. A glimpse at the real 20 carat golden goodies. . . . Be content with this album, which looks to have got the balance between fun, dance and thoughtfulness. One small step for Stevo, a giant foot forward for Futurism!

BEVERLEY GLICK (writing as Betty Page), *Sounds*, January 31, 1981

STEVO There's no mention of the word 'futurist' on the *Some Bizzare Album* cover.

TONY MAYO For an album that was supposed to promote new bands and start a movement, it was a pretty oblique calling card. I mean, no side one or side two, but 'lamp man' and 'fish'?*

The patron saint of Some Bizzare is Sooty, with added influences from Max Boyce, who is about to drop his leek and start using giant fishes.

STEVO to Betty Page, *Sounds*, February 14, 1981

The *Some Bizzare Album* is really not that bizarre at all, although it has some interesting, some promising (and some plain unimaginative) ideas and arrangements. Like most compilation albums.

author unknown, *London Trax*, February 25, 1981

BRIAN MOSS I DJed at the Warehouse, and so did Anni Hogan. She was probably the first female DJ, at least in the clubs in Leeds, along with Claire Shearsby.[†] Stevo gave me a copy of the *Some Bizzare Album* to play out, and it was obvious he had a really good ear. I mean, if you look at who's on that album, it's incredible really. He definitely had a talent for spotting bands, but maybe not so much for managing them.

MARTIN PATTON I do remember encouraging Stevo to sign Depeche Mode, and him saying, 'Nah, they're rinky-dink pop band,' to which I replied, 'Precisely!' His counter to that was, 'I want to sign Blah Blah Blah.' He really wanted the second Some Bizzare release to be their debut album.

---

* *Some Bizzare Album* (BZLP 1) was released on January 30, 1981, on Phonogram.
† The incredibly influential Claire Shearsby has been active on the Leeds music scene since the late 70s, DJing at John Keenan's clubs and the Futurama festival. She was at the forefront of the scene that spawned bands such as Gang Of Four, The Three Johns, and The Sisters Of Mercy. Shearsby was also romantically involved with the Sisters' Andrew Eldritch for a number of years.

CHRIS ANDREWS The *Some Bizzare Album* was a great mix of synth-pop ballads, electronic dance, and experimental pop, and we were happy to be on it. There was a lot of talk about Phonogram and BZLP2 being a Blah Blah Blah album, but Stevo seemed to be most interested in Soft Cell out of all the compilation contributors. We ended up self-financing our first album, thinking we could sell it directly through independent record shops. We subsequently found out our music was too rough even for Rough Trade.

TONY MAYO Phonogram wanted the *Some Bizzare Album* to feature on the BBC's *The Old Grey Whistle Test* and were pushing Soft Cell as the best band to use. The show's producers, however, preferred our track 'Le Femme' and put together a really good avant-garde video, with teacups and men in hats. We really enjoyed it. I must admit, I did phone up Phonogram's A&R guy and just laughed down the phone at him. Serves 'em right.

MARC ALMOND Stevo licensed us to Phonogram as part of a package deal with B-Movie, who were the band the record company really wanted. They were good-looking lads, in more of a Duran Duran vein with strong pop songs, not two odd art students. We were given £1,000, with which we bought some new equipment. Even back then it didn't go far. Stevo's inexperience with the shark-infested music business had already started to show, and the deals were signed for the short-term fix, just two singles for each band. He celebrated by opening a plastic bag of MDMA—back then a pre-med drug used in hospitals that had a hallucinogenic edge—and passed it around. That's how it started, and that's how it continued.

NEIL ARTHUR We would've loved to have signed to Mute but I don't think Daniel was interested. I suppose it might have crossed his mind but we didn't expect it. But we were friends, and we played with Depeche Mode a few times. One gig I remember was at the Hope & Anchor in early '81.[*] Depeche, rightly, should have been headlining, but they had to get back to Basildon with their gear, so we agreed that we would headline so they wouldn't miss the last train. Rather than having a musical connection with Depeche, we all just got on very well. They're all great, and subsequently Daniel and the band asked us to go on with them in late '81.

[*] Hope & Anchor, Islington, January 11, 1981.

MARTIN PATTON After the *Some Bizzare Album* came out, Depeche were with Daniel and Blancmange ended up with London. I don't think Roger Aimes was interested in THE THE, so, as far as Phonogram was concerned, it was basically B-Movie and Soft Cell. And the deal was definitely weighted toward B-Movie. We wouldn't let them have one without the other, and as I seem to remember they gave us £40,000 for B-Movie and £5,000 for Soft Cell. It was almost nothing, but it was a few grand in their pockets that they didn't have already. But the big push was definitely B-Movie, and I do remember going into a meeting with Roger and London Records boss Tracy Bennett, and Tracy playing a white label of Duran Duran's *Planet Earth* and saying, 'If this is the competition, I think we've got it beat!'

STEVE HOVINGTON Then it suddenly took off for us. In January, I was back at university in Coventry, sitting in a lecture theatre and someone stuck their head around the door and told me I had a phone call in reception. So, I went downstairs, and it was Martin telling me a car was on its way to pick me up and take me down to London because B-Movie were recording 'Remembrance Day' for a major record label.* My first thought was, *Who's producing?* And when I got there I found out it was Mike Thorne, who'd worked with Wire.

BEVERLEY GLICK It was pretty obvious to me from start which bands were going to be successful. I was really surprised that B-Movie got a deal. And Phonogram thought they were going to be huge, with Soft Cell as a bit of an afterthought. B-Movie were the big signing for sure.

[Phonogram] have really stuck their neck out. The offer is touching on as good as what the Rolling Stones got, and is just as good as Spandau Ballet got. They're offering around sixty grand for B-Movie, who are now in a twenty-four-track studio with Wire's producer. I've worked hard with all these bands to make sure they get on—they'd do anything for me. Let me sleep on their floors . . .

STEVO to Betty Page, *Sounds*, February 14, 1981

* 'Remembrance Day' was B-Movie's first release after signing with Stevo and the first single to feature the Some Bizzare logo. It was released on March 13, 1981, via Phonogram subsidiary Deram and reached no.61 on the UK chart.

STEVE HOVINGTON I really liked Stevo—he used to stay at my parents' old house in the Midlands, and my dad and mum were really welcoming. He always remembers that, and there was a respect there. Whether he was looking for something that he didn't have in his own life, whether there was something secure and solid about my family, I don't know. I knew about his brother and his reputation. But Stevo never used to talk about him.

STEVO When my brother was incarcerated, his name was everywhere: 'Free Joe Pearce' was written on the walls around Dagenham.* I was damned by association and I lost my surname because of it. There were a lot of lunatics out there who would have thrown acid in my face, right? I had my mum to look after, and it was very easy for someone with a tape machine to put my life at risk.† I had people walk up to me and out the blue headbutt me. They could have been from the left or right, it didn't matter to them. Everything was very sinister.

DAVE BALL Joe was a very intelligent guy, and so was Stevo. But Joe picked up his politics from their dad, who was a really scary man, so it's no surprise he turned out the way he did. Stevo was not involved in any of that at all—he couldn't wait to get out of Dagenham and away from that shit. There was graffiti on the walls where he lived saying, *Kill Stevo* and *Stevo is a traitor*, and the local National Front were onto him. When you've got those sorts of people threatening you, you don't want to stick around.

STEVO You don't know what it's like to be in a pub in Dagenham with my mum and dad with my brother just being released from prison. He's sitting with us, and before I know what going on, there's like fifty or sixty kids all around him like he's fucking God. When your name is painted all over the walls you don't fuck around. I didn't want to alienate people because I didn't want to get a machete in the head

---

* Joseph Pearce joined the youth wing of the National Front aged fifteen and in 1977 set up *Bulldog*, the organisation's openly racist newspaper. In 1980 he became editor of *Nationalism Today*, advocating white supremacy. Pearce was twice prosecuted and imprisoned for his writings under the Race Relations Act, in 1981 and 1985. During his second prison term he converted to Catholicism, and he has since written extensively on Catholic subjects and Christian literary figures such as J.R.R. Tolkien, Oscar Wilde, and C.S. Lewis.
† Writing in *Hoolies: True Stories Of Britain's Biggest Street Battles* (John Blake, 2010), Gary Bushell made a direct connection, stating that Joseph Pearce was the 'brother of Soft Cell's Stevo'.

51

from the Anti-Nazi League or the bloody Nazis. I tried to keep the ambiguities for my own safety.

MATT JOHNSON My uncle Kenny was a successful music promoter in the 1960s, so I'd heard plenty of stories from my own family about how the music business was a bit crooked and dodgy. He and my dad had a lot of friends in the underworld who would enforce things for them.

I remember my dad saying to me once, 'Look, if you ever have any trouble in the music industry, Matthew, or anyone messes you about, let me know and we'll get it dealt with.' Luckily, I never had to take him up on that offer, but I think Stevo was a little bit wary of my dad. But both my parents really liked him because he was very charming and polite around them, plus he came from the East End, which counted for a lot.

>>

TONY MAYO Stevo wanted a new hairstyle, so he went to the same person who did my hair. They cut it all short except for a couple of long bits on top, which they dyed aubergine. It was like he had a purple spider on his head.

STEVE HOVINGTON Stevo was at the meeting with Phonogram and he'd had his head shaved, apart from two tassels of hair sort sticking up from his head. It didn't really complement his pugnacious demeanour. Somewhere along the line we obviously signed a contract with Phonogram, and Stevo told us it was the biggest record deal since The Rolling Stones. But it certainly didn't feel like it. We wanted an album deal [but] we seemed to have signed a try-before-you-buy singles deal arrangement. They were happy to put out a single, and if that did well then they'd put out another one. It wasn't what we as a band wanted at all.

POLLY BIRKBECK Anyone connected to the bands I liked used to pique my interest, and the music press used to write about Stevo a lot. I always remember thinking he didn't look particularly 'alternative' but he was always in the 'Thrills' pages of the *NME*. I guess he must have been inspired by Malcolm McLaren and Andrew Loog Oldham when he started. And in funny way, all those stories about him not being able to read or write but still be able to manage all these really good bands was quite inspiring.

Every Some Bizzare Evening was an event, a party.* I hate normal gigs. Bands just kept phoning me up, wanting me to get them gigs, so about eight months ago I started trying to get the album together. No one took me seriously for a long time, but then I don't take the music biz seriously either. Then two months ago the licensing deal with Phonogram came up. Daniel Miller was against it, but I went with them for three good reasons. They're a good company with good ideas, and they're friendly people too. The most important thing is to only work with people I like. 99.9 percent of the music biz are shits. I even made them give me the 40p a week sweetie money deal, non-recoupable, for a year.

STEVO to Betty Page, *Sounds*, February 14, 1981

CHRIS ANDREWS As we were more like a performance art group than a pop one, the Some Bizzare Evenings were another excuse to dress up. We played Crocs in Rayleigh, Cabaret Futura in Soho, and the big Lyceum showcase. We also supported Soft Cell at the Venue in Victoria, London. Our music wasn't easy listening but the spectacle got us noticed in the press.

STEVE HOVINGTON We played one of the Some Bizzare Evenings in Liverpool and there was literally no one there. The bill was meant to be Depeche Mode and Soft Cell supported by B-Movie, and it was just us. After the show I tried to get paid and was told, 'No chance, mate, I'm not giving you any money for this.' And then we had all our gear stolen.

STEVE PARRY Stevo was larger than life. A lot of us would not have had the opportunity without him. For what it's worth, I don't think anybody made any money out of it. You know, it's very complicated. When I asked him for money he would say, 'I don't have any,' and take me down to a cash machine to show me. He'd say, 'I'm not making any money out of this.'

The recently publicised series of 'Some Bizzare Evenings' have now all been cancelled following the collapse of the tour after the gig at the Limit Club in Sheffield on February 3, when the PA company decided they couldn't cope and

---

* Some Bizzare Evenings were scheduled for January and February 1981, at venues including Electro Disco in Leeds, Sheffield's Limit Club, and Brady's in Liverpool. Adverts listed all the bands on the *Some Bizzare Album* with the caveat, 'Different bands on different nights. Check venue for details.'

packed up their gear. Spokesman for the bands that were appearing, Stevo, said: 'The tour hadn't been well organised, but we decided the bands shouldn't appear in such normal pub and club venues because they are part of the rock'n'roll lifestyle and just rip off bands.' The bands, all of which featured on the Phonogram-distributed *Some Bizzare Album* will now be appearing at selected venues outside the normal rock circuit.

author unknown, Sounds, February 14, 1981

TONY MAYO Although Naked Lunch had severed ties with Stevo, I carried on working with him for little while longer. But it came to an end at the Sundown Club for Duran Duran's debut London show.* B-Movie were supporting. Stevo decided to pour a pint of lager over Ashley Goodall, the senior A&R guy from EMI and I stopped him. I had to pin him up against a wall with my forearm on his throat and tell him to behave. There had been silly bits of behaviour all along where he'd do strange things, but enough was enough.

B-Movie come from Mansfield and have a hint of Liverpool pop, a touch of soul mystique. Tonight [they] break the ice with a dissolute piracy chic onstage and an impressive, searching symphony of sound. They sway with expressionless faces while keyboards and guitars swirl behind a rich voice and beautifully structured melodies.

LYNN HANNA, NME, March 14, 1981

STEVE HOVINGTON We supported Duran Duran in March on their first tour and we'd be sitting backstage and they're having their hair crimped by a hairdresser and fashion people were milling around. We were driving around in the back of a transit van, and they had stage crew and a massive lorry for their gear. It was like, 'Welcome to real life, mate, you're not going to get any preferential treatment around here.' But there was still a credible buzz around us, and the label were still talking about getting us to the top of the charts, but for whatever reason it never quite happened.

---

* The Sundown Club was a venue in the basement of the old Astoria on the Charing Cross Road in Central London. Duran Duran played there on March 4, 1981, supported by B-Movie and Biddie & Eve.

DAVE BALL We couldn't decide on what to release as the single and, confusingly, settled on 'A Man Can Get Lost' as the seven-inch A-side and 'Memorabilia' for the twelve-inch A-side.* The twelve-inch was the most important record at that stage as we were aiming to build our audience through playing at nightclubs, relying on DJ support in addition to playing live. We'd sort of made a conscious effort to become a lot more dance-friendly, and because Marc worked at Leeds Warehouse, he got to hear all the latest New York club tracks every weekend and buy or 'borrow' the best ones.

Oh, give me a home where a thumping rhythm doth roam! The Cellers perpetrate such a warm, tongue-in-cheek type of electro-funk dabbling; all but the vocals are created by synthesizer. Cool as a mountain stream and just as refreshing.

author unknown, *Sounds*, April 4, 1981

MARC ALMOND Our first proper single, 'Memorabilia', and an early version of 'Tainted Love' were produced by Daniel Miller, which was a dream for us. He was a god on the electronic music scene, and there was always part of us that wished we'd been on Mute instead of Some Bizzare. But even at that early stage, we felt a loyalty to Stevo. We felt he had discovered us, and it was him who'd made the recording session with Daniel possible in the first place. And, anyway, Daniel already had Depeche Mode.

'Memorabilia' was based on a James Brown funk riff and was influenced by the electronic repetition of Suicide. I kind of rap over the top about obsessively collecting trash—and human body parts. It was a huge club hit, and DJs like Rusty Egan used to play a thirty-minute mix of it at his club nights. 'Memorabilia' changed a lot for us and Stevo. All of a sudden, we had respect from the club scenes in London and New York. Years later, 'Memorabilia' was cited as being a precursor to acid house in the late 80s.

RUSTY EGAN 'Memorabilia', the Daniel Miller mix—oh my God, I thought that was the fucking future of electronic dance music. But I'd be going into record

---

* The two versions were issued simultaneously through Phonogram on March 21, 1981. The catalogue number HARD only appears on this release and was dropped in favour of BZS for subsequent Some Bizzare releases.

companies and they're saying, 'Have you heard the new Spyro Gyra or Shakatak?' And I'd be like, 'I don't give a fuck, mate!'

DAVID KNIGHT I don't remember a lot about the Some Bizzare Evening at the Lyceum, but I do recall Blah Blah Blah performing their set under artificial rocks in what looked like a planet-scape from *Lost In Space*, complete with twenty-foot multicoloured aliens prowling the stage.* That was great—I've always been a fan of The Residents, and this was more Residents than The Residents themselves. I don't have any memories of the other acts, but I know many of those who were advertised didn't play. I must have been so nervous playing to such a large venue that I blanked most of the evening, although I remember our set and that it seemed to go better than expected. In his gig review, Danny Kelly from the *NME* said we reminded him of Queen—forty years later, I'm still trying to work out if that's a compliment or not.

To say Some Bizzare Evening was a let-down would be like saying Noah had a few plumbing problems. I went along prepared to forget my own feelings about the movement's moral/ideological bankruptcy (the superficiality of its doctrines, the pea brain paucity of its ideas, the horrible elitism and bizism of it all) to be impressed by some of the good pop music which I'm told the movement is all about. Instead I found nothing. Dull youths desperately trying to spark up dull lives with a coating of glamour. This movement doesn't inspire, it doesn't exhilarate, it has no aspirations to greatness.

GARRY BUSHELL, *Sounds*, April 4, 1981

TONY MAYO We were playing up north that night. After splitting from Stevo we went with Asgard agency, and they were seriously thinking about helicoptering us down to play the Lyceum show. It didn't happen, though.

STEVE HOVINGTON By this point we'd started to get the picture that Stevo's organisational skills were sort of *unique*, shall we say. As Depeche Mode and Soft

* The Some Bizzare Evening at the Lyceum on the Strand in London again billed all the bands from the *Some Bizzare Album* as potentially appearing, alongside DJs Perry Haines, Dave Archer, and Stevo. In the event, only Blah Blah Blah, Illustration, The Loved One, The Fast Set, Jell, B-Movie, and, for some reason, The Bollock Brothers played. Depeche Mode claimed they weren't booked; Soft Cell never turned up.

Cell didn't turn up, the Lyceum was our first big London headline show. There were a lot of people there, and it was terrifying.

JULIA ADAMSON We played the album launch at the Lyceum. It was quite exciting and grand. Our manager had made some new outfits for us (think Brian Epstein designing a look for The Beatles), and I remember Stevo finding them amusing. They were supposed to tidy us up, but I'm glad no photos exist of them.

CHRIS ANDREWS Most of our audiences were half angry, half bemused at our act and costumes. I remember ducking cans and insults at the Lyceum in particular.

POLLY BIRKBECK The Lyceum was one of the first gigs I ever went to. I was fourteen. And it was annoying because I'd suddenly discovered Depeche Mode and they were on the bill along with Soft Cell and Blancmange, and none of those bands ended up playing. I was very disappointed. But B-Movie I really liked, and The Bollock Brothers played, who were good fun. I remember Blah Blah Blah getting canned off. I was just gutted that none of the bands I wanted to see played. Although I did get to see Depeche Mode supporting Fad Gadget the month after.

TONY MAYO We played the Hope & Anchor with Blah Blah Blah and The Loved One. One of them, I can't remember who, was using subsonic sounds to try and make people sick. It didn't work, though, and they just sounded awful.

CHRIS ANDREWS We always made the audience feel uncomfortable as we improvised a unique cacophony of synths, processed guitars, and demented singing. We would mix our own sound onstage and give the output to the PA, as most sound engineers couldn't tell who was playing what. The old Mini Korg mono synth had a thirty-two-foot bass sound that would creep into the mix, which could explain the subsonics.

STEVE HOVINGTON We met Matt Johnson and we would hang out with Soft Cell at the Columbia Hotel when both bands were in London. We played with Blancmange, Illustration, and Naked Lunch, but we never met Depeche Mode and there was no real camaraderie as far as we were concerned. We were arrogant little buggers, to be honest—we weren't particularly nice.

NEIL ARTHUR There was a possibility of us going a little bit further with Stevo, and there were definitely management contracts flying around, but I've got to say I was pretty reluctant. There were times when we weren't really sure whether we even wanted to get a record deal. Stephen and I were both working as graphic designers and really enjoyed our jobs, so it wasn't like we were chomping at the bit.

STEVE PARRY Neu Electrikk sort of self-combusted. We recorded an album called *Somnambulistic Limbo* and Derek, our lead singer, wasn't happy with it. He wanted to pursue a more commercial direction and had his head turned by various people. He got a deal and did a few demos, then basically vanished off the face of the earth. Steve Sherlock played with THE THE, then Matt recommended him to Marc Almond, so he ended up joining Marc & The Mambas. I wanted to be more avant-garde, more like the experimental German groups such as Can and Faust, so I went off and did that.

DAVID KNIGHT It was strange to watch that whole scene rapidly melt—as the bands went overground, the club nights went under, and it was obvious a sea change was afoot, as things were rapidly transitioning into the warehouse club scene, with funk, rare groove, and early rap, more of a NYC vibe than a Crocs-in-Rayleigh vibe. Meanwhile, The Human League were at no.1.

JULIA ADAMSON I thought we would do more with Stevo. I do remember him really liking the group and he wanted to release a single. He also put a daft promotion for the album in *Sounds*, where he proposed to me and there was to be a celebration in the Museum Of London or something. I don't have a copy of it, unfortunately. I remember getting a letter from John Peel, too, around the time the *Some Bizzare Album* was released, apologising for not replying sooner to my sending him our demo cassette tape and saying he liked the band. He used to play 'Tidal Flow' as well as other bands' tracks from the album.

NEIL ARTHUR Being part of the Some Bizarre thing was really important to us because, although we had a bit of a kind of around-about-the-houses route to signing with London, it wouldn't have happened if we hadn't been on that album. I think it was really important that we ended up meeting Stevo and allowing him to use 'Sad Day'. I don't know whether we ever earned any money from it—it was a long time ago, and the contracts were very strange.

JULIA ADAMSON It was agreed that our song 'Danceable' was going to be one of the first singles on Some Bizzare, and it was to be produced by Martin Hannett at Strawberry Studios. I found Hannett's production process fascinating; the harmonics creating choirs, and the dry mechanical percussion. Sadly, Ian Cutis had only recently died, and Martin was at loggerheads with Tony Wilson, all of which affected his work routine. He was late for sessions but would then often work through the night, long after the session hours were booked. The routine thing didn't bother me too much, as the work was being done, one way or another. In the end, we weren't happy with the mix, and it wasn't the song it should have been. Martin regretted it not working out as he really liked Illustration. During this time our manager dropped us, and as he had been the communication between us and Some Bizzare, we lost contact with Stevo, too. He must have heard the recording wasn't going well because he didn't pay the studio bill and the single never came out. I remember seeing Soft Cell at no.1 with the fantastic 'Tainted Love', and frankly feeling sick Illustration had split up. I think our single was to be released about the same time, with the same promotion and fuss. The *Some Bizzare Album* remains a visionary and remarkable document, though.

TONY MAYO Stevo wanted me to do the publishing for Some Bizzare, but I didn't know anything about publishing. 'That doesn't matter!' he said. 'What will happen is all the publishing will be assigned to you and you'll get 50 percent of all the bands' money!' Well bearing in mind I viewed most of the Some Bizzare bands as friends, that wasn't going to happen.

In retrospect, I feel bad because if I hadn't had split from Stevo then perhaps some of the bands wouldn't have had the problems they did. The outcome may have been better for all of us. However, it was such a head screw-up dealing with the random and bizarre issues that constantly cropped up. So, I feel a bit of guilt, but on the other hand some got further than Naked Lunch did.

BRIAN MOSS Paul Morley from the *NME* came up to Leeds to interview Marc and Dave, and they were really happy and wined and dined him, and he absolutely hammered them in print. It was a steep learning curve, but I suppose it's just the nature of the beast.

❝ The slight Soft Cell are caught up in the small but protective wind of a trend, trying as hard as they know how not to sweat like clumsy pop predecessors applying themselves with a proper fear of dullness to representing some vague but perhaps virtuous interest in life. They'd like to bend away from the trend that has wafted them this far but are perhaps too brittle.

PAUL MORLEY, *NME*, May 23, 1981

JOSE WARDEN Vicious Pink Phenomena formed before we became Soft Cell's backing vocalists. Dave was the unofficial third member, he was always going to be the silent partner and the producer. The first time we did backing vocals was at Amnesia in Leeds.* Most of the crowd ended up onstage that night. It really was a fabulous show in that everyone in the room was part of it.

MATT JOHNSON Ivo gave me the opportunity to record a solo album for 4AD.† *Burning Blue Soul* was made on a shoestring budget of £1,800, which paid for four or five recording sessions, and I'd record and mix maybe two songs per session. One of the most memorable times was when Ivo and I drove to Spaceward Studios in Cambridge in his little blue Peugeot. We took sleeping bags, so we could have a full day's recording, sleep on the floor in the live room, then get up early the next day to start work again.

JOSE WARDEN We did all the early Soft Cell shows: Rock City, Maximus, Retford Porterhouse, all the venues that were trendy then. Brian drove the tour bus with Marc up front next to him, while me, Dave, and often Stevo and all the gear sat in the back.

Stevo was always just one of the gang—I never saw him in a role of being in control. We had a laugh, it was always about a laugh, I never took any of it seriously, and looking back I never realised how huge Soft Cell were. Not even when the shows got bigger and the hotels got nicer.

* Anni Hogan booked Soft Cell to play the Amnesia Club in Leeds on May 28, 1981. It was the first time Jose Warden and Brian Moss appeared onstage with them.
† *Burning Blue Soul*, which was confusingly credited to Matt Johnson not THE THE, was released by 4AD in September 1981. Along with Ivo Watts-Russell, production credits are given to Pete Maben, and Bruce Gilbert and Graham Lewis from Wire, who had also produced THE THE's debut single, 'Controversial Subject', the previous year. In 1993, *Burning Blue Soul* was reissued under Johnson's band moniker, finally making it an official THE THE album.

BRIAN MOSS I remember Rock City was crazy.* Matt Johnson was there. Ronnie was the support doing a PA, no band, just miming. And they put her record on at the wrong speed.

MATT JOHNSON The *Some Bizarre Album* garnered a lot of interest, especially from the music press, and the major labels were starting to sniff around. 'Tainted Love' hadn't happened for Soft Cell yet, but it was just around the corner, and we did a gig with them up in Nottingham around that time. We met Rusty Egan there, who was very supportive of Stevo and Some Bizzare in the early days.

RUSTY EGAN I first met THE THE at that Rock City gig, and I said to Stevo, 'You're unbelievable, you fucking found another one. This guy's amazing.' But guess what, nobody else agreed with me.

DAVE BALL We'd been playing little clubs for a couple of years, steadily building up a reasonable following, and then all of a sudden we've got this massive record. The transition happened so fast. Stevo had got us loads of bookings and we were committed to them, but you can't really play little clubs when you should be playing place like the Hammersmith Palais. It took us a little while to realise quite how big a band we were.

BRIAN MOSS Soft Cell didn't have an agent or a tour manager, so I would imagine Stevo was probably phoning around and booking all the gigs. He was still thinking small when really they should've been upping the scale. Every single show was busy—like, absolutely rammed. There wasn't any crew or whatever, we just did it all ourselves—everything and everyone in the van. Later on, we even had the padded cell in the back of the van, too.

HUW FEATHER I'd gone to Nottingham Poly to study theatre design, and Marc was at Leeds doing fine art performance. We'd carried on working together, and I would go up and help out with the design and lighting on his degree shows, so we'd established a professional connection as well as a friendship. So, when Soft Cell started getting

* Soft Cell played Nottingham's Rock City, supported by THE THE and Ronny, on June 3, 1981. The flyer highlights the fact that Stevo and Rusty Egan would be appearing for the first time together, along with 'lots of people you wouldn't expect to see onstage'.

61

some interest, it was natural for me to work with them. The first thing Stevo said to me was, "Ere, what's theatre design then?' So I explained it to him, and here said, 'Well, 'ow would you present Marc and Dave onstage?' and I said, 'Well we need to make an actual soft cell—a padded backdrop with sugar pink and baby blue neon bars.' I used my training and contacts to build it, and it was designed so it could be transported in a van rather than a lorry. And they were the only band that had an actual set rather than just a sheet or a television or a tape recorder onstage with them. Soft Cell had a look, and the look was minimal and it was gobsmacking.

As one half of a synthesizer duo, singer Marc Almond is stranded alone at the front of the stage, a position which DAF's Gabi has recently been using with style and skill. To put it politely, Marc doesn't project the necessary personal charisma and whether it was tacit acknowledgement of this, or an understandable desire to create a carnival atmosphere, he's soon surrounded by a variety of extras whose effect is tacky shading down to atrocious.

LYNN HANNA, *NME*, July 4, 1981

BEVERLEY GLICK Soft Cell shows were chaotic because Marc in particular came from a performance art background and wasn't bothered about perfection. It could be a bit crazy, but I liked that unpredictability because a lot of music at that time was overly produced and polished, and I quite liked that feeling of not knowing what was going to happen next. But I thought they were great live in those early days. I remember they played at this New Romantic disco in Dartford, and the crowd just didn't know what to make of them. I mean, Marc used to provoke some extreme reactions.

MARC ALMOND Early Soft Cell shows were messy, chaotic, and confrontational, definitely low-rent events. The sound was often poor, and we had no production values apart from a few neon lights we'd had made which didn't work very well, and things usually ended with the audience invading the stage. We'd have to set up on the dance floor sometimes, surrounded by people nearly knocking over the equipment, which never seemed to be upgraded. Even after 'Tainted Love' we continued playing these tiny venues, places way too small for our stature as a band after we became famous. They were always over-sold, which was stressful, but to be honest the standard of our show at the time wouldn't have translated to the places we probably should have been playing.

STEVE HOVINGTON B-Movie had quite a traditional line-up, especially compared to other Some Bizzare bands, and we were definitely more psychedelic. We had touches of electronica in there, but we were more into experimenting with sounds, using phaser pedals and putting weird effects on my bass. Rick was a brilliant piano player so there were three- or four-minute synth solos, it was more like early Doors or Pink Floyd. We were just trying to mess around sonically more than anything else. I think when Some Bizzare really got going, us having a full-band line-up became a bit of a bone of contention with Stevo, because most of his bands just switched on a drum machine and stood in front of a synthesizer playing a few notes.

NEIL ARTHUR There were opportunities, like supporting Grace Jones at Drury Lane, that must have come off the back of the *Some Bizzare Album*. I can't imagine Chris Blackwell playing *Irene & Mavis* to Grace and thinking, *Yeah, we'll have them support us*. We played with Japan, too. While there may have been an interest in what we were doing musically, which is lovely, one of the reasons we were asked to do these shows was the fact that we were a duo. Just Stephen with a cassette machine and an organ and me with a guitar and a microphone.

STEVE HOVINGTON We supported the Comsat Angels at the Top Rank in Sheffield, a massive venue which had huge curtains across the stage. When we were setting up, their tour manager objected to us moving any of their gear. Stevo went behind the curtain to speak to him, and all of a sudden the drapes started moving and you could see there was some kind of struggle going on behind them. It was like a Morecambe & Wise sketch, the lighting rig started coming down and suddenly the tour manager came flying out. Stevo's approach was always straight to the point—that was the Dagenham way of doing things.

DAVE BALL 'Memorabilia' didn't do much on the main charts, although it did really well in the clubs and reached no.35 in the *Billboard* US dance charts, which, although based only on dance-floor reaction and not sales, was still incredible for an unknown English electro duo. Stevo persuaded Phonogram to give us another chance although they wanted us to use a different producer, which was why Daniel was moved aside and Mike Thorne brought in. They wanted a less-programmed sound, which in retrospective was definitely the right move. That kind of sequencer sound suited Depeche Mode better than it did us. They had perfect three-minute pop gems like 'Dreaming Of Me' and 'Just Can't Get Enough', and it worked so well, they were like Silicon Teens made flesh. We weren't a sequencer band, we were a bit more freeform. Everything on Soft Cell's records, apart from the drum machine, is played by me. And Marc's singing was much more expressive than what was associated with synth bands at that point. Marc was a male version of a diva, and the whole lone synth player at the back and diva up front idea was picked up by Vince when he left Depeche Mode and formed Yazoo with Alison Moyet, as well as Dave Stewart with Annie Lennox in Eurythmics, especially on their early records. It was a good blueprint, and our success proved that it worked.

DANIEL MILLER Of course, I would have liked to have carried on working with Soft Cell. I thought I'd done a reasonable job, and the band enjoyed the experience. But around the same time, Depeche started to take off, and suddenly I didn't have much time on my hands. And I wasn't necessarily aiming for a career as a record producer anyway—that wasn't where I saw myself going. If I was a budding record producer then I probably would have been more pissed off than I was, and obviously Mike Thorne did such a brilliant job, but I was disappointed.

MIKE THORNE I was always interested in working on things that were a little bit off the wall. A lot of people break through with one type of music and then milk it for the rest of their careers, but I always wanted to move on to something new, so when Phonogram got in touch and asked me to do a couple of one-off singles I was interested. I was in London working on a film score and I had my Synclavier with me.[*] The singles were B-Movie's 'Marilyn Dreams' and Soft Cell's 'Tainted Love'.[†]

BEVERLEY GLICK I think Phonogram thought they'd put out a couple of Soft Cell singles to see what happened, and if it didn't work, they wouldn't have lost that much. A lot of record companies had that attitude at the time. And, of course, a lot of new signings were steered toward doing a cover version, so I do think 'Tainted

---

[*] The Synclavier was an early digital synthesizer, polyphonic sampling system, and music workstation manufactured by the New England Digital Corporation of Norwich, Vermont. Popular in the late 70s and early 80s, it appears on records by Genesis, Depeche Mode, Paul Hardcastle, and Laurie Anderson, and on Trevor Horn's ZTT productions.
[†] Released in June 1981, B-Movie's second single for Deram, 'Marilyn Dreams', failed to chart. Released a month later, on July 17, 1981, Soft Cell's second single for Phonogram, 'Tainted Love', reached the UK no.1 spot on September 5 and stayed there for two weeks, selling over a million copies in the UK alone.

Love' was make-or-break for them. Phonogram wouldn't have been interested in the stuff that they did later if hadn't have been for that.

MARTIN PATTON I was definitely pushing for 'Bedsitter' to be the next Soft Cell single. Luckily, I was outvoted, or things could've been very different.

MIKE THORNE B-Movie were a nice bunch of guys and I'd worked with them on 'Remembrance Day'. Soft Cell I'd only spoken to on the phone, but Stevo bought them down to the studio unannounced while we were working on 'Marilyn Dreams', which didn't seem the best way to make the individual artists feel as if their particular needs were being given special attention. Stevo was always an aspiring emperor and not always with smooth social grace. But even then, fresh off the train from Leeds, Marc and Dave had a real aura about them.

STEVE HOVINGTON I don't know whether it's true or not, but the myth is Soft Cell only got signed to Phonogram because Stevo insisted they couldn't have B-Movie unless they took them too, a kind of buy-one-get-one-free deal. And they ended up using our studio time and our budget.

MIKE THORNE For economy's sake, we did the two singles in parallel. Both bands were fairly new in the studio, and I'd do one day with one group and the next day with the other, just to give them time to settle in, get confident with what was going on. I was doing twelve-hour days and was absolutely exhausted.

PETER ASHWORTH The first time I met Soft Cell was at a publicity shoot for Phonogram. I like people who work outside the usual boundaries, and Marc and Dave were doing exactly that. I think they were kind of amused at the time at where everything was going, and how it was going to progress. There were no great plans because they hadn't had any success at that point.

MIKE THORNE It was one of those dream sessions where everything we reached for seemed to fit effortlessly. Whether it was the surprisingly effective horn sustain in the middle or the classic 'bink'. We went for a run-through of Marc's vocal, which I recorded, wisely as it turned out, as it sounded marvellous and became the lead vocal on the final record. A few extra backing vocals, some premeditated and some

65

invented on the spot, and we were done. Although the track was long, most of the mixing and effects generation was done in real time. It was almost a theatre piece: lunging across the room to tweak a sound as the tape was whizzing by. I remember so clearly focusing on the mix and then suddenly noticing that all of us in the control room were dancing as we were working on our feet, completely spontaneously and without being aware of it. It was a good sign. We came to the end of it at about 3am and felt quite pleased. Someone said, 'Well, this one should make the Top 50.'

There was virtual bribery and blackmail going on! Our position's always been unclear, at the moment we're being held to ransom again—we won't know for another four weeks whether we can do an album or not. We've got everything prepared but we're being held back. It's a very frustrating and worrying time. It'll be easier for us all if this single's successful, but I won't slit my wrists if it isn't, it won't stop me from doing what I want.

MARC ALMOND to Betty Page, *Sounds*, August 1, 1981

VAL DENHAM I was doing my MA at the Royal College Of Art, living in a little bedsit in Streatham. One evening I was watching *Top Of The Pops* when Soft Cell came on singing 'Tainted Love'. I already liked the song but had never seen what the band looked like before, so I was somewhat confused and shocked when I saw Marc emoting from the screen.

NEIL ARTHUR What a fantastic record 'Tainted Love' is.

BEVERLEY GLICK Stevo had the first laugh, if you like, as opposed to the last laugh, when 'Tainted Love' got to no.1. It was not the way things were supposed to be, that a band like Soft Cell would have this massive worldwide hit before any of the New Romantic bands did. There was so much competition between them.

JOHN LUONGO I first met Stevo in New York, at the Broadway offices of an attorney we shared. Stevo had a reckless abandon and a personality bigger than the Statue of Liberty, and we became instant friends and bonded in a heartbeat. He had a record by a group from the UK and he wanted to licence it to a label in the US and Canada. He had an offer from Seymour Stein at Sire, but after we met and hung out, Stevo wanted to give me the option. I listened to the track and flipped out, and the next day I went into the CBS offices, sure it was going to blow them away too, and they'd let me sign it to my label. I sat in a room with the head of the Associated Labels and his head of promotion and put the acetate on the turntable, confident they would feel the same way about the track as I did. To my utter shock and dismay, they both looked at each other and said they did not hear it and had to pass. I was crestfallen that they could not hear what was, clearly, a masterpiece, and an innovative new direction for music.

I walked back to my office on West 57th Street feeling gutted and betrayed, and called Stevo and told him the news. He and I went out to dinner anyway, and toasted our friendship and the daft deaf ears of older executives who did not have a clue. Stevo ended up giving the record and the group to Seymour Stein of Sire, a wonderful man but a competitor, which simply broke my heart. The record was of course 'Tainted Love' by Soft Cell.

SEYMOUR STEIN ['Tainted Love'] was incredible. I had to have this record. And I became very, very excited. I knew the song from its earlier version by Gloria Jones.

STEVO We needed more radio promotion money, which is basically cash that goes into brown paper bags and is pushed under the table. And, hey presto, you're on the playlist. But it was an extremely large sum of money, and non-recoupable, so there wasn't going to be a nice way of asking for it. I discussed with my attorney beforehand how best to proceed, and we both walked into Seymore's office and turned his desk over. While he was still sitting at it.

SEYMOUR STEIN He came to my office and said to me if I didn't do a good job with this record he would shoot my kneecaps off.

STEVO I think that he did the deal just to get me out if the room, probably.

BRIAN MOSS Jose and I were just having fun and not thinking too much about it. Initially, we were going to be on *Top Of The Pops*, but behind the scenes I think the record company thought Jose might have been too much of a distraction, so Marc and Dave did it as a duo, which was the right thing to do. We weren't on the record anyway, although we did the backing vocals on 'Tainted Love' live.

BEVERLEY GLICK I found it puzzling why people felt so confronted by Marc. A lot of people talk about the first time they saw him on *Top Of The Pops* with outrage. But he didn't strike me in that way, perhaps because I'd met him in person. But I can imagine seeing him on television, this 'nose with eyes', as he use to refer to himself, and thinking, *Who is this strange creature?* Somehow the way he presented himself was threatening to people, but I don't think he was doing it deliberately. If you think about Boy George and how he went down the cuddly homosexual route, Marc was seen to be much more disturbing for some reason.

KARL O'CONNOR When I saw Soft Cell on *Top Of The Pops* for the first time, my future was revealed. I went into school the day after and I couldn't talk to people I'd been friends with before, they just didn't have the language to speak to me anymore. I had tickets to see The Jam, but by the time the gig came around I hated them, I thought they were awful, because I'd moved so far away from what they were about. I think people of my age were very lucky, because we were hit just when great independent British music got into the charts unfiltered. Something like Soft Cell was beyond subversive. It had nothing to do with Marc Almond's sexuality—I didn't even know what being gay meant at the time—I just felt that he and Dave Ball together were genuinely threatening. You definitely felt they went straight from the TV studio to the life they presented in their songs, which was pretty much the case.

BRIAN MOSS They would have probably been instant millionaires if they'd put one of their own songs on the B-side of 'Tainted Love'. It was Stevo's mistake, but you can't knock him because we were all new to it all.

MARTIN PATTON It was the band who wanted 'Where Did Our Love Go' on the B-side of the seven-inch of 'Tainted Love'. We didn't know what the publishing implications of that decision were at the time. Phonogram wouldn't have pointed it out because it made no difference to them.

MIKE THORNE 'Tainted Love''s commercial story is well-known: number one in seventeen territories, the biggest seller of the year in the UK,* and set the record

* In 2021, the Official Charts Company recalculated the data and retrospectively gave the title to The Human League's 'Don't You Want Me'.

for the longest stay by a single in the US *Billboard* Hot 100 chart.* Nothing had prepared any of us for such a level of commercial success. Marc and Dave were completely swept away, and even at my advanced age of thirty-three it felt almost out of control. I would get goofy, giggly phone calls at home, and the group could barely walk down the street without provoking a mob scene. At home in Leeds, they had to endure a state of siege, from well-meaning social interruptions to being shouted at in the street, and they soon moved to London to try and get a little more privacy.

MATT JOHNSON 'Tainted Love' had a huge impact, for Marc and Dave, of course, but also for Stevo and the other bands associated with Some Bizarre, because in the record industry, as soon as something happens for one label, all the others want to copy it and replicate that success. So, Stevo was running this fledgling record label, while still doing a bit of DJ'ing and promoting gigs, primarily to show off the bands he had. A decision was made to record a THE THE single and shop it around the majors. 'Cold Spell Ahead' was recorded at Stage One in Forest Gate, which was opposite my nan and grandad's house.† They had an excellent house engineer called Pete Maben, who also worked on a couple of tracks on *Burning Blue Soul*. Daniel Miller had been in the night before, producing Depeche Mode, and he'd left some of his gear set up, so we cheekily used his ARP 2600 synth and his drum machine and sequencer.

THE THE was still technically a duo at the time; Keith and myself, although when it came to recording I ended up playing all the instruments as I was now quite experienced in the studio, and it was just quicker. Stevo played it to many labels, and all of them turned their noses up. I even took it up to CBS myself, and Howard Thompson, an A&R man there, actually turned the cassette off halfway through and dismissively said, 'Well, that's not very good is it?' I was just a teenager and felt humiliated. Someone like Geoff Travis would at least listen all the way through and then say, 'You're not quite there yet, Matt, but keep going.' Which is what you need when you're a kid. Stevo was still keen though, and so we decided to put it out independently through Some Bizarre with Pinnacle distribution.

---

* In the US, the single reached no.8 and stayed on the *Billboard* Hot 100 chart for forty-three weeks—a record at the time.
† THE THE's first single for Some Bizzare, 'Cold Spell Ahead' was released on September 25, 1981, on seven-inch only (BZS4). It failed to chart.

MARTIN PATTON Matt's brother Andy did the sleeve for 'Cold Spell Ahead' but hadn't done any labels, so I ended up doing it. I tried to copy the style of a typeface that he had created specifically for the single, but not particularly well I have to say.

DAVE BATES Expect the unexpected with Stevo. The idea of him insisting in his contracts that he wanted X-amount of pounds and X-amount of points and he wanted this and he wanted the other and he wanted a duck. A live duck.

MARTIN PATTON Stevo was running around London, knocking on doors, causing havoc and making things happen. We were trying to make sense of it and put it all together. We'd learnt quite a bit about press, advertising, manufacturing, marketing—we pretty much knew what a label needed. I had trained as a graphic designer, so the artwork was a world I understood. In essence, we were the label and the label managers in a 'creative' way, but feeding things into Phonogram. Occasionally we'd have a meeting whereby we'd say, 'Stevo, really?' Like the proposed Blah Blah Blah album. 'Are you actually going to do this, because we don't see it.' And those types of meetings were becoming more frequent.

STEVO As far as I'm concerned, I did a very good deal with Phonogram—for both them and the artists, I did my job. Y'know, before I came along Phonogram were a bloody rock label, they used to have Def Leppard and Status Quo on their books, they were nothing before we broke the doors down, metaphorically speaking. Although, I did break an actual door down later on. But yeah, I sent Phonogram a teddy bear with a cassette taped to its chest, and the cassette had the terms of the Soft Cell agreement on it. That was the deal because they couldn't negotiate with a teddy bear. But it was a jest, a joke. Of course, the legal dealings were watertight before I sent them the teddy bear. A lot of Stevo stories are fabricated myths that have been pinned on me, but if they're good for the art, then great.

>>

MIKE THORNE The committee had chosen 'Bedsitter' as the second single and I wanted the best resources available, given that we had to follow up one of the best-known records of the era. I insisted the recording take place where I could provide

70

the support of my considerable collection of sound-mangling machines and new-fangled synthesizers. I think it's fair to say Marc and Dave did not have a problem with coming to New York.*

DAVE BALL New York was great. I'd been before with my mum and my sister in 1978, but being out with 'the boys' and working in a studio was something else. We were actually very disciplined: we'd get in in the morning, have a bit of breakfast, start at 10am, and work through until 6pm. Mike didn't like to work long days, which kind of suited the music because it meant we didn't overcook things with unnecessary stuff and just kept it simple. And obviously the club scene in New York at the time was fantastic, and we were getting a lot of inspiration from there and discovering new chemicals along the way. Just having a generally great, debauched time, but getting the work done too.

BRIAN MOSS It was almost like being asked to be an astronaut—I didn't know anyone who'd even been to America. We actually flew over with Marc, as Dave was already there. New York had a bad reputation back then for crime and violence. The problem for me was, I'd had an appendectomy which had gone wrong, so I basically had a hole in my side, which had to be cleaned out and dressed by a nurse a couple of times a day. And then Marc and Dave asked us to go to New York, and the nurse said, 'You can't go like this,' but we said, 'Well, we're going!' So, the nurse showed Jose what needed to be done, and she did it every day while we were there. She's a hell of a woman, is Jose. I spent two weeks in New York recording and going clubbing with a gaping hole in my side.

STEVO I spent a lot of time in New York. The first night I was with Soft Cell, in a swanky apartment at 86th street, between West End and Riverside. And we went to the Ritz and I met a girl who was studying in New York, and I shacked up with her and went back to her place on First Avenue on 91st Street. And I stayed with her for three months, living in Spanish Harlem. Many years later, Dave Ball took me to the Baby Doll Lounge, and she was up onstage dancing.

---

* *Non-Stop Erotic Cabaret* was recorded in New York at Mediasound Studios, with Mike Thorne producing, between September 22 and October 22. Dave Ball flew out for the first week and was then joined by Marc Almond, Jose Warden, Brian Moss, and eventually Stevo.

71

MIKE THORNE I always liked to record the twelve-inch version then extract the commercially all-important seven-inch edit rather than the other way around. Recording the long version gave a better conceptual whole, and often revealed any spaces screaming for something to fill them. That nature-abhorring-a-vacuum approach could be pretty beneficial for the seven-inch version too, with ideas generated for the twelve-inch version rebounding into the edit. It was a very effective way of working, especially on those early Soft Cell singles.

For 'Bedsitter', I built an eight-minute behemoth out of the original song and Marc and Dave rose to the challenge with new musical ideas for the twelve-inch version. Especially creative was Marc's additional centre vocal section, prefiguring the rap centrepiece of dance tracks by at least a decade. That 'Bedsitter' made the Top 5 in the UK charts was an essential confidence boost for Soft Cell. A poor showing with their own song following a gigantic cover version could have been devastating, but their existence was fully vindicated.

BRIAN MOSS Mike was great. He's from Sunderland and was a really down to earth guy. All the people at Mediasound were fantastic. The atmosphere there was really good, and we had great fun doing it. And obviously Jose and I had a lot of spare time, so we'd go and do a bit of touristy stuff. We went with Dave up the Empire State Building and went shopping with Stevo.

MIKE THORNE One of the strengths of Soft Cell's music at that time was its unadorned simplicity. Dave's bass lines were played with something resembling one-finger typewriter technique, and Marc's wordy vocal lines and passionate delivery meant the musical space was filled without fluff or unnecessary fat. Flash was at a minimum, the message maximum. Songs like 'Chips On My Shoulder', which could easily have been delivered by a punk combo; and 'Entertain Me', a latter-day vaudeville transplant with a sharp touch. We also co-opted several top New York session musicians whose technical class and quality in the middle of the simple electronic textures somehow fitted immediately. Dave Tofani's clarinet solo in 'Seedy Films' takes the track away from anything previously heard. And 'Say Hello, Wave Goodbye' became a signature classic and deserved to be their third Top 5 single. Soft Cell were one of the most distinctive and creative acts to emerge from the 80s, and *Non-Stop Erotic Cabaret* remains as fresh as when we delivered it. But we did put the work in, though.

JOSE WARDEN Marc, Dave, Brian, and I had been to see a couple of soft-porn films in some really shifty cinemas in Soho and were trying to recreate that ambience for 'Seedy Films'. When we did the song live, Marc and I would dance behind a screen so that you could only see our silhouettes, which I always thought looked a bit weird as I'm so much taller than him.

I saw this headline in the *News Of The World* that said, 'Sex Dwarf lures 100 disco dollies to a life of vice'! That just has to be a song! Definite trash. It's about this horrible little dwarf who had a harem of sex slaves that he made do disgusting things with him and then he sold them again. Filth! But we can be *very* romantic as well!

MARC ALMOND to Betty Page, *Sounds*, August 1, 1981

BRIAN MOSS The thing is, we never had a single rehearsal. We didn't rehearse for that first Amnesia show, we just had the lyrics written on a serviette. And that's how it stayed—everything just evolved through the live performances. And at the point we came to record the album, we just got on and did it. Yeah, I'm the sex dwarf on the album. I'm about five foot eight, so I don't quite qualify, but I don't know how I came up with the idea to do the voice like that.

MIKE THORNE *Non-Stop Erotic Cabaret* has an assurance unusual for a first album. Whatever the confluence of intent and environment, the record still sets its own standards. And New York contributed greatly. The city energises anyone who experiences it, and Marc and Dave each grabbed the possibilities with both hands.

BRIAN MOSS Marc had met Cindy Ecstasy while out one night, and she joined our gang, along with two other guys, one who used to be Rudolph Nureyev's boyfriend and an early graffiti artist called Skipper. So, there were a few of us, but we still got into every club for free and got looked after. Cindy wasn't a drug dealer—a drug dealer is somebody selling illegal drugs, and ecstasy wasn't at the time.* She might as well have been selling tins of beans! She just had a connection with these two chemists who were making it in Brooklyn, so she was just the hook up. She was a really nice girl and good fun to be around. When you go to a big city for the first

---

* Prior to June 1, 1985, ecstasy (or 3,4-methylenedioxymethamphetamine) wasn't classed as a Schedule 1 substance by the US DEA, making the taking of it for recreational purposes technically legal. In the UK, it had been illegal since 1977.

time, you don't really know where to go, so it was good to hang out with a cool person who lived there who could point us in the right direction. Cindy was more like a tour guide, I would say, but I never considered her a drug dealer, and it's totally unfair to call her one.

MIKE THORNE Cindy is credited with the group's discovery of ecstasy around this time, and she's been obnoxiously described as 'a drug dealer', which is glib and convenient journalistic nonsense. She was a camp follower who contributed to the general party energy level and had her own distinctive style and rasping Brooklyn sense of humour and delivery. She passed on wonderful substances to Marc and Dave et al, but in a street social way. Ms Big she was not. I wonder where she is now. She was very good at hats.

STEVO The whole *Non Stop Erotic Cabaret* album was recorded and mixed totally on ecstasy. Every single part of the recording process of that record was on legal ecstasy. It gave you this great feeling, it was a wonderful drug. I loved it.

BRIAN MOSS As far as I know we only ever took it when we were out or before we went out. No one took it in the studio because we had to be focused—we weren't messing around. We were there every morning, even though we'd been out quite late quite often, we still would still be there on time.

MIKE THORNE Although Marc has said that the two of them were as high as kites on sessions, the truth was more mundane and workmanlike. I was never bothered by what anyone was on, as always preferring just to deal with the personality I found in front of me. Sometimes their eyes shone unusually brightly, but when you're making a record you just get on with the job, and anyone's altered state just becomes part of the equation. The only person who couldn't indulge was the producer, if he was to serve as a constant musical and emotional reference point. Somebody has to play the straight man. I could enjoy myself socially, but in the studio I find that even a half pint of light ale throws me off balance.

JOSE WARDEN The entire trip was a big party. Even the night before we were due to return home we were out living it up. We didn't get to the club Berlin in the East Village until 4:00am that morning. Needless to say, we missed the flight home!

BRIAN MOSS I didn't take ecstasy again until I worked on the rave scene in the 90s. I was persuaded by a DJ friend one night in Bridlington, so I did a half, and it was awful, I just felt crap. It wasn't the same thing at all, and I've never taken it again.

>>

PETER ASHWORTH I was living in a bedsit by myself at that point and I wanted to do something that conveyed that for the 'Bedsitter' cover.* I'd created a formula for my studio shots using quite a long lens for portraiture, separating the subject from the background, allowing to light the sitters separately. I was shooting on a Hasselblad at that time, which is a square-format film camera entirely suited for doing record sleeves. I would shoot a ton of Polaroids to see what I was getting, which was a bit unfortunate on the 'Bedsitter' shoot because the kitchen utensils that were stuck onto a piece of Colorama paper with gaffer tape kept falling off. It seemed every time I went for a shot, a pot would crash to the floor. As I didn't work with assistants, I had to stick the thing back on the wall myself and hope it would still be there by the time I got back to the camera. Marc wasn't happy and told me so. That shoot kind of changed our relationship, and it became very memorable for that reason.

Soft Cell are the essential teases of the modern bop, at once winsomely witty and coyly touching. Marc sings 'Bedsitter' with one eyebrow furrowed and the other firmly arched, while David's sterling stride of composition passes the Hayes morality code by keeping a leg in the bed and the other foot tapping on the floor. Soft Cell are the great soul duo of the moment: sexy, suggestive and soppy. Play them right after your Motown hits and don't worry about the consequences.

author unknown, *NMF*, October 31, 1981

PETER ASHWORTH I'd spent some time wandering around Soho, shooting people wandering through the neon-lit alleyways. Marc and Dave loved the pictures, so it was a matter of recreating that for the album cover. We had to do a studio shoot, partly because of light levels but also because the bouncers outside the clubs would have got annoyed with us scaring off the punters. The background

* Released on October 29, 1981, Soft Cell's 'Bedsitter' reached no.4 on the UK chart and was notable for its eye-catching video, made with first-time director Tim Pope.

is a piece of PVC that's corrugated. Stevo had commissioned two neon signs, but they weighed an absolute ton and there was no way of hanging them in the shot, so they were added to the image later. It was Marc's idea to be pulling a bag out of his jacket, which created a lot of mystique—a talking point to this day—and that was something he wanted to get across. If an artist is going through something, then I'm not shooting a just portrait, I'm capturing a story unfolding. And stories became what Soft Cell and I did from then on, pretty much. It wasn't just turn up and shoot, it was more, *Look we've got this idea, let's see where it goes.* And that became more and more exotic and exciting as we went on.

KARL O'CONNOR *Non-Stop Erotic Cabaret* is absolutely Soho in the early 80s, especially the 'Bedsitter' video.* Director Tim Pope captured London nightlife at that time—he even managed to mythologise St John's Wood tube station. Even though I was only twelve, through this music I'd started thinking about certain topics that were absolutely fucking taboo. Even though I didn't necessarily know what drugs *were*, I definitely knew the people who were making these records were on them. And the whole nightlife thing I found really exciting because it was the opposite of everything I knew up to that point. But it was also very grounded and attainable. And Marc and Dave were a conduit for that life, we saw it all through their eyes. It looked great and they led us into it.

MARC ALMOND Walking down Soho, you'd hear 'Seedy Films' coming out of clip joint or a strip place, and I thought the greatest accolade was to make music for strippers to strip to.

I think it's no coincidence that The Human League and Soft Cell are two of this year's success stories: they both have powerful character singers that croon from the heart, one writing of a more wholesome love, the other of grubby, messy affairs and sordid, secret sex. Both are Soft, both are Human, expressing feelings that connect with a satisfying simplicity of electronic melody. Laugh, cry, love, hate, bump, grind, scream, sing, dance. As they say in the trade, this one will run and run.

BEVERLEY GLICK (writing as Betty Page), *Sounds*, November 28, 1981

---

* Soft Cell's debut album, *Non-Stop Erotic Cabaret*, was released on November 27, 1981. It reached no.5 on the UK album chart, eventually going platinum, and no.22 in the USA.

DAVE BALL I had the most fun around *Non-Stop Erotic Cabaret*. It was before any stress and any drugs were involved, it was a completely naive and joyful experience. We were so grateful for the opportunity to be in a studio with a proper producer. We were like little pop virgins, we were still innocent and hadn't been put through the mill yet. We still thought the pop world was great, going to all these exciting places, partying all the time, we were having a ball.

PETER ASHWORTH The best bands have got opposites in them—different people who have different, sometimes opposing, approaches—and if you get the right two or three people together, it's just so creative. And Soft Cell were a great example of that. Photographically, Dave was usually the straight man, standing as silent witness while Marc preened and gesticulated. But that outtake where he's threatening Marc with a flick knife with that leery smile on his face was the first time he became the story. I'm pretty sure that pose was Dave's idea—I know it doesn't seem likely. It ended up as a double-page pull-out poster in *New Sounds New Style* magazine. I think they got into a bit of trouble for printing it.

JESSAMY CALKIN Lydia Lunch was my first point of contact with that extended Some Bizzare world. I met her through the photographer Christina Birrer, who was working with her. I'd interviewed The Birthday Party for *The Face* but met Nick Cave and his partner Anita Lane properly through Lydia. We all lived in Brixton, so we became friends. I first met Marc when I interviewed him and Dave for *New Sounds New Styles*. That was when I first met Stevo too, as I had to do the interview at the Some Bizarre office, but I didn't click with him at all. I didn't find him funny, I just found him really obnoxious and annoying. Did me being a woman have anything to do with that? Absolutely. Lydia never had time for him either. I did appreciate what he was trying to do with Some Bizzare, but I thought of him like a Throbbing Gristle record: I was glad he was around, but I really didn't want to spend any time with him.

STEVE HOVINGTON Stevo did have a certain loyalty to us probably because we were the first band that he was properly involved with. And 'Remembrance Day' did exceed everybody's expectations, but unfortunately for us, 'Tainted Love' completely eclipsed that, so naturally Stevo started to leave us behind. There were arguments, and I think we made mistakes; I don't know what was going on behind the scenes with Stevo and Tracy Bennett. In hindsight we should have followed up with 'Nowhere Girl' and not 'Marilyn Dreams'. Plus, there was a suspicion that we'd just been signed as a one-hit-wonder type of band, and we wanted to make an album. We'd toured Europe at the end of '81, which was just mayhem. You put a bunch of teenagers from the Midlands in that environment with all the drink and drugs and it was bound to spiral out of control. Things came to a head at Les Bains Douches in Paris, which was a bit of wake-up call, and it took a while to get back on track.

TONY MAYO Stevo was very young, and he was riding the crest of a wave. He was happy, he was excited, and it may well be he was doing things with the best of intentions, but he was chaotic. And when you're chaotic, things go wrong, and it maybe he caused the issues and the problems for the others. When he started it all up his heart was in the right place and he was trying to do the right thing, but he went off on a tangent that may not have been helped by an excessive and random lifestyle, shall we say.

STEVE HOVINGTON Yeah, it was it was definitely exciting, and it was a rollercoaster ride. I remember sitting in the office and the phone was passed to Stevo and he basically said to the guy on the other end of the phone, 'If you don't agree to what I want, I'll break your neck.' I remember watching *Rock Follies* when I was a kid, and my dad saying to me, 'Never ever get into that industry.' There were all these tales of Don Arden and Peter Grant, all those managers who threatened people and dangled them out of windows. And here I was, right in the centre of it with one of those guys. Because, let's face it, Stevo would resort to physical violence and threats to get what he wanted.

RUSTY EGAN Nobody liked me or Stevo. We didn't go to the Groucho Club and hang out with international A&R blokes in suits, we weren't corporate, we didn't play the game. We were people who never changed from being what we were in the first place: fans of music.

Yes, if but why?

Ø, from the sleeve of B-Movie's 'Nowhere Girl' twelve-inch (1982)

1982 I'm lost again and I'm on the run

04

SOFT CELL'S ECSTATIC
DANCING, THE MAMBAS
SLITHER FORTH, AND MATT
JOHNSON LOSES HIMSELF IN
THE US OF A

Best track on the elpee, 'Say Hello, Wave Goodbye' is the most poignant, heartfelt, stunning, magnificent, swelling (cont'd Superlative Supplement) . . . you know the kind of thing. The return of the Grande Ballade complete with lip-biting weepy chorus and meaningful sordid-sex-at-its-saddest lyrics. The twelve-inch version, which has yet to reach my rose-petal palms, is said to contain many horns and the video attempts to turn David Ball into the matinee idol he always should have been.[*]

BEVERLEY GLICK (writing as Betty Page), *Sounds*, January 23, 1982

KARL O'CONNOR Despite their use of synths, a lot of those 80s bands—Duran Duran, Spandau Ballet, Ultravox—had traditional line-ups. But the synthesizer-only bands broke the DNA of rock'n'roll, and that was so fucking offensive to some people. Soft Cell were part Warhol's Factory, part end-of-the-pier seaside act; their image was threatening and real, and the music itself was extremely minimal. Just having two people up there doing it was such a massive 'fuck you' but it was also on the cusp of something genuinely new. Yes, they were pop, but their records were really experimental, too. And when I watched *Top Of The Pops*, I thought,

[*] 'Say Hello, Wave Goodbye' was released as a single (BZS 7) on January 29, 1982, and reached no.3 on the UK chart. The twelve-inch (BZS 712) featured an extended clarinet solo by Dave Tofani, while the video, again directed by Tim Pope, vividly brought Huw Feather's sleeve art to life.

There's only two of them, so maybe I could do that as well. I'd never really felt that way about anything else.

'I tried to make it work,' breathes Marc, 'You in a cocktail skirt and me in a suit.' Oh no. Suits aren't Marc at all. When he snakes his way across the BBC stage doing this one on *Top Of The Pops* I shall expect nothing less than footless tights, a leather off-the-shoulder blouson top and picture hat. A cocktail dress? Probably not. I mean a fellow doesn't want to get a reputation for being a *fruit*, does he.

author unknown, *NME*, January 30, 1982

RUSTY EGAN B-Movie's 'Nowhere Girl' was unbelievable.*

STEVO I mixed the twelve-inch of B-Movie's 'Nowhere Girl', with the piano solo at the beginning. There's still a lot of love and feeling between that band and me.

STEVE HOVINGTON We recorded 'Nowhere Girl' over Christmas and New Year at Trident Studios, after we'd come back from our first European tour. It was produced by the late Steve Brown, who'd recently worked with ABC, and engineered by Flood. We were looking for something danceable, forsaking live bass guitar for sequenced bass, although the drums were played live. We enticed an Italian student off the streets to provide the manic laughter at the beginning and a friend from Nottingham, Maria, provided the harmonies in the middle section. The twelve-inch version was improvised, with Rick's piano intro recorded on the same Steinway used on records by Bowie, Elton John, and Queen. *Sounds* made it Single Of The Week and we headed out on a UK tour in March to promote it. The highlight was a packed show at the LSE in London and a party afterward at the Columbia Hotel with Soft Cell and others from the Some Bizzare crowd. Despite support from Radio 1 DJs such as Peter Powell and Kid Jensen, it failed to gain serious daytime radio play, and entered the lower reaches of the charts at no.67. By the beginning of April, it was out of the chart and that was seemingly the end of the road for 'Nowhere Girl'.

>>

* B-Movie's third Phonogram single, which was released this time by Decca in March 1981, had a Some Bizzare catalogue number, BXX8/BZZ X8. It reached no.67 on the UK chart.

I'm doing a sort of off-beat lowlife sleazo disco thing with various friends! The A-side is called 'Sleaze (Take It Shake It!)' and it's definitely non-BBC! [Dave and I] both like to keep involved in loads of things—being just the two of us we're not tied to other musicians and it leaves us to go off on different paths.*

MARC ALMOND to Betty Page, *Sounds*, August 1, 1981

ANNI HOGAN I met Matt Johnson at a party at the Columbia Hotel and he introduced me to Simon Fisher Turner, who asked me play on a track of his which was just brilliant—my first studio experience, and it was doing avant-garde improvisation! I played it to Marc, and that's when he asked me to play keyboards on what became the first Marc & The Mambas' twelve-inch, 'Sleaze' / 'Fun City'. It was a little bit Velvets, a little bit Suicide, a little bit The Doors. It was Dave's beats, and I just did an improv basically, with a little of Duke Ellington's Caravan at the end. Amazing track.

BRIAN MOSS I did do some of the music on 'My Private Tokyo', but the majority of it was Dave.† He used the pseudonym Ryko on the sleeve. It stood for Revox Yamaha Korg and Oberheim, all the instruments he was using at the time.

JOSE WARDEN Soon after we got back from New York, Vicious Pink Phenomena got a publishing deal and were signed to Parlophone Records. They had us doing PAs every night in clubs around the country, radio interviews in every city from Glasgow to Brighton, so we weren't really around to do Soft Cell. We did become their support act for a bit, but we only had about five songs, and as we were signed we had to start taking things a bit more seriously, unfortunately. Marc and Dave were full-on anyway, flying all over the place, so we just couldn't hang out so much together. I still have all the postcards Dave sent me from this crazy period.

* Although it was released in March 1982, the debut twelve-inch single by Marc & The Mambas carried the catalogue number BZS 512, putting it between THE THE's 'Cold Spell Ahead' and Soft Cell's 'Bedsitter', both of which were released over five months earlier. Despite being listed as a fan-club-only release, some copes of 'Sleaze (Take It Shake It!)' did find their way to record shops.
† Vicious Pink Phenomena's debut single, 'My Private Tokyo', was released on March 19, 1982, by The Mobile Suit Corporation, a label set up by David Claridge via Phonogram to release music from other cultures, including Indian-themed band Monsoon and Germany's Trio. It can only be assumed that Jose Warden's dual French/English heritage was sufficient to fulfil this remit. Around the same time, Claridge started putting on fetish nights at Stallions gay club in Soho called Skin Two. He also went on to create and voice popular children's television puppet character Roland Rat.

BRIAN MOSS There was no animosity or fall out, Dave just didn't have any time for Vicious Pink Phenomena anymore. It was like, 'I've got a proper job now'—he'd signed a major contract and he was committed. So, Jose and I had to knuckle down and continue by ourselves.

MIKE THORNE Marc and Dave had flown into New York from fulfilling their madhouse marketing obligations the day before sessions for 'Torch' started.* I was seriously irritated, although certainly not with them. Someone from the record company was always trying to yank Marc and Dave away for interviews while we were trying to work. It's a struggle to get a record made when you're not successful, but sometimes it's even harder when you're actually winning.

DAVE BALL I'd gone into the studio over the weekend on my own because we needed a single. I wanted to do a kind of John Barry–influenced torch number, so I worked out the song over the weekend and Mike and Marc came in on the Monday. Marc liked idea of having a trumpet play the top line, and that was that really. It did really well—in fact, it should have been a no.1 record in the UK but apparently there were problems with the chart return shops. Adam Ant's 'Goody Two Shoes' had got to no.1 the week before, and we were actually selling three times as many copies as him, but he stayed there for a second week. We were robbed.

MARC ALMOND We recorded 'Torch' in New York, again with Mike Thorne, and it featured Cindy Ecstasy rapping as the voice of the torch singer in my head. The song is about a person in a bar who is moved by a singer and a song. That person was me, and I wrote 'Torch' one night in New York after a bar-room blues singer had brought me to tears. As she had sung, I remember feeling so low, alone, and loveless—an addict's self-pitying: 'Poor me, poor me, pour me a drink.'

MIKE THORNE Cindy's vocal delivery on the record was nervous—even more so before the tape rolled for real—but Marc was, as ever, a good support and teacher of session ingénues. 'Torch' was intended to be a double A-side, but musically it

* 'Torch' was released on May 21, 1982, on seven-inch (BZS 9) and twelve-inch (BZS 912) and featured extended versions of both the A-side and the flip, 'Insecure Me'. It reached no.2 on the UK chart and was Soft Cell's most successful self-penned single.

moved far ahead of the other track 'Insecure, Me'. For me, it's the apex of their creative success during their first period, and years later, Marc and I both agreed that 'Torch' was the best single of the many tracks we made together.

MARC ALMOND Cindy came over to England for the video and a *Top Of The Pops* appearance. But she hated the video. Somehow I'd convinced myself that the singer in my imagination should be bald, which we made Cindy up to be, imbuing her with a strange, androgynous look. She was none too pleased. The result was surreal and beautiful, in a mannequin sort of way, but she thought she had been made to look ugly and that I had done it on purpose. It was the beginning of the end of our friendship.

STEVO What must it have been like for Cindy, turning up and being told that she's got to have a bald head? It may have been all well and good artistically, but she was in tears. Imagine, here was a New York Jewish girl and they wanted her to be made up to look like she had a bald head—think about that for a minute, how bad that would make her feel. I would like to have it on record, I had nothing to do with that bald head.

HUW FEATHER What we were doing visually was a lot more complex than it may have first appeared. For example, the imagery for 'Torch' had its roots in Massenet's *Manon*; Marc and I were acutely aware of how the opera had been represented historically, and that was an influence. The bald thing was really interesting because my drawing just came out that way, but I certainly know from working in the Far East that the cover spoke to a certain element of the trans community, and I was very happy with that. The reaction from the record company was it was too effeminate, too camp, too ambiguous, too purple, and the typical Soft Cell response to any form of criticism was, 'Fuck you and hold on to your seats, because it's gonna get a lot worse.'

MARTIN PATTON 'Torch' had just come out and Steve and I realised we couldn't work with Stevo like *this* anymore, and we both thought, *You know what, life's too short*. So we decided to leave, and although it did go through lawyers, it was all very amicable. We just sold our shares in the label Some Bizzare, which at the time was not really worth very much, because although 'Some Bizzare' appeared on Soft Cell's records, legally the band were signed to Phonogram, and our royalty override wasn't going to generate a fortune.

MIKE THORNE 'Torch' brought together all the classic Soft Cell elements: the world-weariness, the tender bitterness, the vulnerable regret of making avoidable mistakes. It was to be a real pinnacle of achievement. Soft Cell singles after that classic would start a slow decline in quality and chart success. Sometimes those two things do go together. Those days were more halcyon than we realized at the time.

MARTIN PATTON I have no regrets about selling up whatsoever. I made quite a decent amount of money, and, as far as I was concerned, I just got lucky, but most importantly it got me through the door. It gave me an opportunity, and I was in. Some Bizzare was nearly all Stevo's idea, unquestionably—I take almost no credit for it whatsoever. Yes, we'd found B-Movie, and had it gone differently with them, that might have changed things. But it didn't fall that way. I've always been of the mind that Stevo delivered Soft Cell—it came from him knocking on doors and refusing to take no for an answer, and I don't think it would have happened for them without him. Remember, at that time, Stevo was Soft Cell's manager, and Some Bizzare was built on Soft Cell's success. Of course he did some absolutely crazy things, but usually it was what was needed. For all his craziness, Stevo really did care for them, no question.

JANE ROLINK 'Torch' was no.2 or something, and Stevo had arranged this personal appearance at this night club, Cinderella's in Hickstead, in Sussex. It was awful. Marc, Dave, Huw, and I turned up there in a chauffeur-driven limo, all on acid. Stevo was DJing and was winding the crowd up by playing Cabaret Voltaire, Throbbing Gristle, and the Sooty album. The people were dead straight and really didn't like it. Then the DJ got into Dave's face, and it ended up in a bit of a fight. We were all tripping off our faces and had to barricade ourselves in the dressing room all night. It was on the first floor, and all these bouncers were banging the doors, and they were even coming up onto the roof and banging on the windows. It was just so frightening. After a while they sent me out to have a look, and I got thumped—I didn't think they'd hit a woman, but they did. When we did eventually get out, they'd let down all the tires on the Rolls-Royce, and we couldn't get back to London.

MARC ALMOND That night was very frightening—we ended up being barricaded in our dressing room while our hired Rolls-Royce was smashed up and death threats were made. Jane understandably couldn't make it into work next day and she lost her job, so Stevo employed her, and she ended up almost running Some Bizzare singlehanded at times.

JANE ROLINK I was working in a B&B and didn't make it in and was sacked. But Marc said, 'Come and work for us and run our fan club, Cell-Mates,' which was how I ended up at Some Bizzare.

MARC ALMOND It was that night that made me realise that things were getting out of control, that I was getting out of control. Everyone was taking acid and even harder drugs, and things were going in a darker direction with Some Bizarre. I wanted to get out but I didn't know how, and it would be many years before I got the nerve to leave. I'd be almost destroyed before that happened.

FLOOD Some Bizzare were a crucial element in the success of Trident Studios in the 80s.* It was like a symbiotic relationship. Two of the owners at the time were Rusty Egan and Jean-Philippe Iliesco, and they were also involved with Metropolis Music, who Soft Cell were signed to for their publishing. There were loads of clubs springing up at the time—the Batcave, Alice in Wonderland, Skin 2, the Camden Palace—and they were the only places you could get a drink after 11pm, so that's where everyone hung out. Rusty was one of the main players in the club scene at that time, and we'd all end up at these places in the small hours.

RUSTY EGAN I gave Stevo the office in St Anne's Court. There was us [Metropolis Music], Some Bizzare, the Hi-NRG DJ Ian Levine, Carol Hayes Management, and of course the studio. Ros Earls ran that and managed Flood and Mark Stent, and she was a very good at it—the studio was always booked up.

---

* The original Trident Studios was located at 17 St Anne's Court in the heart of Soho. It ran from 1968 to 1981 and was famous for recording classic albums by David Bowie, Elton John, Queen, Marc Bolan, Lou Reed, and Genesis. In 1981, the studio was bought by its senior engineer, Stephen Short, and three new investors: Rusty Egan, producer and publisher J.P. Iliesco, and Mel Morris.

STEVO We did a publishing deal with Metropolis and they had offices in Trident, so it was logical for us to be there too. Of course it was madness—we were all teenagers.

FLOOD Studio One was on the ground floor; the remix room, Studio Two, was the first floor. The next floor was dormant for ages, the third floor was the mastering room and offices for the studio, and the fourth floor was maintenance and accounts. When the second floor was souped up, that's where Some Bizarre moved into. Maybe I'm just speaking for myself, but I felt it was a community of outsiders. It was shambolic but there was no pretence. Everybody knew Stevo was wide of the mark, but that's why the establishment weren't sure how to deal with him. Stevo was not stupid—he knew how to give a good floor show and to leave them wanting more.

IAN TREGONING I first met Stevo through Rusty Egan. I had just signed Yello to my label, Do It, and we put out a white label twelve-inch of 'Bostich'—I think we did two hundred copies. It didn't go down that well in the UK but it went down a storm in America, playing every hour in Paradise Garage. Rusty loved it and was very enthusiastic. He got in touch and said, 'I'm in Trident studios, you should come down and meet my mate, Stevo, he really likes the record and has been playing it out as well.' So I rocked up to St Anne's Court, and it was just chaos in there, but fun chaos. Things being thrown around the room, Stevo ringing people up and abusing them down the phone, Jane holding it all together with her beautiful dry sense of humour. It was all so ridiculous, and I loved it.

JANE ROLINK The Some Bizzare offices in Soho were fantastic. Good lord, how lucky were we? It was brilliant. At the time, I just took it all in my stride, but looking back it was absolutely bonkers. People would pop in and out, and it was a really secure atmosphere for me—best time of my life, that's for sure. We did work hard, though. I'd moved from doing the fan club to doing press, and I was basically Marc's PA, doing all his day-to-day life management and being there at his side whenever needed me. I did press for the all the bands, so it was it busy, really busy and bonkers.

HUW FEATHER The Some Bizzare office had multiple contexts, which were gathered together like an enormous sandwich. And when you've got such a big sandwich, you can't just nibble at the edge, you've got to take a big bite, which means the filling goes everywhere. That's what Some Bizarre was like. I mean, the building had a huge rock'n'roll history, and it was a privilege and quite outrageous that we were even allowed in there. And then you had the offices—and we're talking tiny, cupboard-sized offices—which housed not just Some Bizarre but Metropolis Music, Schmaltz Agency, all these little gangs. And it was all definitely a bit *other*, because of the number of camp and gay individuals wandering around. And the people hanging around were just amazing.

I was tasked with taking them out for tea, because there was literally no room in the office, so I'd always be over at Patisserie Valerie on Old Compton Street with people like Lydia Lunch and Diamanda Galas. And this was where meetings were supposed to happen, music was supposed to be listened to, and decisions were supposed to be made. Add to that the gaggle of Marc fans constantly waiting outside or trying to get in the building in some way, it was like a Marx Brothers movie. It was such a chaotic period and unless you were there, it's very, very hard to describe.

ZEKE MANYIKA I met all the Some Bizzare lot through staying at the Columbia Hotel with Orange Juice.* It was a very odd but fun place to stay. It was a cheap place for the labels to put their regional artists while we were in London doing promotions or whatever. The once grand building was now a bit rough round the edges but was impressive enough for us to play at being rock'n'roll pop stars. There was a good bar with little Pac-Man tables at which many musicians from around the country and the world got to know each other. That is where I met Stevo, Marc Almond, Dave Ball, and eventually Matt Johnson, amongst many others.

MATT JOHNSON I'd left my parents place in Loughton and moved into a small bedsit in Highbury with my old friend Alessandra Sartore and her Japanese flatmate. I had a little broom-cupboard-sized room I'd sleep in with my recording equipment, including a little Fostex eight-track recorder, mixing desk and my trusty Akai 4000DS mk2 tape recorder. I was also begging, borrowing, and stealing studio time and that was how I made *The Pornography Of Despair*. It was supposed to be

---

* The Columbia in West London is set across five Victorian townhouses and has been synonymous with touring bands and musicians since the mid 70s. Prior to this, the hotel served as an American officers' club, and in the early 80s one could find the incongruous sight of nostalgic military men mingling with the latest pop or rock sensation.

the successor to *Burning Blue Soul*, but my life was about to change. I suddenly went from being a struggling independent artist to a well-funded major label artist, and that album slipped between the cracks.

STEVE SHERLOCK I knew Matt and Keith via Steve Parry, and Neu Electrikk and THE THE did a couple of gigs together with Stevo as DJ. I did some work with Matt on an early version of 'Uncertain Smile', and played flute and sax on 'Three Orange Kisses' and 'Waitin' For The Upturn', which we recorded at Phonogram's studios in Bayswater, and eventually came out as B-sides.

ZEKE MANYIKA I was in London for a few days and Stevo played me a cassette of some quite rough demos, but I could hear there was something interesting about them. And he said, 'That's Matt from THE THE. I'm gonna take these to Phonogram to play to Roger Aimes, do you want to come?' I knew Roger because Orange Juice were signed to Polydor, so we went over to Notting Hill. We could immediately tell Roger was in a bad mood, and when we put a Walkman on him, he listened and he said, 'That's crap, it sounds like Jethro Tull!' And he turns to me and says, 'What do you think, Zeke?' And I told him I thought it was really good, and he said, 'Oh, you haven't become another disciple of Stevo, have you?' Anyway, he dismissed it and basically told us to fuck off. Of course, later they wanted to sign Matt, and Stevo refused to give them the album. Later, I saw Roger at one of those record-company Christmas parties, and I called over to him, 'Roger! How's Jethro Tull doing?' And he said to me, 'I was wrong there, Zeke, I'll give you that one.' So that was quite good.

STEVO I was producing records as a finished artefact, I wasn't running around with a cap looking for money. The records would be made, I'd play them to potential distributors, and I'd cut a deal with whoever was most enthusiastic. Artists should be in a situation where they can actually offer their work to all the corporations, and whoever gives them the best feedback, is the most passionate, that's who they work with. So when Roger Aimes turned off Matt Johnson's tape and said he was like Jethro Tull, I took it elsewhere.

MATT JOHNSON Soft Cell were having worldwide hit singles and there was also still a buzz about B-Movie. Stevo was having a lot of meetings with major labels, and it was at one of those that he arranged for London Records to pay for me to go to New York to record a new version of 'Cold Spell Ahead'—which became 'Uncertain Smile'—with Mike Thorne. I remember being at a meeting in their offices with Stevo and their head lawyer, and somehow he managed to get him to sign off on this expensive recording trip without London owning the fruits of it. I don't know how he did it but Stevo could be *very* persuasive. At one point the lawyer was refusing to agree to a specific point in the agreement, so Stevo started shouting and screaming, picked up a chair, and threw it across the room. The lawyer then just signed whatever he had to, just to get us out of the building probably. It was intense.

Well my ideology is: exploit them. Use 'em: use 'em for what powers they've got. They're hungry and they know I've got what people on the street want. Basically I've got something they want and so they've got to pay for it highly. So I take the money from the faceless and give it to a kid like Matt Johnson who has no money and lives in a bedsit.

STEVO to Tony Mitchell, *Sounds*, December 25, 1982

MATT JOHNSON I'd been to California as a teenager but I'd never been to New York before and I was very excited about going because Stevo, Marc, and Dave were always travelling back and forth and telling me all about it. I'd met Mike Thorne briefly in London, when he was working with Soft Cell, and he was a very nice chap. I flew out in May and the whole trip was quite magical. Britain and America back then were so different, and it was quite overwhelming, while being quite familiar too, probably because of the DC and Marvel Comics I read as a kid. I was staying in the Mayflower Hotel, where a lot of musicians stayed—it's unfortunately demolished now—and recorded at Mediasound studios, which was a former church on West 57th Street. The sessions went extremely well, and one morning Mike took me out to Manny's, a very famous music store on 48th Street, and I found this African percussion instrument called a Zylimba. I bought and it used it for the intro of 'Uncertain Smile', and it became the signature sound of it really.

I think about that session and compare it to just a year earlier—suddenly I was in a very nice hotel, working in a very big, posh studio in New York City with a very good producer and with quite a lot of money being spent on me. As it turned out, I prefer producing myself, but Mike didn't do anything wrong at all—he did a wonderful job. Was I surprised how commercial 'Uncertain Smile' was? I suppose so. It was such a leap forward from *Burning Blue Soul* and my other recordings. I remember riding around New York in Checker Cabs at night heading downtown to meet new friends and listening to the twelve-inch mix on a Walkman. It still vividly brings to mind that first trip to New York and the pure magic of it. It has very happy connotations for me.

PETER ASHWORTH I did a location shoot with Matt that was set up by Stevo, and Andy Dog re-created the 'Uncertain Smile' sleeve as life-sized painted backgrounds. I don't know if those pictures were used much, but I did have an exhibition in 2019 and I digitised a full set, and Matt loved them. He got really excited, mainly because they showed off his brother's work.

MATT JOHNSON When I flew back with the tapes of 'Uncertain Smile', everybody loved it and London Records were thrilled—until Stevo pointed out to them that they didn't, in fact, actually own it. They were *extremely* upset and angry— particularly the pair who ran the company, Roger Ames and Tracy Bennett—to the point they even attempted to buy the publishing from Cherry Red in order to stop it being released by anyone else. They were seething and tried every trick in the book to get their own back on Stevo. In the meantime, he'd hyped up various other major labels into a bidding war, which ironically—given Howard Thompson's complete dismissal of the earlier version of the same song—CBS won with the largest offer. I was very happy to sign with them, though. It was home to some of my favourite singer-songwriters: Bob Dylan, Johnny Cash, Leonard Cohen, and Bruce Springsteen—they were an album-artists' label and very glamorous. It felt a bit like how a young footballer must feel signing to Manchester United.

STEVO The CBS negotiations were dragging on, so Maurice Oberstein's office arranged for us to meet at Tottenham Court Road at 11:30pm to sign the deal.[*] So I'm standing outside the station, and Maurice walks by me a couple of times, then he stops, says, 'Stevo?' It was raining, so we jump in his car and drive to Trafalgar

---

[*] Maurice 'Obie' Oberstein was a flamboyant figure in the music industry. Rising through the ranks of CBS in the UK, he was instrumental in breaking British acts such as The Clash, Adam & The Ants, and George Michael on the international stage. Known for taking his dogs to meetings for 'advice', Oberstein was rarely without a titfer, and during disputes he would place it on a table and leave the room, with the parting instruction to 'talk to the hat'.

Square. I told him to stop and he pulls up right on the square, literally opposite the Mall, parked on a double yellow. It was pouring with rain; I jumped out the car and climbed up on one of the lion statues. I tried to get Maurice to join me, but he refused. Then this police officer came along, and she asked Maurice if the car parked on the double-yellow line on Trafalgar Square at midnight was his and told him to move on. So we didn't sign the contract on the lions, but when the media say that we were up there signing away, what am I going to do? We got a load of press, and it was good for the artist.

MATT JOHNSON I didn't go to the infamous signing ceremony because I was embarrassed by the whole tabloid exposure it would entail. I wouldn't have wanted to perch on a lion in Trafalgar Square myself—I thought I'd let Stevo and Maurice do that. He was a legendary figure, Maurice, but a very strange man. I liked him and we got along, he was nice to me. But he and CBS had obviously signed me on the strength of 'Uncertain Smile', which was the most commercial thing I'd done— before or since. So when they heard *The Pornography Of Despair*, they were a bit freaked out. They thought they were signing a young pop act and then realised, too late, that I was more experimental than that. My A&R person at CBS was Annie Roseberry, who, whilst at Island Records, had also turned down the earlier version of 'Uncertain Smile'. But Annie ended up being the best A&R person I ever had and was beyond supportive the entire time I worked with her. She said, 'Look, could you try re-recording some of these?' Which I did, but the company weren't happy with those versions either. So, I said *OK, fine*, and put *The Pornography Of Despair* on the back burner and just started writing new material. Some of those re-recorded versions ended up being used on the *Soul Mining* cassette or as B-sides, and one track called 'Screw Up Your Feelings' eventually became the song 'Perfect'.

MIKE THORNE Stevo may have found the bands and helped them be successful, but he helped bring them down, too. He complicated everything with what I read as destructive personal political plays. Stevo played Marc and Dave like a classic synthesizer, and I felt he was jealous of the close creative working relationship the three of us had developed. Divide and rule is a good tactic of any politician, but in the case of Soft Cell it may have contributed to the destruction of an extraordinary creative combination, one of the most productive I had known. Marc and Dave, without any prodding from me, had already banned Stevo from the control room, because he always wanted to be the centre of attention and was inevitably disruptive. He was usually only allowed to join us for playbacks or at the end of the day. He'd sit on my equipment rack, which still echoes the curve of his backside all these years later.

MARC ALMOND Somebody came up to Dave and me with the idea of remixing some of the Soft Cell tracks for a mini album. We were sent back to New York to work once more with Mike Thorne, both to rework half a dozen tracks and also to record a new single. Dave and I both loved dance music and wanted the opportunity to work with different people on the project. We wanted to get New York's club culture to work with us, to utilise local talent. We wanted to give our songs to young DJs and producers in the clubs to do as they wanted with. Nobody was doing that then, and it would have been a first. But a nervous record company refused to let us. In the end, we went along with what they wanted.

DAVE BALL There were some amazing DJs in New York at the time but doing the album with them was a kind of romantic notion in a way. It would have been difficult to pull off and there was no proof that the quality of the mixes would be any good. Just because someone sounds great in a New York club after you've dropped an E, doesn't mean they'd know what the fuck they were doing in a professional studio. The idea was very forward-thinking because it predated all the big superstar DJs that you have today making records, but back then it just wouldn't have made any sense. Not only might we have ended up with some dodgy mixes but it would've dated it, too. As it is, the album has a uniformity, and the quality control is maintained throughout.

MIKE THORNE The decision was made to record a dance LP, which would be among the first of its kind, and nowhere in the Soft Cell canon is there more sense of brats at play. The wilful, just-for-the-hell-of-it sheer infectiousness of the still-current sound transmits the fun we had making it, and, for me, the standout tracks are the bookends. For 'Memorabilia', we copied the original twenty-four-track tape in segments, kept the excellent original rhythm parts that Daniel had worked on, then built on the superstructure starting with a fresh, new lead vocal. I added the Synclavier and the Serge modular synthesizer, and other extras are John Gatchell's trumpet and Cindy's mid-track rap, written by Marc. It's a great performance. 'Sex Dwarf' appears in a second incarnation *en route* to its final, controversial unreleased video (which I still haven't seen). There are so many odd noises that I can't remember how we did many of them. It's not immodest to say that we invented a few things, facilitated by the new technology and tools that were showering down on us.

PETER ASHWORTH There was a theatre to the *Non-Stop Ecstatic Dancing* cover.* Huw Feather wasn't involved, and I'm fairly certain Stevo came up with the idea of the musical notes. I actually got them made by an old boy who worked on a wood-cutting machine in the basement of Bagley's Warehouse in Kings Cross, where I had my studio. The shot was more of a *Smash Hits* cover than a record sleeve, but there's something great about seeing your favourite musicians at play and being really responsive. A lot of album sleeves are so serious and sombre, even if the music isn't, so this was a nice change. I used a medium wide-angle lens, so when Dave and Marc pushed the notes forward the whole thing popped and really leapt out.

Non-Stop Ecstatic Dancing is an exercise that succeeds and in some cases is an improvement on the original—like 'Memorabilia' re-done with a female rap. However, the best track is a new one, a version of a Northern Soul song once performed by Judy Street, called 'What!' I love Almond's voice and the way he turns its vulnerability into bravery and its limitations into a kind of reedy soul. With Soft Cell's economical electronics and the play with sleazy camp, it all makes for the ideal sound for the modern club, the modern cabaret, while it actually digs below the surface of that meretricious night world. Genuinely, artfully subterranean, and exhilarating with it.

author unknown, The Face, June 1982

MIKE THORNE Disruptive personal undercurrents flowed, but they weren't yet sufficient to break up the party. A launch party was held at Danceteria, one of the best New York clubs of the period, to celebrate the remix album's completion and offer opportunity for yet more promotion to keep the juggernaut rolling. The music worked, and the dance floor duly went crazy. Unknown to me at the time,

* Soft Cell's remix mini-album, *Non-Stop Ecstatic Dancing* (BZX 1012), was released on June 21, 1982, and reached no.6 on the UK chart. For its US release, where it reached no.57 on the *Billboard* chart, 'Chips On My Shoulder' was replaced by 'Insecure, Me'.

a rift with between me and Marc and Dave was beginning to open up. They later grumbled that there were so many interesting DJs in New York at the time and that they had wanted to pull in some of them. I still disagree strongly, since I feel that the coherence of the final result would never have had its unique character if style specialists had been used. And, don't forget, the session also produced a new piece, 'What!', which became Soft Cell's fourth consecutive Top 5 UK single.*

>>

Soft Cell's record company (well, Stevo's we s'pose) Some Bizarrre [sic] has taken the plunge at last with their signing of Psychic TV! In the London West End's trendy Trident Studios, ex-TG perv-isionaries Gen and Sleazy are hard at work with the help of some friends on a debut album which, according to our man's exclusive chat with the former, will contain 'Lots of love songs and lots and lots of guitar!'

It certainly looks set to be a million miles away from Throbbing Gristle's aural terrorism (or even the naff computer-disco side of TG, which the other half, Chris & Cosey continue to recycle). We shook our dazed correspondent on these matters to get some more sense out of him, but all he could remember was that Gen said the LP would be like 'Leonard Cohen meets Ennio Morricone on the set of *Apocalypse Now*.' It's also hoped to use real strings, possibly arranged by Paul Buckmaster (of Elton John and other megarockdom fame) who was apparently so moved by some of Gen's Tibetan thigh-bone trumpet blast stuff that he's attempting to fit PTV into his schedule. We have to admit these men are anything but predictable...

author unknown, *Sounds*, July 24, 1982

STEVO I used to put Throbbing Gristle in the Futurist chart and would play their records when I played out. So I approached Gen because I appreciated him as an artist, and Sleazy too. I gave Gen baby food. Although he did pull a knife on me once—he had a belt a buckle that came out as a knife, because he was always worried he would be attacked in the street.

ALAURA O'DELL I met Gen when I was fifteen or sixteen. I worked in a supermarket in Hackney on Saturdays, and, looking back, I believe he was definitely stalking

---

* Released on August 13, 1982, *What!* (BZS 11/BZS 112) was another Northern Soul cover and reached no.3 on the UK chart. The sleeve notes state, 'One nice pop song—from two nice people'—a veiled reference to the recent 'Sex Dwarf' video controversy.

me. We became a couple in February 1981, when I was eighteen and still in school studying for my A-levels. I was planning on going to college to get a degree in sociology. Throbbing Gristle were playing their last two concerts in LA and San Francisco, and Gen said to me, 'Do you want to go to college or travel the world with me?' So I left school, got a nine-to-five job, and saved up so that I could join Gen in California. Between the concerts we went to Tijuana for a daytrip to Mexico. While we were walking around with Gen's friends—the artist Jerry Dreva and Don Bolles, former drummer of LA punk band The Germs—we saw a sign for marriages and divorces outside a lawyer's office. And with encouragement from Jerry and Don, Gen and I got married. Back to London, Throbbing Gristle broke up, and then Gen and Sleazy decided to start their own band, which became Psychic TV. I gave birth to our first daughter, Caresse, in August of 1982, and within a year after I joined Psychic TV, playing percussion live and in the studio.

GAVIN FRIDAY My earliest relationship with what became the Some Bizzare gang was when The Virgin Prunes signed to Rough Trade in 1980. I met Throbbing Gristle in London, and Genesis and Sleazy were fans of the band. I got to know Geoff through his *Stabmental* fanzine; he was a big Virgin Prunes head and became a very good friend of mine.* The big thing at the time was letter writing rather than phone calls. Not many people had a phone, so letters were really important. It was the sort of the Instagram or Facebook of its day—if you wanted to find out more about a band, write to them. I used to write a huge amount, mainly to Geoff, Cabaret Voltaire, Fad Gadget.

VAL DENHAM For my degree show at the Royal College of Art, I did a performance action piece with my friends called *The Death And Beauty Foundation*. It was dreadful, challenging, and confrontational—exactly what I was aiming for. Genesis, Paula, and their daughter Caresse came to see the show, accompanied by Geoff Rushton, Stevo, and Marc.

Marc and Stevo were interested in my paintings and bought three of them from the degree show. Marc reserved two: one of a bald entity wearing a gold and

---

* Prior to joining Psychic TV and forming Coil with Peter 'Sleazy' Christopherson, Geoff Rushton published seven issues of the fanzine *Stabmental* and was a tireless letter writer and mail artist. He first came into the orbit of Genesis P-Orridge and Christopherson when he interviewed Throbbing Gristle for the fanzine, alongside other bands including Cabaret Voltaire, Clock DVA, and The Virgin Prunes.

bloody Crown of Thorns, and the other a painting of my then-wife Elita pointing downward, which he eventually used on the Marc & The Mambas 'Torment' sleeve. Stevo bought a depiction of deranged laughing clown, which even I thought was horrifying. Stevo phoned me a week after the show and asked to bring the paintings to the Some Bizzare offices, which I did as I was eager to get paid. The office was really welcoming, mainly due to Jane's down-to-earth Northern friendliness—she was quite a motherly character, and everybody was drawn to her. I gave Stevo, who was bumptious yet always entertaining, his painting, and Marc the two artworks which he had reserved, and they paid me immediately, which impressed me no end.

HUW FEATHER The early sleeves were a *fait accompli* done by people Marc knew in Leeds, and they were OK, but Stevo and the record company wanted something that hadn't been seen before. Marc used to show me his lyrics while he was writing and perfecting them, so I was there for nearly every song's creation, in some way, shape, or form. Marc and I lived together at all his different addresses in London, so I was totally aware of what the nuance for the new record would be, what story each track told and I was there for the recording of them too. He and I were playing with images throughout the whole process. So things like 'Say Hello, Wave Goodbye', 'Torch', 'What!'—all that imagery was worked out as we went along. And we would take those ideas with storyboards or mood boards to video director Tim Pope. He knew we cared about the visuals and we that knew enough stage- and film-craft to be able to pinpoint exactly what we wanted to play with, replicate, or pay homage to. The videos became another medium for the band to present themselves.

MARC ALMOND I seemed to remember it had been Stevo's idea to film the whole of *Non-Stop Erotic Cabaret* and even some of *Non-Stop Ecstatic Dancing* as a surreal cabaret. No one had tried anything like this before, and I found the prospect very exciting. It was again to be directed by Tim Pope, who was to direct all Soft Cell's videos and even a few of my solo ones. It was another opportunity to be mischievous and subversive.

TIM POPE [Marc] just had to come out of his front door and walk in front of the camera and we'd begin filming. So, there was a whole reality that was very easy to film at the time. What was really interesting about Soft Cell was there was a certain trashiness to them, a certain rubbish element. I was really honoured once when someone said to me my Soft Cell videos are so grimy that if you ran your hand down the front of the TV screen you'd have dirt under your fingernails, and I thought, *Yeah, that's exactly what we're trying to do.*

JESSAMY CALKIN Marc and I gradually became really good friends and I would do bits of work for him occasionally. I was in the video for 'What!'—I was the Allen Jones table, with a sheet glass of my back.

TIM POPE Within three months of 'Bedsitter', they phoned me up and asked if I could make a video to 'Say Hello, Wave Goodbye', then shortly afterward they decided to do a whole video album of songs, *Non-Stop Exotic Video Show*. We filmed a lot of them around Soho, and it was great fun to dip into that lifestyle and cause as much trouble as we could. In that way I think Soft Cell and I were co-conspirators. Here was a band who had had massive, massive success with 'Tainted Love', 'Bedsitter' went to no.4, but then we made 'Sex Dwarf'.

Soft Cell have made a pornographic video as outrageous as those shown in London's Soho. Lead singer Marc Almond is shown masturbating through his clothes and rubbing raw meat into naked women. He strips down to only a jockstrap throughout the video and appears with a dwarf in the same attire. It was intended to go out to discos around the country, although it will not be going out now, according to the group. *Record Mirror* received a copy of the video last week. The staff saw scenes which feature Soft Cell's keyboards player Dave Ball cutting up raw meat with a chainsaw. He runs wild through the cast with the saw while they rub raw meat into each other. But Marc Almond insists the video isn't offensive.

author unknown, *Record Mirror*, June 1982

BEVERLEY GLICK Marc was always the observer, so it used to upset me when people called him things like 'a sick little pervert'. He was fascinated by the S&M scene, though. But just because they dressed up in all the gear for the 'Sex Dwarf' video, it didn't mean they were necessarily into it themselves. I always got the feeling that he was more of a voyeur.

MARC ALMOND The 'Sex Dwarf' video got us into a lot of trouble because the offices were actually raided. We didn't think about it because I came from this performance art experimental theatre background, and Leeds Polytechnic was known for its kind of very shocking performance art and theatre things. We didn't get it into our minds that we on a pop stage now. A part of us was still experimental artists, Dave was listening to things like Throbbing Gristle and Cabaret Voltaire, and we still thought we were part of this kind of experimental thing. So we did the video and it was really encouraged by Tim and we just got carried away with ourselves. I remember Dave running around with a chainsaw and Tim came in with this big bucket of maggots and threw them all over everybody. So all the screaming and running around is actually real because he wanted to get that affect for real. It made so much trouble for us really.

TIM POPE The reaction to 'Sex Dwarf' was hilarious! It has become a legend in its own lunchtime, mainly because people don't seem to have seen the full version. I don't even have a master copy of it. Really, all that happens is a lot of posturing, people rolling around in meat, me chucking handloads of maggots in which no one knew I was doing, a dwarf jumping out of a crate with a bondage mask on, and everyone having a whole load of fun.

There's a fantastic end shot of Marc as he leers at the camera. I put it into slow motion and noticed there's a writhing maggot hanging from his lip. There were two studios where we were filming it in St John's Wood, and next door some ladies of a certain age were making an aerobics video in blue leotards. When the dwarf was dressed in his bondage gear, I took him on a leash with a zip up mask and decided to break into the other studio and walked through the back of the shot. I know that somewhere there will be a piece of video of these ladies were dancing to Madonna or whatever, with me walking through with a dwarf on a lead. It was just boys having fun!

The 'Sex Dwarf' video has caused the group even more trouble after the dwarf who appeared on the video complained to the Sunday papers that he was exploited. He claimed that he was only paid £40 for the appearance. Marc Almond says that after meeting them at a party the dwarf—Tony Cooper—kept ringing the Soft Cell office to get a part in the video. Eventually they hired him instead of taking a dwarf from an agency, although Almond said that all the people they normally use on videos are 'professionals'.

author unknown, *Record Mirror*, June 1982

STEVO I had a tabloid call me up, saying that one of the young actors from the 'Sex Dwarf' video had gone to them saying that they'd not been paid as much as the others. It wasn't Some Bizzare that paid the actors—we gave the production company a budget, and they paid everyone out of that. Anyway, it turned out that it was the bloke playing the dwarf who was doing the complaining. What could I say? Half the man, half the salary. The headline in the paper was 'Dwarf Exploiter!'

TIM POPE I remember being chased up the street by the *News Of The World* and all these reporters came after me I thought I was going to have to leave the country. And then the porn squad seized the video. It was absolutely fantastic, it was great.

PETER ASHWORTH Soft Cell were beginning to disappear around the world and would return to the UK for a shoot, having had all these new experiences. New York really changed them in all sorts of ways, especially Marc. The seedy night life was more real in New York than it probably was in London. And he also met up with Cindy Ecstasy, and she came back and introduced a lot of people to everyone's party favourite. There was one memorable evening at the Columbia Hotel with Cindy, Soft Cell, Matt, Julian Cope, and me. We all took a little bit of whatever, and I was running up and down the corridors, being very excitable. Matt hated it and had a horrible night. I think he basically kept away from it after that, which is interesting, because that defined him as much as it for those who really did get into it. Another memorable aspect of the evening was ending up in Julian Cope's bathroom with about half a dozen other people, chatting with him while he was in the tub. I remember thinking, *This is pretty weird, but also really good fun.* But yeah, I got into it all.

STEVO It's important to realise that what was actually being consumed came from a hospital. It was a legal drug. It was used in marriage counselling, if a couple were clawing each other's eyes out, give them some ecstasy and they'd soon be kissing each other. As it became bootlegable it just became amphetamine. You see people now that say they're on ecstasy, they're grinding their jaws and have been awake for forty-nine hours. You could sleep on the ecstasy from the hospital.

BEVERLEY GLICK Most of the people who took ecstasy in the early 80s get very snobby about it now. The MDMA in New York was reasonably unadulterated, and taking it was a life-changing experience for me. I don't think it was even illegal at that time. I never got to meet Cindy Ecstasy—she was off the scene for some reason by the time that I got to New York. Didn't she end up with one of B-Movie?

DAVID KNIGHT We were still looking for a permanent front person/singer for The Fast Set, but it never seemed to happen. At one point, Stevo mentioned putting us together with Cindy Ecstasy, but we never met her. Happily, our eternal search for a new singer eventually led me to meeting Danielle Dax from The Lemon Kittens, who, conversely, was looking for a live band to promote her recently recorded *Pop Eyes* solo album. We became great friends, had identical tastes in music, and I began writing and recording with her, as well as joining with her former bandmate, Karl Blake, in his band Shock Headed Peters.

MARC ALMOND I was developing and looking for my own musical style outside of Soft Cell through some of the artists I'd been influenced by, such as Lou Reed, Syd Barrett, and, of course, Scott Walker. That became the first Marc & The Mambas album, *Untitled*, which wasn't really meant to be an album at all, but an extended EP of ideas, some of them quite rough. I was being very self-indulgent on Phonogram's money in this famous studio where Bowie and Bolan had recorded.

ANNI HOGAN *Untitled* was such a fantastic experience. We were booked in on dead time, cheap, late-night, cold-and-closed hours. I remember the first night we started recording, John Barry had run over time with a very drunk Rita Coolidge recording 'All Time High' for *Octopussy*. She had a bottle of whisky in one hand, and apparently she was stuck on one line. John Barry's wife was in the reception area, and she spent the whole time, which was quite a few hours, slagging off John Williams to anyone who would listen. It was a surreal start to the recording. John Barry was my absolute hero. Eventually he emerged knackered but just cool as fuck, and I got to shake his hand. And that was the beginning of the session! Flood was the engineer, and he was just so lovely, we very much bonded.

FLOOD I was training as an engineer, and some of the people who ran the studio by day could be genius but by night were just bully boys, and it wasn't pleasant. However, as a training ground, it was brilliant. I'd been working with Soft Cell doing some very small things, and Marc wanted me to work on the first Marc

& The Mamba's album, *Untitled*. But my immediate boss, who was the studio manager, wanted to work on it so he could get an in with Soft Cell. It didn't work out, though, and Marc said, 'I'd much prefer Flood to work on this.' So I finished it off, and my boss's nose was put out of joint. Then one day, not long after, I was pulled up into the studio management offices and questioned why I was working with the Some Bizzare bands, and told that it was going to destroy my very promising career. I constantly had the management of the studio questioning what I was doing with these people whose music I loved. They just did not understand.

MARC ALMOND I used to play *Burning Blue Soul* constantly, even before I got to know Matt. I thought he was fantastic—a real musician and not a pretender like me. I had so much respect for him and his talent, and we hit it off immediately and became good friends. We co-wrote a couple of songs on *Untitled*, and he created this amazing psychedelic sound with his guitar that I just loved, which was perfect for the title track and 'Angels', a drugged-out trip through Los Angeles.

ANNI HOGAN The album was definitely led by Marc but musically led by me. We started with 'Empty Eyes', I think, which was pretty much an improv. There was an electric piano, and I just started playing this 60s-style progression. Matt came in and out—he was there for his two big tracks, 'Untitled' and 'Angels'—and we all played on 'Twilights & Lowlifes'.

MATT JOHNSON I was friendly with Marc, and he was always very kind and supportive to me whilst I was struggling to get a deal. He really liked *Burning Blue Soul* and 'Uncertain Smile' and wanted to do a project outside of Soft Cell. He had all sorts of ideas that he felt he couldn't do within the electronic duo structure. And he just asked me if I fancied collaborating on some stuff. He was lovely to work with, very enthusiastic and generous. Anni was involved, who was great to work with too, and we recorded at Trident with Flood. I really enjoyed it.

ANNI HOGAN There was a C Bechstein grand piano at Trident that everybody had used, and Marc encouraged me to do a solo piece, which became 'Margaret'. It was a fantastic atmosphere and everybody was into it. Marc had given me Scott Walker's first solo album and the Julian Cope compilation, *Fire Escape In The Sky*, and those arrangements by Angela Mortimer, previously known as Wally Scott, were very influential for me. I was opened up musically, and it inspired me to try different things. Everyone was enormously talented, but I do feel like I led those sessions, musically. It's hard because I don't want to blow my own trumpet, but no one else is blowing it!

FLOOD Up to that point, the only things I'd had the opportunity to work on that musically I absolutely adored were The Cure's first record, *Three Imaginary Boys*, where I was a tea boy—that was my first credit; I'd worked with the Associates; and then I was the assistant engineer on New Order's *Movement*. But everything else was training ground. So, when I was asked to do something where not only do I love the artists but creatively it was so completely different, it was just, like, 'Brilliant!' You could try out all these mad ideas and refine them and still get brilliant sounds, and everybody was like, 'This is great!'

VAL DENHAM I'd never done a record cover before, and I felt simultaneously excited and apprehensive. Marc gave me a commission to do exactly as I wished for *Untitled*, although he hoped it would look something like one of my degree-show paintings. I imagined he wanted an image that was weird, with gradated dark skies, and containing Roman Catholic iconographic undertones, subversive androgyny, gold, blood, death, and big sad eyes. In other words, something very me. I didn't want any text sitting on top of my painting, so I put a big black border around it for the Huw to place the various titles and logos, using either red or gold lettering. I decided to do a portrait of Marc as a religious icon and placed a golden halo above his head. I named the painting *Say Halo*, an obvious pun, and painted it exactly twelve-inch square. Marc loved it and enthused like crazy about the finished result. Around this time I also did a painting for the cover for the single of 'Big Louise', but that never ended up being released.[*]

KARL O'CONNOR *Untitled* introduced me to a musical world I didn't know existed, and from it I developed this really mature taste in music. That's what Marc provided for us, and it was invaluable. And he kept on doing that for most of the 80s, actually; I wouldn't have got into Lee Hazelwood or Tim Rose or Spanish music

---

[*] *Untitled* (BZS 13/14) was released on September 1, 1982. A double set consisting of a seven-track album and a three-track twelve-inch, it reached no.42 on the UK chart.

without him. I got into THE THE through Matt Johnson being on *Untitled*, and the songs he plays on it are still mind blowing—I mean, 'Angels' could have been on *Burning Blue, Soul*, it's so great. And of course there was Anni Hogan—without her the Mambas wouldn't have been the band they were, and Marc wouldn't have had the career he had, no fucking way. She was his Mick Ronson.

ANNI HOGAN *Untitled* was long nights and big hair, existing on a combo of drugs, sandwiches, beer, and chips. We were all knackered because we recorded at night—you think you're going to catch up on sleep during the day, but you never do. There was nowhere to sleep anyway! Despite all that we made this amazing album, and when I think back to what Marc was juggling at the time, it only makes me admire him more.

>>

J.G. THIRLWELL I was really tight with The Birthday Party, and around mid-'82 they had moved to Berlin, so I was going back and forth to see them a bit. Berlin before the wall came down was a really unique place because it was kind of an island unto itself. It was this haven where it was cheap to live and easy to get by. And because of that people would go to Berlin and experiment with their art. I think there was also something unique to Germany at that time, a rejection of American and English culture, which resulted in the ground-up creativity that was going on, a real collaborative and community-based spirit. And it was very daring—people were doing crazy stuff. The isolation was important, and I think people kind of liked the wall being up.

MARK CHUNG Berlin was wild. Being in the midst of the Soviet Bloc and the Warsaw Pact, it was one of the few legal ways of escaping the draft—if you were male and registered in Berlin then you didn't have to go to the army. So, you had a walled city with a disproportionately high number of young males that did not consider the army a good option, lots of drugs, and a feeling that at any time somebody could push the wrong button and the world would be over. And, as we found out later, that was actually true, and we came pretty close a couple of times. But what that gave us was a sense of, *If there's nothing you can do about it, let's have a good time as long as it lasts.* It was a unique place—I don't think there was anywhere quite like it at the time.

J.G. THIRLWELL It was a unique time in Berlin. There was a term, *Geniale Dilletanten* (Genial Dilletantes), which I think Blixa [Bargeld, Einstürzende Neubauten singer] identified himself as, and groups like Neubauten, Malaria!, Die Tödliche Doris, and Mania D were creating this unique vision. New York had No Wave, which is sometimes lumped in with punk rock but was very different. There were musicians who knew how to play, but there were also musicians who rejected those musical conventions and were just exploring sound. And, in some ways, the scene in Berlin had a similar basis. If you look at Neubauten using found objects to make sounds or people who used electronics in unconventional ways. Even the means of distribution were really grassroots, and it was easy to put out a record in those days. People who were not necessarily musicians making music, and people who were not necessarily artists making art. There were pockets of that type of thing in the UK, but because the UK is so small and had three weekly music papers, it was easily communicated. It seemed that Berlin existed in a bubble and could create an ecosystem that was unique to itself, which wasn't getting corrupted by outside media. People were creating things for the joy of it, and it was organic.

MARK CHUNG Neubauten had put out a few cassettes and a couple of releases on Alfred Hilsberg's Zickzack label, including the album *Kollaps*, which I was a guest musician on. After that came out, I joined the band full-time. By comparison to other German groups, Neubauten were doing pretty well and were recognised early on as being quite unique. But we're talking very small numbers, totally independent distribution—five or six thousand, something like that. But even then we were getting responses from abroad and you could tell there was interest from other countries.

J.G. THIRLWELL On one trip I saw Einstürzende Neubauten play—I was aware of their work through their singles, but I had no idea how phenomenal they were live, and the first time I saw them they just blew my mind. That was the classic line-up of with Mufti and Mark Chung. Alex Hacke was actually doing their sound and would run onto the stage and play something then go back to the mixing desk. It was just incredible.

MARK CHUNG Jim was great. He said, 'Look, I'm sure you can get a deal in England, and I'm happy to introduce you.' So Blixa and I came to London, but as we didn't have any money we caught the ferry to Harwich, which was absolutely horrible—everybody was throwing up and the vomit was sloshing around our feet. Jim introduced us to Stevo and also to Daniel Miller. Jim was very, very helpful.

J.G. THIRLWELL Neubauten had released a single with Lydia Lunch and Rowland S. Howard called 'Durstiges Tier', which I loved, so I asked them about licencing it for a subsidiary of Self Immolation I was planning. I went to Rough Trade and they gave their blessing, and I was going to take the proceeds from my second album, *Ache*, and launch a label, Hardt Records. Neubauten then decided that instead of licencing 'Durstiges Tier' to me, they would rather do something more significant and put out a compilation album, which was fine with me. The band and I started putting this album together, which turned into *Strategies Against Architecture Volume One*. Around the same time, Matt had exposed Stevo to my work and he was interested in signing me. So I said, 'Well, I've been working with this band Einstürzende Neubauten,' and I turned Stevo onto them. I'd spoken to Neubauten about Some Bizzare and they were interested and came along for the ride too.

MARK CHUNG Personally, I thought Stevo was remarkable. Obviously, he was quite young and, I don't know if this is true but he actually couldn't read or write very much. And he also seemed quite mad, but I thought he was an interesting guy. I liked him and respected him, and obviously he ran a very interesting label. But what he liked most about Neubauten were the things we considered the least important—aspects of the work that we were trying to steer away from to avoid being pigeonholed as a band who were just about destroying everything. Although we did enjoy destroying things from time to time. He was into sensation and controversy, and always wanted us to play somewhere where we could tear down the whole building and get on the front page of *The Sun* or something. So, he didn't have a strong artistic understanding of what we were doing, but that didn't really matter.

>>

Some Bizzare teen tycoon Stevo is in America polishing up the leather and oiling the chains for Soft Cell and attempting to sign Californian fruit cases The Residents. Stevo is also trying to flog his latest proteges Psychik TV [sic]—formed from half of Throbbing Gristle, they are a group playing some 'extraordinary' love songs and are going to surprise us all with their breadth, variety and sweetness. However, faced with the prospect of Genesis P-Orridge strumming a lilting acoustic ballad on acoustic guitar *T-Zers* thinks it can wait a little longer *(Like forever?—Ed.)* for the record's release . . .

author unknown, *NME*, September 11, 1982

Musick: Should be listenable, intelligent, full of ideas and thoughts, thee lyrics a diary laid open, vulnerable. It should also have longevity.

GENESIS P-ORRIDGE, *NME*, December 11, 1982

ALAURA O'DELL I wasn't surprised when Psychic TV got involved with Some Bizzare because Gen really wanted to be rich and famous. When Stevo negotiated the deals with Warners and CBS, Gen was so happy, exclaiming, 'Oh, we're gonna be rich!' The contracts with those companies gave us a massive advance—maybe £250,000 or something crazy like that—but we never actually saw any money in our personal bank accounts, because the money went into promotion and recording costs, including making brass dildos.

GAVIN FRIDAY A lot of the license Stevo had hung on the huge success of Soft Cell. 'Tainted Love' was one of the most successful singles of the 80s—it was ridiculous. I couldn't believe when the first Psychic TV album came out. I remember them getting a fucking huge advance and phoning Geoff and saying, 'What are you gonna do with all that money?' And he said, 'Oh, Gen and Sleazy have gone out and spent it on making gold [sic] dildos!' Just fucking insane stuff. It was beyond a Sex Pistols–style swindle that Stevo was pulling off, it really was. Because this was not rock'n'roll, absolutely not.

STEVO I can't remember whose idea it was to make the dildos to be honest. All I know is Sleazy supplied the mould. I have no idea whose it was, but a very gifted man. It was reported that all the major labels were engraved on the top, but that's not true. It excluded Warners as I signed Psychic TV to them. When they got the dildo, they must have wondered why they weren't listed on the helmet; well, it was because they were getting the deal.

PETER ASHWORTH I took some pictures of Gen and Sleazy in the basement of

Trident, with the famous brass dildos arranged on a chessboard. I shot Psychic TV a few times and we got on really well, actually. I did a shoot with them where Gen got the whole band to dress in white, which made them look quite angelic, but then they all had really surly expressions, which I adored because I like having a conflict within an image. If you're going to do something superficially nice, it has to have an edge somewhere. And that was where Stevo's heart was, too: he knew how to play with people's minds, and these images have almost become infamous.

RUSTY EGAN Stevo pushed people to the limit, to test them, to see if they were loyal, to make sure they weren't going to try and pull him down. I don't think he'd had anyone in his life who he felt he could trust, and then all of a sudden after 'Tainted Love' he was surrounded by people who wanted something from him. We were both in the same boat. We were completely different people, but we both had the same journey.

PETER ASHWORTH Stevo stood out. He was always different. The gobbledygook comments that no one quite understood, yet mystified and attracted attention because of that, were a constant. And he was always playing tricks on people that really he shouldn't have played fucking tricks on. But that stuff was pure Malcolm McLaren—playing with the game and making fun out of it, usurping people who thought they were involved in creative endeavour, but who actually had about as much creativity in their entire body as Stevo did in the end of his little finger. I personally was shocked by the bravado he showed, but also thought, *Far out*.

BEVERLEY GLICK I don't think Soft Cell's success changed Stevo, really. He just got bolder about the ways in which he could wind up record company people and the things he would do to get them to make fools of themselves.

CHRIS BOHN Stevo had a lot of fun with the labels and making demands on them, asking for ridiculous things, from a weekly delivery of jelly babies for Soft Cell to a dildo chess set for Psychic TV, if I recall it right. Again, quite brilliant to get Psychic TV on Warner Bros, and later CBS. The label heads must've thought, *What the fuck are we doing?* Obviously there are things like 'Just Drifting', which is a really sweet song, and maybe that was played to them first. But once they got the full picture and found out about the Temple Ov Psychic Youth and seen everybody with their Tibetan haircuts and heard about the induction ceremonies, they must have really started panicking. Stevo was pretty canny, so I think he must have known he wasn't going to be able to take it much further than that.

ALAURA O'DELL I grew up in the East End of London and I'd heard some very crude things on the streets of Hackney, but I have to say Stevo was so fucking crass. He was the complete opposite of refined. I believe Gen was just looking for any opportunity, and it came his way with Stevo. I found him exhausting—a non-stop talker, full of frenetic energy. He was obviously a smart guy, but in terms of sophistication and how many books he'd read, I wouldn't put him into the class of an intellectual, more of a streetwise guy who was great at spotting talent and making things happen. I have to applaud him for that.

JANE ROLINK Stevo was brilliant. He messed it up in the end but at the time he was an absolute genius. When he got Warner Bros to sign Psychic TV, he got the MD's chair thrown in as part of the deal—this huge leather chair, which ended up being my chair in the Some Bizzare office. I don't know how he did it, but it was hilarious. Everything was fun, but it could be pretty extreme too. Like the music, it was all in keeping.

ALAURA O'DELL I didn't go to Stevo's house very much—maybe twice. I had a young baby, and I wasn't into partying and all that stuff, but I was at St Anne's Court a lot. Gen had told me he wanted our marriage to be an open relationship, so one day when I was at Some Bizzare there was this person with Jane, very feminine looking, with long hair and wearing androgynous clothes, what we'd now call nonbinary, I guess. And that person was Bee. A talented musician, artist, and writer. I was infatuated with him, and we ended up having a long love affair and a friendship that has lasted decades.

PAUL 'BEE' HAMPSHIRE I was friends with Jane—we kind of grew up together— and she basically ran Some Bizzare while Stevo was off doing his mad things. I was involved in music as well, playing with Getting The Fear, and would regularly visit Jane in the Some Bizarre office. The other connection with Some Bizzare was through Skin Two, the fetish club. I used to do the door and I met David Tibet of Current 93 and Geoff Rushton of Psychic TV through that.

MARC ALMOND One of the most positive things about being involved with Some Bizzare was the roads and avenues it led me down, and the connections I made from that. Through Psychic TV I met David Tibet, and he's been a great educator of music, poetry, and art for me, and I consider myself an honorary member of Current 93. Chris and Cosey, too, I was thrilled to meet and work with them.

Some Bizzare: We are all united in creating mischief in thee business and a total assault on thee culture. To repeat thee question 'WHY' to make people think, however briefly and to keep pushing to make things happen. It's thee unity in Some Bizzare that makes it work and scares people.

GENESIS P-ORRIDGE, *NME*, December 11, 1982

PAUL 'BEE' HAMPSHIRE Jane and I went to see Throbbing Gristle play with Cabaret Voltaire in Sheffield in about 1979. And we'd seen the Lyceum show and stuff—we were really into them. It was really exciting for both of us when Psychic TV signed with Some Bizzare. When I first met Genesis it was like meeting a mentor, it was insane. We clicked instantly because we had the same sense of humour and interests. It became a lifelong friendship. And with Geoff and Sleazy as well, we'd all hang out together.

VAL DENHAM I loved going to the Some Bizzare offices. There was always group of goth urchins outside; young Marc Almond clones in black with lavishly applied eyeliner, huddled together as if to comfort each other in their desperate longing. The place was a hive of activity with people coming and going, boxes of fresh vinyl all over the place and posters of the label's bands on the walls. The phone was always ringing, and sunlight would be streaming through the big windows. I always ended up getting plastered on red wine and going home with carrier bags filled with free records. Plus, everyone kept telling me that I was a genius, which did a lot for my confidence. I almost wished I could work there.

JANE ROLINK We were at the centre of something, that's for sure. Groups like Neubauten were so groundbreaking. It was important to me because that music was what I was into anyway—I loved all those bands. So, signing Cabaret Voltaire and Psychic TV was something else for me. I was just a girl from Barnsley, but meeting Gen and Peter was brilliant. They were normal people but twisted.

MARC ALMOND Jane was a genuine music fan and savvy as well. She really was the heart of Some Bizzare for many years and took all the bands under her wing and provided a motherly shoulder for us to cry on. She eventually left and became a successful DJ on London's early 90s techno scene under the moniker Mrs Woods.

ALAURA O'DELL Some Bizzare did feel like a family. Gen and I would go up the West End with Caresse in her stroller, and I would like to pop into Boots and Mothercare, and then go to Some Bizarre and hang out in the office for hours, having endless cups of tea. People were always coming in and out, and we got to know Marc and Dave and worked with them both. And Matt was lovely, and Stevo would always be running around just being nutty.

MARK CHUNG There were very few bands that we respected, but we were big fans of Throbbing Gristle. They were probably one of the biggest influences for Neubauten in many ways, not musically but more in the approach they took. So, we were really excited to meet Genesis and Peter, that was fantastic for us. And it was new, too, because we didn't really have much contact with the other bands on Zickzack records, partly because everybody was in a different city. But the density of London, in the West End, within a square mile you had all the labels, all the video companies, all the art companies, and you would meet all the bands on the street, and we really liked that. Soft Cell were pop to us, so we didn't really have a musical connection there, but Marc Almond was really charming and a nice guy, and we got along very well with Matt Johnson. And the Some Bizarre office was the place where people would hang out after having what passed for a meeting with Stevo, or if you had to see Jane to sort out some stuff. It was fun and it connected people.

STEVO Some Bizzare is like either a mental hospital or a community. It's for artistes who've got integrity but are paranoid or insecure or who feel that no one can relate to them. They know if they come to Some Bizzare they'll be appreciated and understood.

STEVE HOVINGTON We started to feel that our sound needed to change and develop more toward the pop side of things, the more electronic side of side of things. We did a tour of the States in '82, which wasn't particularly successful. We had a personnel change—I'd stopped playing bass onstage and we got an amazing bass player to fill in—but it kind of broke an essential link to the sound of the band. We'd come out of that tour in a bad way; I was in a mental hellhole. We didn't even know whether we still had a label, but we decided to soldier on.

>>

MATT JOHNSON Everyone was delighted with 'Uncertain Smile' and they wanted a follow-up.[*] I had this track 'Perfect', very simple with just the same three chords repeating all the way through—like 'Louie Louie' or 'Wild Thing'—which I thought could work. So, we arranged another session in New York, again with Mike Thorne. Stevo and I flew over and before the sessions started—we'd been hanging out at Fran Duffy's loft in Chelsea and I'd smoked far too much Hawaiian grass that was far too strong, it was like taking LSD or something.[†] I was tripping and having a really horrible time. Stevo said, 'You know, the best way to deal with this is to take some ecstasy,' so I did and was, of course, even more out of it. So then Stevo suggested a quaalude might help. I then swallowed some quaaludes and could barely stand up, much less walk in a straight line. So I was then in the studio, and poor Mike and his engineer were looking at each other, like, *What the fuck is wrong with this guy?* And I was just stumbling around, bumping into things, playing a bit of organ here and a bit of Omnichord there, desperately trying to get it together. I was not enjoying it at all. It was stupid and highly unprofessional. This went on for maybe one or two days, and I just couldn't stand it anymore and really did not want to be in that studio.

MIKE THORNE I've worked with inexperienced musicians before, and I tend to play to their strengths, to look for their talent rather than think, *Well, they don't know that much yet*. Matt was an ingenue and I tried to take care of him as best I could, but he was going dizzy having so much new stuff thrown at him. If you want to get music out of somebody then you need to shield them from a lot of the realities

* 'Uncertain Smile' (EPC A2787/EPC A13 2787) was released through Epic on October 8, 1982, and reached no.68 on the UK chart.
† Fran Duffy was a music, video, and TV promoter and a fixture on the New York club scene during the 80s and 90s. As the founder of Snub TV, he showcased the burgeoning alternative scene and gave many Some Bizzare bands their first US exposure alongside acts such as The Cure, R.E.M., The Sugarcubes, and Nine Inch Nails. When he died in 2001, he was referred to in his obituary as 'the most famous person in the world who wasn't famous'.

of the record business. Saying that, I thought his behaviour around 'Perfect' was pretty dumb. But Stevo was impossible—he was so self-indulgent.

STEVO The reason I fell out with Mike Thorne was simple: he was told not to bring his Synclavia to the studio for the 'Perfect' session, and he bought it. So we walked.

MATT JOHNSON I was desperately trying to find any excuse not to go back into the studio, and the idea came up, *Hey, why don't we drive to the most dangerous part of America?*, which at that time was Detroit. So, Stevo and I stocked up with pills and drugs, performed the customary rock'n'roll trashing of our hotel rooms, rented a car and hit the road. It was a long drive because we went via Niagara Falls and into Toronto for a bit. I love those big old American cars and I love driving them, but it was getting a bit tiring after so many hours, so Stevo offered to drive for a bit. We swapped positions, and he immediately started driving *really* fast. It was misty anyway but then it started to pour with rain, and he's belting along, going faster and faster, and it was horrific, terrifying. And the more I complained, the faster he drove, so I had to pretend that I wasn't bothered in the hope he'd get bored with trying to scare me and would slow down. It was only after that he admitted he'd never driven before.

STEVO I was driving in thick fog with my foot full down on the accelerator—bearing in mind I can't drive—and watching Matt Johnson clinging to the dashboard, realising that his life wasn't in his hands.

MATT JOHNSON CBS were phoning the Some Bizzare office asking what the hell was going on, Jane was making excuses trying to cover for us, and Mike was freaking out, too. We eventually got to Detroit, and it was really run down with under-lit streets, burnt-out cars, and dilapidated buildings everywhere. We were still trying to find the roughest part, and it got quite scary driving around there at night, and we did have a few frightening experiences, but luckily, nothing terrible happened. The worst thing was the bill when we returned to the UK, which was, of course, all charged back to me! One thing that sticks in my mind though was taking a tour of Niagara Falls, which goes behind the falls themselves and you can throw a coin into the rushing water to make a wish. I wished for my next record to be a big hit and really successful. Stevo simply wished for the health and happiness of all his friends and family. I remember thinking that was a really nice mark of his character—he could be very caring and kind-hearted.

>>

STEPHEN 'MAL' MALLINDER We'd had contact with Stevo because of his interest in electronic music, and he was really keen to sign us. From our perspective, we'd been on Rough Trade for a long time, and we wanted a change. We felt Rough Trade were becoming a different kind of thing and great as they were, it was starting to feel a bit alien to us. It was all very West London—Scritti Politti, The Raincoats, that kind of thing—and we were electronic and a bit different. And, apart from The Fall, we were the only weird Northern band on the label. Mark E. Smith was like, 'What do you mean everybody has fucking lentils for lunch?' We were kind of these Northern irritants, and even though our relationship with Geoff Travis was fine, we kind of wanted to move on. We'd also started working with a guy called Paul Smith, and we all wanted to set up a label to make videos. So, as a show of faith, Stevo lent us the money to do that and get our video label DoubleVision going.

GAVIN FRIDAY Rough Trade basically signed The Smiths and dropped everybody else: The Fall, Cabaret Voltaire, Scritti Politti, everyone on the label. Virgin Prunes had just released our debut album, which Colin Newman from Wire had produced, and it was a big seller in Europe. But Rough Trade had decided to put all their coins into this one band, so we had to find someone else to sign us, which was very tough.

STEPHEN 'MAL' MALLINDER We didn't have a manager at that point, and it was just coincidence both Paul Smith and Stevo got in touch with us at the same time. Stevo leant us the money to set up Doublevision, which we worked with Paul on. And then we signed the deal with Virgin through Stevo. All the early videos Rich and I did either at Western Works in Sheffield or at Stevo's place in Hammersmith because he'd set up an editing suite in a back bedroom upstairs. *Doublevision Presents* was all done in Sheffield, but we did edits on stuff like *TV Wipeout* at Stevo's place.*

* *Doublevision Presents* (DV1) was a VHS and Betamax collection of Cabaret Voltaire's pre–Some Bizzare promo videos. *TV Wipeout (A Contemporary Entertainment For Television)* (DV4) was a one-off 'video magazine' available on VHS and Betamax and released on Doublevision in 1984, featuring live performances and videos from artists including Bill Nelson, Clock DVA, Renaldo & The Loaf, and Cabaret Voltaire themselves. These were interspersed with clips from Warhol's *Heat* and *Flesh*, *Plan 9 From Outer Space*, and an interview with David Bowie.

STEVO I put the Cabs in Trident and said, 'You've got two weeks to give me a finished record.' Which was contra to what I did with Test Dept and Neubauten, where there were endless resources for them until they were happy with it. To be honest, it would not have been a good idea to have done that with Cabaret Voltaire. They would just work, work, work until they've lost the basis of the idea that made it great. Like a painter, you have to know when to stop.

STEPHEN 'MAL' MALLINDER Richard handled all the early conversations because I didn't have a phone, but the idea was to make an album for Stevo, and then he'd sort of auction it out to major labels. As the Some Bizzare offices were above Trident Studios, Stevo did a deal with them, which is how we ended up recording *The Crackdown* there. We didn't have long: the idea was to do the album in a week. We had nothing prepared at all, but that was just how we worked—we figured it out in the studio. We arrived in Soho one night in December '82, tipped out our gear in the studio, were introduced to the in-house engineer, a guy called Flood, and that was it really.

FLOOD After the first Marc & The Mambas album the next thing I did for Some Bizzare was the Cabs. Stevo said, 'I want you to produce this album,' even though at the time I wasn't a producer, I was still an engineer. But that was the way things worked, if you had an engineer who could look after everything and join in a conversation with the band, you were almost considered a producer. So Mal and Richard came down, and it was brilliant—we had such a laugh. Stevo was around for a bit, and it was the first time I'd been involved in something that was, to me, total anarchy. My training was that everything had to sound amazing. And there was this one track where I had to record some cardboard boxes—which poor percussionist Alan Fish had to drum on—and make them sound like they weren't cardboard boxes . . . or were they? It was perfect. They'd come up with all these crazy ideas, and I'd go, 'Brilliant! How are we gonna do this?' And that it was the way it was with the Some Bizzare artists.

STEPHEN 'MAL' MALLINDER Apart from *Nag, Nag, Nag*, everything we'd done so far had been recorded at Western Works.* Flood was our first experience of it of

* Cabaret Voltaire's recording and rehearsal space in Sheffield.

working with a co-producer, but it was great, and he was brilliant. Although I've heard he refers to that whole period as his 'dark years', we did have a lot of fun. He was very collaborative and open-minded. We weren't a rock band in the sense that we brought in sequencers and 808s instead of guitars and drums, so we weren't his normal fare. I think it was nice for him to work with us, and we learnt a lot from him too, which is why he gets a co-production credit.

FLOOD The co-production credit on *The Crackdown* in a way sums up the way that Some Bizarre was in the early days. Obviously Stevo was at the head of it, but in the studio there was no one person in charge—everybody knew each other, and there just weren't any egos. It was always such a laugh and there was always a party going on, at every session. In the end I had to train myself to block out what was going on behind me, which turned out to be a good skill to have.

STEPHEN 'MAL' MALLINDER There was a quite a nice family vibe to Some Bizzare, as the offices were upstairs, so we met Jane for the first time, and we got on really well with her, and all the other artists were kind of flying around. I'd met Matt before, but Marc and Dave were popping in and out. And I think that was when I first met Jim. St Anne's Court was like a little hub.

JESSAMY CALKIN Stevo was no Simon Cowell, but he did manage to lure a lot of really good artists to his label. The disparate quality of the Some Bizzare artists was quite amazing. To have Jim and Cabaret Voltaire and Matt and Soft Cell and Neubauten all on the same label, that was really exciting.

STEPHEN 'MAL' MALLINDER Dave was just kicking around in the office, and I'm sure it was probably Stevo's suggestion to get him on a track. We were a bit limited with the synths and Dave had a Prophet-5 and a DMX drum machine, so he just brought his gear down and played on the album. It was fun, and Dave was into it and happy to play. The album actually took less than a week as Richard's girlfriend came down on the Sunday and he wanted to spend some time with her. Stevo was mortified, saying, 'This is costing hundreds of pounds a day, you can't just take a day off!' But Richard wasn't really that bothered about other people's budgets, so Al and I went in, and I did the vocals.

FLOOD After *The Crackdown*, and through Marc and Dave recommending me, I became the go-to guy at Trident, which meant I never left the building. Maybe I called it the 'dark years' because I never saw any daylight!

>>

PAUL 'BEE' HAMPSHIRE Musically, Psychic TV was very different to Throbbing Gristle, but I bought into it straight away. The instruments that David Tibet got them, like the human thighbone trumpets, and the techniques they used to record everything, still had the same depth and substance. Throbbing Gristle may not have been quite as pastoral, with the strings and stuff, but things like 'United' and even some of *Heathen Earth* are just as beautiful as stuff on *Force The Hand Of Chance.* And things like 'Terminus' and 'Ov Power' were quite dark—plus you know, playing human thighbones was in keeping with where they came from. The whole thing about Psychic TV was, you're meant to question everything, so they weren't going to do exact carbon copies of what they'd done before, because that would just be wrong. To me, it made sense and didn't seem odd at all at the time, because there was a continuity to it.

ALAURA O'DELL Gen, Sleazy and Alex Fergusson, Psychic TV's talented guitarist and lyricist, were in the studio quite a bit. Me not so much, as I had a young baby to look after. I think I only did vocals on 'Stolen Kisses' on *Force The Hand Of Chance*. I believe I did some percussion on that album as well. David Tibet, another exceptional artist, was a neighbour who lived just down from our house on Beck Road in Hackney, and he was around a lot and contributed to Psychic TV and the albums we released at the time. And then, when Geoff Rushton and Sleazy got together, Geoff was also at our house a lot. Gen's attitude was, 'I'm going to make a pop record and it's going to be a no.1 hit.' But Gen was still into the shock factor, too, and making art that pushed the envelope, hence human thighbone trumpets.

MARC ALMOND Psychic TV intrigued me. I liked all the people involved and had admired Sleazy and Genesis since their Throbbing Gristle days, and I jumped at the chance to work with them. I sang 'Guiltless' on the *Force The Hand Of Chance*

* Psychic TV's debut album, *Force The Hand Of Chance* (PST 1), was released on Some Bizzare through Warner/WEA on December 17, 1982. The first five thousand copies came with a bonus LP album, *Themes*. On the same day, a single, 'Just Drifting' (PTV 1/PTV 1T), was also released. It failed to chart.

116

album, which echoed all the philosophies of the Psychic TV project at the time. It was cultish, tribal, and mystical, with shades of Aleister Crowley, Kenneth Anger, and even Anton Le Vey, all put into the Hari Krishna Temple. I loved it.

A huge improvement on Soft Cell's Northern soul excursion 'What!', 'Where The Heart Is' should safely give the boys a respectable chart position over Yuletide.* Sad symphonic waves of melody lap lightly over a nostalgic essay of childhood. One almost senses the vibration from the vocalist's quivering lower lip. It will break a million mothers' hearts.

author unknown, *NME*, November 27, 1982

Marc Almond went down a storm at London's Batcave last week. The secret gig was grapevined as a Mambas session, but in the event Marc appeared alone, intoning half-a-dozen songs, including Lou Reed's Caroline Says with the aid of backing tapes.

author unknown, *NME*, December 4, 1982

ANNE STEPHENSON I'd just come out of the Guildhall School of Music and Drama and Gini Ball [née Hewes] from the Royal College—both classically trained, but we were punk-rockers. We used to go busking together at Tottenham Court Road tube station to survive. There was a pub on the corner where Bananarama and Boy George used to drink, and we loved chatting to them. There were loads of wonderful people around at that time in London, and lots of things were happening. And everyone looked wonderful, punks and goths of all different shapes, sizes, and colours.

As well as the busking, me, Gini, and a cellist from the Royal College called Caroline Lavelle formed a string trio called Humoresque. We used to busk in Covent Garden, and I'd do things like play 'Flight Of The Bumblebee' dressed up as a bee, or Caroline would perform flying splits while we played Vivaldi's *Four Seasons* at breakneck speed. We had a real punk attitude, which was unusual for classical musicians, and we did look rather fab with enormous hair and outrageous clothes.

GINI BALL Caroline was friends with Mike Hedges, and he was producing Siouxsie & The Banshees. One day the phone rang, and it was Budgie from the Banshees

* Released on November 26, 1982, 'Where The Heart Is' (BZS 16/BZS 12 16) reached no.21 on the UK chart.

asking us to come in a do a session, which turned out to be for the single 'Slowdive', from *A Kiss In The Dreamhouse*. After that we did the tour, by which time Robert Smith had taken over from John McGeoch. So we got to meet him, which was really nice.

STEVE SHERLOCK Music was always a passion for me, but not my way of earning a living, although that would have been great. Neu Electrikk had unfortunately finished far too early to release any more of our recordings, and the work with Matt hadn't gone any further than doing those B-sides. Anyway, I was at home and—I'll never forget this—sorting out a blocked sink. The phone rings, and it was Stevo, and he said something along the line of 'Awright mate, how you doing? Wanna play with Marc Almond? Theatre Royal, Drury Lane, in three weeks' time?' I was there with dirty water dripping off my hands, not having thought about music for months. So, I said OK, went to a rehearsal and got a call that night telling me I was in.

ANNE STEPHENSON Gini and I lived in a little flat in Peckham with my son Pete, who was about a year old at the time. We were big Soft Cell fans—we just thought they were brilliant. I remember reading about them and Some Bizzare in the *News Of The World* one day and saying to Gini, 'Oh, that Stevo sounds like a right laugh.' How wrong could I be? But we loved Marc and thought he was a genius—still do.

GINI BALL We used to go to the Batcave all the time, and one night out Marc was at the bar. Anne and I were dithering about talking to him, but I thought, *We've just got to ask him, he can either say yes or no.* So, we went over and said hello and after telling him what great fans we were, we told him we were classical violinists and if he ever needed to use strings, would he use us? And he just said, 'Oh my god, I can't believe it, I've got a concert next week at Drury Lane, would you like to come and play?' Anne and I were just so excited about the whole thing.

ANNE STEPHENSON So, the next day, we went over to the Some Bizzare offices above Trident, and Marc was there, and he was really excited to see us. We'd asked him to buy us some weird pedals so we could put our instruments through them and make strange sound effects. We practiced 'Big Louise' with him and that was that. We also told him about Humoresque and our wild punk-classical performances, and he offered us the support slot at Drury Lane, too. We just couldn't believe it—within a week of meeting him we'd joined the Mambas and become his support act. It was unbelievable.*

ANNI HOGAN Drury Lane was the first live show I ever played. Rehearsal was Marc and me in a small room somewhere in London. There was a Farfisa organ set up and an upright piano. We'd go through things just him and me, and it was always fantastic, and perhaps the closest we ever were in a way. And in those moments, when it was me and the piano and him singing, there was a super-special intimacy there. It was an amazing feeling that I've never had since.

PETER ASHWORTH I played drums at the Drury Lane gig. I was only supposed to go on for one track, playing timpani, but I stayed there for the next track. Marc turned around and looked at me as if to say, *Why the fuck is he still standing on this stage?* And I just looked blankly back at him until someone actually called me off. I don't really know what happened that night, and I feel a bit guilty about it. There was no intention to usurp any of the other musicians, I just didn't really know what I was doing or why I was there. But I did learn you don't really do that sort of thing when Marc's playing a gig—you do exactly what you've been asked to do, and then you leave quickly and quietly.

Due to the fact no review tickets or photo passes were allowed, it would appear Stevo was being somewhat cautious over the (official) debut of Marc & The Mambas. However there was little need for him to worry—Marc Almond can get screams of adulation for sipping a cup of tea before he's sung a note, it would appear fairly obvious the austere Theatre Royal was full of Soft Cell devotees. Backed up by Humoresque (a three-piece string section), Anni Hogan on piano, and later Matt Johnson on guitar, as well as a sax and flute player, this 'Little Black Evening' was devoted to Marc Almond doing non-Soft Cell numbers and his own interpretations of other people's songs.

DAVID CORIO, *NME*, December 11, 1982

* Marc & The Mambas' first live show was at Theatre Royal Drury Lane on December 5, 1982. The band played most of *Untitled*, plus a version of Nico's 'Wrap Your Troubles In Dreams', a ten-minute version of The Stooges' 'Dirt', and Lou Reed's 'Caroline Says'. One of the evening's 'special guests' was Dave Ball, who appeared onstage for a ramshackle encore of Soft Cell's 'Say Hello, Wave Goodbye'.

STEPHEN 'MAL' MALLINDER I loved that mad collective vibe of Marc & The Mambas. I saw the Drury Lane show and I remember being impressed at how professional Marc was. Maybe my ideas of professionalism weren't so well-honed back then!

ANNE STEPHENSON During the support set at Drury Lane, while I was playing, somebody crawled onstage and started biting at my ankle. I thought it was a dog at first, but of course it was Stevo. I was laughing my head off while this a bloke is pretending to be a dog sniffing at my ankles, all while I'm trying to play the 'Sabre Dance' really fast and keep in time with the others. I think that was his way of letting me know he fancied me. There was a party at the Columbia Hotel afterward, and there we were surrounded by people we'd only been reading about a few weeks before. Gini and I couldn't believe it—we were just so thrilled.

STEVE SHERLOCK Siouxsie Sioux was a great friend of Marc's, which is probably how we got the slot for Siouxsie & The Banshees' end-of-year Hammersmith Odeon shows.[*] But as we were the support band, we were all stuck in a single dressing room together. This was not good for Marc as he wanted his own dressing room. But the dressing room was small, and there was nothing in there for us, so Marc had a word with Siouxsie, I believe. Sometime later, Stevo and I were walking up the stairs backstage, and the Banshees' tour manager was coming down. Stevo got in front of him and said words to the effect of 'So what are you doing about the dressing rooms?' and proceeds to list everything we want, punctuating each point by poking the bloke in the chest with his finger. The tour manger takes it for a bit, but then suddenly rears back and headbutts Stevo right on the forehead. Stevo doesn't miss a beat, just continues his list of demands and chest prodding. You could see the bloke thinking, *I've just given him my best shot and he took it*. And, sure enough, Marc got his own room, and we got the food and drink. And Stevo got a massive lump on his forehead, but he refused to acknowledge it, as it didn't seem to matter to him. What mattered, I think, was he got what he asked for.

[*] Marc & The Mambas supported Siouxsie & The Banshees at the Hammersmith Odeon on December 28 and 29, 1982.

MATT JOHNSON Stevo and I did a lot of travelling together, some of it for work, some of it for pleasure but we would always have a lot of fun and get up to mischief. And there were always funny stories because Stevo just would not take any advice about anything. One Christmas we went to Lamu in Kenya, arriving in Mombasa to get a connection to the island the following morning. We were wandering around Mombasa's back streets at night and we found a little bar. We'd been warned to avoid tap water and just drink bottled water or soft drinks, so I ordered a Coke and Stevo asked for a pint of tap water. I said to him, 'Stevo, I really wouldn't do that if I were you,' and he lifted the pint, turned to me with his Cheshire cat grin, said 'Cheers!' and downed it. Obviously, the next day he was rushing off to the toilet every five minutes, whimpering, 'I've got dysentery! I'm sick! I'm dying!' Once he'd got over that, I remember putting on sun cream, and he sniffed, 'That's for wimps' and of course he got completely sunburned and looked like a freshly boiled lobster. He also refused to put the mosquito net up, so he was lying in bed in agony, red raw from sunburn and then covered in mosquito bites. But that was Stevo, he always had to learn the hard way.

A Bizzare Meeting . . . . . .
'You can only have 100% trust in yourself'
'What about me!'
'Indoctrination is the only way'
'Debatable'
'What isn't'
'I don't care'
'Good luck'
'Wake up'
'What's in it for you?'
'Friendship?'

Ø, from the sleeve of Marc & The Mambas' *Untitled* LP (1982)

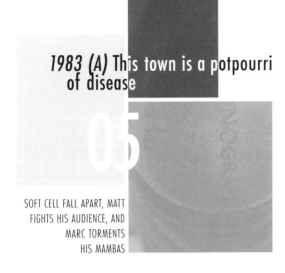

1983 (A) This town is a potpourri of disease

05

SOFT CELL FALL APART, MATT
FIGHTS HIS AUDIENCE, AND
MARC TORMENTS
HIS MAMBAS

MARC ALMOND One of Stevo's strengths was he had a good ear for music—not obvious, easy commercial choices, but often quite experimental, left-field artists. He collected eccentric bands that didn't fit the mould, and then licenced them to major labels. He saw it as a challenge, and he was a genius at it. After the success of electronic-based bands like The Human League and OMD, record-company A&R men were looking for other synth-based new sounds, and Stevo tapped into that. These often bored and jaded record company men were excited by this odd young kid with a funny way of talking, who seemed to have his finger on the pulse of what was happening and was brimming with new ideas. Plus he always made them laugh.

STEVE HOVINGTON At the beginning of '83, Rick left the band, and at that point it probably would have been right to say, 'OK, that's that, I'll go back to uni and finish my degree.' But we were still we were playing live, and the 'Nowhere Girl' twelve-inch seemed to have another life in the clubs—people like Rusty Egan had kept playing it. And we started to being offered big money to play in places like California and Spain (where 'Nowhere Girl' had gone Top 5) so we carried on, just myself and Paul. Of course, the style of the band changed, and we did attempt another single with Phonogram, 'A Chance To Dream', but Stevo was not very happy with it. He literally threw the demo tape at the wall and said, 'I'm not putting that out.' To be fair, it was pretty dreadful.

J.G. THIRLWELL They were very heady days for Some Bizarre, there was a lot of success. Stevo had a golden ticket with Soft Cell—they were huge. They'd continued to have hit singles in the UK, and they were on the cover of every music paper imaginable. Every day there'd be a clan of Marc Almond clones hanging around outside the Some Bizzare office waiting for a Marc spotting, and he'd sign autographs and they'd squeal. But up in office it was quite social, and you would go in and hang out. It was the place to go to find out what was going on and you'd run into people there.

JANE ROLINK I can't speak highly enough Jim—he's an absolute fireball. Honestly, so inspiring, just full of energy and really funny. We laughed a lot.

BEVERLEY GLICK Although they were very different personalities, I think Marc had something in common with Morrissey in terms of the intensity of the connection with his fans, and that kids would see themselves in him. He was expressing something they identified with, that they couldn't express themselves or didn't feel they had permission to express. I remember he had an entire family following him around at one point—a mother and her two daughters basically stalked him. It got quite mad, the intensity of it. I think it was the nature of what he wrote about as well. Even though he wasn't sexually available to women, I found Marc to be highly emotionally available, so maybe that's what they were picking up on. He was not a closed person and wore his heart on his sleeve, which a lot of men did not do at that time. He had the courage to talk about things that other people wouldn't. And while everything else was getting very glitzy and smooth and well packaged, he was talking about the seedy underbelly, real life, which I think was part of it too.

MARC ALMOND After we appeared on *Top Of The Pops*, fans started to gather outside the offices. Their parents were understandably worried about their kids spending so much time hanging out there, and it all became a huge strain, and any privacy I may have had was compromised. I bought a flat in Brewer Street, around the corner from Trident, with my first royalty check from 'Tainted Love', and fans gravitated there too, often ringing on the doorbell late and annoying the neighbours. Some even crossed over into stalker status. The fun of it soured all too quickly.

BEVERLEY GLICK It was obvious to me and everybody I knew who knew Marc that he was gay, but he never talked about it. And then there were these urban myths that grew up around him, which were really difficult to shake off. He was able to laugh about it, but I suspect it got to him at times.

MARC ALMOND I revved up the camp, fey thing just to annoy Phonogram, who constantly wanted me to tone it down. Marc Bolan used to ramp up the camp, but he got away with it because he was straight-ish. But camping it up it just put a big gay spotlight on me at a time when homophobia was running high. At times it could be very scary. I got punched in the face playing live a few times.

MIKE THORNE Soft Cell had an uncanny knack of delivering songs and sounds that mirrored their current mental and psychological state. Unfortunately, when they arrived in New York in mid-1982 to record their second album, something just wasn't right. The pressure of their success had begun to destroy the quality of life for both of them. Dave especially had been feeling at a loss, not enjoying live performance as much as Marc, essentially having very little life outside of writing and recording.

MARC ALMOND *The Art Of Falling Apart* was aptly titled, because by that point it really was.* Dave and I were exhausted by the chaos, no one was steering the ship, and it was all over the place. That was probably partly why it all crashed on the rocks so soon.

DAVE BALL The other bands on Some Bizzare had an influence on *The Art Of Falling Apart*, definitely. *Non Stop Erotic Cabaret* was our pop album, which was great, and very successful, too. But there was a deliberate move toward going a bit darker, and part of that was because we were surrounded by heavier, industrial-sounding acts who were seen as being more credible, if you like, and we wanted to incorporate some of those elements in Soft Cell. Also, I think we were generally starting to get a bit fed up with the machinations of the music business and sick of being a pop band. We deliberately wanted to make ourselves a bit darker and

---

* Soft Cell's second album proper, *The Art Of Falling Apart* (BIZL3) was released on January 15, 1983. Initial copies came with a free twelve-inch single (APART12), and it reached no.5 on the UK chart.

deeper, rather than carry on being a little pop outfit that appeared on *Tiswas*. We weren't chasing chart success anymore, that was for sure.

BEVERLEY GLICK I experienced a bit of the intensity around *The Art Of Falling Apart* because I was in New York with them while they were recording it. Marc was going through a bit of a breakdown. He found himself having to be this shiny little pop thing and going on chat shows and children's TV when that just wasn't who he was. And they were creating this incredibly intense, quite dark music, which Phonogram just didn't want to put out. I thought it was an amazing album. It just made me feel very sad because I could tell that things were literally falling apart, and they didn't last much longer together.

JANE ROLINK I was in New York for God knows how long while Marc and Dave were recording *The Art Of Falling Apart*. I stayed in the same apartment they were, but Dave kept himself fairly separate from the rest of us. He was seeing Anita Sarko at the time and had his own thing going on.*

BEVERLEY GLICK I didn't sense that they weren't getting on, they still hung out with each other. But they'd spent all that time in New York and were having relationships with other people, so I think maybe that was the start of them going in slightly different directions.

MIKE THORNE During the recording, I stopped being seen as a collaborator and supporter, and started to be viewed as a controller, an undercover agent for the record company. It often happens when a new group with little studio knowledge become successful—they feel they want to take control and do it themselves. You can argue for or against that. I always thought it was better when there was another more objective mind in the room. But that's the way it went with Soft Cell, and it was very typical behaviour. There was pressure from the label, but as I was always making records for major labels; I was used to it. It wasn't good for sleeping, though.

DAVE BALL Phonogram weren't totally enamoured with the subject matter of the song 'Numbers' in particular, considering it was the beginning of the AIDS

---

* Anita Sarko was a journalist and influential DJ at the New York venues Mudd Club, Danceteria, and Palladium.

epidemic. Marc had explained to me about the John Rechy novel that had inspired the song, and that it was about casual gay sex. I just went along with it—I was happy for Marc to write about whatever he felt, I never censored him in any way. I wanted Marc to be true to himself.

MIKE THORNE The earlier recording sessions remain crystal clear in my memory, but I can barely remember anything about the sessions for *The Art Of Falling Apart*. Maybe I've forgotten deliberately, or maybe it's just that they weren't very inspired or interesting. The earlier records had been blessed with a whimsical, playful, and unmalicious approach to ordinary, compromised people getting life slightly wrong. There was fun and laughter in the studio for 'Martin', the monstrously over-the-top extravaganza based on the George Romero horror film and 'It's A Mug's Game', used as a B-side, was the old, hilarious Marc stumbling through life's mistakes and laughing at himself. But for the most part, his light lyrical touch had hardened, with some lyrics, such as 'Numbers', becoming just plain nasty. The twinkle seemed to have gone, the song subjects sometimes became objects to despise rather than tweak.

BEVERLEY GLICK I was very into the Skin Two scene and the reinvention of fetish clubs in the UK. Previously, it all used to happen behind closed doors in invitation-only clubs or people's houses, and then all of a sudden there was a nightclub that you could go to in London. But the New York clubs, like the Hellfire and the Anvil, were way beyond anything that was, to my knowledge, happening in the UK, certainly not in public.

PETER ASHWORTH *The Art Of Falling Apart* was the last time I worked with Huw Feather. He arrived with boxes full of trinkets and the bits and bobs, and placed them in the sand around Marc and Dave. I can't remember whose idea it was to shoot different colour versions of it—possibly Stevo. The classic story from that shoot is one of the pictures actually has Dave asleep in it. He actually was audibly snoring and his lips are bit blurred in the shot. Perfect!

HUW FEATHER We wanted things to look slick, but as ever it was done on a shoestring, yet we made it look efficient and answered the brief. Everything was a guerrilla attack—that it was our way of planning something. It was a lot easier for

Peter and me to control things because it didn't feel as hectic or as experimental. Even though what we were doing was incredibly experimental, we could infer that things were on the edge of disaster, without there actually being a disaster.

MIKE THORNE I never think about overall directions, I just work with the material in front of me. When I realised this album wasn't going to be a collaboration, I simply attended to duty and helped with their more ambitious embrace of new instrumental sounds. The result seemed to me self-destructive, the album turning out as monochromatic and sprawling compared with the economy and precision of the first.

SEYMOUR STEIN You need a single or a key track, and there wasn't anything to match the quality of 'Bedsit' [sic] or 'Say Hello, Wave Goodbye', or particularly 'Tainted Love' on that second record.

ANNI HOGAN By now I was living with Marc in his house in Headingley, just me and him, it was great. When *The Art Of Falling Apart* was nearing completion, I remember him designing some of the sleeve artwork on the settee in an afternoon while we watched horror movies on VHS. At that point, things felt phenomenal, exciting, and not falling apart at all. Dave had more influence on the overall sonics of this album, as the sound was beefed up and huge, particularly the bottom end. Like the Elmer Bernstein and Bernard Hermann soundtracks we loved. It was a New York epic, massive melodies driving a noir narrative that oozed lost minds and disturbing dreams, a cast list of the beautiful and the damned.

Soft Cell will never fall apart, which is why Warhol courted them. He recognised that their vision of degradation was like a totally unjaded version of his own. Almond is one of the few people New York can't take prisoner. He is the *naïf* who receives the keys to the city. Falling away and apart from almost everything else, *The Art Of Falling Apart* is a stunning display of the duo's range and diversity. They've now progressed so far beyond both post-Krafticide electrobeat and the tight compression/repatterning of Motown/Northern Soul that one scarcely recalls the skimpy 'Memorabilia', the unwieldy 'Where Did Our Love Go?', the timid 'What?'. Keep luring those dollies, guys.

BARNEY HOSKYNS, *NME*, January 15, 1983

MIKE THORNE As part of Marc and Dave's self-assertion, they and Stevo insisted the second single taken off the album be the unpleasant 'Numbers'.* The record company demurred, using expressions like 'commercial suicide', which just egged the group on. 'Numbers' was released to wide disinterest and, in a classic display of lack of imagination, the record company had bundled the new single with a free copy of 'Tainted Love'. The contrast in attitude and spirit between the two tracks could not have been more poignant.

STEVO It was another example of disrespect. To suddenly find out that the message of 'Numbers'—which is serious song about a serious subject—is lost because someone at Phonogram's marketing department decides it makes sense to pair it with 'Tainted Love'. We only found out about it when it was in the shops. The band were trying to get away from 'Tainted Love', to move forward, and they didn't agree to it. It pissed me off too. I certainly had no intention of any criminal damage when I went into Phonogram, but when people came running around the corner saying, 'Marc has gone berserk and is smashing all the gold discs!', what could I do? Well, you've got to support the artist, haven't you? So I pulled up a plant, picked up a fire extinguisher, and smashed it through a glass door. I then grabbed another fire extinguisher and walked through the door spraying everything.

DAVE BATES Marc stuck his head round the door and made a token gesture toward kicking my jukebox and then stormed off down the corridor, screaming and smashing a few more bits and pieces.

Ever on the case, *The Maker* [got over there quick] and found the floor covered in dirt, plants and pots broken, and a couple of cleaners vacuuming up glass. They claimed that, indeed, Stevo had up rooted plants and although they denied that gold discs had been damaged, they admitted a music centre had been smashed. A more official spokesman for Phonogram . . . told *MM* that as far as he could tell one gold disc had been smashed but he couldn't ascertain whether there has been any

---

* 'Numbers' (BZS17) was released as a double A-side single with 'Barriers' on February 25, 1983. Worried about its commercial chances in the UK, Phonogram shrink-wrapped a free copy of 'Tainted Love' to the twelve-inch. Despite this promotional push, the single only reached no.25. Almond called it 'a complete kick in the face', and it irreparably damaged the label's relationship with the band.

other damage. On being told that Stevo's attack on the Phonogram offices had been prompted by the manager's annoyance at losing 'marketing control' he retorted, 'If Stevo thinks he has control over marketing he has another think coming.'

author unknown, Melody Maker, March 12, 1983

HUW FEATHER I was a trained theatre designer, so I knew how to build a set, and Marc and I had been in a Southport theatre group together, so we knew how to tour. And because Soft Cell had a worldwide no.1 that lasted two and a half years, we were able to do anything we wanted. So we approached the . . . *Falling Apart* tour like a proper production.* The backdrop was commissioned, the show was rehearsed; I was the lighting designer as well as stage designer. Plus, I designed all the T-shirts, the badges, the programs, everything. I was the absolute epicentre of Soft Cell's visual presentation, and the fans knew it too. Why else would they ask for my autograph?

ANNI HOGAN I loved DJing on the . . . *Falling Apart* tour. I could play anything I wanted, and my sets included Suicide, Siouxsie, Velvets, Stooges, DAF, Gun Club, Lydia Lunch, and plenty of classic movie soundtracks. It started with two sold-out gigs at Hammersmith Palais. I loved seeing Huw's flames on 'Heat'—so camp, proper theatre. Dave was in full-on Jack-Nicholson-in-*The-Shining* mode, and Marc was transformed into a larger-than-life dervish, whirling in all the energy from the room and spinning it back out there. At the Liverpool Royal Court gig, I sat with Marc's mum and sister in a box to watch the show, getting a sneaky kick out of being recognised by fans. The atmosphere for the whole tour was intense and celebratory. My nose was a bit put out of joint that some of the other Mambas were doing the backing vocals, so I was glad to be DJing, but I think Marc wanted to keep me separate.

GINI BALL Marc wanted backing vocalists for the . . . *Falling Apart* tour and he didn't really know anyone, so Anne told him that I could sing and that he should ask me. Then the next thing you know, all of us are doing it. We did some European dates and a few in the UK, it wasn't very big tour.

* The . . . *Falling Apart* tour ran sporadically between March and July 1983. The UK leg started with two nights at London's Hammersmith Palais before moving to Belgium and Germany, then back to the UK. Further dates in Spain and the UK were added for May and July, winding up at Coasters in Edinburgh.

MARC ALMOND We just couldn't seem to move beyond our art college, post-punk roots and grow into a band that befitted a string of hit singles and albums. But that's why people liked us, we were unconventional, edgy, and rock'n'roll. My look was modelled on Suicide's Alan Vega and Johnny Thunders' Puerto Rican junkie chic, not on the smooth, big-shouldered couture of the 80s.

>>

MATT JOHNSON My main partner in the studio for the *Soul Mining* album was Paul Hardiman, who'd previously engineered with Mike Thorne, not only on Soft Cell but also with Wire. There was a connection because I'd worked with Graham Lewis and Bruce Gilbert on a couple of tracks for *Burning Blue Soul* and the first THE THE single for 4AD. The first thing Paul and I did was finish off 'Perfect', and I was really happy with it.* I liked Paul a lot—he's got a great sense of humour—and we got on very, very well. So we started looking around for studios to record an album and we found the Garden in Shoreditch, which was owned by John Foxx at the time. I was living in East London—I'd moved to Braithwaite House in Bunhill Row with my new girlfriend, Fiona Skinner, who was soon to design the new band logo for me. I'd written a few songs at the Highbury bedsit, and I was writing some more at her flat.

ZEKE MANYIKA I was getting the train to and from Glasgow quite a bit. One night, Stevo wanted to go clubbing, but I had to get a train, so he said, 'Let's put a stop to this now, I've just bought a house in Hammersmith, so why don't you move in with me? You'll get your own floor, and you can pay me what you want.' And I thought, *That sounds good*, but everyone else thought it was the worst idea ever!

ANNI HOGAN Zeke should get a medal.

ZEKE MANYIKA I was very fond of Stevo. We just got on well, which seemed inexplicable to some people—and to me too sometimes, because on the face of it we were so very different. I think it helped that when we first met we had no

* 'Perfect' (EPC A 3119) was eventually released as a single by Epic on February 11, 1983. It reached no.79 on the UK chart.

professional relationship, we just laughed and talked a lot. He was a very curious soul and wanted to learn stuff. He could also be very kind and thoughtful. There was something of an old spirit about him, and you could forget how so much younger he was than everybody else. Then suddenly he would turn and behave like a rude spoilt little brat!

J.G. THIRLWELL When the whole Postcard and Orange Juice thing appeared, I did not identify with it at all—I thought it was it was a bit weak and wimpy. I had a friend who knew Edwyn, and I was like, 'Fucking Edwyn Collins, that wimp, when I meet him I'm going to push him down the stairs.' And when I did meet him, Edwyn came up to me and said, 'Oh, Foetus, I hear you are going to push me down some stairs?' And after that we became really good friends. He's a great guy with a great sense of humour and we had a lot of similar reference points. Then I became friends with the others—Davey, Malcolm, and Zeke—and we started hanging out.

ZEKE MANYIKA Stevo woke me up one morning to tell me Orange Juice were going to be on *Top Of The Pops* with 'Rip It Up'. Jim was a good friend of ours and him and Edwyn got on really well, so, as we didn't have a sax player, we asked him to mime the solo for our appearance. What used to happen at *Top Of The Pops* was everything had to be camera rehearsed, and you had to stick to that routine. So, we thought, *Let's change everything.* The cameramen went mental—I don't think we were asked back again.

J.G. THIRLWELL For some reason, for about five minutes, I became the go-to sax player. I had taught myself how to play as I wanted to have brass instruments on Foetus records. So, I borrowed a sax from Katy Beale, who was Mick Harvey's partner (now wife), and I learnt the fingering and just enough to do overdubs and James Chance–influenced solos, stuff like that. I wasn't particularly great at playing it, but I was the only sax player people knew. So, I ended up playing sax with Lydia Lunch on a tour of Scandinavia when Rowland S. Howard dropped out, and then Virgin Prunes asked me to play on one of their albums, which I did. I also played with The Birthday Party at a festival in Athens, which was the first one that new wave bands had ever played. The headliners were The Fall, New Order, and The Birthday Party. I played sax on the encore, which was The

Stooges' 'Fun House', and it was absolute mayhem, the stage was invaded, and I barely got a few toots out. But it did end up on one of their live albums. So, when Orange Juice got offered *Top Of The Pops* for 'Rip It Up', they asked me to come and lip-sync the sax solo. Which was fun. And then, weirdly enough, they were headlining the Lyceum and I got a call—I don't know where I was, but it wasn't my house because I didn't have a telephone—saying, 'You've got to get down to Lyceum because Orange Juice want you to play "Rip It Up" with them.' So, I went over there with my sax and played the encore, a very skronky solo!

CHRIS BOHN Stevo didn't accept that there were differences between high and low culture, that this is pop and this is not. A good example was when Jim appeared on *Top Of The Pops* with Orange Juice. It was a very unusual mixture of things and not something you'd expect to see. And that was one of the great things about Some Bizzare and the associated artists, this strange refusal to acknowledge that popular automatically equated something to hum or tap your feet to. Obviously Some Bizzare weren't alone in this; bands such as The Human League mk II, Heaven 17, and The Associates were all opening up the idea of what popular music could be, what being popular meant. The problem with most of those bands was they soon started compromising their ideas for further success. This is something Some Bizzare did not do, and that was a major point of difference. They kept being as daft, as extreme, as noisy as possible within the context of being signed to major labels. Those deals may not have lasted very long—Psychic TV got out two albums before going independent and Neubauten only the one—but for a time it really broadened the definition of popular music, and by extension the possibility that popular culture would not accept compromise.

STEVO Someone came up to me and said, 'Stevo, the trouble with you, your artistes and Some Bizzare is that you're too bigoted.' And I said, 'Yes, you're right, we are bigoted and we've got every right to be because we're superior.' The music of Some Bizzare is not a projection to the masses. It is something which is very self-indulgent. And yes, it's a shame that you're 'elite' if you put over music that's intelligent, original and projects attitudes. Some Bizzare has got its own variety in a very anti-structured framework. Maybe you can compare Neubauten to Cabaret Voltaire or PTV to Foetus; to me, there is no comparison. We widen variety, we support creativity, we discourage sycophantic adulation.

ROB COLLINS I was at the Lyceum when Einstürzende Neubauten supported The Birthday Party.* I saw Stevo and the Some Bizzare crew there—I knew them but hadn't started working for them yet. I loved Neubauten—I had the 'Kalte Sterne' double seven-inch and was blown away by them live.

Einstürzende Neubauten [at the Lyceum] were a phenomenon totally unfamiliar in their inspiration and totally inspiring in their destructiveness. One figure, trapped in white light, screamed a frenzied release into a microphone while another hammered on an unidentifiable percussive device with a huge staff and a third roamed the stage, his shirt abandoned, arms swinging, fixing the audience with an eye-popping stare of malicious delight. Einstürzende Neubauten were pure, caressing hatred, an enlivening phenomenon concealing a level of terrifyingly bleak alienation.

DON WATSON, *NME*, March 19, 1983

ROB COLLINS Stevo was operating Some Bizzare like a production company. So, he'd sign the band, make the record, and then shop it to record labels. And the deal would be between the label and Some Bizzare, not the band. Cabaret Voltaire were already making *The Crackdown* when he contacted me. He came into the office and played some songs, and that was the first time I met him. He was a lunatic, a complete character, but he made me laugh, and he did take you over with his enthusiasm and craziness. We got on, but I was a bit intimidated as well—he had this manner about him, and you never knew whether he was going to go one way or the other. I went over to St Anne's Court to listen to some more tracks and met some of the other Some Bizzare people.

Then it got to the point where I had to go to Virgin and say, 'I want to do this Cabaret Voltaire deal.' Understandably, they wanted to hear the record, and I had to tell them that Stevo won't bring it over and we all had to go to his office to listen to it. There was a bit of grumbling, but eventually we all jumped in a couple of cabs and went over there.

STEPHEN 'MAL' MALLINDER We were around for the mad, fun stuff, the parties at Stevo's house and all that. Gen and Sleazy were there with Psychic TV, which was

---

* Einstürzende Neubauten supported The Birthday Party at London's Lyceum on March 7, 1983.

reassuring, and Jim was doing his Foetus albums. So, there was a kinship, but it all revolved around Stevo and his personality kind of overrode everything, we were a bit like little satellites in front of this mad guy. Obviously Soft Cell had kicked off, which had empowered him. And he'd started his relationship with Seymour Stein, and it was a time when someone like Stevo could be this maverick label boss. And that's what we liked—he wasn't industry, but he had their ear, and he could talk to them. But he just didn't give a shit, and I suppose there was something quite Dada about him—he fitted in with this idea of a completely mad character in the music business. If we were going to work with anybody, we would choose to work with someone as mad as that.

ROB COLLINS Stevo's an entertainer, a jester, the devil, whatever he wanted to be. He had all these people from Virgin in his office looking pretty worried as he held court. But eventually he played the record, and everyone really seemed to like it, and so we did the deal. I wasn't super-involved in the finances, but I know it wasn't an expensive deal. It was like, *These are the recording costs, and you need to pay us back for these, and pay us a royalty.* Stevo always had good legal advice.

>>

MATT JOHNSON I was offered a residency at the Marquee Club in Wardour Street and decided to put together two 'underground' super-groups with some of my favourite people and friends.* So I had Jim Thirlwell, Thomas Leer, Jean-Marc Lederman, Marc, Zeke, Mal, Simon Fisher-Turner, Colin Lloyd-Tucker, Peter Ashworth, Edwyn Collins, Steve James Sherlock, a couple more. I divided the groups up initially into 'aggressive' and 'mellow' for a large part of the set, and we'd all get together onstage at the end, wearing all black and balaclavas, playing a single chord on our guitars very loud—sort of Glenn Branca-ish, though I'd never heard of him at the time.

The shows went very well, packed every week, a great atmosphere, except on the very last show, some idiots in the audience started throwing glasses and bottles and a big fight ensued. But it transpired we were fighting with the wrong people because the missiles had come from the back of the audience, but we couldn't see

---

* The Marquee residency—known as *Rock'n'roll With THE THE*—ran every Thursday throughout March 1983. Only one very rough recording, from the second show of the run on March 10, is known to exist.

that because the stage lights were in our faces. So, this fight started, and everyone ran off the stage, leaving just two other people to support me. No one would be surprised to hear that Jim was one of them, but a lot of people are when they find out the other was Marc. He was ferocious.

STEVE SHERLOCK It was a series of gigs, one a week for four weeks, at the old Marquee on Wardour Street. I found it fantastic as the place is steeped in musical history, the changing room walls had signatures of all the famous artists who had played there over the years. There had been no rehearsals—well, I hadn't been to one—as Matt wanted to keep an improvisational feel. And on the first night, certain elements of the audience didn't seem to get it, beer was thrown at the stage, and one-by-one the band walked off. Matt did manage to quieten the situation down, and we were back the next week as if nothing had happened.

STEPHEN 'MAL' MALLINDER I think me and Edwyn were the guests for one night. Anyway, Matt did his set, and for the encore he gave me a guitar and went, 'Right, you're playing now, off you go!' and just shoved me out there. I didn't even have a plectrum, I had to use a 10p piece or something. I'm just stood there on my own at the Marquee, playing scratch guitar. I was lucky, I played the safe night—there weren't any riots when I was there.

PETER ASHWORTH It was a really interesting idea, and it consolidated a lot of friendships. Foetus was another person who used to hang around St Anne's Court. Jim and I got on and I really liked him. There were quite a few of us involved in the Marquee shows, with Zeke and me both on the backline and a stage-wide row of guitarists standing in front of us.

J.G. THIRLWELL Matt got offered the shows, and I helped him put them together. We were driving around London, and we saw a kitchen sink lying on the side of the street. So, we stopped, picked it up, and it became part of the set—literally everything *and* the kitchen sink. There were several different iterations of THE THE for those concerts. Matt had a band version, which I was in playing keyboards, guitar, and doing backing vocals. There was also a duo version with Thomas, and then, for want of a better word, an acoustic version with Simon. And then we all came together at the end and performed a Glen Branca–inspired, atonal, one-chord-bash thing. Those shows were really good, and I played all four. At one of them, people started throwing beers or something, and when that type of thing happens, you don't know where in the audience it's coming from, and sometimes the wrong person gets victimised. And I think that's what happened that night with Marc, and it turned into a big melee, and everyone jumped in. To be honest, it wasn't the only time something like that happened.

MARC ALMOND The audience were wild, and someone threw something that hit me in the face, so I retaliated by hitting them with my guitar, which I regretted straightaway. The guy wasn't hurt, but a fight ensued in the audience, and it all ended in chaos. Just another Some Bizarre show!

ZEKE MANYIKA Oh God, those shows were punk rock reincarnated. Two drummers (Peter Ashworth and myself), Marc, Mal, Jim. There were no rehearsals—it was literally a discussion in the dressing rooms and then, 'Right let's go!' One night, I don't know what happened to him, but Marc just lost his mind, 'cos he hit someone with a guitar, and it was so sudden and so unlike him as well. I think someone in the audience had been needling him, so I'll give him a pass for that, but backstage no one was happy because that was crossing a line. Those shows were chaotic, but it was so exhilarating. There was something so free about it, and scary as well. It had no form to it, and to this day, I still think, *What were we doing?* It was so risky and could've seriously ruined reputations. But that's what was so exhilarating about it, there was a sort of Wild West gang togetherness about it, going into a little town and mashing it up.

ANDREAS MCELLIGOTT I first met Marc backstage at a Siouxsie & The Banshees concert, and we'd just released a single which he loved, and we got chatting. The next time we met was at the Music Machine, and we had a more serious and less distracted conversation.* Marc suggested we should do something together, which I thought was great, because I really respected him as an artist, and still do. He said to me, 'Too many people think from the wallet and not the heart,' which really chimed with me. So we were having this intense conversation, and we

* Soon to be taken over by Rusty Egan and Steve Strange and renamed the Camden Palace. It's now known as Koko.

soon realised we were surrounded by this circle of people all leaning in trying to hear what we were saying. And Mick Mercer was photographing us, and a picture ended up in the gossip columns of the weeklies.

ANNI HOGAN The place to hang out was the Batcave, which was fantastic. I DJed when it was in the basement of Foubert's and the place was decorated with webbing and nets. You had a sex cinema in one room, and Danielle Dax looking amazing in another, and the music was brilliant. I just adored everything about the place. Siouxsie & The Banshees used to be there a lot, and that's who I was hanging around with then. I was involved in their *Play At Home* film for Channel 4—we were all tripping when we made it. It was very messy.

ANDREAS MCELLIGOTT Marc and I had decided to do something, then the idea of *The Whip* came up. I think it was the brainchild of Sex Gang Children's original bassist, David Roberts, in connection with Kamera Records, as a kind of showcase for new bands, I guess. So Marc and I did 'The Hungry Years', and we just donated it to the record. We recorded it at Trident and it was engineered by Flood, who was fantastic to work with. He didn't say much but he worked nonstop—he was like a machine. You'd suggest something to him only to find out he'd already done it. We didn't have a damn clue as to what we're going to do, but Marc had put together a drum track, which sounded really good, so I just added a bass part to it, and it sounded great. Marc had this idea for us to do our vocals separately, without hearing what the other was doing, except for the chorus section, which I worked out on a piano. I was in the live room, doing my vocal, and a lot of people from Some Bizzare were in the control room watching me.

ANNE STEPHENSON We all used to hang out together at the Batcave. Marc, Siouxsie, Severine, and Robert Smith. Gini and I were asked to do a track on the Batcave album called 'The Dance Of Death', which we did as The Venomettes, a name that Jane had come up with.

ANDREAS MCELLIGOTT Everyone used to hang out at the Batcave, especially at the beginning. Gini and Anne played with Sex Gang Children and played on 'The Hungry Years' too. Severin and Siouxsie would be there, and bands like King Kurt had started to go there too—loads of people you wouldn't normally bump into.

And they used to play great music, the Velvets, Sweet, T Rex, Roxy—the music we all loved. It was a good hangout and a private place too, you know.

GINI BALL Marc was due to appear on *No 73*, an 80s kids' TV show, but for some reason he couldn't do it, so he suggested The Venomettes as a replacement. Amazingly, the producers were OK with that, so Anne and I went along, with Martin McCarrick and Billy McGee. The other three did the strings while I sang, and we played 'Dat's Love' and 'Dere's A Café On De Corner' from *Carmen Jones*. So, Marc was indirectly responsible for Bizet getting played on kids' TV on a Saturday morning.*

>>

ZEKE MANYIKA Matt and I became friends, and just started hanging out together. Matt is a naughty boy and we just made each other laugh. So, when we started working together, it was just an extension of the friendship. What Matt was doing was so momentous and new, and he didn't want to be struggling to explain himself to a bunch of session musicians. At that point, he could have had any players, but he wanted to work with people who had an instinctive understanding of where he was coming from. And I think that's why he asked me, Jim, and Thomas—he was close to all of us, and the album has an intimacy because of it. It was a great atmosphere and quite painless because we were all mates. It was fantastic.

MATT JOHNSON I was lucky to be able to bring in some of my friends to play on *Soul Mining*—people like Zeke, Thomas, and Jim. And Jools Holland, of course, who was suggested by Annie Roseberry and who I didn't know at the time, but I got to know after that session for the new version of 'Uncertain Smile'. I didn't want a producer, what I needed was a great engineer who could share production responsibilities with me. And Paul was superb, really professional, very much old school. This is pre-digital, obviously, completely analogue, we didn't even use any sequencers. So, for certain songs like 'GIANT' and 'Waiting For Tomorrow', I devised a way of playing each part live, building up layers, which we would then mix manually with mute buttons and faders, all-hands-on-deck style. Nowadays,

---

* Almond would return to the 1943 Broadway musical for the next Marc & The Mambas album, covering another song from it, 'Beat Out Dat Rhythm On A Drum'.

it wouldn't take that long to do some of those things via MIDI in Logic or Pro Tools, but in those days it was a time consuming, handmade process.

J.G. THIRLWELL Matt was in the studio, doing his thing, and I just went down there and played some percussion on 'GIANT'. I was around, but that was about the extent of my involvement with those recordings. It's Zeke who deserves a lot of credit for that track.

ZEKE MANYIKA Matt tells everyone I was a week late to the sessions, but that's bloody wrong! It wasn't like that. That was probably when he wanted me to be there, but I wasn't available. When Matt wants something done, he wants it done now. He's very impatient. With Matt and Stevo, there was a kind of Some Bizarre philosophy, everything had to be hard, *hard*! And that's what Matt wanted for 'Waitin' For Tomorrow'—something punchy—so I just went for it. With 'GIANT', Matt needed something for the ending, so I suggested the chant. Him and I went in and started layering vocals, so it sounded like a big crowd. We got Stevo to sing on it too, but he was so bad we had to chuck him out.

J.G. THIRLWELL We did another track, I can't remember what it was for but it was me, Zeke, Matt, and Mal from Cabaret Voltaire. We recorded it at Abbey Road. It was called 'Hit Me Where It Really Hurts' or something like that. I think we might have done a version of that at the Marquee.

ROB COLLINS The job offer from Stevo came totally out of the blue. They needed someone to work in the office because they were so busy and he said, 'You signed Cabaret Voltaire, you can come and help me manage them.' It was as simple as that. I did try and use it as leverage to improve my position at Virgin, and they improved a couple of things, but ultimately I felt like an outlier there. It may have been because of my age, but I'd wanted to sign a few things and kept being knocked back, so I was probably like, 'I'll show you!' So, the following weekend, I was up in the Some Bizzare office going, 'Well, what do you want me to do?' I just sort of made it up.

STEPHEN 'MAL' MALLINDER Stevo saw himself as a provocateur rather than a manager, and after he'd set up the deal with Virgin, our connection with him was much less. He'd turn up to shows and be a perennial nuisance, but we saw ourselves being managed by Rob, really, while Stevo got on doing whatever it was he did. I was living in London, and I saw Stevo more than Richard because of that, so there was a social connection. Creatively, we connected less with the music and more with the videos, that became more of a link than the record label.

ROB COLLINS One of the first things I had to do at Some Bizzare was sort out some equipment for Peter 'Sleazy' Christopherson. Because the office had an open-door policy, people were in-and-out the whole time, and I was sitting there on my first or second day, on my own, and Sleazy comes in and I didn't know who he was, so he explained he was in Psychic TV. He then gave me a list of equipment, told me where to get it from, and then walked out. So, I just rang the places up, ordered the gear, and then it all arrived at the office. And I thought, *Ah, that's what management is all about: getting shit done.* And I suppose it built up from there. A lot of it wasn't work—it was three years of just having a mental time, coming across crazy people and crazy situations. I don't think there will be anything like it ever again.

JANE ROLINK I didn't have a background in the music industry like, say, Rob did. I taught myself everything—I just stayed behind and learnt how to type and how to run the office. But the music was everything, and I was already up to speed with that because I loved it all already.

DAVE BALL Jane was the only sane person at Some Bizzare. Everyone loved Jane— she was great and kept the ship steady. Stevo didn't know what he was doing half the time—she should have been in charge, not him. He should've been the creative director and just let Jane deal with the business side of things.

ANDREAS MCELLIGOTT Jane was the drill sergeant at Some Bizzare. She ran the place. I used to hang out there a lot, with Marc and Dave, and getting some advice from Stevo, whether I wanted it or not. I still have every respect for the guy, he's cheeky but shrewd, like an Essex barrow boy.

MARC ALMOND When Stevo really got Some Bizzare going, the great thing about it was the camaraderie and interaction between the bands. We often hung out with each other, supported each other at concerts, and played on each other's records. Friendships were made that have lasted over the years. There was almost a Warhol's Factory feel about the St Anne's Court office—it was a very creative atmosphere. If we didn't have to be anywhere else, we hung out there all day, every day. It's amazing any real business work happened at all. Often it didn't. It was a bit chaotic, to say the least.

DAVE BALL Stevo created a kind of an art collective, and for a while it was a quite healthy atmosphere. As far as Soft Cell funding the lesser-known bands, I think that was probably quite true, but we welcomed it because we liked that approach. Us and THE THE may have been generating the money, but I didn't mind putting it back into something so creative. I got to play with Cabaret Voltaire and meet and work with Genesis P-Orridge, who was my hero. And I liked the fact that there were radical bands like Neubauten and Test Dept on the label. We were a lot more extreme when we started out—we toned down our act in a lot of ways—so we felt a kinship.

GAVIN FRIDAY The Some Bizzare office in Soho was quite an extraordinary place to visit. It was the Soho you read and heard about on the Soft Cell albums; it really was a different place to what it is now. It was fucking great—insane, to tell the truth. We were all young and a little crazy, you know what I mean? A lot of antics, lots of drugs and not going to bed and just working all night in the studio.

ROB COLLINS Honestly, the office was a tip. We didn't have carpet; we had that old green-baize fake-grass matting that you'd get on fruit and veg barrows. Stevo thought it would be funny to use as carpet and picked a load up from Berwick Street market. There were three or four rickety old desks and piles of old studio kit, microphone stands, and leads. It was pretty rough.

PAUL 'BEE' HAMPSHIRE One day there was a big kerfuffle in the office because they'd put a few months' receipts into a black bin liner, and the maid had thrown it out thinking it was rubbish. Things like that would happen all the time. There were always weird and wonderful characters hanging about, and because it was in the middle of town, people would pop in and out—you never knew who would

141

be there. It was complete chaos, but Jane was a real anchor for the company. It just would not have run if it hadn't had been for her. I mean, people were working on acid there. You'd go in and everyone was fucking tripping, making international calls and trying to sort stuff out. It was a miracle that they managed to get anything done.

ROB COLLINS We kept regular hours, 10–10:30am start, but Stevo would come in later, saying, 'I've done my morning's work at home, let's go down the pub.' So, it very quickly revolved around long drinking sessions in the George and the Ship on Wardour Street. Then we'd head back to the office for a bit, then go back out to the pub or Marc's place in Brewer Street, Stevo's place in Hammersmith or Jane's on the Edgeware Road, and carry on.

ANNI HOGAN The office at Trident was pretty mental. Everybody was on speed of one form or another, and were just buzzing around like mad. It was a crazy atmosphere but at the same time, very inspiring, and it felt exciting. I was totally drawn to it.

PAUL 'BEE' HAMPSHIRE The Some Bizzare crew were some of the first people to take ecstasy in the UK, and it was cheap and legal. It resurfaced a couple of years later with the Taboo crowd. I remember being at Maximus, and someone came up and said they had some ecstasy, and I was like, 'Give me it!' But it had gone from costing £6 to £18.

ZEKE MANYIKA There was a very strong connection with New York at Some Bizzare, and that's how we got to have the very best first batch of ecstasy. Very clean, no hangovers. It was fun and a lot of ideas were formulated under the influence.

JANE ROLINK I arrived just after Cindy, so she wasn't around a lot when I was, but I did know her. Speed was the big one for me at the time, but we all took ecstasy. It was so fantastic, it was gorgeous.

ANNI HOGAN I do remember when I first tried ecstasy—I was in London with Cindy and a few others. I'd previously been a bit scared of it, but Cindy talked me round. I was more into speed and LSD—just listen to 'Twilights & Lowlifes'.

ROB COLLINS My first exposure to ecstasy was not knowing that other people were taking it and then hearing people talk about it. The first time I took it was at Stevo's house in Hammersmith. It felt pretty cool, it was warm, it was nice. But there was so much other stuff going on at the same time. Alcohol was a big part of Some Bizzare, maybe not for everyone, but for me and Stevo it was a big part of each day. Pints in the pub, spirits in the office, go back to his house for a line, take ecstasy at whatever time in the evening and go and lie in the bath. I didn't get hugely caught up in it, though—it was more about going out drinking, and I enjoyed a line of speed more than anything else.

MARK CHUNG We had very good speed in Germany, so we did do long sessions overnight locked in the studio. And the speed gave us the tenacity to stay with an idea until we got it right. One time, we were in this tiny cellar studio right beside the Berlin wall for three days working on 'Armenia' [from *Patient O.T.*], trying to get it right and getting so hung up on tiny details. Chris Bohn and Anton Corbijn turned up to interview us for the *NME*, and I remember the look of horror on their faces when they opened the cellar door and saw the state of us. It puts you in a weird space when you spend three days underground on speed.

DAVE BALL It started to go dark when one of the guys in the office who had a heroin problem killed himself. That was very sad, but there was a lot of heroin around at the time. I was more into coke and speed, so I never really got into that side of things. Metropolis Music, who dealt with Soft Cell's publishing, had an office next door to Some Bizzare, and Steve Strange was always around, bless him. He was always a bit of a cokehead, but then he started getting into smack too, and once he was on it, he was *on* it. I really liked Steve, though, and I got on with him really well when he wasn't off his tits.

STEVO Steve Strange gave me my first pizza. He was on Kings Road eating outside a restaurant, and I said, 'I've never had a pizza,' and he like looked at me like I was joking. He said, 'Come sit down, I'll get you one.' That was my first ever pizza. The funniest thing Steve Strange told me was his vision for the Camden Palace when he and Rusty took it on. There were four levels in the building, and he said that people down on the dance floor would envy the people on the second tier. And the second tier envy the third tier, and the real *creme de la creme* would get to

143

the top. He meant it, too, this working-class kid from Caerphilly in Wales. I never saw any greatness in that class thing.

>>

ANNI HOGAN I had my upright grand piano in the basement of Marc's house in Leeds, and the first tune ever written there was what turned out to be 'Black Heart'. Apparently I'm descended from a Spanish Armada galleon sunk off the coast of Ireland, and one of my favourite musical styles to improvise are Flamenco-influenced chords. Marc was equally Spanish-influenced, and when he heard me playing my Spanish flavours, a tune started to emerge. So I recorded it on a cassette player and gave it to Marc to write lyrics to. I wish I still had that tape.

VAL DENHAM The next record sleeve Marc asked me to do was the 'Black Heart' single.* He already had an image in his head—a mad female Flamenco dancer for the front and a male Flamenco dancer on the reverse. I still hadn't realised that works created to be reproduced needed to be made larger than the finished product as the printer's photographer shrinks them down to give it greater clarity, so I actually did the finished paintings exactly seven inches square. I had to trawl through Thomas Cook holiday brochures to find images of flamenco dancers. I used the same brochures for the *Torment And Toreros* album.

STEVE SHERLOCK I was a permanent member of the Mambas as much as anyone could be in that sort of mix, along with Anni and guitarist Lee Jenkinson. We were told *Torment And Toreros* was going to be a double album, there was going to be a tour, and I was to be paid of eight grand. *Fantastic,* I thought, as that was good money back then. I recall an initial instalment was paid, but the rest of the money never materialised.

ANNE STEPHENSON Marc told us he was going to be making a double album and asked us to do the strings on it. Gini and I said yes but Caroline was really pissed off because we never really got properly paid by Some Bizzare, so she left and joined the Fun Boy Three and had a career as a solo artist. Gini and I were really

* 'Black Heart' (BZS19) was Marc & The Mambas' first commercially available single. Released by Phonogram in June 1983, it reached no.49 on the UK chart.

144

idealistic, saying things like, 'It's the music that counts,' but Caroline was right, of course, because you have to pay the bills. We needed to find a really good cellist to replace Caroline, because she was so brilliant, and I remembered my friend Martin McCarrick from Guildhall. So, I got in touch with him and told him we were playing with Marc and asked him if he would like to join us. He came along and brought a friend with him, Billy McGee, who played double bass.

ANNI HOGAN I understand that *Torment And Toreros* is a phenomenal record, but it really was traumas, traumas, traumas.* Musically, again, fantastic, but it was very much 'do everything in one take', which I found a terrible pressure. It wasn't the same as *Untitled*, where it had been freer—Marc had some more definite ideas this time, and there were a lot more people involved. Everyone was sucking up to Marc unbelievably—which he was enjoying, of course—and there was a lot of playing this person against that person. Anne was going out with Stevo, Gini was falling in love with Dave, and Lee Jenkinson and I were getting close, even though he kept going off with Marc to take lots of E. It was just a lot of late nights, a lot of drink, a lot of drugs. Genius and jealousy.

STEVE SHERLOCK I was in the band but I never really felt part of the gang. The others seemed to socialise together to all hours, whereas I had a wife at home and was working during the days. So, whenever they said, 'Right, we're recording tonight, 8pm at Trident,' I'd do day's work, get changed, and then drive up to Shaftsbury Avenue, park up, and get there for 8pm. Sometimes I'd sit there with Flood—who was a lovely guy—until gone midnight before the others turned up.

MARC ALMOND I did all the sessions for *Torment And Toreros* at Trident, recording late at night, using dead-time hours as it was cheaper. We worked through the night until morning, and wore out Flood in the process—he used to sleep on a sofa in the studio, exhausted.

FLOOD Every record I was involved in at that time was a great training ground, but *Torment And Toreros* in particular. My memory is that it took two weeks to make,

* The second and final Marc & The Mambas album, the double LP *Torment And Toreros* was released by Phonogram on August 16, 1983, and reached no.28 on the UK chart.

which is no time for a double album. There was a period of time when we were at Trident, and then we moved to Jacobs to finish it off. And it was really intense. It was a good job I was only about twenty-one or twenty-two.

GINI BALL Most people were taking something—I think I was the only one who wasn't. There were darker things creeping in, too, but I can't really remember too much about that. I just remember the late nights.

FLOOD I mean, there were definitely things that were helping us get through, although I didn't know at the time the extremities of which that was going because it never impinged on the sessions. I was the person who was sitting there every day; assistants came and went, but none of the interpersonal stuff ever came to the fore in the studio. A lot of that only came to me after the fact.

GINI BALL Normally, we'd just play what we were told to, as we were quite new to composition. That was an interesting thing to do, especially in that Spanish style, which I loved. And it was nice that we got to do our own track as well, 'Once Was'. We never expected that to happen. Anne and I wrote that in the lounge of her flat in Peckham. I do feel really proud to have played on that album. It was a very creative time.

ANNE STEPHENSON No one cared about what time it, was and sometimes we'd go on all night. It was great because they'd set up a backing track and tell us just to go in and put some strings on. We were kind of fearless in those days and would go straight in and improvise the whole thing, and it always used to work out really well. My favourite moment was when Marc put the vocals on 'Once Was', and the sound inside the studio was just amazing. Flood was fantastic, an absolutely brilliant guy. It was just an amazing experience, the whole thing was great. I remember listening to Martin improvise on 'The Animal In You' and thinking, *Oh my god, we're really doing something quite special here, this is going to be a classic*. I think people realise that now.

FLOOD Marc wanted each side to have a flavour, so I was trying to keep that in mind, while so many people were coming in and out of the studio. It was also where the Mambas first really came to fruition, and we had such a great relationship. I'd always wanted to record strings, and here were people who looked like me and were my age, and I could say to them, 'Can we try it like this?' and they'd say, 'We've been waiting ages for someone to ask us that!' The attitude was, 'Oh, brilliant, let's just do it!' And Marc was so inspiring. He was always there, every day, scribbling things down and suggesting ideas, his momentum drove everything.

STEVE SHERLOCK Anni co-wrote the majority of the Mambas music, I believe, but I don't know what the process was between her and Marc for this. However, for 'Narcissus', for which I got a co-write, Marc did his vocals first and then I did the sax backing after. I took the mood and atmosphere from his lyrics and voice to create the sounds for it. Marc wanted to do something from *Carmen*, so Martin, Bill, Gini, and Anne found a quiet room with a record player and the Rodgers & Hammerstein album and the original Bizet. And they sat there with blank music paper, listened to the albums twice and wrote all their parts out by ear. I had never seen anything like it—such skill!

ANNI HOGAN I felt intimidated because it seemed everybody had been to Guildhall and could play anything. Things like 'Catch A Fallen Star', which I'd just worked out the piano for, I had to go in and play it there and then in front of everyone. Thank God for Flood, you know, just as somebody to feel OK with. Flood was amazing guy to work with—he was so kind to me, and he really, really got me through *Torment And Toreros*, and without him I'd have gone mad. Just a super-duper guy.

FLOOD I got thrown out of choirs at school because I sang so far out of tune, so being intimidated and stressed that there are other 'better musicians' there was something I could relate to. But my advice was always, 'Don't think about their technical abilities, just be yourself, because that's far more important.' And, in a way, those 'better musicians' are just as stressed by trying to shake their technical skills and be themselves. I just encouraged people to try things they hadn't tried before and at least have a laugh.

ANNI HOGAN When we were recording 'Black Heart' we'd got everything down and we needed Steve to play this motif and he just couldn't get it. It went on for hours, but he was just frazzled and fucked, as everybody was. It was kind of a metaphor for the whole album. Everyone was speeding, it was chaotic and exhausting, but finally rewarding.

J.G. THIRLWELL When Marc was recording the Mambas stuff, he asked me to write a track for him which became the song 'A Million Manias'. That was a really magical time for Marc—the confluence of influences that were on *Torment And Toreros*, the mood of the songs, both his own and the covers, was really dark but really heartfelt. It's almost perfectly curated, a great distillation of what he was into at that time. Marc was very eager to expand his musical horizons beyond the shackles of pop music. I don't know how it did commercially, but I think it was a really successful crystallisation of his vision.

MARC ALMOND I adored working with Jim, whether as part of the Mambas, The Immaculate Consumptive, or Flesh Volcano. The 'genius' label is used all too freely, but I will put myself out there and say Jim is definitely a genius. The way he worked on 'A Million Manias' was incredible to witness, the way he built up layers of percussion and sound, one instrument at a time. When I got to perform the whole of *Torment And Toreros* in 2012 as part of Ahnoni's Meltdown Festival, I was thrilled to have Jim onstage as part of the huge ensemble.

Never one for understatement, Marc Almond now delivers his most intense, extreme and radical attack on the accepted parameters of pop music to date—it'll repel and exhilarate its customers in roughly equal proportions and will surely come to be recognised as some kind of gaudy milestone in rock. More over-the-top than 2 Para, Marc is way beyond preposterousness, sending us all up with manic overkill as he erratically pursues his self-styled mission to destroy all rock's established guidelines, without pausing to put up any new ones. Not content with simply ignoring the No Entry sign, he tramples it to the ground in that feverish, seemingly un-calculating enthusiasm of his.

COLIN IRWIN, *Melody Maker*, August 13, 1983

STEVE SHERLOCK I was originally an engineer by trade, and I used to really enjoy being in the studio watching Flood and, when appropriate, ask a few questions about equipment and things like that. I liked him. The write-ups for that album were pretty bad, and I thought, *No, Flood did a bloody brilliant job*.

FLOOD The music press was totally different in those days. I mean, the *NME* was the bible for this type of music. Everybody got hammered in the press, or eulogised and then immediately cut to shreds—I could go on about what happened to Nick [Cave]. And it was the same for Marc. I was getting a lot of bad press, too, in trade journals like *Studio Sound*. It became a running war with me and one of the journalists, and he'd just badmouth anything that I was involved with. It hurt, but because everybody was in a similar position, there was a sort of collective response of, 'Well, fuck you.'

I don't know whether Marc regards his work with the Mambas as a bit of light relief away from the serious business of making money, but it sounds like that. *Torment And Toreros* is haaaard going, four sides of ill-disciplined doodling. It deals with familiar Almond obsessions: i.e., the generally scabrous side of life. I'm afraid I find Marc's murky travelogues neither outrageous nor daring but simply tedious.

JIM REID, *Record Mirror*, August 13, 1983

JANE ROLINK I tried to stop Marc from going over to *Record Mirror* with the bullwhip. He was so volatile, though, it was kind of brilliant. And, you know, the feeling at Some Bizzare was, 'Slag us off and you'll get what's coming to you.' The journalist Jim Reid was really horrible about Marc, so it was fair enough. But every day was like that at Some Bizarre—it was really on the edge, and you never knew what was coming.

A bullwhip brandishing Marc Almond certainly lived up to his sadomasochistic image when he came storming into the *Record Mirror* offices last week and thrashed boy hack Jim Reid for his scathing review of the new Marc & The Mambas album, *Torment And Toreros*. And by the end of the week things had got so bad that Marc announced the Mambas had definitely split and the future of Soft Cell was hanging in the balance. It all started when Reid's purple prose landed on the Almond black leather sofa and burnt a hole through to the carpet. A small dark streak was spotted careering through the streets of Soho and, seconds later, the foaming frothing heap of rage arrived at Jim's desk and throat. 'You're not fit to review my album,' Almond screamed, while lashing at the mild-mannered reporter with his favourite specially imported Zambian rhino whip. 'You got a grudge against me? I'll give you something to have a grudge about. I've lost friends and money making this album. I've made myself ill. You write anything else about me and you're a dead man!'

SIMON TEBBUTT, *Record Mirror, August 20, 1983*

BEVERLEY GLICK I wasn't in the office that day, and I honestly don't think it would have happened if I'd been there. I think I probably could have defused the situation. But God knows Jim told me the story enough times afterward. I felt a bit bad for him, and I think he was quite scared by it actually, but then made a joke about it afterward, as if it was a big laugh. I can imagine it must have been quite shocking. That was the problem with Marc—he took things so personally. Because I knew what he was like, I vowed to never write bad review about Marc's music; if I didn't like something, I just avoided writing about it.

ANNI HOGAN Marc was authentic. I love his singing on *Torment And Toreros*. I didn't want him to change his vocals because it was so honest and real. He's not just a great singer, he's a great performer, too, it was like he was delivering his lyrics as if it was the end of the world. I can see now that it's a brilliant album, but it's not something I would put on and listen to, ever. Whereas *Untitled* I can go back to sometimes. I don't know if I was relieved or not relieved when he announced the Mambas split. I knew I was always going to be involved at that point, so I was probably excited to move on to the next thing and put that album behind us.

STEPHEN 'MAL' MALLINDER As we were working in an electro and electronic area, we saw ourselves connecting more with club culture than pop culture. Twelve-inch singles were far more important to us than radio play—that was something that came as a result of editing a club track down, rather than the other way around. We didn't see ourselves as commercial, but we saw a synergy between what we were doing and what the outside world was doing. Particularly in terms of what was coming out in New York, the early electro stuff: D-Train, George Clinton, electronic music with a funk kind of feel to it was where we were coming from. As well as being avant-garde, Richard and myself particularly had come from a soul background, so it wasn't it wasn't as if we were trying to shoehorn those things into one we were doing. We were very rhythm-based anyway.

150

JOHN LUONGO Being invited to London's famous Trident Studio to remix Cabaret Voltaire's 'Just Fascination' and 'The Crackdown' for their debut Some Bizzare twelve-inch was one of my favourite experiences in the studio. That I was able to help them enjoy crossover success, not only in Europe but in the United States too, was a great achievement.*

STEVO You have to understand that 'Tainted Love' was the longest-running record in the history of the American charts and in the *Guinness Book Of Records*, forty-eight consecutive weeks. My point is, when you've got 'Tainted Love' and you have a new record that's connected to Some Bizzare, it's not gonna be too difficult to find a producer who wants to work with you. John had a great track record, I loved the music he'd produced, and I had a lot of time for him.

STEPHEN 'MAL' MALLINDER I'd always been the vocalist in the Cabs, and it was a role I kind of grew into rather than him something that I wanted to particularly do. But with *The Crackdown* it became more of a thing.† The story goes that Stevo told us to drop the effects on my vocals, but he didn't—it was just a natural evolution. And I wasn't an overt frontman anyway, I was just the member of the band that happened to do the vocals.

TEST DEPT We had been working independently, releasing cassettes through Rough Trade, but wanted to get our work out to a wider public. Some Bizzare had some of the best post-punk and new electronic music credentials, mixed with an intriguing attitude to shake things up a bit and challenge the way the major labels were operating. We had approached a number of labels including Some Bizzare, and we were considering a few offers, when Stevo turned up at our door, giggling in a typical Stevo manner, and said, 'Who shall I sign, Test Dept or Yello?' He chose us, and I guess that was the fatal attraction.

JANE ROLINK Test Dept were my thing—they were great. Their live shows were so fantastic. They used to just take your breath away it was so physical.

* 'Crackdown' / 'Just Fascination' (CVS1-12) was released on seven-inch and twelve-inch in July 1983 by Virgin. It failed to chart.
† Cabaret Voltaire's first album for Some Bizzare, *The Crackdown*, was released via Virgin on August 18, 1983. It reached no.31 on the UK album chart, a full thirty places higher than their previous highest entry.

TEST DEPT We were quite taken by his maverick approach, which had echoes of Malcolm McClaren with his attitude to major labels and retaining artistic independence. We were also interested in the overall Some Bizzare project, which was very eclectic but had a serious collection of alternative creativity. He got us a deal working through Phonogram, which gave us access to some serious studio spaces and technology, all very different from our New Cross squat cellar. This opened the door to new ways of working and the opportunity to link up with some top producers such as the genius Ken Thomas. On the visual side of things, we also had access to the video studio that Sleazy had set up in Stevo's house in Hammersmith.

STEVO Sleazy got an inventory of equipment that he made me buy, and it was all kept in my house, and I used it to edit all the episodes of *Some Bizzare Show*. I got people in to help me and whatever, but I was making all the decisions on the in-and-out points of the editing. Sleazy would use the dead time when I wasn't working and editing my shows, and he said to me one day, 'Can I can use the editing suite for Pink Floyd?' I said, 'No, problem,' so he's up there bloody editing Pink Floyd for no money. And *TV Wipeout* and *Gasoline In Your Eye* were both done up there, and a Cabaret Voltaire documentary, which was on USA Network, which I put together.

STEPHEN 'MAL' MALLINDER Stevo would badger us about the editing suite, saying, 'You've got use it, come down, come down!' He just wanted someone to play with while he drank gin and tonics and acted the goat. So we used it and Sleazy used it, although he was probably there more than us, as he used it for some of the early Psychic TV things. When Rich and I did *Gasoline In Your Eye*, that was all edited up in Sheffield, with the Film Co Op, using better gear.

STEVO I was the director and the editor of *Some Bizzare Show*. I would intercut drama with music, which still today no one else has ever done. You'd be watching something you're familiar with, i.e., actors in a domestic scene, and then it would cut into music. I put on Orchestral Manoeuvres In The Dark, The Smiths, Tom Waits, loads of other artists, it wasn't just Some Bizarre stuff, but it was called *Some Bizarre Show*. And it went straight through to Night Flights on USA Network. I believe we delivered nine shows, which were broadcast at 9pm on a

Friday evening in New York, and then across the country from Miami to Alaska, it was nationwide. Night Flights were the competitor, if you want to call it that, of MTV. What happened is, Universal bought the network, and subsequently we were thrown off the air. It was an absolute outrage really, because about the same time there was *The Chart Show* on ITV, and then suddenly there was a UK version of *Snub TV*, both of which were very similar to what I was doing. I've still got the masters of all nine episodes of *Some Bizzare Show*, but they're in storage and dilapidating. It's heartbreaking, really.

There is no musical barrier of peoples acceptance
The only musical barrier is the media.
(Music press, radio, television.)
Remember what people cannot see or hear
They cannot think about.

Ø, from the sleeve of Soft Cell's *The Art Of Falling Apart* LP (1983)

1983 (B) This is the day your life will surely change

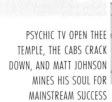

06

PSYCHIC TV OPEN THEE
TEMPLE, THE CABS CRACK
DOWN, AND MATT JOHNSON
MINES HIS SOUL FOR
MAINSTREAM SUCCESS

Finding myself increasingly confused and unhappy within the music business I no longer wish to continue on the recording side of the music scene, whatever that may be, and whoever I may be. The Mambas no longer exist and the finishing of the new Soft Cell album, currently being recorded, is in doubt. I no longer wish to sing on records, in fact, I no longer wish to sing. I don't want to be involved in any more interviews—this is no disrespect, or show of petty arrogance, to those that have written constructively, fairly and favourably about me—there are those whose writing I respect and also whose friendship I respect, that will continue, I hope—to those on the other side of the fence—go to hell! I don't seek praise or glorification, I just seek constructive and fair critique, though whenever I get praise, I feel confused and filled with self-doubt—one of my major problems at the moment—the bad things I'm afraid I take to heart—that's my problem. If there are any future recordings, there will be extremely few if any, which will come as a great relief to those who find my singing a pain to the ears. I don't know about my future, but it could possibly involve working on the other side of the Some Bizzare fence working for other bands—on the invisible side. I may however continue some live work of some form which I enjoy, but not under Mambas or Soft Cell guises and it is unlikely they will be at all commercial, though commitments abroad will have to be fulfilled. To the fans that have supported me I hope they will understand my reasons and to keep their ears open for anything I may do. Thanks to those who have supported me—confused? Not half as much as I am.

MARC ALMOND, Some Bizzare press statement, August 1983

A 'confused and unhappy' Marc Almond suddenly quit the music business this week. In an emotional open letter to the press, Marc announced both the end of the Mambas and Soft Cell, claiming he was filled with 'self-doubt' and that 'I no longer wish to sing on records, in fact I no longer wish to sing'. His shock announcements follows two bizarre incidents. In one he threatened a *Record Mirror* journalist with a whip, and in the other he was assaulted outside his home by a passer-by.

author unknown, *NME*, August 20, 1983

DAVE BALL I read about us splitting up in the music press like everyone else. I was in the office and someone showed me *NME* or something, and it said, 'Soft Cell split!' and I thought, *Have we?* Marc never mentioned it to me, although he is renowned for having theatrical moments. He just gets carried away and makes sweeping, dramatic statements, that's just the way he is. He did like to shock people, to say something outrageous and make people sit up and say, 'What?' He loves the drama.

MARC ALMOND After a couple of days of retirement, unrestrained and feeling carefree, I began to regret my premature resignation and began to back-pedal furiously. Of course I never intended to actually retire, not really, surely everyone must have known that. My letter had been a public cry for help, a metaphysical suicide attempt. I'd wanted to hurt and punish everyone– my friends, my fans, especially my critics—but instead, as usual, I'd only hurt myself. I began to retract my statement.

Marc and I are still working together, we want to finish this LP (due out in February). I think it's the best work we've ever done together, because we're both so aware that it will be the last album—and it *will*. It's just got to the stage where we're both fed up with the pressure of being Soft Cell and, more importantly, we've got to the point where we feel we've explored most of the possibilities of being together. After this album I really don't see what we could do. It's not impossible

155

that in the future we'll occasionally work together, but not as Soft Cell. Also, to rehash an old cliché we need to break from this situation to be able to change both musically and as people. I know we've both been working on separate projects as well for the past year, but that wasn't enough.

DAVE BALL to Helen Fitzgerald, *Melody Maker*, October 29, 1983

TEST DEPT There was some serious talent on Some Bizzare, quite stunning when you look back and see all those artists under one roof. We met most of them and had some positive relationships—we shared stages with Foetus in New York and Cabaret Voltaire in Sheffield and worked with some of them on different projects. The Cabs mixed 'Pulsations' on our first single, 'Compulsion', and both Genesis P-Orridge and Mufti [Neubauten's FM Einheit] worked with us on tracks for *Beating The Retreat*.* Marc Almond even worked on the door for our Titan Arch show in December, getting nicked into the bargain, as we all did that night.† So there was definitely a kinship.

Once inside, their megaphones sparred for attention amidst the din and as they mounted the stage massive applause broke out. . . . Plain clothes drugs officers, probably with cropped hair, ponytails and studded belts, were rumoured to have bought tickets in advance, and were inside before the raid happened.

author unknown, *Sounds*, December 1983

The group wasn't charged but their equipment was confiscated on the grounds they're potential offensive weapons. More disturbing, the 350 people inside found themselves being photographed and forced to fill out cards as they were channelled out of the club. Some, including Marc Almond and Some Bizzare's Jane were subjected to more rigorous shakedowns.

author unknown, *NME*, December 1983

---

* Test Dept's first Some Bizzare release was the 'Compulsion' twelve-inch (TEST 112). The title track was co-produced with Flood and Ian Tregoning; the B-sides, 'Pulsations 1' and 'Pulsations 2', were produced by Kirk and Mallinder.

† Test Dept would constantly look for unconventional sites to perform in outside of the usual music-venue circuit. This led to a long-term association with British Rail, with their first event being held in a disused railway arch near Waterloo Station. On November 30, 1983, they staged another event, *A November Reprisal*, at Titan Arch No. 14, under the station. The location was kept a secret, but it was still raided by the police and shut down.

STEPHEN 'MAL' MALLINDER Rich and I did a remix for Test Dept at Britannia Row. We were just given the track to rework and the guys came down later. We all had that attitude of, we wouldn't tell other people what to do, so they asked us to do a remix and they trusted us to do it. In that sense, it wasn't collaborative—we were given their material and reworked it. It wasn't a production job—you can only remix Test Dept, really, you can't ask them to go in and do a dustbin-lid solo or anything like that.

FLOOD Stevo asked Ian and me to do Test Dept's 'Compulsion' twelve-inch and said to us, 'Right, I want this to really stand out.' We did it all at Trident, and we'd recorded the sound of a pinball table being pulled across the floor, which we'd spent hours in mastering, getting it so it was the loudest part of the track. We mixed and mastered it and took it up to the offices. Stevo was like, 'Come on, then, let's hear what you've done,' so we put it on, and it starts with these little tinkling bell-like sounds, pretty quiet. Stevo immediately says, 'Fuck, this is shit!' and turns the stereo up as loud as it can possibly go. There's about 20 seconds of the bell sounds and then the pinball table crashes in, both the speakers flew off the wall and hit the deck, and Stevo shouts, 'Brilliant! I don't need to hear any more!' And in a funny way that was the greatest appreciation we could have got, because he knew that it was special and that it was going to do something.

MARC ALMOND I was struck with Jim from the moment we met. Just to see him was striking—this stick thin, tall Australian with a mane of red hair in a quiff and piercing eyes and razor cheekbones—like Ghost Rider himself. We sang that Suicide song together on a UK TV show, a full on-fire performance that probably dropped a few jaws in suburban sofa land.

KARL O'CONNOR I was at my grandparents' house when Soft Cell were on *Switch*. We were all sitting watching it, and they did 'Soul Inside', which was the new single and fucking great.* Then J.G. Thirlwell appeared and started screaming his head off. Halfway through, my grandad said, 'They've lost control! They've lost control of television!' and he just got up and left. And I was thinking, *Who's this*

---

* 'Soul Inside' was released on September 19, 1983, and reached no.16 on the UK chart. The video recreated the infamous Phonogram office-smashing incident of earlier in the year.

Clint Ruin guy and what's this song they're playing? And then you found out about
Foetus and Suicide and your world opened up yet again. And you know, there's
absolutely no fucking way a normal record company would have allowed that
performance to happen. Remember, we only had four channels back then, so there
was a good chance hundreds of thousands of people were watching. And on that
day Soft Cell did absolutely nothing to help the record company shift units. What
they did instead was create history.

J.G. THIRLWELL Working with Marc started with just hanging out in the Some
Bizzare galaxy. We did a track for the Mambas album, and then Soft Cell invited
me to sing 'Ghost Rider' with them live, which I did a few times and on a TV show.
Marc and I then recorded the Flesh Volcano EP, and we did a one-off show opening
for Cabaret Voltaire under the name Bruise 'N' Chain.* It was unannounced and
really thrown together. Marc had put some backing tracks together on cassette,
over which I played sax and guitar and he sang. It was pretty scrappy.

STEPHEN 'MAL' MALLINDER I remember all those kind of mad things going on
and hanging around with Jim a lot of time, and Marc too, so it doesn't surprise me
that they played with us. I do vaguely remember it, but I've got no mental picture
of what I saw. Or heard!

J.G. THIRLWELL I don't know why I became the connective tissue, for want of a
better phrase, at Some Bizzare. I was collaborating a lot, but I was known as a
kind of audio alchemist, I guess, and I was brought in in that context. I was really
interested in studio work, and a lot of the collaborations were studio-based at the
time. It started with Matt Johnson, and then one thing led to another, and I ended
up collaborating with pretty much everybody. What can I say, it was a close-knit
community in London back in those days, and there was a lot of crosspollination.

KARL O'CONNOR Everything starts with J.G. Thirlwell. Foetus wasn't just part
of the Some Bizzare constellation, he was at the centre of it. He was involved in

* Flesh Volcano's three-track *Slut* EP (SLUT 1) was recorded in 1984 and 1986 and eventually released by Some
Bizzare in 1987. The one and only performance by Bruise 'N' Chain was supporting Cabaret Voltaire at St Albans'
City Hall on August 20, 1983. The songs played were 'Switchblade Operator', 'Slut', 'Your Love Is A Lesion', and
'Body Unknown', and an audience recording can be found online.

everything: Nurse With Wound, Come, PragVEC, Swans, Birthday Party, The Bad Seeds, Neubauten, Coil ... he was fucking here, there, and everywhere. Mind-blowing one-man-band studio techniques, the unique visual identity, his comic-book rock'n'roll image, the gravity-defying hair. And his lyrics—Beefheart meets Vivian Stanshall, just pure absurdist genius. I just don't know how he did it and how he had the energy. Maybe the drugs did work after all.

>>

STEPHEN 'MAL' MALLINDER We definitely thought what we were doing could have wider appeal, but it wasn't a case of, 'We want to be more commercial." We'd had a level of success making electronic music, and we felt we were the zeitgeist. We'd seen other people come through, people we felt connected to, who were having success without making overtly commercial music. Matt was doing well, and people like Orange Juice were reaching people with music that wasn't shit.

IAN TREGONING I started hanging out with Stevo a lot. He loved Yello and what was going on in European electronic music, and he had a DJ's ear but also an eye for the unusual. And Yello were, and still are, quite unusual, but back then, in the UK, I couldn't get arrested with them. It was good fun because I was connecting with some interesting people who really dug it, like Stevo, but it was a really small percentage.

ROB COLLINS I wouldn't have said there was really a hierarchy at Some Bizzare. Everyone was hanging out in the office and playing on each other's records in the studio. Soft Cell had pretty much split up by the time I got there, so it wasn't like there was Soft Cell and everyone else. If anything, Matt was the one who wanted to be separate from everything else and have his own career, but even he played on other people's records.

MATT JOHNSON I think *Soul Mining* has a certain vitality that comes from the range of instrumentation. Most bands with a fixed line-up, for good or bad, sound the same whatever they do. But because THE THE wasn't a standard group it meant that every song could have a unique instrumentation. I could have marimbas and cellos on one track, and accordion and fiddle on another. I've always been a fan

* In September 1983, Cabaret Voltaire released the standalone single 'The Dream Ticket'. It failed to chart.

159

of film music and atmospheric soundtracks, and this approach gave me a freedom to create something very cinematic. I was attempting to combine traditional songwriting with film music in a way.

IAN TREGONING I was at this sort of poetry evening at the Raymond Review Bar, and I was bored out my tiny mind, so I left the theatre area and bumped into Stevo, who was in the bar with Matt, and he introduced us. We never went back to the theatre, just stayed in the bar rabbiting away. At the end of the conversation, Matt said, 'Oh, this is my new album,' and gave me a white label of *Soul Mining*, which I've still got. I remember playing it thinking, *Fuck, this is incredible.*

MATT JOHNSON There was a lot of pressure on me to tour around the time of *Soul Mining*. Major record companies like CBS knew how to 'break' an act and had a certain set of tools that historically had been very effective for them. You would release your three singles with videos, and you would arrange a tour to sync with the release of the album. You would go on tour, play concerts, appear on television and radio, and give endless interviews all over the world. Hard work but very simple and effective. But I didn't want to do that because I knew it was going to be very difficult to re-create *Soul Mining* live. Bearing in mind in those days, a sampler was the price of a house and someone like me didn't have access to that kind of money. And I couldn't afford to have thirty musicians onstage either. I couldn't figure out how to do it, so I didn't want to tour *Soul Mining* and CBS weren't very happy with me. I was told, 'Look, you've got to tour or the album is going to disappear without trace.' But I stuck to my guns, whether it was the right thing or the wrong thing to do, I don't know, really. *Soul Mining* probably would have been a far more successful album at the time if I had toured, but I didn't feel I could do it justice.

Soul Mining is a classic slice of everyman's everyday music, ready-made for the radio, the dancefloor and those thoughtful interludes late at night. From pounding beats and punchy melodies through to passionate lyrics and personal propaganda. Just slip it on and watch as any room of your choice becomes awash with colour and excitement. Submerge yourself in a sea of electronic sophistication as it vies for position against structures developed from contemporary rock'n'roll. The time in indie isolation has served him well. All the little tricks in the tracks and subtle references have been mixed perfectly to present a powerful pulsating concoction. Yes, there's all that and songs too.

DAVE HENDERSON, *Sounds*, October 22, 1983

MATT JOHNSON I'd written 'This Is The Day' at Fiona's flat, and I remember crying when I was writing it.* I felt that I was expressing something very truthful, and it made me very emotional. I do sometimes cry when I write songs—I guess it's a more extreme version of getting goosebumps. I was very proud of 'This Is The Day'.

KARL O'CONNOR Some Bizzare had all these extremely flamboyant, amazing looking people: J.G. Thirlwell was a cartoon rock god, Genesis and Psychic TV resembled a Tibetan cult, and Soft Cell just looked amazing. But in the middle of all this peacocking was Matt Johnson in double denim and moccasins. But that's what made him brilliant and I loved him for it. I bought *Soul Mining* on tape, and the shop had a deal on *Burning Blue Soul*, so I bought into the whole history of it. I got really heavily into him and again it was a completely different thing. Actually, Matt reminds me more of London than even those Soft Cell albums do. His lyrics spoke with urgency and you could hear London's past and present in his music. He walked the (Lambeth) walk and sang the ugly truth over the top of his beautifully crafted music.

MATT JOHNSON The reviews and sales for *Soul Mining* were OK when it originally came out, but over the years its reputation has grown and grown, and it's become a bit of a classic.[†]

ALAURA O'DELL Geoff became a member of Psychic TV during *Dreams Less Sweet*, although I can't remember him really being with us in the studio.[‡] I think they must have had recording slots when I wasn't there. Ken [Thomas, producer] was a really

---

* 'This Is The Day' (A 3710) was released by Epic on September 5, 1983. It reached no.71 on the UK chart. A limited-edition double seven-inch (XPS 184) included tracks from the abandoned *The Pornography Of Despair* project.
† THE THE's debut album, *Soul Mining* (EPC25525) was released by Epic on October 21, 1983. Initial copies came with a free twelve-inch (XPR1250) that included a new version of 'Perfect'. The album reached no.27 on the UK chart.
‡ Psychic TV's second and final album for Some Bizzare, *Dreams Less Sweet* (CBS 25737), was released by CBS on October 21, 1983. Initial copies came with a free twelve-inch EP, *The Full Pack* (XPR 1251).

lovely man. The studio in Guildford, Surrey, was residential, so there were many late nights, and we did the Holophonic recording there too. We wanted to create the sound of someone being buried alive, so we bought a coffin and—with the recording device inside it—buried it in a deep hole we'd dug in the studio grounds. And that's the sound of the soil hitting the coffin lid you hear on the record.

GINI BALL I met Gen and Alaura in the Some Bizarre office, when Dave and I first got together, and we used to go over to Beck Road for dinner. We never saw the coffin, though! After we had our son, James, we used to hang out together as families, with the children, and have picnics. I have some really nice memories of that time. It's funny, because some people might say, 'Isn't he really weird?' and my answer was always, 'To me, he's just my friend Gen, who's an amazing dad to his children.'

ALAURA O'DELL The music was always important to Gen. There were some people who were Psychic TV fans who were interested in our music and then became members of Thee Temple Ov Psychic Youth. The two things went hand in hand. I have to say, Gen was one of the most intelligent people I've ever met in my life. However, people who are as intelligent as Gen was can also be dangerous if it's not used in a healthy way. And to be honest, I really do think Thee Temple ov Psychic Youth definitely had many of the attributes of a cult, although it was disguised as a sort of fan club. People would follow the sacred rites and do sigils for twenty-three months, then mail them to us at Beck Road, and we'd have to open these packets of blood and sperm and hair and God knows what. Then these people would get their Eden or Kali name, which I came up with. I think it was filling this niche. Britain was pretty depressed in the 80s, with strikes and Thatcherism, and there was this need for community. Those who were attracted in Psychic TV and Thee Temple Ov Psychic Youth were mostly white, some women but mainly men. There was this demographic of working-class people looking for someone speaking their language, who weren't telling them that they were stupid and worthless.

ROB COLLINS I find, in general, the more extreme the artist, the easier they are to deal with. Genesis was always really nice when I met him, he was really lovely. Obviously, I was told that the whole Thee Temple Ov Psychic Youth was a bit odd, but it looked great to me. I shaved my head, got the crucifixion T-shirt—it was just a brilliant look. Part of what Some Bizzare wanted to do was buck the trend, to disrupt. I suppose I'd always kind of enjoyed that, being slightly rebellious and into doing things a little bit differently. I wanted to operate outside of the normal channels, and I was at the right place to do that.

PAUL 'BEE' HAMPSHIRE Thee Temple Ov Psychic Youth was multi-layered and multipurpose. In some ways, it was like the internet, in that it had good and bad sides to it. And, like the internet, it created networks and pathways of communication. So, freaks in Arkansas could connect with freaks in Barnsley through Thee Temple, and find out that they weren't actually freaks at all. It was a medium for the outcasts and the disassociated to come together. It wasn't about making carbon copies, it was about finding collaborators, and it was an excellent chance for people to get involved and do something. Those who just latched onto the identity and shaved their heads and got all the things, that was almost a sign that they didn't really get what it was about.

ALAURA O'DELL The East End of London has a history of fascism, but the Battle of Cable Street happened because people objected to it.* The National Front were born of ignorance and fear, and Thee Temple Ov Psychic Youth were offering this other narrative: 'Don't feel threatened by immigrants and people of colour, feel threatened by your government.' That was Thee Temple Ov Psychic Youth's message, and that was why I believe Scotland Yard raided our house, in cahoots with certain members of Parliament and the *News Of The World*, and a group of Evangelical Christians. Suddenly there was an organisation saying, 'You're worthy, and here's a platform for your voice,' and that's really where Thee Temple Ov Psychic Youth was coming from. It was an alternative, and that's why it was so popular. And I also think that, even if people aren't aware of it, Britain is innately pagan. The deep national consciousness is that we've come from a belief that is pre-Christian. And with the younger generation in the 80s, it was like, *Fuck, we're not going to church, that's what our parents did*. And there's magic—the veil between the worlds is thin—and that's what we were offering people.

* The Battle of Cable Street occurred on October 4, 1936, and was a series of skirmishes in London's East End between the Metropolitan Police, who were protecting a march by Oswald Mosely's British Union of Fascists, and anti-fascist demonstrators. The fascists were driven out by the counterdemonstrators, who were estimated to number anything from 100,000 to more than 300,000.

PAUL 'BEE' HAMPSHIRE If you listen to 'Message From The Temple' with Mr. Sebastian from *Force The Hand Of Chance*, I feel that a lot of it still stands up today as principles of how to live your life and be creative and choose who you really want as friends. Plus, Thee Temple was also an amazing merchandise vehicle as well. A lot of the behavioural stuff was taboo at the time, and people would be ridiculed and bullied. But today it's commercial, mainstream, the norm. Thee Temple was a good thing, but it did change over time and become something that it didn't set out to be, which caused problems.

MARC ALMOND Psychic TV was art, and even though some of the more squeamish elements made me uncomfortable, I liked the fact it was against the grain. I'm just a middle-class boy from Southport who ultimately loves musical theatre at heart, but I still had that thing of wanting to shock people, upset the establishment, to be subversive. Although I never read too much into all the Psychic TV philosophy stuff.

ALAURA O'DELL I really feel that if Gen could have had a proper cult with many, many followers, he would have done. But most of what was done under the Temple Ov Psychic Youth name was on an artistic level. But it was going to be controversial because it was going against the grain. We didn't feel that [the ritual videos] were done to shock, but we were pushing the envelope. They were more like art films, and some of the footage was even used in one of Derek Jarman's shorts. Derek had worked with Gen and Throbbing Gristle, and continued to work with Psychic TV for many years. I felt pre–Throbbing Gristle Coum Transmissions were far more transgressive. I just could not get my head round some of the art performances by Coum, but then I was very young, and this was a completely new world to me.

>>

MATT JOHNSON Stevo and I had been in New York promoting *Soul Mining*, and then we were flying to Rome to do some promotion over there. It was like a dream come true, standing on top of the Empire State Building one day then wandering around the Colosseum the next. We were at Roma airport about to fly home, and Stevo said, 'Why don't we go to Cairo?' And I said, 'Yeah, OK.' We found a flight and twelve hours later we had climbed all the way up inside the Great Pyramid and were in the King's Chamber. This was the sort of youthful exuberance we had.

164

Anything and everything was possible. I then had to call my mum from the hotel and tell her I wasn't going to be coming for lunch as I was in Egypt.

ZEKE MANYIKA Living with Stevo was fine, even great fun sometimes. We were both very busy, and I was away a lot with Orange Juice, but when we were at home, we just went clubbing and stuff. And then Jane moved in too, and it was all right for a while. But then it became an issue because Stevo couldn't handle being reminded of his work responsibilities when he was at home. That coupled with the fact that the artists were always around led him to behave appallingly.

STEVO I don't drive, so I spent a fortune getting cars every day from Hammersmith over to St Anne's Court and back again. I spent about £30,000 on taxis—the local cab company were very happy. I still had my home in Hammersmith when we moved to New Cavendish Street, and I'd commute there too. We never worked from Hammersmith except for the editing suite, and when I sold Hammersmith that moved to New Cavendish Street as well. Any credible artist was hanging out at my house. It was cool. There's was Nick Cave, Edwyn Collins, and Diamanda Galas; Lydia Lunch and Jim were upstairs in one of the rooms; Zeke and Jane were in another room. Even Marc Almond stayed at my place when he was in between homes.

MARC ALMOND I stayed at Stevo's house in Hammersmith for a while, and shared a room with Jane.

JANE ROLINK We didn't just share the room, we shared the bed. How bonkers is that? We were so close, like brother and sister really. It was really lovely.

>>

PAUL 'BEE' HAMPSHIRE I don't actually know why Sleazy left Psychic TV. I can remember being on walks with him and Gen, with Geoff and Paula, and having a really heated arguments. Maybe Sleazy and Gen just weren't getting on as well. Or maybe it was the wives. In fact, the wives weren't getting on, definitely! It was a tough time for me in some respects, because when I first met Psychic TV, I became very close friends with David Tibet and Geoff, and then when they all fell out, initially people were saying, 'Well, you can't be friends with Tibet, Geoff, and

Sleazy if you're friends with us.' And even though I admired everything Gen was doing, and s/he was like a mentor to me, I stood my ground and said, 'No, I'm not going to stop talking to them.' And I didn't. Years later, s/he did apologise to me for it, which was a real fucking surprise.

ALAURA O'DELL Gen and Sleazy had this falling out, and I think partly it was around Geoff. Gen didn't really warm to Geoff, who triggered him for whatever reason. So Sleazy and Geoff went off to form Coil, and then we had all those reinventions of Psychic TV. Despite Gen thinking, *Oh, these labels are coming in and advancing us a quarter of a million pounds, we're going to be on Top Of The Pops and make a fortune*, the reality was we were being charged for everything, so we ended up being in a deficit. Gen was like, 'Fuck this, we could start our own record label and keep the money.' So that's when we started Temple Records Limited and Rough Trade distributed us. But those two record deals that Stevo got us really got the publicity out there, posters all over London or wherever in the country we played on tour. It helped us become a known name and set us up for running our own label.

STEVO I don't think Psychic TV could have produced those records without Some Bizzare. After *Dreams Less Sweet* I wanted to do the follow-up, and I was very disappointed, because I wanted to make something that was their *Dark Side Of The Moon*, but instead they went the other way and recorded a hundred cheap albums.

Gen sent me an email just before he died, which was nice. It said, 'How are you? How are you, you madman?'

>>

J.G. THIRLWELL The Birthday Party had dissolved, it was a mutual thing, and Nick asked me to be involved with whatever was next. And that started with us writing the music for 'Wings Off Flies', on a piano at Lydia's house. And then we went into the studio with Mick Harvey and Blixa. I played some guitar on an early version of 'From Her To Eternity', which was totally different to the one that we all know. From about March to October, I was also in the studio recording *Hole* and the twelve-inches that came out around the same time, at Wave Studios in Hoxton Square. And that was where I started working with Warne Livesey and Charlie Grey. That was my first time in a twenty-four-track studio working on Foetus stuff. I had only just finished mixing everything, right up until the eve of going to New York for the Immaculate Consumptive shows—I was doing edits on 'Cold Day In Hell' the day before I left. So, *Hole* was finished by October 1983, and it didn't come out for another year. Stevo shopped it around, but I think there was a lot of the resistance to the Foetus name.

MARC ALMOND I have a favourite story of Jim's. When he was on the verge of signing a major American deal, the record-company executive said, 'Hey Jim, we have a little problem with the name You've Got Foetus On Your Breath.'

'OK,' said Jim, 'I'll change it.' And he did. From then on he was known as Scraping Foetus Off The Wheel.

J.G. THIRLWELL The *No New York* compilation put together by Brian Eno was a seminal album and had a big impact on me and a lot of people that I knew. I was particularly drawn to the Teenage Jesus & The Jerks tracks, which was Lydia's first band. The Birthday Party had met Lydia in New York when they played there, and she got involved with them and moved to London. I was roommates with Mick [Harvey] and Katy [Beale] for quite a while, and Mick introduced me to Lydia. I used to write the press releases for The Birthday Party when they were on 4AD, which were quite fanciful and prosaic, and Lydia had seen them and asked me to write one for her, which is how we got to know each other. Eventually we started doing music together, and we'd already done a lot of stuff before we got together romantically. We recorded the first version of *StinkFist* around the same time as we did the backing tracks for The Immaculate Consumptive. Anni Hogan, Barry Adamson, and Mick were involved in putting those together. Once I'd moved to New York we fleshed *StinkFist* out and added some other material, which we recorded with Norman Westberg from Swans, and that became a set called *Swelter*. Lydia and I performed that with Cliff Martinez, who'd been playing drums with Captain Beefheart and the Red Hot Chili Peppers at the end of '83. We did a bunch of shows out west in Portland, Seattle, and San Francisco, places like that.

ANNI HOGAN It was an open-door policy, for sure—everybody did play on everybody else's records, but that was just the vibe. The Trident building was a very creative place, and of course you had a studio there, so and it was happening the whole time. I mean, nobody had any money—I don't remember ever being paid by anybody except Marc. We were just helping each other out. Plus everyone was so fucking talented, just phenomenal, interesting and unique voices. Everybody knew everybody, and everybody worked with everybody. We were just all members of the same musical family. In retrospect, I don't know if all the family members were that nice and giving, but it makes me feel better to think of it like that. If Some Bizarre was a family, it would have been *The Munsters*.

JESSAMY CALKIN I remember lots of meetings at Marc's flat with Lydia about us all going to New York to do The Immaculate Consumptive for Halloween. It all sounded brilliant. And it was brilliant, but it was a bit more complicated than we thought.

CHRIS BOHN Covering The Immaculate Consumptive shows for the *NME* was a total dream trip for me. The idea of an old Weimar-style cabaret, but without the dancing and comedy—although there were certainly comedic moments—was really inspired. It wasn't as fully realised as one would have hoped, but the setup—having four very different people working separately and then doing something together at the end—was wonderful.

J.G. THIRLWELL So few people got to see it, and there's no official documentation of it, so it's gone into this sort of legendary status. It was short-lived but really interesting. It may have seemed like a weird collision of people, but we were all friends, and we'd all worked together before in one way or another. I had done stuff with Marc, Lydia, and Nick, so for me it made total sense.

JESSAMY CALKIN I sort of tour managed it, even though I had no experience of doing that. There were three shows, one at the 9:30 in Washington DC and two at Danceteria in New York, between October 31 and November 1. I didn't know what the fuck I was doing—I was just kind of hanging around and helping out. It was a brilliantly incongruous group of people. Marc was the ingénue of the whole thing, really, and quite thrilled to be part of it, because he was still seen as this pop star and he wanted to move on from that. He and Nick got on really well. It was a very good combination of people, but there were a lot of fights. Chris Bohn was covering it for an *NME* cover feature, and I remember him writing that Nick was playing good-natured mongoose to Lydia's cobra. That was such a good line because that was exactly what it was like.

CHRIS BOHN Nick is kind of sharp, but he's not as sharp as Lydia. Few people are.

JESSAMY CALKIN Lydia had a big thing for Nick, but I can't remember if he'd rejected her or what. At that time, Nick on tour was a bit of a nightmare because he took so many drugs. Jim was drinking quite a lot too. I think he and Lydia had got together by then, so there was a bit of tension between him and Nick. I can't remember what it was about, but during the show Jim trashed a piano that Nick was about to play on. There was a touch of the apocryphal Jerry Lee Lewis and Chuck Berry 'Follow that . . .' story, although I can't remember if that was just me and Chris talking about it, or if Jim actually said it to Nick's face.

CHRIS BOHN Nick was not in the best of shape, and if I remember it right, he only got through one song all the way through, 'A Box For Black Paul', during his solo slot. Jim went on to write 'Sick Man' from *Hole* about Nick. So only three out of the four were working at full strength, really. And then, at some point, there was some tension, maybe even anger between Jim and Nick, and Jim got really annoyed and smashed up the piano. It was a great performance, but then suddenly everything is broken, and who's crawling around the floor fixing things? It's Marc, picking things up, trying to get stuff ready for Nick's performance. It was a wonderful thing to see because Marc was obviously the biggest draw—the star of the show, really—and he did not behave like that at all. He was one of the troupe. And Jim was probably the least well-known at that time. So you had all this tension going on, and Marc was fantastic—he had a real let's-get-this-show-on-the-road attitude.

J.G. THIRLWELL Marc and I did a segment, we did 'A Million Manias' and I played sax, Lydia and I duetted on Alice Cooper's 'Blue Turk' and a couple of other tunes. I played two Foetus songs. We did one song when all four of us played together, and the set finished with Nick singing 'In The Ghetto' and 'A Box For Black Paul'. The Immaculate Consumptive was the first time I played live as Foetus, and it was also super-significant for me because it was while doing those shows that I decided to move to New York.

MARC ALMOND The show, though chaotic, went quite well. Nick and I sang one of my songs, 'Body Unknown', and I sort of sang 'Misery Loves Company' with Lydia. Nick came on at the end and stole the whole show with his rendition of 'In

The Ghetto'. What the show lacked in substance it made up for later in legend. It was the kind of show that improves in the memory, and with the telling: by the time you had heard about it third hand, it sounded bloody brilliant. We performed another show in Washington, but it was even more uncontrolled. Then we all knew never again. It was for the best.

FLOOD I got the Nick Cave gig because of Marc. The Birthday Party were over in London playing their last shows and I was doing some stuff with Soft Cell, I think we were doing twelve-inch versions or preparing for the live shows. And Nick asked Marc if he knew anybody who was worth working with, and to his eternal credit Marc suggested me. And that's how it worked. You go out of an evening, and there'd be Marc and Dave, but then there might also be Jim Thirlwell, a few members of Neubauten, and Rowland and Nick from The Birthday Party. Everybody knew each other, and it was like, 'Yeah, sure, I'll play on your record.' And who knows who would turn up? And money was never talked about, ever.

DAVE BALL Phonogram didn't ask me to make *In Strict Tempo*, I just fancied doing a solo album.* Funnily enough, Marc was a bit perturbed by it, because I'd already done stuff with Vicious Pink Phenomena as a separate project, and now I wanted to do a solo album. I think he got a bit paranoid, and in a way that led to him doing more solo stuff, which was great. I think we both needed to develop our own individual personalities musically, just so we weren't always reliant on each other, to try working with some other people and learning a few new things. *In Strict Tempo* was an experiment, really, and I just wanted to learn more about the studio and mess around with sound. Some of it is a bit like a sketchbook and some of it more structured, it's a bit of both.

FLOOD In 1983, Dave and I were brothers in arms. Not only was I doing Marc's solo stuff but there were a lot of Soft Cell remixes, and I also did a Soft Cell US tour as the live sound guy, so I was always on the periphery with what the two of them were doing. But I spent most of my time in the studio with Dave. When he asked if I'd work on his solo record, I was very happy to.

* Dave Ball's debut solo album, *In Strict Tempo* (BIZL 5), was released by Phonogram in November 1983.

GAVIN FRIDAY I bought the Some Bizzare compilation and became a die-hard Soft Cell fan. It was through them that I first read about this Stevo character and his extraordinary antics. There was always this cross-fertilization thing going on with Some Bizzare. Marc and Dave were into Throbbing Gristle and alternative music much more than the pop New Romantic stuff that was in the charts. And Geoff knew Marc, and it was then I found out that Marc and Dave were big Virgin Prunes fans as well. That's how we ended up asking Dave if he wanted to produce *The Moon Looked Down And Laughed* in '83. We were on the verge of breaking up, but Dave came over to Dublin with Flood anyway, and we recorded for about two weeks before finishing it off at Trident. And it was during that session he approached me about doing *In Strict Tempo*.

FLOOD The Virgin Prunes' *The Moon Looked Down And Laughed* was my first ever freelance gig. Dave was just like, 'Fancy coming over to Dublin to help out?' so I did, and we had an amazing experience. And Gavin is amazing—I've got him to thank for so many gigs over the years.

We finished the Virgin Prunes album at Trident, and as soon as it was done I got a cab across town to the Garden to start working on Nick's first solo album. That's how it was back then. It was mad.

GAVIN FRIDAY I think Dave sent me over a rough instrumental mix on cassette, and I lived with it for a bit, wrote some lyrics, and just went in and improvised. My memory is it was quite a quick recording, and it was done and dusted in a few hours. It was quite beautiful in that it was all immediate; there was no overthinking and there was no agenda. It was just, 'What do you want to do? What do you want to say? Do it.'

I don't know if Dave had the title already—maybe he did, maybe I came up with it, God knows—but it lent itself to the relentless drumming. It just felt like the strict tempo was a given, you know. It was done, it came out, we moved on. I don't even think we talked about money. We just did it. I love Dave—he's this sort of a gentle giant, almost like a bricklayer making synth music. 'All right, that'll do, next, fucking hurry up! Don't bring out your fucking lyric book, just fucking sing it!' He's very raw, but then the sensitivity of what he writes, it's quite extraordinary. With Dave, it's always been very immediate and done. He likes that minimalism thing.

FLOOD Dave was experimenting with different styles and techniques to make up for the fact that he probably missed Marc's presence up front. The way we did the record, he probably could've done with a foil to bounce off of. And for most of *In Strict Tempo* there isn't one, but when there is, it's fantastic, which is why the tracks with Genesis and Gavin work so well.

DAVE BALL Both Genesis and Gavin were people I really admired and wanted to work with. I'd produced a Virgin Prunes album, and I knew from working on that Gavin would sound great on my album. I'd always wanted to work with Gen, and we really hit it off in the studio. He said to me, 'You're the first person that's shown me how to sing, Dave.' He always thought he couldn't sing, Gen, although he had a pretty good musical career for someone who was a non-singer.

PAUL 'BEE' HAMPSHIRE Mark Manning [aka Zodiac Mindwarp] was in the Some Bizzare office all the time, as he did a lot of the artwork layouts and stuff like that, including Dave Ball's *In Strict Tempo*, with Geoff and me on the cover.

PETER ASHWORTH The cover for *In Strict Tempo*, which was art-directed by Marc even though he wasn't at the shoot, was far bolder than any sleeve of Soft Cell's. Marc chose the image for Dave, and he went for it. I had the kettle drum up front and well lit, with a 12-foot Colourama in the background. If a background is a long way away from the subject, it can go black, even though you've got a lot of bright light in the foreground. It allowed me to create this 'rolling cloud' effect, which when lit red looked quite hellish, which seemed really apt for what we were shooting.

I'd met Geoff before, at St Anne's Court—it really was the place to hang out. I remember having very strange conversations with Peter Christopherson and Gen P-Orridge there. For some reason, I wasn't allowed to show that it was Geoff in the picture—I can't remember why—and I'd shot Bee previously.

PAUL 'BEE' HAMPSHIRE I got paid £25 for the *In Strict Tempo* cover, but I'd have done it for free. It was amazing. Marc's concept, shot by Ashworth, laid out by Zodiac Mindwarp—it was a real gang that put that together. Was it a long shoot? Fuck yeah, I had to have someone holding my head up. Try supporting the weight of your head when it's hanging over something. It's insane. And it took fucking hours and hours—it was a really, really long shoot.

PETER ASHWORTH It was a weird shot, but I recognise a powerful image when I see one, especially if I'm shooting it. I actually got into a lot of trouble with the record company over that sleeve. They claimed it was impossible to reproduce because of the richness of the colours; it was quite damaging to my reputation at the time. I since discovered it was down to the fact they used cheap ink and crap cardboard for the sleeve of *In Strict Tempo*.

The album is littered with fragments of stunning sounds, intricate and delicate playing interspersed with aimless jamming and Godawful vocals. He just refuses to take it, himself or us seriously. The flawed masterpiece syndrome is never more evident than on Sincerity. I know Genesis P co-wrote the song but why the hell was he allowed near a mike? His horrendously out of tune, turgid vocals trail through the powerfully chugging music like a line of snot.

JULIAN COLBECK, *NME*, November 19, 1983

FLOOD Soft Cell were only three years into their career, so realistically—and this is just supposition—I don't know if there was really any pressure put on Dave to release a solo record. But we had a total laugh making it, and I can understand why retrospectively he maybe feels like it could have been more. But the fact is, it's very difficult to make an instrumental album when you're from a band with a such a strong personality at the front. It's sad that all the things Dave was trying on *In Strict Tempo*, all the really forward-thinking ideas that are on there, weren't taken into account at the time. It's a fantastic record.

KARL O'CONNOR For me, *In Strict Tempo* is the bravest record of them all, on many levels. For a start, it was so great that Phonogram released it, because normally major labels only support the singer. I also think it's more of the finished article than *The Art Of Falling Apart*—at the very least it's a sister album to it. Sonically you can really hear that. And it's so fantastically Dave Ball, it's his pure vison. I don't think the album misses Marc at all—personally, I think Anni and J.G. Thirlwell get better performances out of Marc as a singer. But Genesis P-Orridge and Gavin Friday were inspired choices, and Dave worked really well with them both. The cover is perfect too: the colours, the image, the art direction; everything about it was rich, deep, and menacing. And if you think in that short period of time, from '81 to the of start of '84, how many records Marc Almond and Dave Ball produced, together and apart, and the sheer quality of them all, it's incredible.

STEPHEN 'MAL' MALLINDER When Dave and I used to go drinking, because it was a time when there weren't really late-night licences in the UK apart from night clubs, we used to go to some weird restaurants that could serve drinks after-hours with food. We always used to end up in this Greek place in Ladbrooke Grove, and invariably there'd be a massive fucking fight. Not with us—Dave may look intimidating, but he's a gentle giant, a big softy—but we'd have to move the table out of the way as people came rolling past. I've got lots of memories like that of late-night drinking with Dave.

ANNE STEPHENSON Things started to go a bit strange in the background. Even though Marc had announced he'd split the band, the Mambas still existed.[*] And we'd realised that we weren't getting paid properly—and definitely not MU rates. Stevo always use to say musicians were 'ten-a-penny' and that he could get them anywhere. He never valued the contributions we made—he really did think we were worthless. And, at the same time, we were expected to do a US tour with Soft Cell as backing singers, but we were told they only wanted to take two of us. I was still going out with Stevo, and he basically told me and Martin to fuck off. But Marc wasn't having that and insisted that we all came. The whole thing was a bit of a disaster anyway, and they only did a few dates before it all started going tits up and they cancelled it. I don't know why—they just hated touring back in those days.

FLOOD I did the live sound on US leg of the *Irony* tour, as it was known, and I think it's fair to say that on some level they didn't want to do it.[†] I can't remember who objected to it particularly, but there were elements of that which I was privy to. But as Marc and Dave always did, they made it into something that they would love, so they brought the backing singers and Gary Barnacle along, and Jim come

---

[*] 'Torment' had been released as a twelve-inch single (BZS 2112) on November 27, reaching no.90 on the UK chart.
[†] The North American leg of the *Irony* tour ran from October 9 to November 20, 1983, starting in Toronto. It included shows in Montreal, New York, Chicago, San Francisco, and three nights at the Palace Theatre, Los Angeles. A recording of one of these LA shows was released in 2018 as part of the *Keychains & Snowstorms* box set (UMC 6741996).

out to do Suicide's 'Ghost Rider' for the encore. And the shows were packed and really well received.

>>

J.G. THIRLWELL Once the deal was done with me, Neubauten, and Some Bizzare, Stevo decided he didn't want to put out *Strategies Against Architecture Volume One*, he wanted to do something new. They proceeded to go into the studio to start working on what became the *Drawings Of Patient O.T.* album, so I took *Strategies Against Architecture Volume One* to Mute, and they were happy to put it out. Daniel actually offered to put the Hardt logo on there, to which I foolishly said, 'No, my work here is done!' The stupidest thing ever—I really wish I'd kept my imprint on there.

DANIEL MILLER I knew Jim a little bit, mainly because he was at he was at every gig I went to. He introduced me to Neubauten—he brought me some of their music and enthused about them greatly. I just thought they sounded amazing, and when he told me about the whole performance aspect of it, I just really wanted to get involved.

MARK CHUNG I felt Stevo was very generous because we were a pretty crazy band, and there was nothing for radio or anything that had commercial potential. And he put us into Trident, which was one of the top studios in London at the time. We never rehearsed as a band generally because we didn't want to lose the spontaneity. But when you're in the studio, that quickly catches up with you, and you end up sitting around going, 'Right, so what do we do now?' And we spent weeks at Trident—a really long time—and I knew enough about the music business to know that no one else would have let us do that. Stevo was completely hands off and *laissez faire*, and gave us complete artistic freedom, and we obviously had a lot of respect for that.

RUSTY EGAN I was into Neu! but not Neubauten. Can, La Düsseldorf, Michael Rother, Wolfgang Reichmann, DAF—I get all that. But Stevo would play me tracks by Foetus or Swans and I didn't get it. I wouldn't tell him not to release it, but it was more for someone like John Peel than me. I was really open-minded—I'd play Throbbing Gristle's 'Hot On The Heels Of Love' at the Blitz—so it wasn't like Stevo was bringing me stuff that was too off-the-wall, it was just Psychic TV or people banging bits of metal together didn't really work for me.

STEVO In a situation where you would speculate on an investment, you would look at something like Neubauten the first album, which probably sold a couple of thousand copies, you'd look at that and invest accordingly. You wouldn't give them tens of thousands of pounds. And it's the same with Throbbing Gristle. You wouldn't give them an orchestra.

CHRIS BOHN Stevo released Neubauten's *Drawings Of Patient O.T.*, and for me it's one of their best records, it's simply outstanding.* This was a time before samples, so artists were creating new sounds and finding ways of making them work together, to fall into rhythm even though they're completely arhythmical, and taking different drones and atonal sounds and mixing them with melody.

MARK CHUNG Initially, we didn't write any songs or rehearse. At some point, we got a bit bored with that and decided to actually do a rehearsal, but when we turned up at Trident we didn't have a plan. We spent a lot of time building tape loops, because there was no sampling at that point. We wanted to use the sound of a breaking milk bottle as a snare, but to get it in time we had to run the tape loop right across the studio around a pencil. We would cut holes in the tape, especially the big sixteen-track tape, to just see what effect that had. It basically created dropouts, but things were gone in a random way. We had fun.

STEVO I put them in Trident, for as long as they needed, and I walked in there one day and they had the multi-track tape out, and they were cutting holes in it. Random patterns, triangles and circles, in this big two-inch thick tape that costs a lot of money. It was total anarchy.

FLOOD I did a bit of engineering on *Drawings Of Patient O.T.* The first day, I was handed a bunch of contact mics and Blixa asked me to attach them to his body so they could record Mufti punching him in the stomach.

---

* Einstürzende Neubauten's one and only LP for Virgin, *Drawings Of Patient O.T.* (SBVART 2), was released on November 21, 1983.

Teenage DJ Stevø playing 'the weirdest sounds ever heard this side of Venus' at his parents' Dagenham home. *Photograph by Margaret Pearce, courtesy of Stevo*

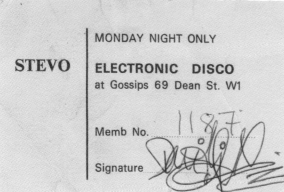

MONDAY NIGHT ONLY

STEVO | **ELECTRONIC DISCO**
at Gossips 69 Dean St. W1

Memb No.

Signature

David Knight's of The Fast Set's membership card for Stevo's nights at Gossips. 'I'm not sure about that membership number—it looks very much like my handwriting, so I'm guessing Stevo told me to just make up a number!'

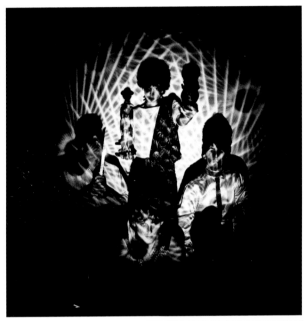

Alumni of the *Some Bizzare Album*: newly-signed B-Movie come out of the shadows (Steve Hovington, top middle) . . .

. . . and smock and roll with Naked Lunch (Tony Mayo, second from left). *Both photographs © Peter Ashworth*

From top left The one that started it all, the *Some Bizzare Album*; the label's first ever single, B-Movie's 'Remembrance Day'; Soft Cell's 'A Man Can Get Lost' seven-inch, with 'Memorabilia' on the B-side, which was promoted to the A-side on the twelve-inch; 'Marilyn Dreams' by B-Movie; the one that changed everything, Soft Cell's 'Tainted Love'; THE THE's first single for Some Bizzare, an early version of 'Uncertain Smile' called 'Cold Spell Ahead'; Marc & The Mambas made their debut on the 'fan club only' twelve-inch 'Sleaze (Take It, Shake It)'; Psychic TV were the first artists who weren't on the *Some Bizzare Album* to release a single on the label.

'And you're going to hang what behind us?' An out-take from the shoot for the 'Bedsitter' sleeve. © *Peter Ashworth*

When THE THE were still a duo, hanging around at their first official photo shoot. © *Peter Ashworth*

'Genius and jealousy.' Marc &
The Mambas, *left to right*:
Anni Hogan, Steve Sherlock, Lee
Jenkinson, Billy McGee, Gini
Ball, Martin McCarrick, Anne
Stephenson, and Marc Almond
(*front*). © *Peter Ashworth*

Beverley Glick, Marc Almond,
and Jose Warden (of Vicious
Pink Phenomena) enjoying a
quiet night out. *Photograph by
Steve Rapport*

From top left Huw Feather's painting and design work (*top four images*) not only defined Soft Cell's public image but was also the basis for some of their best-known videos, particularly 'Say Hello, Wave Goodbye' and 'Torch'. Val Denham's idiosyncratic work adorned the sleeve of many a Marc Almond release as well as the cover of the compilation album *If You Can't Please Yourself You Can't, Please Your Soul.*

The art of falling apart. Marc Almond and Dave Ball prepare to call time on Soft Cell with one final photoshoot. Seventeen years would pass before they worked together again as Soft Cell. *Both photographs © Peter Ashworth*

Stevo would often be present at his artists' shoots and would sometimes appear in them. Here he is with Matt Johnson at a session for *Sounds* in September 1982. © Peter Ashworth

Matt's brother, Andy 'Dog' Johnson, recreated his 'Uncertain Smile' painting for this shoot. Stevo supplied the props. © Peter Ashworth

Stevo and friends help Zeke Manyika celebrate signing to Some Bizzare for his 1989 album *Mastercrime*. © *Peter Ashworth*

Jane Rolink pictured post–Some Bizzare in the guise of Mrs Wood, the persona under which she enjoyed considerable success in the 90s hardbag and UK techno scene. © *Peter Ashworth*

Hats the way to do it: Marc Almond shows his naughty and nice sides as he launches his solo career with 1984's *Vermin In Ermine*. Both photographs © Peter Ashworth

Andrew Johnson's paintings are synonymous not only with his brother's work in THE THE but also with Some Bizzare generally, from early flyers for Naked Lunch to sleeve art for Zeke Manyika and various Some Bizzare compilation albums. 'Andy Dog' also exhibited at the Discretely Bizzare gallery under the New Cavendish Street office.

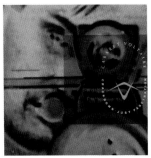

From top left 'Crackdown' / 'Just Fascination' (1983) was the first Cabaret Voltaire release on Some Bizzare, with sleeve designed by Neville Brody; 'Yü Gung' (1985) was the fruits of Einstürzende Neubauten's first collaboration with producer Gareth Jones at Hansa Tonstudio; Swans' 'Dollar Sign' series (1986), with artwork realised by Paul White; *Hole* (1984) was the first album J.G. Thirlwell released on Some Bizzare as Scraping Foetus Off The Wheel; Malcolm Poynter's sculptures featured heavily in the presentation of Test Dept's 1986 Some Bizzare releases; Coil's *The Anal Staircase* EP (1986) on K.422; Wiseblood's sole album, *Dirtdish* (1986), released on K.422 in a very expensive-to-make sleeve; Renaldo & The Loaf's ill-fated album *The Elbow Is Taboo*, which resulted in the band's demise.

Opposite page A selection of Jessamy Calkin's collection of Polaroids taken in the 1980s in London and New York: Blixa Bargeld; Anita Lane and Nick Cave; J.G. Thirlwell; Anni Hogan; Thirlwell and Calkin; Michael Gira.

J.G. Thirlwell, aka Clint Ruin and Frank Want, of Scraping Foetus Off The Wheel, You've Got Foetus On Your Breath, Foetus Art Terrorism, Foetus Uber Frisco, Foetus All-Nude Review, Foetus Interruptus, and Wiseblood. *Photograph by Peter Anderson*

Test Dept spot Stevo in the distance. *Photograph by Kenny Morris*

Cabaret Voltaire in New York in 1985. *Photographer unknown*

Psychic TV's Genesis P-Orridge and Peter 'Sleazy' Christopherson hang out with the big knobs.
© *Peter Ashworth*

Koot filming the video for 'Mississippi Soul' in Atlanta, Georgia, just before the music industry imploded. *Photographer unknown*

In the 90s and early 2000s, Stevo popped up in the most unexpected places. Don't bet against him doing the same again soon. © *Peter Ashworth*

MARK CHUNG The truth is, we were always trying not to get caught up in doing things we'd already done. Our approach was, we wanted to challenge ourselves, to put ourselves in situation where we produced something we wouldn't have produced by just thinking about it. Blixa played a key role in that, as he always had a very conceptual approach to music. Initially, he just improvised lyrics based on the sounds we were making, and that informed his text. But this approach changed over time, mainly driven by the wish not to repeat ourselves.

For anyone expecting something similar to other groups who have used such materials as instruments, this LP will come as a great surprise—and for anyone expecting a more accessible but enjoyable follow up to *Kollaps* (Neubauten's first LP), there's a shock or three instore. Neubauten have moved on, way beyond your wildest expectations.

DAVE HENDERSON, *Sounds*, November 22, 1983

CHRIS BOHN One of Stevo's dumb-yet-genius slogans was 'Conform To Deform', which was exactly right for the time. You had all these really fascinating, interesting, bizarre artists who were socially, culturally, musically, and artistically confrontational. They were seeking different forms of expression and communication, and Stevo facilitated this meeting of popular and outside culture. At Some Bizzare, the extreme and mainstream weren't divorced from each other as they were elsewhere. Plus, there were the fantastic deals he made on the back of Soft Cell's success. He got a great deal for Cabaret Voltaire from Virgin, and convinced them to put out Neubauten's *Drawings Of Patient O.T.* as well.

ROB COLLINS Stevo was definitely seen as difficult, awkward, and uncompromising. And in some ways we all tried to live up to that. We did a distribution and manufacturing deal with Virgin for Neubauten's *Drawings Of Patient O.T.*, and part of the packaging was supposed to include a tiny bit of silver. Blixa always said silver was so important as it showed decadence, a beauty within the greyness of Berlin. And the silver wasn't printed properly on the cover and wasn't exactly the way band wanted it. So, myself and a couple of Neubauten went over to Virgin, and I was really stroppy about it. I instantly regretted it, as I think I was just showing off in front of the band a bit. Also, I knew the people at Virgin, and I could tell that they were just thinking, *Fucking wankers*.

PAUL WHITE I was aware of Some Bizarre from the first compilation album with Depeche Mode's 'Photographic' on it, and I saw B-Movie play around the same time. But the first album I worked on for them was Neubauten. I rented a desk space in a studio in Kilburn Lane, and there was another guy there called Ken Ansell who was doing a lot of work for Virgin at the time. He used me as a kind of overspill when he had too much work on, and one of the things that came through was *Drawings Of Patient O.T.*

I met with Blixa, who obviously had his own very specific vision, so there wasn't a hell of a lot for me to do, it was just a case of gathering his ideas and making them all hang together. That was also my first introduction to the people at Some Bizarre—Stevo, Rob, Jane, etc.—too.

MARK CHUNG We had nothing to do with the deal with Virgin and to be quite honest, we didn't care that much. What was great about Some Bizzare was that it gave us the opportunity to work in the studio, try things out, and do what we wanted to do. What Stevo did with it afterward, the business side of things, didn't matter to us at that point. Of course, it did later on. But at the time we just thought maybe he had a label deal with Virgin, or something. But, you know, when those bigger labels did a deal with a company like Some Bizarre, who had great success with Soft Cell, it's because they hoped they'd find something else just as commercially viable. And if they had to put out other stuff that they wouldn't normally in the meantime, well, that was a price they were prepared to pay.

FLOOD The music industry was a very different place back then. Stevo could go in waving the 'Tainted Love' ticket, and majors would go, 'Great! What else have you got?' And he'd say, 'I've got B-Movie and Matt'—things the majors would really respond to, that were commercially viable—'and I've also got Neubauten. So, if you do me this, I'll do you that.'

This is just my perspective. And, remember, Stevo was operating in a time where the labels were not corporations—there weren't shareholders, there were still individuals. So, people like Seymour Stein and Maurice Oberstein still ran things, so it was a very different environment. So, somebody like Stevo, even though he could be extreme, was still an individual and those people responded to him totally differently than a load of faceless people who are just into music as a commodity would.

STEPHEN 'MAL' MALLINDER For all of Stevo's sins, he backed his artists, and he encouraged people to be more out there than less so. That was his thing, that was the agenda, that was the surreal new world that Stevo wanted to push and get major labels to bankroll. It was a belief we all had, and Stevo encapsulated that: the idea that all music would be appreciated, and indulged by people, if they just had the chance to hear it. So, he encouraged his artists to make the music they wanted, because the issue wasn't that it needed to be commercial to be successful, it was more most people don't get to hear it, because it's not presented to them through the usual channels, it's labelled as weird or avant-garde and kept on the sidelines. Stevo's thing was, don't change the music, just get major labels to put it out and people will make their own choices about what's good and what's bad—they don't need gatekeepers. In retrospect, I was probably slightly naive about his intentions, but at the time I always felt that was his philosophy throughout.

DANIEL MILLER The labels were thinking, *Well, he did it with Soft Cell, he could probably do it with somebody else,* but as time went on, it was clear that the musical direction that Stevo was going in was not aligned with what a major really wanted to do. And that affected his relationships with those labels, even the people who were on his side, because even though they were trying to help him, he did not respond in necessarily the most positive way.

STEVO People who use false smiles are the enemy, and the record business breeds stereotypes, which I don't like. I don't think they understand any integrity whatsoever, other than selling records. The people inside those structures climb the bureaucratic ladder by false smiles, and they end up with a permanent one. I have no time for these people. International companies are there to be used and that's all they are for. The people in these companies are sycophantic parasites.

PETER ASHWORTH I saw Stevo as an artist more than more than a businessman, really, and he gave me room to create some of my most powerful pictures. We had such a good relationship. He really sold me to his bands, so they would trust me implicitly to do the right thing. But if I did a shoot they didn't like, I would happily allow it to be thrown away. I really felt I had an ownership of what I shot—I didn't realise that record companies believed they had absolute ownership too. But Stevo always made sure I was paid for reuses, which was unusual. That being said, he also instigated a bunch of shoots that, when I tried to get a PO number, the label said, 'Who told you to do that? We never gave permission for that shoot to be done.' And I would say, 'Well, I've done it, so now you need to pay for it!' I don't know if things like that vexed them. The pics were always good, though.

STEVE HOVINGTON I think, generally speaking, the whole euphoria of the post-punk, New Romantic thing was starting to waver a little bit. Whereas before you could get away with not being a particularly great musician, I think it started to change around '83–84. No disrespect to any of them at all, but when acts like Wham!, Go West, and Nik Kershaw appeared, you had very competent musicians suddenly on the scene. B-Movie should have stuck to the core sound we had when we first were signed to Some Bizarre, and if we'd have done an album at that particular point, along the lines of the John Peel session we did in '81, then we would have made a great record, which would have been a foundation we could have built on in the future. And as our manager, Stevo really should have sorted that out, frankly, and prioritised B-Movie a bit more. I think probably we could have done with somebody a bit more business-minded and sober. But it was a crazy time, and Soft Cell's success was unprecedented, and of course Stevo was only eighteen years old.

STEVE SHERLOCK The Mambas only ever played in London, apart from one show in Israel.[*] Marc had said to Stevo, 'Find us a gig in a nice place,' and he came back with a gig in Spain, which suited the theme of the album, but there was also an opportunity to play a club opening in Tel Aviv. When we arrived, we were given a tour bus with a guide every day we were there, and we got to do all the tourist sights. We went to the Wailing Wall, but the girls weren't allowed in, and us blokes had to wear skullcaps. We went down in the catacombs, and Marc's dressed in occult-looking garb, tattoos on show. Suddenly, all these armed guards descend on us. They'd had complaints from other tourists, as they thought Marc was a devil-worshipper or something. Just as we were being marched out, one of the female soldiers, service weapon on her belt, turned to me and said, 'Is there any chance we can get Marc's autograph?' Hilarious.

[*] At Kolnoa Dan, Tel Aviv, on December 20, 1983.

ROB COLLINS I think Stevo had to deal with a lot growing up. He didn't publicise his brother's involvement with the National Front, but he never hid it either. He was just like, 'Yes, that's my brother, but I'm Stevo.'

ZEKE MANYIKA One of the reasons why I love Stevo is that he came from this pretty heavy right-wing environment, and even though he was only seventeen or eighteen, he fought against it. He would play black music and world music at home because, being Stevo, he didn't just want to leave it—he wanted to confront it. His mum was very sweet and his dad was very polite, although I think his political sympathies were more in line with his brother's. It was an education for me, because Stevo was opening a door to a world that I knew was there but had never seen. I'm socially fearless myself, but it was a seriously dodgy time, especially in Dagenham.

So, it's Christmas eve, and Stevo wants me to go with him to see his mum and drop off some presents. I'm wary, but he uses every weapon he has to emotionally blackmail me, so we call a taxi. It arrives, and the driver is the biggest, tallest Rasta, with dreads down his back, and I'm thinking, *Well, this should be interesting*. We get to Dagenham and Stevo asks the taxi driver to wait, but instead of staying in the car, he asked him to come into his parents' house with us. As soon as his mum opens the door and sees the three of us, she starts to panic and goes off to the kitchen. Stevo gives his dad a cheeky look and we sit down in the living room. The taxi driver doesn't know what the vibe is here, and he notices that Stevo's dad is smoking roll-ups, so he says, 'Don't smoke that, smoke this,' and starts skinning up.

About half an hour later, Stevo's brother, who's a spokesperson for the National Front remember, arrives, and is confronted with the sight of two black guys in his mum and dad's living room, one who's smoking spliff with his dad. Stevo jumps up, big grin on his face, and says, 'Merry Christmas, Joe!'

"With every kick in the face and every hurdle you pass the rewards get greater.
STEVØ, from the sleeve of THE THE's *Soul Mining* LP (1983)

1984 Then sometimes, someone, cracks down

07

SOFT CELL SPLIT, MARC
COMES BACK, FOETUS
ERRUPTUS, AND TEST DEPT
BREAK COVER

STEPHEN 'MAL' MALLINDER Cabaret Voltaire's relationship with Stevo was different to most other people on Some Bizzare. But the underlying thing was always money, which underpins any relationship with him.

J.G. THIRLWELL I had socialised with Stevo and the whole Some Bizarre clan for a while before I signed with them. I don't want to go too deeply into the details of the contract, but I signed as a recording artist for several albums, and by the time I'd fulfilled my commitments I'd become pretty disillusioned. But what I gotta say about Some Bizarre is, even though I was starting to get a little notoriety by myself, they facilitated me moving from eight-track studios to having a budget where I could make the leap to twenty-four-track studios. That's when I could really realise the sounds I had in my head. It was a huge leap in terms of the amount of time and the technology available to make the music I wanted to make. And you can hear it in those albums—it's suddenly in Technicolor. It became the way I wanted it to sound.

ROB COLLINS I don't think Stevo could get a deal for Jim in the same way as he did for Psychic TV, Test Dept, and Neubauten. And I was much more interested in releasing music independently. So, I just said, 'Let's do a deal with Rough Trade and put Jim's stuff out ourselves.' And it did really, really well. I was of the mind that Some Bizzare should be releasing music that really confronted people, that was disruptive and physical and more than just music, in a way. It seemed the logical route for the more extreme music to just put it out independently. There really wasn't that many indie labels putting out records and trying to push boundaries like that at the time. And there was definitely an audience for it.

J.G. THIRLWELL I had already decided to hang up the You've Got Foetus On Your Breath name and had chosen Scraping Foetus Off The Wheel by the time I signed to Some Bizzare. I know particularly in the US that there was resistance to the name, that it was a problem. I didn't know what Stevo was doing [about getting a deal with a major]. He never said, 'Well, I went in for a meeting with CBS or Warners and they're not interested,' or anything like that. A decision was made to put my stuff out independently and I was like, *OK, fine*. He did get me a big publishing deal, and he convinced me to spend it totally on promotion, which I did, stupidly. There were these massive posters of me being crucified fly-posted across London.

MARK CHUNG The *Concerto For Voices And Machinery* at the ICA came about partly because interests within the band had started to diverge.* Blixa was a bit tired of construction machinery at the time, but Mufti and I felt we hadn't done it properly yet. With Neubauten, the machinery was more of a side effect, and we thought it would be interesting to expand that and focus just on that side of things. So, we were the driving force behind the concerto. It wasn't billed as a Neubauten show because Blixa didn't want to do it, and we had Genesis and Frank Tovey on vocals. But on the night, Blixa obviously thought, *Actually this is quite good, I should be part of it*, and jumped onstage at the end. I think Stevo jumped onstage too at some point. It was free-for-all.

ALEXANDER HACKE Because we were using petrol-driven chainsaws, very soon the whole room was filled with smoke, the stench of petrol everywhere. It sounded like a cross between a building site and war. Because I was very young, the others wouldn't let me near the heavy machinery, so I stood, wearing protective gloves and a visor, throwing milk bottles into the cement mixer, which smashed and flew into the crowd.

* The performance was held at the Institute For Contemporary Arts on January 3, 1984, and has gone into legend as one of the strangest events held at the Central London venue.

IAN TREGONING I took some people along and their jaws were on the floor. They had an angle grinder onstage with sparks going twenty feet into the air, which looked amazing. And Alex had this big stack of milk bottles, and he was just chucking them right across the stage. He was a very good shot, and I don't think missed, but of course, there was still glass flying everywhere.

J.G. THIRLWELL I don't know if it was Neubauten's intention to drill into the foundations of the building, I'd never known them to do that before. But apparently Stevo got hold of a drill and, you know, I could imagine him doing it.

ALEXANDER HACKE We had this utopian idea of leaving the stage from underneath. The plan was to dig through the stage into the tunnel system underneath the venue, which is supposed to go all the way to Buckingham Palace. Obviously, the venue had no idea of our intentions. We'd already been banned from a lot of venues for using fire and drilling the walls, but the *Concerto For Voice And Machinery* was billed as a highbrow art thing. There was no connection made to rock music.

MARK CHUNG Drilling into the tunnels wasn't in the preparation, but I think we had heard about them and there was this approach of, *OK, we've got this machinery, let's see how deep we can get until they stop us*. We didn't get very deep, but it did get the ICA staff going. We stopped after twenty minutes because the piece was over. It was written as a kind of Wagnerian overture, so twenty-to-thirty minutes long. I actually wrote a full notation, but it was a case of *no plan survives first contact with the enemy*. It was all sketched out, but at some point it just went off track.

DAVID KNIGHT Danielle and I had gone along, but had got waylaid talking to friends in the ICA's bar. By the time we got into the performance area there was a stream of people exiting, and inside, standing amidst the debris, was Stevo, with a big grin on his face.

STEVO My art is people's expectations and being one step ahead and helping other people's careers. I'm not a frustrated musician. I've never picked up an instrument in my life. But I played a shopping trolley once—I just picked it up and banged it on the floor. It sounded fantastic. And I think I've got rhythm . . .

>>

MARC ALMOND Everything always seemed to be on the edge, too many drugs and too much alcohol, and heightened emotions getting out of hand. Stevo seemed to relish this though, and even at times instigating it like some kind of master of ceremonies.

STEVO I'm not gonna take any blame, they did everything, it was their thing. I just allowed them the freedom to do it. Soft Cell could've been bigger than Depeche, they were definitely the bigger band when they split up. Marc wanted a solo career, but I said, 'You can have both, why one or the other? That don't make any sense.' He could've had the best of both worlds, there was no reason for them to split up. But that was it. No more Soft Cell.*

MARC ALMOND Part of me regrets it a little bit now. Because at the time everything was so dramatic and full on and we got burnt out very quickly. We did the first three albums in America, were constantly promoting them and in each other's faces all the time. But we were actually quite different people, had different friends and different things that we liked to do. When we were recording *This Last Night In Sodom* Dave just said to me, 'I don't want to do this anymore, I want to just work in the studio [and] I don't want to play live.' And I said, 'Well I want to keep playing live,' because I quite enjoyed it. So we kind of shook hands and said let's call it a day. But it was so final you know, it was like, 'OK, right, we're finished, that's it, we're gonna go our own way.' And when I think about it now, I wish we'd have just stood back and taken a break for a year or so, then come back with a really good producer and made another record and we'd probably be where Depeche Mode are now.

DAVE BALL I almost think that maybe Marc was scared of going up to the next level, although we weren't on the ascent at that point. We'd done the pop thing and moved on from that, going a bit darker, and we didn't know where to go from there. Maybe if we'd have taken a break for a year and then got back together, but it wasn't to be. And Marc immediately launched his solo career—his first solo album came out the same year as Soft Cell's last.

---

* Soft Cell played two 'farewell' shows at London's Hammersmith Palais on the January 9 and 10, 1984. They still refused to play 'Tainted Love'.

HUW FEATHER The brief for *This Last Night In Sodom* was disillusionment, anger, political upheaval, capitalist record-company doctrines, and being misunderstood—a response to being fucked over, basically. It was a very honest transfer of emotion to a visual identity. And when viewed in the context of a rack filled with poptastic, shiny, brightly coloured photos, the sleeve stood out like the sorest thumb in the world. Which was brilliant, because people picked it up thinking, *What the fuck is this?*

DAVE BALL We'd announced we were breaking up before we'd started *This Last Night In Sodom.*[*] We'd actually reached the point where we were fed up with the record company, fed up with Stevo, and we'd both been doing too many drugs— we were just at our wits end really. If we didn't stop, someone was going to end up in hospital, or worse. So we approached the album with a real fuck-you attitude, and just went for it. Surprisingly, it still got into the Top 10, and even the single 'Down In The Subway' charted. It's not the most commercial album, but it's got some good songs on it—'Little Rough Rhinestones' and 'Surrender To A Stranger' are quite nice pop songs, really.

This LP is a shambles. It sounds like it might have taken thirty-seven minutes to record. Lucy [O'Pawn] tells me it took five months, during which Marc quit at least three times. What a fragile little brat. That might be the nicest thing I say about him in this review. I might not even mention that odd Ball figure. Piss off Soft Cell. So say all of us. So say Almond and Ball. By the sound of this.

PAUL MORLEY, *NME*, March 17, 1984

DAVE BALL And that was it for Soft Cell, and the beginning of my wilderness years. I amicably parted company with Stevo and Some Bizzare and started hanging around with Gen more. I basically became a part-time member of Psychic TV, and started doing gigs and recording stuff with them.

GINI BALL It was really sad because Dave got dropped after Soft Cell split. But the pair of us actually got to make an album with Mike Hedges. Mike approached

---

[*] Soft Cell's 'final' album, *This Last Night In Sodom* (BIZL 6) was released by Phonogram on March 24, 1984. It reached no.12 on the UK chart.

186

Dave about producing an album for him, and Dave asked me to sing. So we went out to Bavaria, with James, and I think we did it all in about a month. When we got back, we tried to get a deal for it and no one was interested, so we just thought, *Oh, well, that's that.*

ZEKE MANYIKA I played with Marc a couple of times. I was with him on *The Tube* at the beginning of the year, and I played on the demos for his first solo album. That was really good fun, but I couldn't do the actual sessions for it. I was doing so much stuff at the time.

STEVE SHERLOCK I got a phone call one day from a lackey in the office to say, 'Oh Marc's broken the band up.' Neither Marc nor Stevo told me. So that was the end of my dealings with it, really. I fulfilled an ambition that I thought was never going to happen, and the band collapsing kind of did me a favour as it had a definite end, and I could move on from it. After that I carried on making music, but in a very low-key way.

>>

CARLOS PERON I first met Stevo when Yello appeared at the Camden Palace in 1983, when we were signed to Stiff Records. Rusty Egan was DJing, and Steve Strange was there. Yello's manager, Ian Tregoning, introduced me to Stevo, although I was more interested in the beautiful girl from Stiff's promotional department. I later invited her onstage with us to sip champagne. Critics said Yello were better than the Marx Brothers, although I don't think Dieter and Boris were happy with that. Stevo wanted to sign Yello to Some Bizzare but couldn't make it work financially.

IAN TREGONING That Camden Palace show was extraordinary. It was a playback of *You Gotta Say Yes To Another Excess*, and we figured it would be great to get the band to turn up and just have them onstage, smoking cigarettes and drinking champagne, just as a bit of a joke. But the day before I got a phone call from The Residents, saying, 'We're in town, could we come and do something at the Yello gig?' And I thought, *Fantastic, let's do that.* Thing was, aside from the industry bods, none of the Camden Palace crowd knew who The Residents were. And there were about fifteen of them onstage with the eyeballs on. A lot of people didn't know what they were looking at.

187

BRIAN POOLE We met Ian Tregoning first, when Do-It Records had licensed our album *Songs For Swinging Larvae* from Ralph Records for UK release. After the demise of Do-It we still kept in touch with Ian, who went on to manage Yello, and he invited us along to the *You Gotta Say Yes To Another Excess* playback, as The Residents were appearing too. It was supposed to be some surreal event, but due to sound issues and a backing track failing to play, it went embarrassingly wrong. Nonetheless, Stevo was also present, and Ian introduced us. We had a chat about our mutual fan-ship of The Residents, and we gave him a quick introduction to Renaldo & The Loaf and our work with Ralph. Stevo really liked the 'Songs For Swinging Larvae' video and wanted to include it on a new visual magazine concept called *TV Wipeout*, being created by Cabaret Voltaire. That didn't actually come out until 1984, but we stayed in contact with Doublevision and occasionally Stevo.

CARLOS PERON I recorded 'Frigorex' in 1980 with punkette Isa Nogara for my debut album *Impersonator*, and 'Der Komtur' was from the 1983 *Die Schwarz Spinne* soundtrack. Both were hits with British DJs. One day, Ian showed up at my new studio and told me Stevo wanted to put out a twelve-inch with those two tracks. I agreed, and we started to work on remixes and also some new tracks, including 'Room 101', which was a reference to the year the EP came out, 1984. I don't know why it was on K.422—maybe Some Bizzare had too many releases. But for me it was nice, as I like to release music for many different labels.

IAN TREGONING Carlos didn't really do that much with Yello, it was all Boris. Carlos would just play around with some noises and whatever—he's a very inventive guy, but it wasn't in the same category. He released an album in 1981 called *Impersonator*, very strange stuff, but it's really good. I played a track to Stevo and he really liked it, so we remixed it and put it out on K.422.

ROB COLLINS K.422 was a spin-off of Some Bizarre. I suggested it because I wanted to do Swans, and we all felt that they didn't really fit with the Some Bizarre way of doing things and using a major label. We wanted to go purely independent with Swans and do everything ourselves. Stevo was really friendly with Yello and wanted to do the Carlos Peron record, 'Frigorex', which was the first thing that actually came out on K.422. It didn't do very well, and I was a bit underwhelmed with it, and thought, *Well, that's the end of K.422.* But Jim was always finding great music. He'd started seeing Lydia so was back and forth to New York. And he sent us some tapes: one of them was Sonic Youth and the other one was Swans.

J.G. THIRLWELL I'd heard Glenn Branca's music while I was in London, I think he played at Riverside Studios, which was phenomenal. Overwhelmingly and crushingly loud. Lee Renaldo and Thurston Moore from Sonic Youth had been playing with him. So, when Sonic Youth's *Confusion Is Sex* album came out on Neutral records, I knew it was Branca-related. I was also aware of Circus Morte, which was Michael Gira's pre-Swans group, and the first Swans twelve-inch. So I knew those records, and through the connection with Lydia, those guys were some of the first people I met when I moved to New York. I became really good pals with Michael, and we used to go out every night, getting up to mischief.

MICHAEL GIRA The No Wave scene was kind of over by the time I moved to New York. I started one band, which isn't worth talking about, and a year after that I started Swans. We'd met Sonic Youth and we sort of supported each other because no one else around was really interested. Swans recorded an EP and an album *Filth* for a label called Neutral records, which was formed by Glenn Branca, who was a great musician, a true genius. We went on tour with Sonic Youth around the US, called it the Savage Blunder Tour, and played to virtually no audiences.

J.G. THIRLWELL The first time I saw Swans, at the Pyramid in New York, they absolutely floored me. It was it was one of the most visceral things that I'd ever seen. It was it was such an extreme outpouring of emotion and bodily fluids—it felt like saliva and snot and sweat and blood, a kind of excruciating but ecstatic exorcism. It was so intense—I heard echoes of the Stooges in it, that kind of rawness. Also, with Roli Mosimann's drumming, he was almost channelling John Bonham, and I could hear Black Sabbath in there too. But the desperation and anger—both visually, because of the amount of energy and exertion Michael put into it, and musically too—really had no precedent. This was post-*Filth* and pre-*Cop*, and it was, *Woah*, just incredible. My motivation for turning Rob on to

---

* Carlos Peron's 'Frigorex' twelve-inch (KDBB 112) was the first release on K.422. Released on May 3, 1984, it was limited to 2,300 numbered copies.

Swans was I just thought they were amazing and wanted them to be exposed and have an avenue to release their records. And it worked out.

MICHAEL GIRA Swans had embarked on a tour of Europe that we just pasted together through far-flung connections of people we knew. We had no money, the gigs were few and far between, maybe one every ten days or something. We were subsisting in some old stone house somewhere in France in the middle of winter, freezing and not having anything to eat. So it was really not an ideal circumstance. Somehow we ended up in England, and the cornerstone of this whole tour debacle was an opening slot for The Fall at Heaven.* And on Jim's recommendation, Rob came to see us.

ROB COLLINS Me, Stevo, and Jane went down there, and the gig was just like, *What the fuck are we listening to?* It was so loud, so intense, and the singer was just a lunatic. There was a noose hanging from the ceiling, and he spent most of the time singing with one arm though it.

MICHAEL GIRA I started putting a noose onstage way before the Heaven show. It wasn't meant to be this big deal, it was just like, *Well, there's always* this *option.*

JARBOE I was not a member of Swans at that time, but I was at the Heaven show. The audience waited outside the venue as a deliberate dismissal until Swans finished, and then they burst through the door to see The Fall.

STEVO What was happening in New York at the time—Sonic Youth and Swans—were all part of the same thing. The scene wasn't that big. There was a handful of bands. When I heard the Swans, it reminded me of a slave-gallery ship, where they hit a hammer to beat out the rowing speed. And it would grind you down.

MICHAEL GIRA I've never really been forthright enough about how important Jim was to the continued existence of Swans. He told Stevo and Rob how great we were, how important it was to put us out, and lobbied them to sign us. There would be nothing without him kind of forcing them to come see us. I mean, the

* Swans' first UK show was supporting The Fall at London's Heaven on June 11, 1984.

situation was pretty hopeless. I don't know how long we could have continued. So, Jim really gave us the opportunity to exist as a musical entity and provided me with a fulcrum for the rest of my life. He's such a mensch—at some point I have to sit down with him and give him a huge hug.

ROB COLLINS The band came over to the office the next day, and Michael was pretty full of himself. He sat down on my rickety old chair and put his feet on my rickety old desk. He was quite intimidating.

JARBOE At that time, the view was that American bands had to be 'discovered' in London to move forward. I had of course heard some of the bands on Some Bizzare, but I didn't know much about the label. There were a few fans outside on the street waiting to see Marc Almond, and the room where we met with Rob Collins looked like a typical office. I personally don't remember seeing Michael putting his feet upon a desk—he was very happy for the opportunity.

MICHAEL GIRA I don't think Stevo really cared about Swans, but I admired his chutzpah. If you're in on the joke, you can admire the inventiveness and imagination, and he was really good at it. It was so funny to watch, jumping up and down on the desk of some major label to get Soft Cell signed—that was great. And the Psychic TV brass dildos with the names of all the record companies on it, fantastic.

STEVO Of course I liked Swans. I didn't put things out if I didn't like them. I don't think you could get any more extreme than Swans. If you produced those records now, they'd probably be banned. There are actually criminal laws now to stop kids from going into a recording studio.

JARBOE The offer was made, 'Yes! We want to put out your record out and we want to record you.' And I remember walking through the streets of London after that meeting, and Michael was on cloud nine. He had a big smile on his face, he was almost dancing on the sidewalk, he was so happy. It was a huge, huge moment.

MICHAEL GIRA Rob responded very strongly. He got us plane tickets home, because we didn't have money ourselves, and we went back and we made plans for an EP and the next album to come out on K.422. The deal itself was not a lot of money, but just having that little opportunity meant I could get off my construction job, which I was still doing into my mid-thirties, and gave me the impetus to work at my music, to start making money as a musician and do what I love.

PAUL WHITE Once the connection was made with Some Bizarre, more things started to come to me direct, such as the Cabs and Test Dept. In the meantime, Rob had set up K.422 and signed Swans, and asked if I'd be interested in working on the sleeve for the album *Cop*. I met Michael, we got on, and I liked his ideas, which were already pretty well formed. He knew what he wanted everything to look like, so for me the exercise was one of getting those ideas across accurately in a printed form.

ROB COLLINS The first release was the *Raping A Slave* EP, which got Rough Trade in a tizzy.* We had to go up against their ethics committee or pastoral committee to argue our case as to why the record should be distributed by them. But there was a lot of support for the band in the UK music press—*Cop* got five-out-of-five album reviews, and there were big features and front covers.†

MICHAEL GIRA The one thing about Swans, and this may sound like I'm bragging but I'm not, is there's nothing else like Swans. And that's been a hinderance as much as benefit. Swans doesn't fit into any world except its own.

CHRIS BOHN Musically and lyrically, Swans were pared to the bone. Everything about them at that point was fantastic, really quite extraordinary. But one of the problems with popular music is the tendency of most audiences to identify the voice with the words, assuming the 'I' character in the song is stating the opinion of the singer, or the band as a whole. Lou Reed had it, as did Nick Cave, and so did Michael. Of course, there is a confessional element to a lot of singer/songwriters, but there is still an objective distance, and the fact that it is still a performance, no matter how heartfelt it seems. And it's very important to remember that, especially in the case of a group like Swans, where there's an absolute immersion and commitment to the art, because it's hardcore. And hardcore is expressing some inner

---

* The *Young God* EP (KDE112) was released by K.422 in May 1984. It's also known as the *Raping A Slave* EP, although the band refer to it as *Young God*.
† Swans' first LP for K.422 was *Cop* (KCC 1), released on June 7, 1984.

being or inner feeling that doesn't automatically translate opinions. It was there to interrogate the subject, not endorse it. So yes, *Raping A Slave* was a confrontational title, but when you listen to it it's not endorsing any form of violence, rather it's highlighting the violence perpetrated by others on society in general.

MICHAEL GIRA I don't know how much I needed validation, but it gave me fuel to continue. The press attention in the UK in particular was an odd thing for me because I still had this sort of underdog mentality, having worked really shit jobs most of my life. And coming fresh from that and then having this attention, it was an odd thing. I had kind of a perverse take on it, because it wasn't like I felt I deserved it or anything, I was more like, 'Ugh, who *are* you people?' I didn't trust it, I suppose—wisely, as it turns out. It was great at the time but, you know, fuck 'em.

STEVO Michael gave me my first ratatouille. He offered it to me and I said, 'I'm adventurous, Michael, but I don't eat rats.' Turned out it was eggplant, which I'd never heard of either.

JESSAMY CALKIN I offered to tour manage Nick Cave & The Bad Seeds' first US tour in June 1984, thinking it would be a good way to travel with my friends while being paid for it. But I didn't have any idea of what I was letting myself in for. They all took a lot of drugs except Mick Harvey, and he ended up trying to keep everyone in line. Nick was quite ungovernable at the time, while Barry Adamson was in a very dark and paranoid place. Those two had a terrible, terrible relationship, and the whole tour was nightmare, really difficult. They were all off their heads, and there wasn't much money involved. I ended up losing Nick's air ticket and had to buy him a new one out of my fee. I thought I was coming across as quite professional, but I think they knew that I was just as chaotic as them and found it quite funny. Blixa was quite separate in the Bad Seeds. He didn't really care what anybody thought and just went his own way. And he and Nick really respected each other—they didn't have the tortured relationship that Nick and Barry had, or even Nick and Mick.

>>

Test Dept make one hell of a noise but it's a disciplined cacophony. When in full flight, they're like demons, caught in a trance. Metal on metal on a Trans Europe Express. A steamrolling Steve Reich, primeval yet precise, with water tanks and oil drums in place of piano and strings.

author unknown, *Sounds*, December 1983

ROB COLLINS I worked pretty closely with Test Dept. They were lovely, really good, knew exactly what they wanted and how they wanted it done. They were so self-sufficient in terms of recording, visuals, artwork, and organising these amazing, huge shows. They hated playing regular venues and they wanted to put on events, so they did shows at Cannon Street Station and Paddington Station.* The band did all of it, though—the label wasn't involved in the organisation of those shows at all.

TEST DEPT [Being involved with Some Bizzare] helped raise our profile and got us press, which helped to build a strong base for working on large scale projects. Through Jane at Some Bizzare we made connections with people like Kevin Milles of Final Solution, who were the foremost underground music promoters in London in the 80s. This led to a re-scheduled gig at Heaven after the police raided and prevented our Titan Arch event near Waterloo. We worked together on the Cannon Street Station show, which was an incredible coup at the time. After that we became more independent and adept at creating large scale events such as *Unacceptable Face Of Freedom* at Paddington, working via the GLC, and *Second Coming* in Glasgow for their European Capital of Culture in 1990. We also worked in collaboration with Brith Gof on the epic *Gododdin* in Wales, and across Europe while working largely with NL Centrum in Amsterdam to create large scale events in Europe during the 80s.

STEPHEN 'MAL' MALLINDER I went to the Test Dept Cannon Street event, and also one under the Westway as well. It was a funny time—it was quite good being in London because Ken Livingstone and the GLC put on free events and supported the arts. I remember going to see events on the Thames, all these mad performances, and Test Dept slotted in with that. They weren't isolated. They fitted this nonconformist, almost European notion of theatre; there was this mad

* Test Dept's *Program For Progress* show was held at Cannon Street station in London EC4 on June 23, 1984.

anarchist circus from Spain doing things around that time, and there were the Mutoid Waste Company events, too. Test Dept were more South London, but they did seem to fit in the vibe. There were certainly more anarchic elements on the edges of society back then, which also fed into the early Shoom stuff and things like that as well. London was quite an interesting, volatile, nonconformist city, and Test Dept were part of that.

IAN TREGONING I really liked Test Dept's vibe, and they were great guys. They were doing experimental theatre and installations really early on. I thought the Mutoid Waste Company events were just a little bit too druggie, just a little bit too loose. I went to a couple of them and there was running water next to live wires and people writhing around in mud next to it all. Whereas Test Dept were really into the spectacle, and it was almost like they were channelling the Russian Constructivists and that bold Eastern approach to the concept of industrial machinery.

>>

 Hole is somewhere between a terminally sick joke and a masterpiece. In the analogy: pop music in the 80s is a tattered circus-shooting stall, the gaudy peeling paint no longer attractive. Along the target line run a series of plastic heads, each one more or less the same as the other and for the most part beyond the range of anyone with the guts to try and shoot them. As for Foetus—he is a whole different rollercoaster. *Hole* will leave you exhilarated, slightly shaken and maybe just a little nauseous. But more than ready to go through it all again.

DON WATSON, *NME*, September 29, 1984

WARNE LIVESEY The first time I worked with Jim, I was hired by the studio as a freelancer to work on that particular session. There was a few smaller studios around town that I hooked up with in my pursuit of breaking into production, generally speaking twenty-four-track but not the big name places. So, they would have been asked to supply an engineer, and I got the call. That first time with Jim was at Wave Studios in Hoxton. There used to be quite a few studios around there, as at the time East London was a no man's land, and the property was considerably cheaper. Jim was a very unique character, of course, but it wasn't that unusual at that time to come across people that were, how do you say, very *original* in their look. So he wasn't completely outlandish, but it was his intensity that really struck me, and he had a very different work ethic to most artists I'd worked with.

J.G. THIRLWELL I feel very affectionate toward *Hole*, and it was real crystallisation of what I had been doing for the years prior.* It has a lot of energy and is full of ideas. I already had a lot of the material before Some Bizarre came along; all the lyrics, song frameworks, and arrangements were written. But I got to work with two great engineers, Warne Livesey and Charles Grey, and they indulged and gave me the time to really explore the sound of the record. It's a really good snapshot of that period of time. It was also a hell of a lot of work.

All my records up to and including *Hole*, and beyond, have been evolutionary leaps. And that was the next leap on from *Ache*. There's some really dark stuff on *Hole*, but it's dark content that has a light context. There's also some really interesting sonic exploration in there, a lot of different stuff. But it's also really frantic, and probably a good reflection of what I was like at the time.

WARNE LIVESEY Jim was essentially a solo artist without necessarily being a musician. He had no real technical ability on any instrument. He was musical, for sure, had great ideas and could write, but he didn't have chops, if you know that expression. When I first worked with him, I was hired as an engineer, but there were a few conversations early on when I would offer to play parts for him or offer to get someone to come in and play them for him. But Jim was determined that it was all him. Because I'm relatively musically literate—I'm not the greatest musician, but I can play quite a few instruments—I started to help Jim get around his technical limitations to enable him to achieve the sounds he had in his head. For example, at the time Jim's guitar playing didn't extend much further than playing a single bar on open strings and moving it up and down the neck. So, I'd work out which chord he was hearing, tune the guitar to that chord, and he'd play the part. If it shifted to a minor key then I'd retune the guitar and drop that in. But he had a very clear vision of the sounds and the melody and knew how he wanted the harmony to move in relation to that. It was just a question of working it out. I'm credited as an engineer on the earlier records because that was how I was hired. But when Jim started to see how I was able to help him musically as well as

---

* *Hole* (WOMB FDL 3) by Scraping Foetus Off The Wheel was released on Self Immolation/Some Bizzare in September 1984—the first fruits of J.G. Thirlwell's association with Some Bizzare.

sonically, and also that I was willing to let him do things the way he wanted to and respect his method of doing things, he started to give me a co-production credit.

J.G. THIRLWELL Around the time of *Hole*, I'd never really heard the term sampling but what I was doing on a lot of my records was what sampling turned into. I would make cassette compilations of the different sounds I wanted to use, and then I'd cue up the cassette player with my finger on the pause button, have the engineer start the tape. When it got to where I wanted the sound to go, I'd lift the pause button and hopefully get it in the right spot. We would change the Varispeed on the multi-track to get it in the right key. On *Hole*, I had a very elaborate system which was of kind of a homemade Mellotron, where I recorded my voice on sustained notes, and then created tape loops out of multiple voices. I'd have several tape loops playing back at different speeds, so there would be different pitches playing, creating this choral kind of thing, muting and unmuting the voices on the mixing desk. I did finally rent a Mellotron and added that as well.

WARNE LIVESEY We were doing things in small little chunks. We'd put down a tempo map and then do the rhythm track, which would be maybe some drums but mostly oil cans, pieces of sheet metal, and all sorts of other weird stuff. And Jim would play them one at a time. Then we'd get some chords on guitar and another guide vocal. We would just utilise what we can get our hands on. Sometimes there'd be a real bass drum or snare, but often those roles were taken by something Jim had found on a building site. We'd find the best place in the studio area to put that specific thing to get the right sound, often in a stairwell or in the bathroom.

J.G. THIRLWELL At that time, AMS had a digital delay, which you could lock sounds into—I think it was under two seconds, but that was the dawn of sampling. And when MIDI was introduced, you could interface a keyboard with the AMS delay, and that was really revolutionary. And then they made the AMS delay that had ten seconds of sample time, and that was followed by the Emulator and then the Fairlight. It was all rolled out pretty quickly. We rented an Emulator for Coil's *Scatology*, and for the next Foetus album, *Nail*, I rented a Fairlight—that was the speed that technology was moving at the time. The drums were always played live, but as I played them one drum at a time they sound sequenced, but they weren't. And then there's other live instruments on top of it.

A lovely, horrible, stupid record that disappears up its own hole which remains in the middle but ought to be somewhere over there (waves hand vaguely) on the very edge. An honourable near extremism with a noble sense of nihilism. A 'brilliant advert' in itself for Baby Foetus and his ever-expanding head.

CHRIS ROBERTS, *Sounds*, September 29, 1984

PAUL WHITE Ken Ansell had set up a design agency with Virgin but I decided I wasn't going to get involved as I wasn't keen on the corporate side of things. But he very kindly let me work from their dedicated design office for six months, rent free, while I sorted my shit out. I was doing stuff with Jim Thirlwell and a number of other Some Bizarre kind of bands, so he and Lydia would visit. It must have been very strange walking into this posh building and at the end of this plush carpeted corridor was an office blaring out Swans and Neubauten.

>>

MARC ALMOND Bursting with inspiration, I began to think seriously about recording a new album. I felt it was important to do something soon—the music business has a very short memory, and I feared that unless I made a record promptly I'd be forgotten. The only problem was that I wasn't entirely sure what kind of album to make.

FLOOD 'The Boy Who Came Back' was such a bold statement, it was really exciting.[*] I wasn't privy to all the stuff that was going on in the background, but I was just like, *Wow, this is brilliant*. And I know a lot of people were sort of questioning why I was still working with Marc, but I've always found him to be so incredibly inspiring. I love his voice and his lyrics, and with *Vermin In Ermine* he was trying something new. He was putting himself out there, and that's what I respond to. That's a human being.

ANNI HOGAN *Vermin In Ermine* was an odd one.[†] Stevo and the record company were desperate to credit Marc as the main songwriter, which became a bit of a bone of contention. Nowadays, the work that I and various other people did would

---

[*] Marc Almond's debut single as a solo artist, 'The Boy Who Came Back', was released by Phonogram in May 1984. It reached no.52 on the UK chart.

[†] *Vermin In Ermine* was released on October 1, 1984, and reached no.36 on the UK chart.

count as writing. So I don't remember it feeling like a job promotion, it was just the same, although I may have been paid a tiny bit more. Marc couldn't play a thing—certainly not back then—but he'd sing me his melodies and I'd work out the arrangement from there. I mean, he got his points across really well, but it was basically, *La, la, la*. And he'd suggest a style based on whatever he was listening to at the time. But *Vermin In Ermine* isn't one of my favourite albums, although I know other people love it. It seemed I had the same amount of input, but it didn't count as much, and that didn't feel good.

FLOOD Anni is brilliant—she's one of the few people I've worked with whose persona so comes out in what she plays. It's so beautifully fragile in such a way that you cannot fail to notice it. And there were so many things she did that were just like, *Wow*, and she really pulled herself up for *Vermin In Ermine*. It was so brilliant to see her raised right up like that, because it should have been done earlier. But that's the type of person she was—she was always playing the supporting role, and it was like, 'Come on Anni, you're amazing!' That sensitivity and the real struggle that Anni had was a perfect marriage with Marc's music, and, as another musical voice, she was just as strong. I love that woman.

ANNI HOGAN We recorded both *Vermin In Ermine* and *Stories Of Johnny* at Hartmann Digital Tonstudio in the Bavarian mountains, which was phenomenal. Not only was it the first digital studio in the world, I think, but you'd do a day's recording, go for a sauna, and come out and jump in a mountain stream. Mike Hedges was producing and went bananas. We'd go out to get food, and he would buy the whole supermarket. We had Californian grass flown in—we couldn't have been more spoilt– although obviously it was all going on the bloody record company, but we just went along with it. It was a mixture of real good fun and, you know, the usual drama. It was a lot of being off your head and a lot of creative talent going on. But Mike just compressed everything to hell. The demos sound so much better to me.

GINI BALL It was always fun being around Mike and out in Bavaria with the gang. James was still a baby and I had him with me. We spent a lot of the time in the studio, but we went out sometimes, and it was really beautiful around there. Marc put on the sleeve notes that James was gnawing away on his finger and cut his first tooth, which was so funny. Recording was quite the opposite experience to *Torment And Toreros* in atmosphere.

MARC ALMOND Eventually the album was completed, but I wasn't sure whether I was pleased with it or not. I could see that it was flawed, some of the songs not sounding fully realised, rushed out, tarted up. There were some good songs like 'You Have' and 'Tenderness Is A Weakness', but other tracks like 'Shining Sinners' and 'Solo Adultos' were too long and repetitive. There was a lot I liked about the album however: it had something of the glamorous trashiness that I'd wanted, and Mike had made my voice sound better than ever before. I thought I was finally starting to sound like the singer I wanted to be.

>>

IAN TREGONING Flood and I worked on the first Test Dept twelve-inch, 'Compulsion', and then Mufti from Neubauten and I worked on 'Cold Witness' and 'Plastic' from *Beating The Retreat*. Mufti was fantastic. We were at Jacobs studio down in Farnham, and we hired this huge fuck-off air compressor. We fired it up and the earth was shaking from this thing, and Mufti grabbed a Neumann U 87—a really good quality condenser mic—and was straight in there, trying to record it. He makes up this fantastic loop of little noises, and we stuck that down as a backing track. Once we'd finished with it, he's got this great big, long loop of tape, and he goes off to the studio kitchen and comes back with one of those cereal multipacks, opens one, chucks the Cornflakes away, and just rolls up the tape and pops it in. Another time, he wanted a pint of milk but didn't have any English money on him, so he walked into a Tesco and came out a couple of minutes later wearing a Tesco overall, carrying two pints of milk. He'd just walked in, grabbed the overalls, picked up the milk, and walked out. Very inventive, those Neubauten, guys, in many ways.

TEST DEPT Many people still regard *Beating the Retreat* as our best album, and there are certainly some powerful moments that capture the period well.* Ken Thomas and his studious tape op, Mark Stent, who went on to become a top producer in

* Test Dept's *Beating The Retreat* (TEST 2-3) was released on Some Bizzare via Phonogram on July 30, 1984. It was initially available as a double twelve-inch box set with inserts featuring text, photos, and artwork. It was reissued as a single album by Mercury records in 1987.

200

his own right, were great to work with. Ken was so open to experimenting and trying out new ideas. In that sense, it was very much a studio album.

ROB COLLINS That was the most amazing thing about Stevo: he could take these bands and get them deals with major labels. I mean, who would have thought Phonogram would ever give a band like Test Dept a deal? And they would let us do their first release as two twelve-inch singles, in a box with loads of postcards in it?

STEVO There isn't a label out there today that's operating like that, doing what I was back then and saying, 'We've got this band here which everyone's going crazy for, and here's something else, that don't sound anything like them—because I tried not to repeat myself—which is coming out on another corporation.' That model don't exist today. Why is that? Well, that's what this is about, isn't it? They don't want people like me to exist. It doesn't fit into their psyche.

CHRIS BOHN The problem was the financial issue, which became the thing that drove all the artists away, except Marc, who was incredibly loyal but possibly to his detriment. The records were selling, but nobody could get an audit. And these ridiculous situations like Test Dept, whose records were brilliant and came in fantastic packaging, but cost a fortune. It was similar to the New Order 'Blue Monday' sleeve debacle—they were losing money with every record they sold.

TEST DEPT I remember Geoff and Sleazy from Coil saying how live they thought *Beating The Retreat* sounded—they loved the production on it. Strangely, we all thought that Ken Thomas had done a great job on the production, but we felt it definitely didn't have the raw energy of our live performances. Jack, our sound person, didn't like it and thought we should have released a live album for our vinyl debut. We treated the studio and live performances very differently. It was very difficult to capture that live raw energy with the same intensity. So it goes.

STEPHEN 'MAL' MALLINDER We were well aware of what was going in New York, club-wise, and we'd already worked with John Luongo on 'Just Fascination', so there were already elements on *The Crackdown*. But by *Micro-Phonies* time, that electro-funk influence was fully embedded. And not just the music being made but also the

DJ culture at the time—New York was like the new punk for us. People don't bang on about it, probably because it was black Americans rather than white suburban people doing it, but that was where the really interesting stuff was coming out. It was where people were using drum machines and beatboxes and messing with technology in a really interesting way. So, we were very switched on to that early electro stuff. *Micro-Phonies* was a completely different process to *The Crackdown*. One of our motivations for signing to Some Bizarre was to upgrade Western Works and build it up to sixteen-track, then twenty-four track, studio. And the Virgin deal gave us the money to do that, which meant by the time we came to do *Micro-Phonies*, our studio was compatible with other commercial studios. So, we could do the original production stuff in our studio and then take it elsewhere to mix it. Flood actually came up to Sheffield and stayed with us, and I remember taking him out clubbing to Occasions, when Parrott, Winston, and Jamie were DJing there.

ROGER QUAIL I was friends with the Cabs, and they worked with a good number of Sheffield drummers, one of which was me. The thing about playing with Richard and Mal, you had to keep it pretty simple—they didn't want lots of fancy drum roles and fills. 'Can you play that a bit more simply please, Rog?' You ended up being a bit of a human drum machine, which was fine. That's me on 'James Brown', and the little drum intro is actually based on the handclaps from 'Car Wash' by Rose Royce. I played on a couple of the tracks on *Micro-Phonies*, which was mostly done of at Western Works, although we spent some time at Sarm West with Flood. I don't remember Stevo being around at all.

STEPHEN 'MAL' MALLINDER Because we'd invested in Western Works, we weren't wasting money on studio time, which left us a bigger budget for mixing. Which is how we ended up at Sarm West. We took all the tapes that we'd worked on at Western Works down there, and used all their outboard gear for the vocals, production, and finishing touches. So, with *Micro-Phonies*, we took advantage of our own space to do the recording and then mixed it in a far plusher studio. It was the best of both worlds, really.

FLOOD I think there was a feeling that they wanted to move out of the Some Bizzare maelstrom a bit. They just said, 'Do you want to come up and work in Sheffield at our gaff?' and I was like, 'Yep!' There was a lot of time spent up there experimenting and working on different ideas. I was trying to push the dance side and help them bring that out. The experimental side was still there but it was balanced, so it didn't weird people out so much. We just tried loads of things out, and again had loads of fun.

STEPHEN 'MAL' MALLINDER The single version of 'Sensoria' is a hybrid of two separate tracks on *Micro-Phonies*.* We wanted to work with Robin Scott from M, and we put him in a weird position, really, because even though he hadn't done a tremendous amount, we were fans and thought he had a good pair of ears. So, we asked him to do a remix, and that was when it got really interesting because Robin listened to the album and picked up, correctly, that we didn't vary too much, and that 'Do Right' and 'Sensoria' were in the same key and tempo. Robin was massively influenced by Malcolm McLaren, and [1983 single] 'Buffalo Gals' in particular. So, we went into a studio in Soho, duped the multi-tracks of both songs, and then literally cut them together. It was the most insane bit of work we'd ever done, in the sense that we were physically cutting twenty-four-track tape to make two records into one. I'm sure Flood wanted to kill us by the time it was finished.

Robin suggested getting the African singers on it, and that shaped the visuals, as the video took its cues from the track. The 'Do Right' refrain became the preacher, the African vocals became the dancers, and we've always loved derelict buildings, so we filmed it in the old Sheffield Infirmary that was used in [1984 BBC nuclear war drama] *Threads*. The 180-degree visual effect was achieved with a contraption invented by a technician from Sheffield art college who director Peter Care knew. We just thought, *Pete wants to use this thing, it's fine*, but we'd probably get busted for health and safety if we tried to use it now. For a brief period, every job Pete got was recreating that effect. Everyone wanted it: Scritti Politti, ABC, It's Immaterial, loads of people.

JOHN GRANT When I was thirteen or fourteen, 'Tainted Love' was everywhere. It was something that grabbed my attention immediately. I was starting to become aware of certain things, and hearing those synths was having quite an effect on me below the waist. About a year after, 'Sweet Dreams' by Eurythmics caught me,

---

* Cabaret Voltaire's 'Sensoria' (CVS 3) was released by Virgin on September 24, 1984. It reached no.96 on the UK chart. Their second album for Some Bizzare, *Micro-Phonies* (CV 2), was released by Virgin on October 29, 1984.

too, and 'Just Fascination' by Cabaret Voltaire. I love the twelve-inch of that so much—it was one of the greatest things I'd ever heard. And 'Sensoria' was such a huge track in the States—not in a mainstream way, but the clubs I was going to would play it. I worked backward from there, trying to get my hands on anything that I could. In England, I'd always hear people talking about 'Nag, Nag, Nag' and 'Do The Mussolini-Headkick', but I was quite unaware of that era. For me, it started with *The Crackdown*, and then *Micro-Phonies* became pretty much the centre of the universe for me for quite some time. That had such huge impact on me—when I first heard 'Do Right', I just about lost my marbles.

FLOOD There were so many things happening at Trident. I'd been doing some remixes with Ian Levine for Record Shack, at night, people like Communards, Sylvester, Linda Lusardi, Sinitta. He'd leave me to do it, so again, a brilliant training ground. The Six Sed Red single came in, and I was like, 'Great, let's go for it." Rick had been in B-Movie, and I loved them—they were just amazing—and Cindy had been mentioned by Marc and Dave. She was totally out there but brilliant too. On the Cabs' first record, John Luongo had come over from New York and did a couple of remixes. I was a bit jealous that I couldn't do them, but then I learned so much from watching him, this big-shot producer, brilliant guy. So, with things like the second Cabs record and the Six Sed Red twelve-inch, there was this underlying feeling of a groove that wasn't quite disco, wasn't quite hip-hop. It was something else.

STEPHEN 'MAL' MALLINDER I've actually got strangely vivid memories of being in the studio doing that twelve-inch with Cindy and Rick, because I had some weird flu at the time. Marc was good friends with Cindy, and I think she was a fan of ours, so it was an easy fit. Cindy was lovely. She was great. It was quite collaborative as well, as we were all in the studio at the same time—I played some bass and Rick had a Jupiter 8, which I hadn't used before. We did it in Manchester because Cindy and Rick were living together in Mansfield, which seemed like a strange place for New York's legendary Cindy Ecstasy to end up!

---

* Six Sed Red was erstwhile B-Movie keyboard player Rick Holliday and Cindy Ecstasy. Their one-and-only single, 'Shake It Right' (SIR 4059T), was released by Sire in 1984. It was recorded at BAS in Manchester and remixed at Trident in Soho.

" The Holland Dozier and Holland of hardcore! In the best, truest sense of the word, Foetus Art Terrorism has a rock'n'roll heart.* There are no stated tinges of satisfaction on this record—a full frontal assault on stamina and desire—just a head full of crazed dreams, wild connections, explicit and determined fantasies. But even as he drenches himself in the style and fury lost and found at various points during the last three decades—thrashing the Memphis Flash, Good Times rap mix splattered and tormented into submission—Foetus Art Terrorism displays a mastery of studio technique that would put any number of competitors, in any number of areas to withering shame and envy. He has it all down in terms of echo, impact attack and overlay. Nothing is overplayed, everything is lethal, could be the motto here.

author unknown, NME, November 24, 1984

J.G. THIRLWELL When all that new Foetus material started coming out through Some Bizzare, I was actually exploring a new life in New York—another one of my great career decisions. I started doing shows with backing tapes and visuals, the visuals being mainly blinding white lights and smoke machines, but it was quite theatrical too. I was still in the UK a lot, and most of the Some Bizzare bands were back and forth to New York. Psychic TV and Cabaret Voltaire were touring, and Matt would be over recording, so it was pretty fluid.

ROB COLLINS Some Bizzare were well ahead of the game when it came to going to New York and establishing a base there. When I started, Stevo already had a thing going on, and Soft Cell and THE THE had recorded over there. Now Jim was living over there, and we had Swans, so there was always a lot of conversation about New York in the office. And obviously there was the ecstasy connection. One day, Stevo said, 'Rob, you need to come to New York.' I managed to get a bucket flight on Air India, and I went out thinking I was going to be out there for a week or something, just to hang out and help him get a US deal for Cabaret Voltaire. Stevo picked me up from the airport in an old yellow Checker Cab and gave me a guided tour as we went in, and it was like I'd fucking died and gone to heaven.

---

* The 'Calamity Crush' twelve-inch (WOMB FAT 11.12) was released under the name Foetus Art Terrorism in October 1984.

JANE ROLINK I'd met Madonna in New York when she was working behind the bar at Danceteria. Me, her, and [artist] Martin Burgoyne used to knock about together—we were all really close. When she came over to the UK, Seymore Stein wouldn't pay to put her up in a hotel—which I reminded him about ten years later in a business meeting!

I had a bedsit on the Warwick Road in Earl's Court and Marc had one on the next floor up, and Madonna needed somewhere to stay, so she crashed at Marc's bedsit and we used to have breakfast together every morning. She was great—she was just like us. She used to come up to Some Bizzare all the time when she was in London, because Warners was just around the corner. But I do remember watching her perform and thinking, *Oh, I'm not sure about this*, because it wasn't my cup of tea at all. I was into Throbbing Gristle, you know what I mean? I was thinking, *Oh, I don't know how she's gonna do, she's not going to get anywhere with this stuff!*

ROB COLLINS I remember when Madonna phoned up the Some Bizarre office. We'd moved out of St Anne's Court, so we were in the New Cavendish Street office, and Madonna called to speak to Jane, and I was the one who picked up the phone. That was my one and only conversation with Madonna.

STEPHEN 'MAL' MALLINDER Virgin were really good because they knew we were willing to do whatever they wanted, but that the stuff they weren't interested in we could put out on Doublevision. There was a big point of difference in that there wasn't direct competition between the two. And Doublevision enhanced our kudos in terms of us still creating interesting cool stuff, even though we'd signed to a major.

The irony was, we used to have loads of trouble getting our stuff shown on TV, because networks felt it wasn't broadcast quality. We had to tell them it was supposed to look that way, it was intentional, that it was a counterpoint to what they were doing. It was more suited to things like *Snub TV*, which was started by Fran Duffy in the US and ran on the US cable network Night Flight. They also used to run the *Some Bizzare Show*, which Stevo put together. It was basically a showcase for all the Some Bizzare acts. We were quite happy for our material to be used on it, and although we weren't actively involved in putting the programme itself together, it had our blessing.

ROB COLLINS Stevo always used to stay with Fran Duffy, a promotor and TV producer who had this amazing loft in Chelsea. Fran was crazy, and his family were just brilliant. It was like going to stay with a really close relative. On a typical night we'd have a bit of a party at Fran's, head out with a half a bottle of tequila and a line of something to Nel's or the Palladium or Danceteria—all the places that have gone down in history. It was just like a holiday, and I fell in love with the place. I ended up being out there for three months. I had my wages sent out to me and I had my *per diems*, although I didn't really spend much money, because Stevo was just fronting it all on his credit card. New York was a right shithole back then, but it was magical.

MICHAEL GIRA I'm sure New York had an influence on the music, especially considering what an extreme place it was at the time. It was at the tail end of an economic fallout, which left it kind of devastated, with burnt-out cars on the street, what we now call homeless people but back then we called 'bums' everywhere, heroin rampant. Where I lived on 6th Street and Avenue B in Alphabet City was an extremely dangerous neighbourhood. There was machine-gun fire at night, and I was mugged with a knife to my throat. It was a harrowing kind of place in certain areas. I'm sure if you had money it was fine, but I had none.

ROB COLLINS We used to go to the Pyramid Club, which was on Avenue A, and it was this sleazy underground kind of rock/drag club. Back then, Alphabet City was fucking dodgy. A was all right, B was just about OK, C was pretty bad, and D, just scary. And when places started opening on D, you knew you had to tread really, really carefully. I remember when I first went to where Michael lived, and walking out of the subway station like, *Where the fuck am I?* It looked like a warzone.

STEVO I always saw Some Bizzare as a global label, not just a UK one. Look at all the deals we did in America. I spent almost as much time in New York as I did London. The thing is, when you produce the records yourself, you have the finished artefacts before I meet with a distributor. So I'm not going there saying, 'Can you give me money so I can produce a record?' They've already heard it, and I know they want it. So you're in a strong position, and an even stronger one if you've got a record that five or six companies want at the same time. Now that, as a precedent, isn't something that these corporations are going to encourage, right? Because that'd be giving normal people clout. Most independent record labels wanted to be independent of corporations, but I wanted to be independent and work within the corporations. And that was difficult—next to impossible in fact. I can't name one label out there now who does what I'm trying to do. The corporations want everything, lock, stock, and barrel. Everyone's been bought out. I mean, some of these corporations are financially bigger than some countries. I've just watched these guys get fatter and fatter and fatter.

On Some Bizzare (the crazy empire of Ø),
the label that brings you the very best of chaos!!

from the sleeve of Soft Cell's 'Soul Inside' twelve-inch (1983)

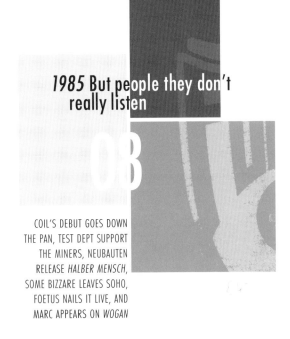

1985 But people they don't really listen

08

COIL'S DEBUT GOES DOWN
THE PAN, TEST DEPT SUPPORT
THE MINERS, NEUBAUTEN
RELEASE *HALBER MENSCH*,
SOME BIZZARE LEAVES SOHO,
FOETUS NAILS IT LIVE, AND
MARC APPEARS ON *WOGAN*

ANNE STEPHENSON I really thought Matt Johnson was a genius. In fact, if I have to choose my favourite album in the whole history of the world, it would be *Burning Blue Soul*. I actually love Matt—I think he's brilliant. And Jim Foetus is another genius and a really lovely guy, too.

Stevo was trying to get as many geniuses together for Some Bizzare as possible, which I think he did accomplish. And I thought he was a genius too, at first. When I was going out with Stevo, someone asked me to sum up Some Bizarre, and I said, 'It's a record label run by a genius for geniuses.' He was nice to me for about a week after that.

ZEKE MANYIKA I never got a sense of any hierarchy at Some Bizzare. Stevo never treated it like that. Obviously, whoever had a record out at the time was the priority, but there was always cooperation between the bands. For example, Matt and Marc really respected each other and worked and played together. Matt is the kind of guy that if he wants something done, he will come in the office and get it done, even if he has to do it himself, and I don't know if behind the scenes some people were fighting for attention. But Stevo always tried to create an atmosphere where things were complimentary when they were happening. It was one of the things that attracted artists to Some Bizzare: you could call anyone at any time and get them to come and help you out. It was a great vibe.

'Why kill time when you can kill yourself?' says everyone's favourite uncle Jim Foetus, with a startling lack of originality—said line first appeared in Tony Hancock's *The Rebel*. 'Wash/Slog' continues his joyful trail of electronic havoc, shouts and wails, hooklines and the irony of a drunkard. Drums and bonking noises urge Jim onto evermore ludicrous heights as he shouts, 'Gimme gimme a man after midnight!' for no apparent reason, and generally has good time.*

DAVID QUANTICK, *NME*, January 19, 1985

J.G. THIRLWELL I'd met Keith Allen through being a squatter in the early 80s and looking for a place to stay. He'd told me about this squat that was near Rough Trade, off of Portobello Road. It was this block of flats where developers had skimped on the building materials and there were cracks in the walls, so they couldn't rent them out. We got into one of those and Keith lived in the one next door. Keith was doing stand-up comedy at the time, and would constantly shoot himself in the foot, because he would just do perverse things. At that time, the whole Comedy Store thing and *The Young Ones* was really successful, and that kind of comedy was seen as a little bit edgy. But Keith was always outside of that scene because he was a little bit *too* edgy. He would do things like go onstage at a stand-up gig totally naked, things that were a little bit too against the grain. Though I feel he was quite influential. Later on he found his feet and did a lot of acting and stuff, which is how I ended up in an episode of *The Comic Strip Presents* on Channel 4 [playing guitar in a bar in *The Bullshitters: Roll Out the Gunbarrel*]. Later on, that crowd also hung out in Soho, so you'd go to a pub near the Some Bizzare office and Keith would be there with all the alternative comics.

STEVO Remember, at the end of the day, it's night-time. So, when our offices were in St Anne's Court, after a hard day's work we'd go down to the George on Wardour Street, and half the pub was Some Bizzare and the other half was *The Comic Strip*. You'd have Jim Thirlwell and Genesis P-Orridge sitting there with people like Alexei Sayle and Robbie Coltrane. I wouldn't say we were close friends or anything, but at that time in our lives we'd all have a drink together, so most evenings we were with *The Comic Strip*. Keith Allen wanted to do this song, 'I

* Released under the You've Got Foetus On Your Breath moniker, 'Wash/Slog' (WOMB FGH 8.12) missed its intended 1984 release date and didn't appear in the shops until early 1985.

Want To Marry Harry When I'm Grown Up', with Simon Brint, and it came out under the name The Champagne Kindergarten. It's probably why my career was ruined—I'd probably pissed the Royal Family off before, but this was the icing on the cake. I thought it was funny. And it was my mum's favourite record.*

>>

ROB COLLINS Sleazy just came into the office one day and said, 'I've got a new Coil record, do you want to put it out through K.422?' And I just said yes straightaway. There was no reason not to. Some Bizzare kind of felt like a family, everyone was really close. It wasn't a regular setup.

PAUL 'BEE' HAMPSHIRE I stayed friends with Geoff and Sleazy throughout the whole Some Bizzare period. Sleazy was the true genius out of all of them, musically, visually, creatively. He was responsible for so much of what people remember as Throbbing Gristle, Psychic TV, and Coil.

GAVIN FRIDAY Geoff and I were quite close and wrote to each other an awful lot and we would hang out whenever I was in London. There always a connection. Geoff told me they were gonna make an album with their new band, Coil, called *Scatology*, and asked if I wanted to contribute. He sent me a cassette of the backing track, which was even more minimal than how it ended up. I think Alex Fergusson from Psychic TV played guitar on it. Geoff suggested the title, 'The Tenderness Of Wolves', which is from a Fassbender movie. I sort of revised the lyric so it was about vampires. Basically, most of us are vampires, and it's quite a heavy vocal. I just went into my complete desolate angst zone on it. And they just loved it, and they were suggesting, 'Do you want to do more backup vocals?'—really just trying to suck anything out of me in a positive way. Jim from Foetus was involved, too, and he was really great.

J.G. THIRLWELL They asked me to produce it, and I consider it a production job. The lines are a bit blurred, because we all played on it, but I was definitely honouring what they wanted it to be. I became good friends with Geoff up at the

---

* Thankfully the sole single by the novelty act The Champagne Kindergarten, 'I Want To Marry Harry When I'm Grown Up' (HRH 1) was released early 1985.

Some Bizarre offices—we talked about music a lot and we had a lot of common reference points. He really liked the way my records sounded, so that's how it came about. I'd go over to their place and listen to their demos, and I think one or two of the demos ended up on the album untouched. But with other tracks, we took the demos and they transferred them to a twenty-four-track and we put overdubs on them. And then some stuff we started from scratch. So it was a mixture of things. It was an interesting point for them, because their trajectory up until then had been more instrumental. *Scatology* was a mixture of sonic experiments, songs, and even kind of poppy things. So they'd kind of broadened their palate. It's an essential chapter in their history, and although they covered so many different things in their time it's probably one of the corner stones.* And around the same time, we did the 'Tainted Love' single, different sessions but they kind of blur together.

Through Some Bizzare and their sub-label, K.422, Coil are about to release the debut LP. Entitled *Scatology* ('frequent references to excretory processes in literature; study of fossil excrement; gross obscenity', according to the *Penguin English Dictionary*) it's a remarkable record that sees accessibility meet surrealism in an orgy of Emulators, chants, high-technology and low anti-technology. And with the added delights of Clint Ruin and Gavin Friday of the low-lying Virgin Prunes. You can be sure there's something there for every fun-lover. Surely the boys could have managed something more extreme. Is this a bid for the pop market?

DAVID TIBET, *Sounds*, early 1985

GEOFF RUSHTON/JOHN BALANCE *Scatology* was the way we wanted it! Jim Thirlwell was an invaluable collaborator. The sounds were 60 percent made before we asked him to produce it: preconceptions in listeners' ears are easily answered by saying it sounds like Foetus records. We admit that we were looking for a powerful, pulsating sound. The common element of the record is the strength of the sounds. Some Bizzare had nothing to do with the choice. Jim is a friend regardless of the label. We did what we wanted to do. At the moment we can only

* Coil's debut album, *Scatology*, was released on January 28, 1985, on their own Force & Form imprint and distributed by K.422. The first three thousand copies came with an 'Anal Staircase' postcard stuck to the front, while a further two thousand had a 'Sexual Architecture' postcard in its place. The deal with K.422 and Some Bizzare would be the source of much rancour in the following years.

record if we get paid. Some Bizzare will release our next record. They have had some financial problems.

STEVO With Coil, Some Bizarre owned the rights, but the artist had their own ident, which was Force & Form. It was the same for Jim—he wanted the records to come out on Self Immolation—and Test Dept with Ministry of Power. I allowed people to have their freedom of expression. But it doesn't mean I agree with what they did in private.

GAVIN FRIDAY I stayed with them in a little house in north London, which was in the middle of suburbia, although you opened the front door and it was like a different world altogether. Peter was sort of quiet and foreboding, more business-oriented. Whereas Geoff would talk non-stop, be fidgety and precarious. He was really Yin and Yang musically; in that he was in the alternative world but had a real soft spot for pop stuff. He used to love Strawberry Switchblade and Marc Almond's more commercial stuff. He collaborated with everybody—let's just say he put his fingers in everyone's pies.

CHRIS BOHN Coil are a deep immersion band in same the way that Swans are a deep immersion band. Geoff was a fascinating person, always interested in many different areas: psychic, physical, spiritual, and magical. And he investigated them all through a combination of substances, behaviours, and sound. All those aspects he absorbed into his being, and what came out through his mind and body went into these really great records, and Peter had the technical nous to make them sound incredible. Of course, Peter had his own interests—Sleazy by name—which is why the first album was called *Scatology*. So, you have this very strange interest in shit and bodily fluids, which is transformed into an album that takes you places you're not sure you want to go to. But what a fascinating journey it is. The combination, Geoff and Sleazy, two men who were really so close, and people like Jim, Marc and Gavin Friday, created something very unique.

ROB COLLINS Coil were just part of the of the of the look and feel that I wanted to put out in the world. They were confrontational, they weren't traditional, they were electronic. And there was this attitude of, let's dispense with regular bass-guitar-drums philosophy.

CHRIS BOHN At a time when AIDS was still openly—and incorrectly—referred to as a gay plague, Coil took 'Tainted Love' and transformed it into a record that addresses this notion of love as a disease and killing the people you're close to.* Then they released it as a fundraiser for the Terrence Higgins Trust. It was such a powerful statement, especially when combined with the video.

GEOFF RUSHTON/JOHN BALANCE 'Tainted Love' was the most successful song that Some Bizzare ever released, it was on the American charts for the longest time and made the most money, and so it was an unspoken taboo to cover that song— meaning it was the first thing we wanted to do. After we recorded it, we sent a tape to Marc Almond, who promptly got really excited and pushed us to release it.

Coil, the Some Bizzare bad boys of British noise, ever searching for new thresholds of confrontational taboos in an aural assault on the conventional morality of the Western World, have already disposed of S/M, Charles Manson, the Virgin Birth, necrophilia, scatology, Christianity, drug orgasms, Aleister Crowleyism, and gay porn. Coil is succeeding in what Some Bizzare founder Stevo calls 'their uncanny ability to always do the unexpected.' And in seducing and provoking people into dealing with the reality of AIDS, by artfully bringing the devastation of a dreadful disease into the fantasy filled world of music video.

JIM FOURRAT, *Spin*, 1985

GEOFF RUSHTON/JOHN BALANCE We did 'Tainted Love' because it's a good song and we put a new meaning to it, and we wanted to deflate the thing that supposedly makes Some Bizzare great and is an albatross around Marc Almond's neck. So we did everybody a favour by recording it but not just for parody sake, it had a meaning behind it.

TEST DEPT We grew up during the end of the Labour government when there were piles of rubbish in the streets, blackouts were commonplace, and the fabric of society seemed to be breaking down. Under Thatcherism that disintegration continued, although this time driven from the top down and in a more systematic

* Coil's 'Tainted Love' / 'Panic' twelve-inch (FFK 5.12) was released on Thought & Form via K.422 in May 1985.

way, and opinions rapidly became polarised. As our understanding of politics grew, we felt the need to position ourselves collectively, to give ourselves stability against the chaos we saw around us. We came to realise that our way of living was positioned outside of the system, and by the time of the miners' strike we aligned ourselves with a more definite political line, although we refused to align ourselves inside a political camp or join affiliated groups, such as Red Wedge, for instance. We worked directly with those actively involved in struggle.

Shoulder To Shoulder is a remarkable example of the uncommon bonds that can be forged in the face of an uncommon enemy.* It is a souvenir of the only union between mineworkers and steelworkers on tour throughout last winter's discontent. . . . The sympathy of emotion between the contributors compounds resolve, with a well-focused resolution as opposing fragments of the musical sphere follow one after the other and finally unite. . . . *Shoulder To Shoulder* is a timely reminder that some people have not lost sight of their idealism.

TED MICO, *Melody Maker, March 1985*

And this is important: a successful adventure for two unsuspecting cultures, traditions drawn together with inspiring invention, surging forward with spirit. A lasting, essential (new) solidarity. Made with understanding, effort and respect (all profits from this record go to support the miners' strike).

ROBIN GIBSON, *Sounds, March 1985*

The moment when Kent miner Alan Sutcliffe's impassioned speech explodes into Test Dept's *Shockwork* is amongst the most thrilling I have heard. The drama of that split-second crystallises the epochal circumstances of this LP in a flash . . .

MAT SNOW, *NME, March 1985*

>>

GINI BALL I never had an agent—it was always a word-of-mouth thing. I played with This Mortal Coil, Crime & The City Solution, Peter Murphy, loads of people. The first time I worked with Nick Cave was on Anni's solo mini-album, *Kickabye*.

---

* Test Dept and the South Wales Striking Miners Choir's joint album, *Shoulder To Shoulder* (MOP 1), was released in February 1985.

I was so excited about working with Nick, and there was an amazing atmosphere while we did the track 'Vixo'. Marc also sang on one of the songs on *Kickabye*, and I played strings on that too, but 'Vixo' was amazing.* A few years later, Nick asks us to play on *The Mercy Seat*, which was an unbelievable thing to be part of.

ANNI HOGAN I'd started what became the *Kickabye* EP back in '83, while I was staying at Lydia's and working on the backing tracks for The Immaculate Consumptive with Barry and Mick, but I didn't finish it until '85. I loved doing it because it was a chance to spend time in the studio, but Jessamy was a big a reason for it coming out—she wrote most of the lyrics and really encouraged me. I was very shy, but I wasn't hiding behind the guests as much as they were the friends I was hanging around with. But I did play it down a hell of a lot, and I was almost embarrassed that Nick, Marc, Jim, and Budgie were happy to be on it, and that Richard and Mal wanted to put it out.

STEPHEN 'MAL' MALLINDER Doublevision was intended as a video label—that was the whole point of it really—but then we wanted to bring out complementary records, soundtracks, and stuff. And then it became a bit of an outlet really for records made by friends or artists we admired.

ANNI HOGAN I was really happy for *Kickabye* to come out on Doublevision, but you'd think Stevo might have at least offered to release it on Some Bizzare. I don't know why he didn't. Stevo was pretty confused by me, I think. The whole thing was like a game to him.

>>

MARK CHUNG To be fair, Gareth Jones deserves the credit for 'Yü-Gung'.† We always liked using other sounds rather than normal instruments, not least because we weren't very good at playing normal instruments. Gareth had a state-of-the-art AMS sampler—you couldn't pitch it, but you could move the timing and

---

* *Annie Hogan Plays 'Kickabye'* (DVR9) was released by Doublevision in April 1985. Its five tracks were recorded between 1983 and 1985 and feature guest appearances from Marc Almond, Nick Cave, J.G. Thirlwell, and Budgie from Siouxsie & The Banshees.
† Einstürzende Neubauten's 'Yü-Gung' twelve-inch (BART 12) was released by Some Bizzare on March 11, 1985. Gareth Jones's AMS sampler would become a massive bone of contention for Some Bizzare and Mute Records in later years.

build rhythm tracks on the computer. I think he'd been using it with Depeche Mode, and although 'Yü-Gung' existed previously and we'd been playing it live, the machine *rigueur* came from him. We had quite a long discussion about that track because Blixa didn't like being made to sing to a machine. The rest of us thought it was great and something we should absolutely do, but Blixa was, 'I can't sing to this, it's too regular!' It ended up as quite a big argument in the band and Gareth had to do what good producers do. In this case, take Blixa for a walk and talk to him. I suspect Gareth got him to give it a genuine try on the basis that he guaranteed it would not be used if he was not happy with the end result. Anyway, when they came back, Blixa sang on it, and everything was cool.

JESSAMY CALKIN I was working at *Tatler* when I did the Neubauten tour in May 1985. They gave me a sabbatical so I could do it, as it went all over Europe, Japan, and the US. While they were easier to handle as people than the Bad Seeds, a lot of their instruments were stuff they picked up from scrap-metal yards, and they kept adding bits that they wanted to take on to the next concert. We'd turn up at airports with pieces of really lethal looking scrap metal to go in the hold, and obviously the airlines were worried it was going to cut up people's Gucci suitcases. While I was dealing with that, the band would disappear one by one to go off to get pissed, so I then had to round them up and get them on the plane.

STEVO I was with Neubauten once when they were playing in America. It was at JFK airport, waiting at the luggage carousel, and the conveyor belts are coming around, and there's a pneumatic drill coming through, a chainsaw, bits of metal. All the other passengers are looking at each other and I'm just laughing.

MARK CHUNG Playing live was a bit dangerous. It wasn't so much conceptual, but Mufti is obviously somebody that doesn't think twice if he's inspired, and he was working with quite big heavy metal shit that could just come down beside you. We always thought it was good because it kept you on your toes—it was kind of the mental state we were looking for, a heightened awareness. The aim was to get ourselves to a point where it was just about the music and there was nothing else. But there were injuries. At some college gig in Kansas, we looked around and said, 'Where's Mufti?' And he was in hospital! During a song he'd gashed open his arm or leg and had a big bleeding flesh wound, so Jessamy had taken him to hospital.

Because of the smoke and the noise and the chaos, none of us had noticed. We were always looking for a transcending moment, and it's quite fascinating why that happens and also why it doesn't happen. You cannot switch it on and off. We were always looking for ways to get to that point, how to trigger it, and definitely a routine approach was not a good way to do it from our perspective, which is why we tried not to repeat stuff.

JESSAMY CALKIN I was tour managing when they set fire to the stage at Danceteria, which made things really fucking awkward for me. It was at the beginning of the tour, which affected the other concerts, because promotors and venues were worried that it was going to happen again. It was rather amazing, though, and funny. Andrew knew what he was doing. It was an evening I'll never forget.

Although Andrew was responsible for the fires, they all planned it. I couldn't know about it though as I was the one who had to sort out all the contracts and the insurance and the mess afterward. But actually it was good that I didn't know because I could convincingly plead ignorance with the promoters.

MARK CHUNG Andrew had this habit of setting things on fire. Blixa hated it, but Andrew wouldn't stop doing it. He was rebelling in some kind of way. He would smuggle in a canister of petrol and at some point, when he felt like it, he'd wander across the stage and pour the petrol somewhere and throw in a match. Often we would only notice when it suddenly got really hot onstage. And Blixa would turn around, furious, and shout, 'Andrew! Stop!' I quite enjoyed the undeniable impact open, uncontrolled fire in a closed space immediately has on the surroundings, but after a while, Blixa was so harsh on Andrew that I tried to moderate and quietly encouraged Andrew to keep it up from time to time. In America the promoters were really nervous about it because the venues usually have a direct line to the Fire Department, so if there's smoke in the venue, the Fire Department gets called out and they get a big bill. Also, a lot of theatres have a metal fire curtain, which comes down when there's smoke, and we always thought it would be great if we could get it to come down while we were playing. We just needed to decide which side of the metal curtain we wanted to be on. We never managed it, though.

JESSAMY CALKIN Neubauten wanted the PA to be 10kW, and it was always in the contract. I'd check with the venue beforehand, but we'd get there and it wasn't anywhere near loud enough. The venue didn't understand it wasn't just about volume—they'd say, 'Oh, we had Iron Maiden here last month and it was fine.' And then Blixa would refuse to play, and I'd have to sort that out. He did that a lot, and then the band wouldn't get paid. And I was responsible for paying all the crew and the sound people, so I was in a really difficult position.

MARK CHUNG Neubauten weren't really popstars in Japan, but it was certainly different by our standards. We were playing large venues and we had very well informed and quite excitable fans. The audience was a lot younger, too—a lot of girls, a lot of screaming and being chased at the airport, which we really weren't used to. That was quite an experience.

JESSAMY CALKIN I never really saw myself as a professional tour manager, and I certainly wouldn't have done it for any bands that weren't my friends. I was also freelancing for music magazines, but I wasn't really a journalist then either. I just think of it as a garish and fun time where I made friendships that I still have. I didn't go to university or anything, so that kind of felt like my education. Those years were the most intense period of my life, but in a way that was really inspiring. A lot of it was really difficult, and a lot of people died and whatever, but it was such a creative time, and an incredibly vivid and formative period of my life.

MICHAEL GIRA Jessamy was going to meet Francis Bacon to do an interview with him, and she asked if I wanted to come along. Bacon was a god to me—I just completely admired his painting and everything about him. And I was so fucking intimidated by the thought of meeting him, I didn't go out of some kind of self-deprecating timidity. It's one of the biggest regrets in my life.

STEPHEN 'MAL' MALLINDER With *Drinking Gasoline* we wanted to tie it in as a Virgin release because it meant we'd get some budget from them to make videos to accompany it.* If we'd have released it on Doublevsion it would've been me and Kirky and a Super 8, but because we went with Virgin we could get Pete involved and film it on 16mm. And that's what became *Gasoline In Your Eye*. We

---

* Cabaret Voltaire's *Drinking Gasoline* (CVM 1) was released on Some Bizzare/Virgin on July 22, 1985.

also saw them less as abstracted, arty pieces and more clips for clubby tracks that we could use with the TV screens onstage. That the montage stuff was hit and miss live was intentional, because we didn't do the same set every night. The film stayed the same, so sometimes it would sync up and sometimes it wouldn't. The inspiration for the visuals was as much Andy Warhol's Exploding Plastic Inevitable and certainly the psychedelic side of things. We also brought in a kind of political eighties post-punk world, using our reality rather than referencing the sixties, but the effect was the same, and it was designed as such.

>>

J.G. THIRLWELL Wiseblood started originally as a project for four drummers and voice, and the first drummer I wanted to ask was Roli Mosimann, who was playing in Swans at the time. I checked in with Michael to see if he'd mind if I approached Roli and he said, 'No, go ahead.' So I met up with Roli and we talked about this idea. He was setting up a studio in his loft in Tribeca, so we started messing around, and it just went in a different direction and just ended up just being the two of us. It was appealing as a way to do something outside the solo atmosphere of Foetus, where I played all the instruments and called all the shots, and it was a good way to get some other ideas out of my system. The first iteration was called Foetus Flesh, and we opened up for Test Dept at the Ritz under that name, but eventually we settled on Wiseblood and it developed into its own thing.[*]

ZEKE MANYIKA I don't remember the St Anne's Court office as a lot of the business was done in Stevo's house in Hammersmith, where the living room was basically an office. When he sold that, he bought the New Cavendish Street place. Stevo had the flat at the top, then there were the Some Bizzare offices, and he had an art gallery on the ground floor. He was putting on exhibitions by young artists years before the YBAs became a massive thing. Stevo was there right at the beginning of that, and he doesn't get any credit for it at all. It's incredible, really. Around the same time, I made my first solo album, and it was actually kind of an accidental record. Orange Juice had just become the two of us, and the relationship with Polydor had become so toxic, particularly with Edwyn. So, Polydor said to me, do you want to do an album? I told them I wasn't ready, but the thing was there was a

* The first Wiseblood twelve-inch, 'Motorslug' (WISE 112), was released on K.422 in May 1985.

220

load of studio time and budget for a new Orange Juice album that was just going to go waste. So, I thought it was a good learning opportunity and I could just go mental without any expectations. So, I got Dave Ball, Anni, Edwyn, Dave Gregory from XTC, all the girls from Amazulu, Thomas Leer, Dennis Bovell involved, and I just wanted to learn the craft in being in charge of a project. It wasn't on Some Bizzare, but it was a template for stuff I did in the future.*

CHRIS BOHN I happened to be in Berlin when Neubauten were making *Halber Mensch.*[†] Coincidentally, Sonic Youth were playing at a venue called Sputnik. On the way to the gig, I stopped off at Tritonus Studios, where Neubauten were recording, to speak to Blixa for a piece I was writing for some magazine or other. They were working on the title track, an a cappella piece that necessitated recording a few different vocalists. They had some great singers from the German alternative scene coming to record their parts, including Ma Gita, who'd played in Abwärt with Mark Chung. When I arrived, she'd already been there for hours and was getting kind of annoyed with the whole process. So I cut my losses and went to see Sonic Youth, and then went back to the studio after the gig, and they were still working on the same part of the same song and had been the whole time. Tritonus wasn't a cheap studio, so you can imagine the cost.

MARK CHUNG We didn't really think too much about the positive press coverage, frankly. Obviously, as a musician, you're always happy if somebody likes your record, but you also know that just as often somebody is going to think it's shit, so I think most musicians learn to have a mental distance to that. You always appreciate people who appreciate your work, and we did feel that we were giving it our best and if somebody liked it, great. We'd often be on the bill at some festival, and within the first minute, two-thirds of the audience would leave, but the third that stayed were cool and we got along and had fun with them. We liked that separation, so, in that sense, we always knew there were people who appreciated us. And we always knew other people hated it and thought, *What the fuck is this?*

---

* Zeke Manyika's debut solo album, *Call & Response* (ZMLP 1), may not have been a Some Bizzare record (it came out on Polydor in 1985), but Andy 'Dog' Johnson's cover art certainly made it look like one.
† Einstürzende Neubauten's *Halber Mensch* (BART 331) was released on September 2, 1985, on Some Bizzare. Initial copies came with a free seven-inch.

CHRIS BOHN *Halber Mensch* cost an absolute fortune to make. Gareth Jones was working with them and really enjoying himself. 'Das Schaben', which is a nine-minute extension of 'Der Tod Ist Ein Dandy', was in many ways the peak of Some Bizzare. It's an incredible piece of music that took a long time to make and cost a lot of money, but the result is extraordinary. Would Neubauten have been able to make *Halber Mensch* without Stevo? Well, yes, they'd have made something, and it would have been different and equally as strong, but it would not have sounded so fantastic. But then suddenly Neubauten were in massive debt, so they made their next record much more quickly and cheaply. Then Stevo could no longer pull that kind of money from the major labels, and, with all the advances gone, suddenly everybody is going hungry and then that's when relationships started to break down between the artists and Some Bizzare. So Stevo, with the best of intentions but not the best economic management, had created this circumstance where incredible groundbreaking records were being made, very silly things were happening in the name of marketing, yet no one was making any money.

KEVIN FOAKES Some Bizzare was like a badge of quality but also of an alternative, left-field attitude. It wasn't for the faint of heart and definitely wasn't for everybody. It certainly wasn't commercially minded in the traditional sense, but you'd know that if Some Bizzare was on the sleeve of a record it was probably worth investigating, if you were that way inclined. Like all the best labels, not everything was good, but there was an intent behind every release, and that intent wasn't purely commercial. The most important thing was to make an interesting record.

MATT JOHNSON I worked with Paul Hardiman on 'Flesh & Bones', which had probably been intended as the start of my next album but ended up on the second Some Bizzare compilation, *If You Can't Please Yourself You Can't, Please Your Soul.*＊ That track is a bit of a lost classic, really, and more should have been made of it. Sadly, it was the last thing Paul and I did together because Paul's manager and Stevo had a very bad falling out over a business matter. And seeing as Paul's

＊ The second Some Bizzare compilation album, *If You Can't Please Yourself You Can't, Please Your Soul* (EJ 26 0663 1), was released via EMI and featured new material from the label's current roster, including Foetus, Cabaret Voltaire, Test Dept, Marc Almond, THE THE, Coil, and Einstürzende Neubauten. Psychic TV were also on the album, despite having left the label, and Yello and Virginia Astley also had tracks included, despite not being Some Bizzare artists.

manager is also his wife, it made it impossible for he and I to work together on the next album. Which was a real shame because I really liked and respected him, and we worked very well together. He's a brilliant engineer, and I would've loved working with him on the follow-up to *Soul Mining*.

IAN TREGONING Stevo was a big champion of Yello, so when he asked if we could give him a track for the *If You Can't Please Yourself You Can't, Please Your Soul* compilation he was putting together, we said yes as favour for his enthusiasm. We did an edit from the *Live At The Roxy* video, but the album came out in this disgusting sleeve and we never got paid for it. I don't think anyone did. That was the real unseating of Stevo. He had all this amazing talent that still shines a beacon from all those years ago—Soft Cell, Matt, Neubauten, Foetus—and they were all in this sort of battle together, but none of the artists seemed to make any money.

GEOFF RUSHTON/JOHN BALANCE There's only one thing that we did that I could ever say was a pop song, called 'The Wheel'. That was supposed to be the first thing we ever did, and it was, but Stevo [took] two years to release it on a Some Bizzare compilation album. That's a pop song—it's like early Wire or something. It's much more poppy, and I did one vocal out of tune, Syd Barretty, and we just left it at that because we're not that interested in what will happen to it.

KEVIN FOAKES From a design perspective, the packaging on *If You Can't Please Yourself You Can't, Please Your Soul* was very strong, and the insert that featured the different artists was totally Dadaist. You got the sense it was telling you something important, even if it wasn't clear what that was. That's what I loved about record labels like Some Bizzare, they seem to create a world of their own. And those worlds ended up crossing over into the mainstream for a little bit, here and there. They would touch the surface of the charts but they didn't dilute the formula or talk down to the audience to do so, which is still pretty unusual.

CHRIS BOHN Because of his background, Stevo was fundamentally a lad—a very strange lad but a lad, nonetheless. And those aspects of his personality cast a long shadow over Some Bizzare. All the artists he signed to the label in the 80s were male, there were no women. Because he was very young when he started, he got away with a lot, but that is no excuse.

MATT JOHNSON I didn't really think about it at the time, as there were always women around—Jane, Anni, Gini, Anne, plus many girlfriends and partners—so numbers-wise it always seemed equal, but yeah, there were no female artists. Virginia Astley had a track on *If You Can't Please Yourself You Can't, Please Your Soul*, but she didn't do anything else for Some Bizzare after that. But the label didn't feel sexist or macho because there were always strong-minded women around. Jane certainly didn't put up with any nonsense.

ROB COLLINS In terms of the office, it was 50/50 male/female. It was totally equal, and who would have thought such a thing back then, especially in the record industry?

STEVO There were plenty of women involved in Some Bizzare in the 80s, they just weren't the artists. If you went to see Psychic TV or Neubauten, 98 percent of the audience was male, that's just a fact. I mean, literally, 2 percent would be female, and they would look like men. It was hardcore.

ALAURA O'DELL Whatever creativity was going on at that time, I feel that, as a woman looking back, it was the same old same old. It was still the patriarchy, the men were calling all the shots, although under this umbrella of, *We're artists therefore we're interesting*. Yet it was still the white-male narrative. So, for me, the lens that I saw it then and the lens I see it now are very different. Today, I'm all about shifting the paradigm and dismantling the patriarchy.

GINI BALL Stevo was a bit of a joker and used to call everyone 'Perk', and then he used to come out with things like, 'Behind every man is a great woman, and behind every great woman is a great behind!' I don't think anybody else would have got away with it. I know he could be really not very nice at times, but I didn't experience that. I just remember the silly side.

IAN TREGONING Yello got a £3,000 promo budget and Stevo said, 'What the fuck's that? That's just a big lunch—let's stick it on a horse!' The thinking being, we'd get so much publicity it didn't matter if it came in last. Stevo was full of ideas like that.

>>

224

BEVERLEY GLICK I didn't really mix with any of what I call the slightly darker end of the spectrum. I was very aware of Genesis but was slightly spooked by him. And Sleazy spooked me even more in a way. Genesis was more obviously weird, but Sleazy was weird in a quiet way, and I was told some stories about him that made me feel like I didn't want to be left on my own with him. There were some very interesting characters wafting around that I didn't really get involved with because by that time I'd moved on to *Record Mirror*, and it was all about chart music there.

ZEKE MANYIKA The place in Hammersmith just got too intense for Stevo. It was so easy to forget he was the manager, as he was so very young. He was younger than everybody and he was still growing up. And there was no separation between his home and his work. He used to love it when I came back from tour, and it was just the two of us having a laugh because it had nothing to do with Some Bizzare. The house was supposed to be an escape for him, but people would just turn up literally any time, day or night. It got a bit more intense when Genesis was around—he brought these hardcore guys with him, and it could get a bit scary.

MATT JOHNSON Stevo's house became very, very intense. Zeke and Jane lived there, and even Marc was living there at one point. Stevo used to have parties all the time, and many of the bands would be there, hanging out together and sleeping over, bodies collapsed all over the house. He had these huge speakers installed and eventually removed the toilet door—to make it less comfortable for those people he didn't like! And he was always doing these psychic experiments with this little electronic device, like a Magic 8-Ball, and he became quite skilful at predicting things, particularly when he was high. You could say it was nonsense, but some of his predictions were peculiarly—and consistently—accurate. Things got stranger still when me, Stevo, and Zeke tried to see if we could live nocturnally. We'd sleep all day and stay up all night, going out for walks across the city when everywhere was deserted. In those days, London didn't really have a night-time economy, so virtually everything shut at 10:30–11pm. I think we did it for about four or five days and it was quite an interesting mind experiment.

I don't know whether the Temple Ov Psychick Youth coming round all the time started to bother Stevo. We all knew and got on well with Gen and Paula, and Sleazy and Geoff, but the outer circle was basically a cult, and they all started

225

showing up uninvited. I think Stevo eventually did get fed up with it, but it wasn't in his nature to tell people to get out.

JANE ROLINK I never really picked up on any trouble with the Psychick Youth lot, but one time they were round, and Gen's dog came into my room and ate a load of chocolate laxatives, a whole box. I don't know the outcome, I never asked, and they never said, but it would have been mayhem! I can only guess, because they were all into various bodily substances and stuff, it didn't bother them too much!

ZEKE MANYIKA The weird videos that Genesis and Sleazy were making started to freak Stevo out, and his behaviour became quite intolerable. Instead of having a sensible discussion about boundaries, he started doing extreme things to put people off coming around, including taking the toilet door off to make people feel uncomfortable. So Jane and I got a flat together off the Edgware Road.

DAVE BALL Stevo's place was in a nice street and had about three or four bedrooms. It would be worth a fortune now. And it was nice for a while, before it went completely downhill. People would go around there all the time—it was like a speakeasy. You'd get the more credible people from the music industry, like Nick Cave, Neubauten, Genesis P-Orridge, Edwyn Collins, all sitting around talking about what they were doing and making plans. It was quite the community, everyone relaxed and chilled, being amicable and getting to know each other. There was no professional jealousy or anything because no one was stepping on anyone else's toes. But it just got more and more crazy the more drugs that Stevo took, and he became unpredictable. He was a heavy weed smoker, and he used to get paranoid. He used to play 'Get Out of My House' by Foetus at full volume, literally ear-splitting, when he wanted people to leave. Everyone got fed up with it in the end and stopped going 'round.

JANE ROLINK Stevo used to drink too much, and it could be hard work, but we used to look after each other. And we did have legendary parties where everybody came 'round. I can't even think about the neighbours, the poor buggers—it was so loud, ridiculously loud. It got a bit much at times and Stevo could be a handful. He was funny, though, because one minute he wanted us all there and then the next minute he didn't. It was like, *Make your mind up!*

ZEKE MANYIKA When I moved in with Jane to the flat on Edgware Road, every Friday people would come over, like Jimmy Sommerville, Mal from Cabaret Voltaire, and Marc with all his Willing Sinners. One of the funniest ones was, I came back from an Orange Juice tour about 3am, absolutely fucked, desperate for my own bed. I got dropped off, and I'm carrying my bags into the flat, get to my room, open the door and, fucking hell, the stench! In my single bed, three black-leather-clad bodies sleeping head-to-toe. Blixa, Nick Cave, and Jim. God knows what dark club they'd been to. So, I just picked up my bags again and went to a hotel down the road.

JANE ROLINK That's how it was—they all needed somewhere to stay so all round to mine! It was a madhouse, honestly. It was brilliant, a great little flat. I remember we had Neubauten round for dinner one night, it was only a tiny two-bedroomed flat and there were about twelve of us in there. And the downstairs neighbours came around because the ceiling was bowing because it was so heavy with people and asked, could we please stop making such a noise? And we were like, 'Fook off!' And Diamanda Galas as well, I used to knock about with her—she was fantastic.

ZEKE MANYIKA Jane was really important, not just as a secretary but because she had very good ears. All the bands used to come to our flat to play her mixes to see what she thought. She had that Yorkshire attitude. Some guys in LA had done a mix of one of my songs, and I wasn't sure if was good enough, so I played it to Jane and she said, 'Oh, Zeke, it's fooking shite!' But she was like that with everyone, it didn't matter who it was—Marc or whoever.

The single 'Stories Of Johnny' was merely a taster to prepare the way for a fuller yet softer sound. The rasping bitterness that made so much of his earlier work so difficult to live with has subsided somewhere along the line, the warmer more mellow side of Marc Almond has at long last been fully allowed to come out from under the covers.[*]

NANCY CULP, *Record Mirror*, September 1985

* Marc Almond's first single for his new label Virgin was 'Stories Of Johnny' (BONK 1), which was released on August 12, 1985, and reached no.23 on the UK chart. The album of the same name (FAITH 1) followed in September and reached no.22.

227

ANNI HOGAN Going on *Wogan* was a nightmare—not Terry, but the kids, the Westminster Boys choir. Martin and I were left to deal with them, and they were just running around, of course, because they were young lads. Absolute nightmare. And I remember everybody laughing because they were on *Wogan* with Marc— you know, *tee-hee-hee* sort of thing.

MARC ALMOND Somebody had the bright idea that I should appear on Terry Wogan's early-evening show singing 'Stories Of Johnny', but with a different twist to it. An alternative version of the song was recorded, and I had to sing with a school choir of thirty children, a twelve-year-old alto taking the lead with me.

Now, bear in mind the song was a tale of heroin addiction . . . but the record company said they wanted the choral version as they felt that children accompanying my performance would appeal to the teatime family audience. There was just one snag: right in the middle of this choir of scrubbed angelic children was going to be me.

ANNI HOGAN With *Vermin In Ermine* and *Stories Of Johnny*, Marc was trying to please everybody. It's not like there's some roadmap; he had phenomenal success with Soft Cell, and he'd done the Mambas thing, so the record company then wanted Marc Almond solo hit records. And that is an enormous pressure, especially when you've already taken the money. Until you've been in that situation, you just don't realise what that actually means. I think he was just trying to do something well and be successful. People love those albums, and they're part of Marc's creative arc, but he obviously felt much more himself when he did *Mother Fist*, because he wasn't allowing the record company to control him so much. You know, creativity and money, do they go together ever really?

J.G. THIRLWELL Like most concept albums, *Nail* didn't start off as one, but as the songs started to emerge, I noticed that there was this leitmotif of oppression running through them.* One is set in a concentration camp, a couple are about serial killers, another is about the suffocation of being in Los Angeles. And the last

* Scraping Foetus Off The Wheel's *Nail* (WOMB FIP 4) was released on Self Immolation/Some Bizzare in October 1985.

track on the album, 'Anything', rejects all of the oppression by declaring, 'I can do any goddamn thing I want!' The bombastic ending of the song was kind of influenced by Prince. Lydia and I were living in Spanish Harlem on 109th Street, and the downstairs neighbour would play 'Let's Go Crazy' when he got home from work, really loud, just that one song. I guess that was his jam at the time. The end of that song would thunder up through the floorboards, and I got a sense of the person below getting some kind of release from whatever oppression he was feeling. So I stole that ending.

WARNE LIVESEY Jim always had copious amounts of notes. Every day he'd take a rough mix of the track we were working on home, and the next day come in with even more notes. We were working really, really long hours—I was only getting four or five hours sleep a night—so I was always surprised when he'd come in with at least two hours' worth of analysis of what he wants to do to the track. Obviously, there was a certain amount of enhancement, but it was still driven by the fact he just had this intensity where he wanted to work every hour he possibly could. On later albums, we actually had to use Charles Grey as a second engineer because Jim would work all day if he could. I think we mixed *Nail* in a week—luckily we didn't kill ourselves.

Positive negativism, he says. OK, let's jump in the deep end pretending it's shallow. Ah, we have a mouthful of water. What else? Pigs. Cry. Agony. Cocks. Destroy. Tracheotomy. Stab. Isolation. Heart. Glory. Zap! Drop Out. Justice and vengeance. I can do any goddam thing I want—*anything! Power!* Seems like a nice boy. Is it alright if I approve of this record more than I enjoy it?

CHRIS ROBERTS, *Sounds*, November 23, 1985

J.G. THIRLWELL I'd decided to play live to promote *Nail*, but without a band. I was very performative, but because I was the only person onstage, I wanted there to be a visual foil. I created an atmosphere with ACL lights, some pointing into the audience and some pointing dramatically up at me, and tons and tons of smoke. I did a pretty short set, thirty to forty minutes. It worked because somehow I was able to fill up the stage using lights and smoke, and the music was thunderous. It was good to get out there, but I didn't want to perform that way for too long. It got to a certain point where I wanted to have more of a live element to it.

Despite laryngitis that reduced his vocals to a raspy growl, the London-based New Zealander [sic] put on a hypnotic and physically exhausting display of emotional anguish, detailing the malingering maladies of a distorted world. In the best Iggy Pop tradition, he often moved into the audience when not crawling, twisting, and gyrating about the stage. Even in the midst of his most brutal frenzies, Thirlwell can appear sensitive, haunted or delicate. The result was a one-man psychodrama that resembled an LSD-soaked Broadway musical.

CRAIG LEE, *Los Angeles Times*, March 11, 1985

J.G. THIRLWELL The idea for the pigs' heads onstage came from a photo session I did with Peter Anderson for the *Nail* album. I wanted to reference Stallone's *Rambo* and *Lord Of The Flies*, so he went out and got all these pig heads from a butcher, and we set this up this scenario where I had a machine gun and I was wrapped in bandages with these pig heads on spikes in the background. Peter's dedication to creating stunning photos was amazing. So when I went out on tour, I would put the pig heads on the rider. So, it would be a bottle of vodka, a bottle of Jägermeister, and six freshly slaughtered pigs' heads. Some venues were more obliging than others—some places would hang them for me, other places I'd have to hang them myself. In Minneapolis, a butcher actually came and hung them up, and then stayed and watched the show, standing there proudly in his blood covered apron. Normally I would just leave them up there, but one night I took one down and was kind of humping it, and a guy in the audience grabbed it by the snout and took a big bite out of it. Which is instant trichinosis, really.

WARNE LIVESEY Jim really embraced the fact that there very few limitations when it came to creating the sounds that he had in his head. He had copious notes, in esoteric emotional language rather than musical language, but he communicated his ideas very well, enough for me to figure out the technical requirements to achieve it. Everything I did with Jim was on twenty-four-track, and, as he wanted to play everything himself, it was going to use a lot of tracks. There was an element of a kid in a candy store, and for me, too, as I was just starting out as producer, and being in those studios using Fairlights was a great exploration.

J.G. THIRLWELL The nuts-and-bolts of running the day-to-day stuff at Some Bizzare was done by Rob and Jane, while Stevo got on with just being Stevo. I had the freedom to say, 'This is what I'm doing,' and it would get done. I had this idea of releasing an empty box to put the three twelve-inches and *Nail* album in, and the label were like, 'Great idea—let's put a T-shirt in there, too.' Hence the *Foetus Of Excellence* box. And that seemed normal—it wouldn't be so easy to do something like that now.

If only more releases were given such lavish care in their creation as this one. And what a brainwave! Just what every twentieth-century boy or girl needs, a box to store their precious Foetus records in away from nuclear war's harm. And what an heirloom to hand over to the next brat generation, a box full of violence ready to go off. To wipe the baby brains off the wallpaper there's also a rather cheap Foetus of Excellence T-shirt enclosed. Alternatively, you can wear it to show the world that you paid up for a box full of air. Consumerism. Don'tcha just love it?

EDWIN POUNCEY, *Sounds*, November 1985

>>

STEPHEN 'MAL' MALLINDER We went back to basics for *The Covenant, The Sword, And The Arm Of The Lord* and did it all at Western Works. We'd invested in gear and could apply what we'd learnt from the previous two albums and working in other studios so were quite happy to make a more homegrown record. Plus, as it was the final record of the contract, there maybe wasn't the budget for doing a big mix at that point. But honestly, it's my favourite Cabs album. After the stuff we we'd done with Flood, working at Sarm and getting in big-name remixers, it was really nice to get back just me and Rich. And we were really happy with that record, even if it's a bit rough and raw. We thought of it as a natural summation of everything we done up to that point. We were aware that it was the last record for Virgin and that they weren't exactly breathing down our necks to re-sign us, so it was the end of a cycle as far as we were concerned.*

I think we achieved everything we wanted to from the relationship with Some Bizzare. It was an opportunity to go down a different path, and we took it. Stevo was a catalyst—we probably wouldn't have gone and negotiated a deal with

---

* Cabaret Voltaire's third and final album with Some Bizzare, *The Covenant, The Sword, And The Arm Of The Lord* (CV 3), was released via Virgin on October 13, 1985. It reached no.57 on the UK chart.

Virgin, for example—so it helped us get a bit further along, although we didn't overthink it.

BEVERLEY GLICK At the beginning, at least, Stevo was passionate about the music. But even after all the success, he was still an outsider, and he played on that—he was a complete maverick and a provocateur, even though he wouldn't have used that language. He just did what he wanted to wind people up, and he did it very successfully. He was aware that no one took him seriously, but then he always used to say he didn't take the music business seriously either. He thought 99.9 percent of the industry was comprised of shits, and he would only work with people he liked.

With danger comes pleasure.

Ø, from the sleeve of *If You Can't Please Yourself You Can't, Please Your Soul* (1985)

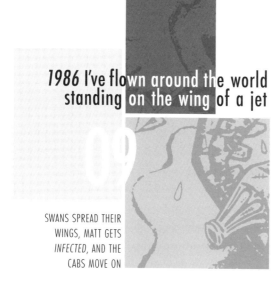

1986 I've flown around the world standing on the wing of a jet

SWANS SPREAD THEIR WINGS, MATT GETS INFECTED, AND THE CABS MOVE ON

MICHAEL GIRA I had no idea what I wanted to get out of the relationship with Some Bizzare. I just wanted to eat. And through the good graces of Jim, I was provided with a venue where I could continue to make music and magically get paid at least a small sum. And that was one step along the way of continuing to have a musical career, and that was great. The association with the other artists, of course, did not hurt at all, and I'm grateful for that. We'd met Neubauten in New York and I loved them—I thought they were great. And Jim, too. Even Soft Cell, who really had nothing to do with us at all but were great in their own way. We were all so different, but there was some kind of common approach toward sitting in opposition to consumerist society, and that made sense. I also liked Cabaret Voltaire and Psychic TV; Genesis was a long-term hero of mine even in the early days. There was definitely a feeling of affinity for a lot of those groups, for sure.

Swans was always my band, but I had to defer to other people. I wanted it to be this kind of collaboration, but it never really was that way. People, of course, contributed greatly, Norman [Westberg, guitar] in particular, but when Roli [Mosimann, drums] and Harry [Crosby, bass] left, I decided that I had to take charge as a producer and figure out how to do it. And, you know, if people come and go, that's got to be OK. I'll pull it together somehow. So that's when Swans became whoever the hell I decided, or what circumstances provided it to be. And that's been the mode ever since.

KARL O'CONNOR I bought *Cop* by Swans completely on spec. I found it impenetrable at first, but I knew it was important—the artwork communicated that. I remember putting it on and thinking I'd got it on the wrong speed. I didn't know if I liked it, but one thing I did know was it was fucking heavy and I might need a bit of time with it. It sat at the front of my collection on my bedroom floor for months, but gradually the message was decoded. And when you get it, you fucking get it. All the scales fell from my eyes, and I thought, *Jesus Christ, this man is singing about the life he's actually living*, and the music was the perfect shroud around him. I believed in Swans—they were the real fucking deal, on every level. For some reason, I always had an aversion to bands with that traditional rock line-ups, until I heard Swans. They showed what could be done within that format, and put everyone else to shame really.

MICHAEL GIRA I was a huge admirer of John Cale's productions and his solo records. There was a tendency at the time in independent music for the vocals to be buried in the music. I don't know why, and I don't know that I intentionally did that. But Cale really heard that in *Cop* and the *Young God* EP, and he told me, 'The kids need something to grab on to!' He was definitely right, I mean, can you imagine listening to a Dylan record and the vocals are buried? What's the point? If I'm going to write words that I think have some meaning, and I think I can sing, why am I putting it back inside the music. It didn't make sense. Jarboe encouraged me greatly to learn to extend notes and be more musical in my singing, rather than shouting and declaiming.

JARBOE I moved to NYC because I wanted to be in Swans. I brought my skills, and those skills were utilised the entire time I worked with Michael. I was in the recording studio in Switzerland, outside the vocal booth, when Michael was recording his vocals for *Greed*, and I heard what he was doing and I suggested he hold notes and bend them down instead of only shouting the lyrics. I talked to him about singing deeply from his core and not his throat.[*]

MICHAEL GIRA The volume felt right in the live situation. The guitars resonated correctly at that volume, and the way the bass was played in Swans in those days,

---

[*] Swans' *Greed* LP (KCC 2) was released by K.422 on February 28, 1986.

these dissonant, thudding chords which were meant to impact on your solar plexus, wouldn't have sounded right at a low volume. So, everything was about the experience of being inside the music and being pummelled by it. And I'm talking about us—not the audience necessarily, but the band, and how we respond to that. The things that I did onstage started out very simple but gradually, as the tour progressed, it became more elaborate.* But it was just what felt right—it wasn't planned, it was an authentic reaction to the music and helped us reach whatever mental state we were going toward. It wasn't some kind of brutalist aggression. It had to do with very high ideals, actually.

ROB COLLINS When it came to *Greed* and *Holy Money*, we got involved a little bit in terms of the production and who they worked with for remixes.† But with Jim and Roli for Wiseblood, no, what they gave us was it. Yeah, it was finished. Wiseblood was a little bit more direct and darker, and I think that was Roli's influence as much as Jim's.

MICHAEL GIRA I don't remember if it was Rob, but someone at the label suggested doing these dance mixes. I don't dance, I've never even been to a fucking disco, so I don't even know anything about it. But I thought, *Well, sure, we'll try that.* Music is sound, you know. *Let's try arranging these sounds in this way and see if it works.* I don't know how successful it was.

JARBOE The whole foray into industrial dance music—'Time Is Money', 'A Screw', 'Money Is Flesh'—that came from me.‡ The clubs had these big sound systems, and it was something that was happening at the time that resulted in those singles, which were very exciting: they had this intense club drum sound. We walked into the Palladium on 14th Street—a huge disco on different levels in an old movie theatre with balconies way up high, people dancing in suspended cages. MTV filmed there for a while. Michael and I were going up the ramp to the main dance floor, and 'Time Is Money' was echoing through the massive venue. It was exciting

---

* Swans played a small UK tour in February 1986 that included a show at the ULU in London and, in Manchester, a Some Bizzare night at the Hacienda, which promised 'never-before-seen exclusive videos of Some Bizzare bands'.
† Swans' *Holy Money* mini-LP (KCC 3) was released by K.422 on March 27, 1986.
‡ Swans' 'Time Is Money (Bastard)' twelve-inch (KDE 212) was released by K.422 on January 31, 1986. The 'A Screw' twelve-inch followed on September 1.

to hear that. I told him at the time, 'This is the best thing I've ever heard!'

MICHAEL GIRA There was the necessity to just keep putting shit out to make a living. And I think Rob encouraged us to release *Public Castration Is A Good Idea* to make some extra money, as well as capture the band at that time.* I can't listen to it now, but I think it does present a clear picture of what was going on musically then. A big part of that record is the ULU show in London. I don't remember the show per se, but I remember it being a moment where I thought, *Wow, that was amazing.* I was completely enthralled by being a musician and just felt so privileged to be able to do something like that. And the T-shirt design was inspired by Frankie Goes To Hollywood shirts that were around at the time. They had 'Relax, Don't Do It', we had *Public Castration Is A Good Idea*.

STEPHEN 'MAL' MALLINDER I don't really know what triggered the idea of moving on from Some Bizzare. Obviously, Virgin decided not to pick up the option after the third album, so, as with the situation with Rough Trade, we felt it was time to change up. We'd been working on the DoubleVision stuff with Paul Smith, who was very different to Stevo, and we thought, *Well, maybe we don't need a manager who's quite so mental.* It was as basic as that, really. It had got a bit mad, but it was fun as well, although by this time we were working more closely with Rob. There was also a feeling that if we carried on working with Stevo, then the next record or the next deal is going to be more about him. He was larger than life anyway, but he was getting more so.

MATT JOHNSON If a radio or TV interview came in for one of the bands, they had to get in quick, otherwise Stevo would grab it and go on in their place. And increasingly in Some Bizzare press releases, he started giving himself top billing ahead of the bands, so it would be all about Stevo and then mention a band and their new record at the bottom. Things like this were starting to happen more frequently as he started to get a bit megalomaniacal. And, of course, all the bands started to get fed up with it.

* The Swans live album *Public Castration Is A Good Idea* (BURN ONE) was self-released in order to capitalise on interest in the band from the tour supporting the K.422 releases. The release had the blessing of Rob Collins.

236

STEVO I was on a college-radio promotion tour in North America with Matt Johnson and each time we'd turn up with at these stations with a CBS rep, they'd be introduced to Matt, and then as soon as they were introduced to me, the DJ and producer would run out to the station's library and come out with copies of *Some Bizzare Album*, *If You Can't Please Yourself* . . . and even things like *The Crackdown* and ask me to sign them. I'll never forget Matt's expression, while I'm signing all these records and he's like, 'Huh, when're they gonna talk to me?' In the time it took him to produce *Infected* from *Soul Mining*, I'd probably produced thirteen or fourteen albums.

STEPHEN 'MAL' MALLINDER We thought if we move on to another deal, we should probably run it ourselves, which is what happened, although that makes it sound quite simple. But stopping working with Stevo was never going to be that easy. It affected him on a pride level, because I don't think anyone had left Some Bizzare before. Marc and Matt were still there, as were Neubauten; Psychic TV and Test Dept had kind of drifted off, but we actually made a decision to leave. So, one afternoon, we took him out to an Indian restaurant around the corner from the office to tell him. Obviously he wanted us to stay and was really pissed-off and very Stevo about it. Eventually, after quite a few pints of lager and gin and bitter lemons, which Stevo used to love, he did finally agree to release us. But we needed it in writing—a spoken agreement wasn't enough. So Stevo got a napkin from the restaurant and wrote something like, 'I hereby release Mal and Richard from their Some Bizzare contract' on it, and that's all we ever had. We were later reassured it was legally binding!

ROB COLLINS The job always got done at Some Bizzare—the records got manufactured, the sales notes got written, and the records came out. Whether or not they financially made sense—and I made many a fuck-up on the packaging versus the dealer price kind of thing—is another matter. But if you want an overview of how Some Bizzare worked, the artistic decision always came before the commercial decision. It was always about the music and the art and what the artist wanted. That had to be right.

>>

PAUL WHITE I loved Test Dept—I thought they were great, amazing live. The show under the Westway where Malcolm Poynter installed a number of sculptures was a pretty extraordinary event. They used them again for the *Unacceptable Face Of Freedom* sleeve.* I was very much trying to push the envelope on what could be done with a record sleeve, and the idea for the fold out crucifix design was definitely mine. In terms of budgeting, if the band wanted something then the label would nearly always say yes. That was very much the nature of independent record labels at that time. It was about making sure the record came out exactly how the band wanted it.

The Unacceptable Face Of Freedom is a colossal advance. What this group do, to the unfamiliar, is construct great panels of noise using industrial elements harnessed through the opportunities of technology—furnace metal turned into monolithic drumbeats, for instance. Over this monstrous beat they methodically pile up the debris of contemporary Britain—politicians, radio cutups, the savage testimony of a miner beaten by a policeman. Its impact is overwhelming, dangerously so—it could be seductive nihilism we're listening to.

RICHARD COOK, *The Wire*, June 1986

CHRIS BOHN I saw Test Dept play at the *Unacceptable Face Of Freedom* event at the Bishopsgate rail depot, outside Paddington station.† There was a huge sculpture of metal instruments, speeches from striking miners and choreography from dancers and circus performers. They really used the space and the sounds from the instrumentation circulated the room and combined with the speeches to create a real politically charged spectacle.

PAUL WHITE The way of working depended on the record really. Initially, the bands might bring things to me, and as long as it didn't look crap, I'd be completely fine with it. Michael would certainly work like that. But later on, things become more conversational, more collaborative. There were different ways of doing things and, to be honest, I didn't feel I had to stamp my personality on anything, so it didn't really bother me. In fact, for the longest time, I would try to dodge having my name anywhere near the artwork.

---

* Test Dept's *The Unacceptable Face Of Freedom* LP (MOP 2) was released by Some Bizzare on March 14, 1986. Initial copies came in a fold-out sleeve that opened into a crucifix shape.

† This multimedia event was assisted by the GLC and included sculpture, gymnastics, and pyrotechnics. It ran from March 28 to 30, 1986.

ROB COLLINS I was a huge fan of Factory Records—more the packaging than the music—and I loved 4AD. I just wanted to carry that on. So, I definitely wanted the embossed gold effect on the Swans records, and that carried over into the Wiseblood mirrored sleeve. Geoff and Sleazy really wanted the reverse board and the postcard on the front cover of the first limited edition run of *Scatology*. I felt it was really important to have amazing packaging for amazing records.

MICHAEL GIRA The 'dollar sign' records were absolutely a complete statement. From the music to the sleeves, from the little prose pieces inside describing these kinds of psychic states to the words themselves, it was all tied together, turning the tenants of advertising around against itself.

PAUL WHITE With the 'dollar sign' records, Michael drew the original designs on tracing paper, I think, and then I basically redrew it. All of that material was hand drawn because computers weren't used back then. A lot of what I did on those sleeves was technical as much as anything else, using a number of different processes to ensure that everything looked as pure and as sharp as it could possibly be. The idea of the Swiss typographers and the Helvetica and the simplicity of that, stripping away quite a lot of ornamentation and delivering the message in as simple and clean way as possible. And there was humour as well. I have to say, they still look pretty strong even today. For me, Swans was easily one of my best projects, I was such a huge fan, they were one of my favourite bands and one of the best live acts I've ever seen.

MICHAEL GIRA The whole gist of my interest in writing words was the psychic infiltration of one's consciousness by modern consumerist society. The forming of your needs and the forming of who you are as a person, so that you would then consume the items that are presented to you. You end up in these roles or jobs in order to consume, and why does it have to be that way? These needs are created inside you, and it's even worse now.

At the time, I suppose my focus would have been on television advertising, and just the advertising that was all around us, and how that infiltrates every aspect of your psyche as you grow up in a modern, First World so-called society. And that to me felt like rape. You had no personal freedom because the whole concept that you could be outside of this system didn't even exist. I suppose having worked really shit jobs most of my life in order to survive, I felt it very deeply, like, *Why am I doing this? Why am I stuck with this?* And I was entering my thirties, so it was kind of becoming an emergency. And I just said, 'No more, I will not take this,' and just threw everything into music. I was doing the one thing I had an aptitude for, which in an idealised society one should be able to do, and that I was able to make a living out of it to me was the whole point.

>>

MATT JOHNSON 'Sweet Bird Of Truth' was the first track from the *Infected* album to be released as a single, although CBS would only put it out as a twelve-inch and actually deleted it on the day of release.* I'd written and recorded the song way before America bombed Libya in April '86. It was banned by the BBC, but it wasn't my intention to cause controversy. I was just writing about war, aggressive American imperialism, and, you know, the nature of man's relationship with God and mortality. All quite reasonable things to be interested in at the time, I thought.

Around the same time, a journalist mentioned to me that Billy Bragg had told them, 'Oh, Matt Johnson just hides behind drum machines and refuses to play live,' as if that undermined my authenticity or something. And I thought that was a bit of a rude thing to say. But eventually Billy and I met—in Australia of all places—and found that over a few drinks we got on fine, and he asked me to play at these Red Wedge gigs he'd arranged to support the Labour Party in the run up to the June 11 General Election. Now, I hadn't played live for a number of years, so I thought, *What sort of format can I do?* I couldn't do a whole show, so I chose three songs that were politically relevant for the time, and with Zeke on bass we played 'Flesh & Bones', 'Perfect', and 'Heartland'. We did two shows, one at Islington Town Hall and one in Notting Hill at the old Acklam Hall under the West Way.†

ZEKE MANYIKA The guy who was our road crew for the two shows was the drummer in my solo band, so was just doing us a favour really. Anyway, he plugged my bass in wrong and I couldn't hear anything through the monitor, so I just started to play my part, and for the first few seconds it sounded awful. I remember a girl

* THE THE's 'Sweet Bird Of Truth' twelve-inch (TRUTH 1) was released by CBS in May 1986 in a limited edition of 7,500 copies.
† The Islington show was on June 6, 1986, and also included Tom Robinson, Lloyd Cole, and The Style Council.

in the row front just pointing at me, shouting, 'He's rubbish, get him off!' It was sorted out very quickly, and it ended up being great fun.

>>

GAVIN FRIDAY Those first two Coil albums are extraordinary. Fucking hell, you play them today and they're still really up there. They didn't compromise which is quite beautiful. To have the freedom of no barriers, to just go there, and they actually believed it—these guys weren't just doing it for the sake of doing something weird. Everything is so overthought nowadays, before things are even fucking released. Where's the spontaneity and wildness and the freedom? It's a very different world now.

MARC ALMOND I became good friends with Geoff, and when Peter and Genesis fell out, you were either on one side or the other. Musically, I preferred Coil to Psychic TV—I loved the experimental soundscapes and film soundtracks they were doing and was glad to be a musical contributor.

GEOFF RUSHTON/JOHN BALANCE The Horse Rotorvator was this vision I'd had of this mechanical/flesh thing that ploughed up the earth and I really did have a vision of it—a real horrible, burning, dripping, jaw-like vision in the night. Actually it might have been at dusk. The Four Horsemen of the Apocalypse killed their horses and use their jawbones to make this huge, earth-moving machine. Which was the Horse Rotorvator.

J.G. THIRLWELL I'm on one track on *Horse Rotorvator*.* I can't remember what I did.

GEOFF RUSHTON/JOHN BALANCE Everyone says [*Horse Rotorvator*] is our best album. It's probably our most realised album in that we'd got over the anger of the first one and settled into a more pastoral or twisted lyricism. I got a bit more confident with my vocals, which I wasn't on the first album. We had a lot more time to work on it—the first one was done in an amphetamania, the second was more thought out, the themes had blossomed. We'd just been to Mexico, which was a major thing, and we'd seen how they deal with death, and we'd been to all

* Coil released *Horse Rotorvator* (ROTA 1) on Force & Form via K.422 in August 1986.

the Mayan temple complexes—all round the Yucatan peninsula. That's really what influenced me with the lyrics and stuff. How sacrifices were made so the world would keep turning and that's how I saw people dying of AIDS at the time, how my mind could deal with it, that they'd died to keep the world turning.

JOHN GRANT Coil's *Anal Staircase* was something I heard in the clubs and I immediately went out and bought the twelve-inch.* I couldn't get enough of it, and I'm still a huge Coil fan. I was really into Test Dept—I had that beautiful piece of vinyl that folded out into a giant cross. I can't tell you how much I love that record. And I'm a Chris and Cosey freak, too. All of this music is still a huge part of my life because I simply haven't heard anything better yet. But I was so conditioned to think that all of this stuff was evil, actually for real. And that I wasn't allowed to go anywhere near it, and that I shouldn't have anything to do with it. I was told that if I were to do something like that, then I would be evil myself and that would separate me from my family. I was so indoctrinated I wasn't allowed to let my mind go there. And so it was like, *That's not for you, you can't do that.* There was a lot of that in my upbringing. A lot of these guys had no fear and they experimented with things, because there was no wrong way of doing it. I grew up playing classical piano, and there was *only* wrong ways of doing it. Thank God for these people who were completely unafraid.

CHRIS BOHN Geoff's magical interests became more prevalent after the first two albums. The funny thing is, I have absolutely no interest in magic at all, but Coil are one of my all-time favourite groups. It's to do with how they transform the listener. They take their interests and tastes and almost magically turn them into music that gets deep into heart of the subjects and kind of explains them. And not just through language but through sound, too, communicating with the listener physically and connecting intellectually. I think the combination of these two men and the work they did together was wonderful.

PAUL 'BEE' HAMPSHIRE When the relationship with Some Bizzare was good, it was great, and when it was bad, it was really bad for all of them, both Psychic TV and Coil. You know, it was like any relationship—the honeymoon period was all

---

* Coil released the EP *The Anal Staircase* (ROTA 121) on Force & Form via K.422 in December 1986.

bliss and amazing, and then when it wasn't working it got really awkward and frustrating. I don't know if they ever made up with Some Bizzare. I know that no one ever held anything against Jane, but with Stevo I don't think any of them had any regard for him afterward.

>>

MATT JOHNSON I was living at a place in Stoke Newington where I'd put together a studio for demoing. I had a nice sixteen-track studio with a Fostex P16, an Allen & Heath desk segment, and a certain amount of outboard. I'd also bought an Emulator II—one of the first in the country, which cost £9,000, a huge amount of money back then. I wanted to demo extensively for the new album, and the plan was to use lots of brass and strings and interesting percussion and double bass. It just made sense to me because THE THE didn't have a fixed line-up—it could be any instrumentation that I choose, really—and I had the budget to do pretty much whatever I wanted, which was really exciting. But the demoing was a slow and quite intensive process.

I started with 'Heartland' and 'Out Of The Blue', and those two alone took about eighteen months to write. Around the same time, I'd given Annie Roseberry—who was my A&R person at CBS and very supportive—a list of potential producers. There was Tom Waits—I loved *Swordfish Trombones* and had seen him live, which totally blew my mind—Brian Eno, and Can's Holger Czukay. We didn't hear back from Czukay, Eno was sort of lukewarm, but Waits came back very positively, and Annie arranged for me to go to New York to spend some time with him. I was staying in Greenwich Village and we met up numerous times, to play pool and hang out. I remember he'd just quit alcohol, so he only drank soda and bitters. He really liked my demos, and we even got as far as looking at studios together. But after I got back to the UK, he got in touch to say he'd so much going on he couldn't commit to producing an album for someone else. He did give me some really good advice and suggested I just get a good engineer and produce it myself. I already had a good engineer in Paul Hardiman, but because of the situation with Stevo and Paul's wife, I had to find someone else.

WARNE LIVESEY I was recommended to Matt by Jim, and we just went out for a drink in Islington one night. I didn't—and I still don't—pay much attention to what the press said about people, so I didn't have any expectations of him. I knew

Soul Mining, and we hit it off pretty quickly. Matt had already done a couple of tracks with Gary Langan, then he did a couple with me before going to New York to Roli Mosimann's place and then coming back to do another couple with me again. I then mixed the whole album.

MATT JOHNSON First of all, I did a couple of tracks with Gary Langan, 'The Mercy Beat' and 'Angels Of Deception', but then another project came in and suddenly he wasn't available. I didn't want to wait for six months, and Jim had mentioned Warne Livesey to me, as they had worked together on the Foetus records. So I met with Warne, and we got along very well, and he ended up working with me on 'Infected', 'Out Of The Blue', 'Heartland', and 'Slow Train To Dawn'. And again through Jim I was introduced to Roli Mosimann—they were working on the Wiseblood album. I met up with Roli in New York, and we really hit it off, so I worked on 'Twilight Of A Champion' and 'Sweet Bird Of Truth' with him over there.

WARNE LIVESEY The thing with Matt is, all of the songs tend to change during recording—quite a lot, actually, more so than any other artist I've worked with. There were demos, and something like 'Heartland' probably didn't change that much from the original version structurally, but other songs changed quite a bit. The lyrics to the track 'Infected' were originally the ones for 'Out Of The Blue (And Into The Fire)'. Matt decided they didn't match the music so built a whole new song around them and wrote new lyrics for 'Infected'.

There were quite often cases where Matt would want to add extra verses after we'd recorded the backing tracks, so we'd edit together new arrangements from the existing recordings. With 'Infected', while we were mixing we completely changed the bass drum part, which was a bit of a nightmare. So even though Dave Palmer played drums on that track, we took his kick drum part out of the recording and replaced it with a sample playing a more phonetic part. There was a lot of tinkering, and you'd be thinking on your feet.

ZEKE MANYIKA I was away for most of the *Infected* album, and Matt was taking a different approach to it anyway. But he did ask me to sing on the title track. I took the wrong train and got lost on my way to the studio, which feeds into his story about me always being late! I wish I'd played a lot more on that album, though, as it's amazing. Talk about development!

WARNE LIVESEY Matt never let CBS get involved with the music. He never played them his demos and he never allowed them down to the studio. And they weren't involved in hiring me for *Infected*, either—that deal was done between me, my manager, Matt, and Stevo. So I'd been booked, and then I got a call from the A&R production manager, who is the bean-counter, really, saying he'd like to take me to dinner so we could have a chat. It was a bit weird, but because I'd never worked with a major label before this point, I didn't really know what to expect, so just went along with it.

So, we're at this restaurant, generally chit-chatting, and he tells me he's just come back from a staff weekend conference at some manor house where the MD walked onstage to do his keynote speech with a tiger on a leash. It might have even been two tigers. He's telling me about this and all the expensive wine and champagne that was drunk, so I ask how much it all cost. And he says, 'Oh, it was about a quarter of a million pounds for the weekend.' So I was like, *Wow, OK, good times!*

We progressed to talking about the actual album, and I mention that Matt and I have been talking about putting strings on a few songs and he said, 'What, like a quartet?' And I said, 'No, no, we want a proper twenty-piece string section.' And he started to get a very twitchy, saying, 'Hmmm, I don't know if the budget take a full string section,' so I just came back saying, 'You just told me how you spent £250,000 on a fucking party, and now you're telling me we can't spend twenty grand on a string section?' I told Matt, and I never heard from the A&R production manager again, and neither did they question anything we wanted to spend.

STEVE HOGARTH I first heard Matt when I was in a boutique in Holland and they were playing 'Uncertain Smile', and I thought it was Jethro Tull. Matt has a very similar voice to Ian Anderson and there was the flute on it, and I thought, *Wow, Jethro Tull have gone really cool*. And then I sussed out it wasn't them at all, it was THE THE. I was a big fan.

WARNE LIVESEY We needed a piano player, as Jools wasn't available. I'd worked with Steve Hogarth on the Europeans records, and we were good mates. He did a really nice job. Obviously Jools is great, but at that stage, at least, he only really had that one kind of vibe, that honky-tonk thing, which worked fantastically on 'Uncertain Smile'. But Steve was maybe a bit more diverse, and more able to fit his style to what the track needed.

STEVE HOGARTH I'd worked with Warne a lot and I had a very high regard for him, as I still do. He phoned me up one day and said, 'What's your blues piano-playing like?' and I asked, 'Well, who wants to know?' When he said Matt Johnson, I replied, 'Tell him it's excellent!' Once in the studio, which was somewhere in Surrey, I met Matt, listened to the track, and I was still trying to get my head around it while we were putting down takes, so they were all a bit sketchy and lumpy. They didn't have a piano in the studio, so I was using a Kurzweil, although you'd never know as their keyboards usually feel good. We did a few takes and Warne pieced together what's on the record. But it isn't really bluesy at all because it's too fast and it's impossible to play the blues at that tempo, so I was doing the blues licks but it kind of came across as quirkier than bluesy. But I was really pleased with it when I heard the final mix. It's a great song with great lyrics, as you would expect from Matt. So I'm very proud to be on it—I mention it every chance I can.

WARNE LIVESEY I was very aware of the lyrical content and knew by that point what to expect from Matt, that it was going to be very political and very astute about state of world. My contribution was always musical, Matt was very self-sufficient when it came to his worldview and lyrics. When working with Jim we'd experiment with musical palettes, looking at how they can be used to enhance the emotional content of the lyrics. When you have artists who write very poignant and often very critical lyrics about how human beings treat each other, and the corruption and politics that serve corporate rather than people's interests, it's my role as a producer to try and offer ways of manipulating sounds to enhance that aspect.

STEVE HOGARTH Nothing's changed one jot, really. We've come in complete circle and we're right back where we were. There's the new Tory austerity, we're still in the pocket of the USA, and the shopping centres still smell of piss. Once you get north of Watford, anyway.

MATT JOHNSON Going into *Infected* there was again a lot of pressure on me to tour but the way the album was developing I knew, like *Soul Mining*, it was going to be very difficult to do it justice live. So, the idea for the film came at a fairly early stage with discussions between Stevo and Paul Russell, who had recently taken over from Maurice Oberstein. Stevo was saying, 'Look, we're not going to tour live but we want to do a video of every track and we promise to tour that instead,' and initially CBS scoffed, 'That's ridiculous, nobody's ever done that before.' And it *was* a very unusual thing for an up-and-coming young artist. And as the album became more cinematic, so too did the ambition for the film, and to Stevo's credit, he really twisted CBS's arm and hammered them to release the funds so we could do what we wanted to do. And the funding was massive: it was over half a million pounds back in 1986, which I guess is a couple of million pounds in today's money.

STEVO First and foremost, getting the funding was really, really difficult. We're talking large sums of money, even by today's standards. But I was passionate about it and believed in Matt's vision, and I was happy to fight for it, but it was exhausting, it took me so long. I kept saying to CBS, 'Look, we've done it with Soft Cell, we've done it with Neubauten, and we've done it with Test Dept.' It was a theme—we'd make a film to accompany the music. And I approached CBS with THE THE in the same way as I did Phonogram with Soft Cell: if you're not going to produce it then don't stop me, because that's a restraint of trade. So, either CBS pay for *Infected* to be filmed in its entirety or they let me go elsewhere. They'd still get a royalty, but I'd broker a deal with someone else because they didn't have the faith. So I kept fighting and fighting, and in the end I was at Heathrow Airport, and Paul Russell was getting off a plane, completely jetlagged, and I grabbed him. And that was a final straw, and he said, 'OK, OK!' and gave me the budget.

PETER 'SLEAZY' CHRISTOPHERSON I wasn't involved until quite late in the project, and most of the music had been recorded. Matt and Stevo came to me with the notion that there was quite a large amount of money to make a promotional video, or film, really, of the whole album and all the ideas that were in it. I already knew Stevo well, because I've worked with him with my band Coil, and so he knew that I did videos and TV commercials and that I would be a sympathetic match. Matt had some quite strong ideas of his own and there was a look going on within the collective, which I could [work with] and make into a film that had an identity of its own.

TIM POPE Matt had gone from being this sort of small indie thing, to this, 'Bang!' this massive, ambitious project. But it's there in the music, you know, you listen to those horns on 'Twilight Of A Champion' and they're incredible and it's a very ambitious piece. My job was to reflect the music because all I ever do with my videos is I go in there and I redescribe the song.

MATT JOHNSON Making the film was really gruelling, and there was a lot of flying around and it could be very stressful, but it was also very exciting and a lot of fun too. Particularly in Peru and Bolivia, which were wonderful. The crew had got there before Stevo and I, so they'd scoped the place out. Sleazy's producer, Aubrey Powell, knew a guy down there called Freddie who was ex-Peruvian army and he had access to certain things, shall we say. We'd decided to go to Iquitos to film part of it, which is where Werner Herzog filmed *Fitzcarraldo*. We were warned in advance about altitude sickness, and the crew implored us not to drink alcohol on the flight but to drink plenty of water and be sensible. So, of course, Stevo starts quaffing large brandy after large brandy immediately after take-off, getting absolutely plastered, and really annoying the other passengers. I stayed sober.

We arrive at La Paz, which is the highest capital city on the planet, and we've been there for less than five minutes when Stevo keeled over, gasping, 'I can't breathe! I can't breathe!' He ended up being carted off by medics. I went to see him in his hotel room later—it was dark with the curtains pulled tight and he was lying there, motionless on the bed with an oxygen mask on. He motioned for me to come closer and whispered, 'I'm dying, Matt, I'm dying.' I couldn't stop laughing. He never learned, but he was always good fun.

PETER 'SLEAZY' CHRISTOPHERSON Going all that way with camera crews and people, and not knowing really what you're going to find when you get there [did create] some serious madness. Even within the film crew itself, all the messages were pretty garbled because we were in the middle of the jungle, and it was 100% humidity. There are hotels in those places, but they're the kind of hotels where you're not quite sure what's going to crawl out from underneath the toilet seat when you sit down. And it's pretty weird.

MATT JOHNSON So we filmed 'Infected' and 'The Mercy Beat' in La Paz and Iquitos. During the latter, we came across a big political rally—about a thousand or so people, very angry, they were marching through the streets. Sleazy was able to think on his feet, 'Let's just keep filming, keep filming.' That's my second favourite video ever because it was just so authentic. The snake, monkey bite, and blood ritual—all completely spontaneous. And in the evenings Stevo, assistant director Phil Richardson, and I ended up sneaking out into the jungle late at night to these weird gatherings and misbehaving. You can imagine the sort of party favours that are available in Peru.

PETER 'SLEAZY' CHRISTOPHERSON The skill is to is to exploit situations that you're not expecting and make them work for the film. And I think that if you can do that, and if you have an artist who is prepared to take those risks, because a lot of rock musicians are not prepared to take any risks whatsoever. And that's one of the good things about Matt, he is prepared to stand up in the middle of 2,000 people all completely out of their heads on cane alcohol or drugs or whatever, and go through that experience. And hopefully that intensity comes out in the film.

STEVO The filming was OK until I suddenly got a phone call saying that CBS had gone into dispute with all the retailers, and they won't stock any of their records. And this was the week 'Heartland' was coming out, so I'm in Bolivia and I needed to jump on a plane via Miami back to London.* I arrive back, jetlagged, and then went into CBS to employ an independent strike force so the records would get to stores. The retailers that were in dispute with CBS deemed Some Bizzare an independent label, hence they stocked it. The single still charted, but it was as Some Bizzare, not CBS.

TIM POPE We decided to shoot 'Out Of The Blue' in a real brothel, but first of all we had to do some shots in Spanish Harlem. What we didn't realise was we were near the biggest crack dealer in New York, so it was a pretty unfortunate area for us to be in. I was standing there with my producer, just as the sun was going down, and I was sensing a vibe, I was thinking this place is really, really edgy. And suddenly, I'm standing there and this large rat—and this is not made up, it probably had been poisoned—came out and ran around in front of my feet and then fell on its back, had an epileptic fit, looked at me and died. That was like the start of the evening.

---

* 'Heartland' (TRUTH 2) was released as single on August 4, 1986, reaching no.29 on the UK chart.

ANDY 'DOG' JOHNSON I didn't go [on the shoots], I got left behind. I did design a car and I thought it would be a really great idea if I went out to supervise the painting of it, but it wasn't deemed necessary.

TIM POPE For 'Twilight Of A Champion', we went to this poor guy's apartment, and we bought these cockroaches, because I wanted the whole place to be flooded with cockroaches. I gave Matt a video camera, which I think was probably pretty out there in those days, and he sort of goes through the apartment, shoves his head in the fridge, and that was all, you know, just very exciting stuff to do.

STEPHEN 'MAL' MALLINDER *Soul Mining* felt like a personal, one-to-one record, whereas *Infected* felt like a record that was a message to everybody. I remember going down to Portobello Road to the Electric Cinema and watching the film, and it felt like someone who was really confident, and going, 'I'm making another record, and I'm going to make a statement with it.' *Infected* was a really brave record and a dark record, a tough record. And it felt like the right record to make at the time, because you look at '83 and *Soul Mining* and the period that record came out, there was a level of optimism and youthfulness, but by the time *Infected* came out it had become darker. Even though Matt didn't deal directly with such specific political things, it reflected what was going on at the time, with AIDS emerging, with Thatcher, the miners, Falklands War, all those things, it felt like it was a record of its time, it reflected some of the dysfunction, and some of the tension that was underneath the surface for everybody. It was a more significant record in some respects.

MATT JOHNSON *Infected—The Movie* was a massive project: sixty-two musicians, four video directors, three co-producers, painters, photographers, as well as all the other people usually involved in making a film.* And I was good to my word to CBS and I travelled across America, Europe, and Australia with the film, doing endless screenings and interviews and TV shows. But the experience of making and promoting *Infected* changed me, and mainly for the worse, I have to say. I became obnoxious, particularly to my partner at the time, Fiona, and she actually left me for about six months because of my disgraceful behaviour. I was only twenty-four

* THE THE's second album, *Infected* (EPC 26770), was released by Epic on November 17, 1986. It reached no.14 on the UK chart. *Infected—The Movie* was broadcast on Channel 4 on December 16, 1986, with a specially filmed introduction from Matt.

or twenty-five, and that first flush of success is extremely toxic. Over time—and with experience—you learn to take praise and criticism with a very large dose of salt and ignore both but, at that early stage of a career, you can become extremely egotistical. I don't think it did me any favours on a personal level.

BEVERLEY GLICK Stevo was extremely persuasive. There were times when he put quite a lot of pressure on me to put certain artists on the cover of *Record Mirror*, one example being Matt when *Infected* came out, and that was because Stevo just kept pushing and pushing and pushing. He really fought for his bands. Matt and I actually became friendly for a while after that, and we'd hang out when he was in London.

>>

STEVO All the artwork for THE THE came through Some Bizzare first—everything was approved in my office before it went up to Epic. And it was a real challenge to get some of it past CBS and into production—it was a real battle at times.

MATT JOHNSON Working with my brother Andrew was always completely collaborative. The sleeve of 'Uncertain Smile' was based on an original painting of his which I loved, so he did a version with my face. The *Soul Mining* cover was something he'd already done, and I felt the vividness of the colours really summed up the atmosphere of the album, particularly the closing track, 'GIANT'. But other things like 'Heartland' and 'Sweet Bird Of Truth' were responses to the music and done specifically. So it was a combination: I'd sometimes see things in his art studio, and say, 'That would be perfect for this,' or he would listen to new recordings I did and show me fresh ideas.

ANDY 'DOG' JOHNSON I've only had one piece of work ever rejected by Matt. Most of the time, whatever I come up with, it's sort of what he had in mind to begin with. Even if he's having problems with lyrics, sometimes I can come up with a line and throw it in, and just help shape the overall look of the thing. I was involved [with *Infected*] all the way along the line to a certain extent, to one degree or another.

MATT JOHNSON Well, the masturbating devil sleeve for the single release of 'Infected' was something he'd already done. Again, there was outrage from people, but we couldn't stop laughing about it. I don't know, probably it was a bit childish, but we used to get a kick out of shocking people back then.

KEVIN FOAKES Andy's work stood out a mile—it was so unique. I loved his THE THE sleeves, and I treasure those records. And Jim's design stuff, I mean, wow, the whole Russian constructivist propaganda thing he had going on then was incredible. I would credit Jim's stuff as being the biggest influence on me as a graphic designer, along with ZTT. One of the first things I said when I met Jim was, 'Have you got any of that original artwork as I'd love to buy some?', and he said, 'Nah, all that stuff went to the printers and never came back.'

J.G. THIRLWELL I'm interested in packaging design as a mode of propaganda. I used the red, white, and black colour palette in a lot of my artwork, and mixed up Spanish revolutionary and WW2 and Chinese communist images together, in a kind of blur of totalitarianism and pop art. I was doing that type of stuff in that colour palette in art school, and still am.

MARC ALMOND [In 1984] I made an appearance at the Bloomsbury Theatre in a night dedicated to the French erotic writer Georges Bataille. Of course, I was flattered. I'd heard of Bataille, but I must admit I'd never read him, so I thought I'd better brush up. I read *Blue Of Noon* and *The Story Of The Eye*, pretending to all concerned that I'd read them years earlier. I performed four songs on the theme of love and murder, including 'Body Unknown', which I'd performed with Nick Cave at The Immaculate Consumptive's show in New York. The Bataille evening was a beautiful presentation. I sang the songs from a black leather sedan chair, while religious images were projected onto the back of the stage.

ANNI HOGAN Seeing Marc at the Bataille show was amazing. He performed solo with backing tapes we'd pre-recorded, including my composition 'Blood Tide'. It then ended up coming out as the *Violent Silence* EP, which is another one of my very favourites, a real high point. It's a bit of a lost classic, a really wonderful record.*

* Marc Almond's *Violent Silence* EP (208 050) was initially only released in Germany by Virgin but was made available elsewhere on import.

MARC ALMOND To some I seemed to be able to straddle both commercial and experimental musical landscapes, and there were times when people couldn't reconcile Marc Almond the 'Tainted Love' *Top Of The Pops* singer with some of the darker more experimental things I was doing. Coming from five years at art college, I couldn't see the joins—it was all experience to me. I loved doing all kinds of music, as long as I could relate and find a place in my world for it.

JOHN GRANT I'm quite embarrassed to say I never really went beyond Soft Cell at the time. It wasn't until I started working with Biggi Veira from Gus Gus that I started to discover all of Marc's solo stuff and understand what was going on with him. I didn't realise how amazing he was back then, and the more I learn, the more I realise he's an absolute genius. Marc is sort of a hero now, and he's one of those guys I really worship. He's the most incredible singer and a beautiful beacon of individuality, and it makes me feel emotional because these people are worth their weight gold.

BRIAN POOLE Stevo contacted us again and expressed an interest in releasing Ronaldo & The Loaf's next album, whenever it might come along. This was discussed with him on a few occasions, during visits to the New Cavendish Street office, and also one memorable evening at his home in Hammersmith. In terms of detail, that visit is a blur, but we probably drank quite a lot, and he gave us a fragment of a Soft Cell gold disc. He also travelled down to Southsea to see us and take in the sea air. We took him out for a curry and drinks—it was enjoyable, he was a fun guy, but I don't think we could ever fully relax in his company.

Working with Stevo was a steep learning experience for us. His personality was, for sure, larger than life, but also in many ways it could be overwhelming, and that was very different from our experiences to date. Our music might have been weird but, on the face of it, as people, we weren't.

The whole Some Bizarre/Stevo scene was strange to us, in some ways perhaps intimidating, but we were excited to have a significant UK label interested in us and we went with the flow. Our prior experience of record production had been simple: we completed an album at home, sent off the master tapes and artwork ideas to Ralph, and several weeks later a box of LPs would arrive. Circumstances and distance meant that we couldn't have much control over what happened, but working with Some Bizarre meant that we could. Also, it could show us how labels with, presumably, larger budgets went about the process.

During 1985 and 1986, we recorded tracks for *Elbow Is Taboo* in our home studios. Some Bizarre did not have any involvement in the recordings. Stevo and Ralph both were sent cassettes, and both liked what they heard. Stevo asked for a twelve-inch single to precede the album, so 'Hambu Hodo' was released on Some Bizarre.[*] Stevo commissioned Paul White to create the cover artwork based on our initial ideas of Morris Dancers and fractured lyrics, and the result was strange and humorous, which suited us.

STEPHEN 'MAL' MALLINDER We were the first ones to leave, really, so we'd gone by the time all the fractious shit started. Because we'd come from the independent world—we'd worked with Rough Trade, Factory, Les Disques du Crépuscule—our relationship with those labels was very much about never relinquishing control, and because of that we never got ripped off. So, we went into the relationship with Stevo with the idea that we were in control, and I'm not sure if some of the others had that. We had an understanding about how we wanted things to work, and as it all started to unfold, we made sure that we felt we were in control of what was going on. It was a different dynamic and certainly, in terms of finances and sense of control, it meant it was a lot much easier for us to leave.

RUSTY EGAN Stevo needed some help around the office, so I introduced him a couple of personal assistants and he handcuffed them to a chair, literally, went home, and left them in the office. We were ringing him on the phone trying to get him to come back and release them.

MATT JOHNSON It's not that I—or any of the other bands on the label for that matter—was happy to go along with Stevo's 'methods', but he was his own man and did his own thing. Some of the shenanigans made me wince whilst others I found hilarious. I have mixed feelings, looking back. I'm never comfortable with people feeling bullied or humiliated, but I didn't have such a problem when

---

[*] Renaldo & The Loaf's debut for Some Bizzare, the 'Hambu Hodo' twelve-inch (rD4) was released on November 17, 1986.

certain people in the industry got what they deserved. But for good or bad, he was a larger-than-life character in an industry that's now so grey, corporate, politically correct, and sterile—it seems like a lost world, looking back.

PETER ASHWORTH That early period at Some Bizzare felt era-defining and introduced industrial music to the mainstream. It was an interesting mix: bands that were flirting with pop and getting Top 10 hits, and bands who were right on the edge of what you might call music. It was an extraordinary age for music as well because it was defined by the rebirth of the synth. It was like punk, except you didn't have to learn a single chord, let alone three. You just needed one finger! It brought in all sorts of people trying stuff out, non-musicians, performance artists, one-offs—even Soft Cell was an art experiment at the very beginning. And Stevo was a man with a vision, which brought a lot of very interesting people together. Yes, there was insanity, but there was an absolutely solid logic there, too, and, for a time at least, it all worked together in harmony.

Affected, you disregard and disgruntled blindfolded comfort, connection can not be true.

Ø, from the booklet accompanying *Redefining The Prologue 1981–2006* (2006)

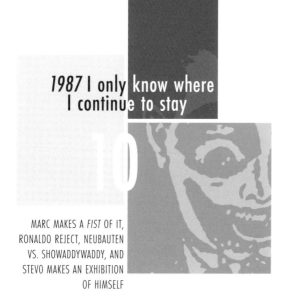

1987 I only know where I continue to stay

MARC MAKES A *FIST* OF IT, RONALDO REJECT, NEUBAUTEN VS. SHOWADDYWADDY, AND STEVO MAKES AN EXHIBITION OF HIMSELF

STEVO Once something becomes a commodity in the sense that it's selling on the strength of the name, rather than the merits of the music, that is the time when it will please a capitalist, but, at the same time, it's a disgrace for art.

JANE ROLINK Marc was so brilliant. He looked after me so well. We went everywhere together. We took brilliant trips to Spain, drank absinthe in back bars in Barcelona, and went to all these drag clubs and burlesque cabarets. It was so different and so gorgeous, just drenched in Spanishness.

MARC ALMOND Bordellos were everywhere [in Barcelona]—whole streets were lined with neon-lit brothels. My favourite place became the notorious Baghdad club, where live sex cabarets and magic acts were performed. The shows featured many post- and pre-op transexuals, a flamboyant homosexual Spanish comedian in sequins and thick white make up, mutilated dwarfs, a black-and-white sex display, a rodeo porn queen called Vanessa, who rode upon a mechanical horse on which was strapped an enormous plastic phallus, and a weightlifter who lifted weights via hooks attached to his nipples and penis. I will never forget an embarrassed Anni Hogan being dragged across the stage on a go-cart attached to a hook on the end of the weightlifter's penis. On that same night another performer invited Jane to insert a knife through holes in his arms. Jane nervously inserted the knife incorrectly, and blood spurted all over her dress, leaving him bleeding profusely.

ANNI HOGAN The writing for *Mother Fist And Her Five Daughters* was mostly done in the studio, and it was recorded at Milo in Hoxton Square, and I think everybody was happier to be recording in London again, not up a mountain in Bavaria. It was the peak Willing Sinners really, but it was the last album Martin did with us, and it was a real shock when he left to join the Banshees.* The whole period was just really, really creative and experimental. Musically, I was doing a lot more again, and everything just occurred naturally—nothing was forced. Mike obviously was a big presence because he was producing it, but I don't have much recollection of him on that particular record funnily enough. I wrote five of the tracks and arranged all of them. Now, I'd look back and say, 'Hello?', but I just didn't really think about things like that until later. Marc was definitely present on the album and focused. And we had some really great musicians—people like Enrico Tomasso on trumpet and Nigel Eaton on hurdy-gurdy—all coming together and doing really interesting things. It was an exciting time and Marc was the leading force, it was totally his thing, and he was very engaged with it all artistically. And his look for the album—the sailor's hat and DMs—was fantastic.

HUW FEATHER The same attitude the music on *Mother Fist* had followed through to the live shows, and we did exactly what we wanted. With candlelight-effect footlights, masonic imagery, tatty fringed velvet drapes, and a bare stage, the vibe was as if the show was being done out of a suitcase. The Soft Cell shows were fabulous, because they were chaotic and anything could happen, and it often did, but Marc's solo shows around this time were more about his mood and what the band were doing. Every number had a set look and set stage directions, which allowed us to change things around quite easily and be spontaneous. We were proficient and professional enough to be able to do a couple of rehearsals and then take it out and develop it on the road.

MARC ALMOND Anni Hogan wrote some beautiful tunes for the album, such as 'The Room Below', written about the basement flat below a brothel where I used

* Martin McCarrick left The Willing Sinners on good terms at the end of the *Mother Fist* tour to join Siouxsie & The Banshees. He has maintained an association with Marc Almond ever since.

257

to live in my Leeds art-college days. The song 'The Hustler' was based on a book by John Henry Mackay about a young male prostitute in Berlin. My favourite track on the album is a hymn to destructive drag queens and divas, the dark 'Saint Judy'—which refers, of course, to the most destructive diva and role model for tormented homosexuals everywhere, Judy Garland.

ANNI HOGAN The whole *Mother Fist* period had a wonderful feeling of freedom after the constraints of the previous two albums and I think Marc was reacting against that. If he'd have wanted a phenomenally successful record, he'd have never called it *Mother Fist And Her Five Daughters*, would he? I'm sure he was still under a lot of pressure from Virgin to be commercially successful, but he shielded us from a lot of things. There was a lot going on, and although Marc did absorb a lot of the pressure, it did spill over into the studio.

HUW FEATHER Marc and I had our own visual language and our own way of reacting to things. Marc had very definite ideas about the ambience and mood he wanted to create, and it was my job to come up with solutions to achieve that with lighting, scenery, staging, and blocking. But we were all learning as we were going along. For example, I was the production designer on all the videos, and I look at the early ones and just get really embarrassed. But by the time we get to things like 'Ruby Red', they're some of my favourite videos of all time.*

MARC ALMOND So what was the problem with the video of 'Ruby Red'? Where to begin? It featured writhing naked devils, scantily clad dancing sailors, disturbing drag queens, and all kinds of homoerotic nonsense. I had successfully made an expensive video that would not be shown on television anywhere. The record company put their heads in their hands and despaired. Then after talking openly about the theme of the song being masturbation and blood, I wondered why radio stations had stopped playing it.

VAL DENHAM My gender identity issues were beginning to rise to a conscious level, and you can see that in the cover of 'Ruby Red'. The painting is of an imagined

* The first single from the *Mother Fist And Her Five Daughters* album, 'Ruby Red' (GLOW 3), had been released back in October 1986. It reached no.47 on the UK chart.

female portrait of myself with long red hair, set within a Yorkshire landscape. The 'Melancholy Rose' cover was based on a Polaroid of Elita which used a coloured wine bottle over the flash to turn everything into blue tones.* Both these paintings were quite large, on coarse canvases. I also painted the cover for *Mother Fist And Her Five Daughters*, which featured a musclebound man covered in tattoos. When doing that painting, I attempted to draw my own puny white body from my reflection in a mirror but, to quote the song, 'Well, it just wasn't me.' I needed some reference material, so I walked up the road to my local newsagents and perused the top-shelf gay porn magazines, full of erotic photographs of musclebound guys flexing their biceps and looking very butch. Once I'd found something suitable, I then had to buy the damned thing. The newsagent knew me, my wife, and my baby daughter very well, so I also picked up some chocolate, asked for 20 Marlboro lights, and then nonchalantly plonked down the magazine on the counter too. He gave me a look that said, *I always knew you were gay*, which I compounded by saying, 'It's to help me paint a record cover—I am an artist, you know!' I don't think he was convinced. Neither were Virgin: they deemed the painting to be way too gay, so instead it was used for the twelve-inch single of the title track.† To be honest, I prefer the photographic cover that was eventually used for the album anyway. It's so evocative of a silent movie still.

Almond was born out of time. Secretly wee Marc has always dwelt in the backstreet of Marseilles or Madrid, hosted bohemian parties in snowy Montmartre and practised, all the while, for the Conservatoire. Heroes, if he has any, must be Hemmingway and the savagely gored Manolete, matador par excellence. *Mother Fist And Her Five Daughters* reeks of sadomasochism and blood on sand, fired by a torrid southern sun.

ADAM SWEETING, *Q*, March 1987

---

* 'Melancholy Rose' (GLOW 4) was released as single in February 1986, reaching no.71 on the UK chart.
† The final single to be released from *Mother Fist And Her Five Daughters* was the title track (GLOW 5-12), which Virgin begrudgingly released on twelve-inch only prior to the album's release. *Mother Fist* itself (FAITH 2) was finally released on April 6, 1987. This would be Almond's last album of new material for Virgin bar the compilation album *Singles 1984–1987* (FAITH 3), released on November 20, 1987, and two CDs of B-sides, *A Virgin's Tale* volumes I and II, released in 1992.

BRIAN POOLE When *The Elbow Is Taboo* was ready, Some Bizarre spared no expense in realising our album. We were booked into the Townhouse Studios with Ian Cooper for mastering, which was a whole new experience for us—a top-notch mastering engineer was working on our record! The cover concept had been in our heads for some time—a pair of elbows slung in a bra—and Paul White was again engaged to do the cover. Plaster casts were made of a woman's forearms and marble effect painted by a BBC artist. But then the perceptions of Renaldo & The Loaf and Some Bizarre diverged somewhat. When the photos for the cover emerged, the bra-clad elbows had been positioned in front of a guy's hairy chest, and, in our opinion, it tipped the idea from surreal into sleazy, which was not a Renaldo & The Loaf thing at all.

PAUL WHITE Oh, that wasn't me. There was sometimes a bit of to-ing and fro-ing over artwork, and sometimes the relationship with some bands didn't work as well as with others, which isn't a comment on Renaldo & The Loaf particularly. Although I do remember there was some controversy about this sleeve, but we definitely would have been handed that picture—we wouldn't have been involved in in shooting it at all. It does sound like the sort of thing Stevo would have done, though. That was definitely his type of humour.

BRIAN POOLE We rejected those images and asked for the elbows to be sent to us, and we undertook our own photo shoot at the local art college with a friend of ours, Dave Warden. The resulting images were exactly what we had in mind. But all this took time and effort, and it delayed the release of the album by some months, and in the US, where it was being released by Ralph Records, an interim 'Desperation Issue' version had to be issued to pre-order customers. Under normal circumstances, as soon as we sent a master tape over to Ralph we would be sketching ideas for the next project, but the protracted process of *The Elbow Is Taboo* somehow exhausted us, and we found it hard, ultimately impossible, to get going again.*

We were very happy with the final product—the album sounded great and looked great too, but at a cost not just in our energy but in monetary terms as well. As far as we are aware, Renaldo & The Loaf received zero royalties for the

---

* Renaldo & The Loaf's *The Elbow is Taboo* (rD5) was finally released by Some Bizzare sometime in 1987. It was issued in the US by The Residents' Ralph Records label.

original release of *The Elbow Is Taboo*. Stevo started to talk to us about ideas for another album. He liked the idea of us creating an album from audio fragments and samples. Those fragments would come from an open recording session in a disused gents' toilet where anyone who turned up could perform for thirty to sixty seconds. We would then sift through the recordings and make of them what we wanted. Needless to say, this never happened, but if it had it would have been ahead of its time. Ultimately, our time with Some Bizarre was in many ways enlightening for us as a band, but it could be argued that, in combination with a certain naivety, the rigours and frustrations of getting *The Elbow Is Taboo* out possibly hastened Renaldo & The Loaf to call it a day in late 1987.

>>

Wiseblood is the latest project for the man with a thousand names and backing tracks, Clint/Jim/Foetus/Ruin. Aided and abetted by another sonic terrorist Roli Mosimann, Wiseblood on record can sound like Stravinsky on bad acid, zapped-out Looney Tunes from Camarillo driving a Harley through hell. Like his paramour, Lydia Lunch, Ruin is one more of the prodigious artists when it comes to lancing those sociopsychic boils. But it takes more than a Sisters of Mercy-like fog show, harsh lighting, getting fucked up on stage and occasionally flashing pubic hair to transform somewhat dreary dronings into some form of either terrifying, aggressive, or transcendent music-vision. Great musicians, haphazard performance, same old attitude.

CRAIG LEE, *LA Weekly*, August 14–20, 1987

CHRIS BOHN I loved Jim as a person and I really loved his music, and sonically he was always inventive and pushing forward. But lyrically, things like, 'I'm a two-fisted fucker getting hard in my pants' from 'Bedrock' and the character he created for Wiseblood was not helping him sell records. I often wonder if Jim was trying to live up to his idea of what Lydia was. She would go deep, but there was always something else going on alongside it. And even after they'd separated, Lydia was very close with Jim and was trying to pull him back. Wiseblood started great but it was a short-lived project, and I'm glad it stopped.[*]

[*] J.G. Thirlwell and Roli Mosimann's first album together as Wiseblood, *Dirtdish* (WISE 003), was released by K.422 in May 1987. They promoted the album as a duo on the *Yank 'Em, Crank 'Em, Don't Stick Around To Thank 'Em* tour of 1987.

261

J.G. THIRLWELL They're all different versions of you, but it's so hard to unwrap, you know. The things that I was expressing through lyrics and my presentation in terms of the art and the whole package, I was speaking about transgression in the first person because I'm really interested in getting into that psyche and exploring that darkness. But although I'm singing in the first person, the truth is that I believe the absolute opposite. I'm inhabiting a character to illuminate those things. Especially with Wiseblood, that character was macho, sexist, and talking about decapitating hitchhikers, and nothing could be further from what I'm like as a person. But I was liberated by Dada and punk rock, and I wanted to push against the system, rebel, and transgress. I can't deny that there was an element of shock to using the Foetus name, and then to step onstage and inhabit those songs, that was a very liberating experience, and I felt very comfortable the first time I did it. Those songs are violent and confrontational, and that's how I was onstage a lot of the time—or that's how I portrayed myself, at least. I wasn't sitting down in bed of daisies, cross-legged with an acoustic guitar. It's confrontational stuff. But just because that's my art, it doesn't necessarily mean that's what I'm like when I get home. Of course, I can look back and cringe at some things, but I own it.

God help us! The Neubauten event, where a crowd bereft of company was eventually to dissipate without pleasure, a crowd consummately tired, deservedly cheated and weirdly overestimated by a mind who's ideas have outgrown even speculation. The fact that the names Showaddywaddy and Einstürzende Neubauten are faintly amusing when they share the same poster is really no apology for having the realities sharing the same stage. Boredom is one of the few things beyond humour.*

THE STUD BROTHERS, *Melody Maker*, September 19, 1987

DAVE BARTRAM We had a new album and single coming out, and we wanted to up the ante a little bit. Our promotor, Derek Block, came to us saying we'd been offered a gig at the Kilburn National Ballroom with Einstürzende Neubauten.

* Einstürzende Neubauten's *Funf Auf Der Nach Oben Offen Richterskala* (BART 332) was released by Some Bizzare on June 22, 1987. To promote it, Stevo organised a double bill of Einstürzende Neubauten and 1950s rock'n'roll revivalists Showaddywaddy at the Kilburn National on September 7.

I immediately said, 'Who?' I wasn't into goth rock, never have been, so it was a weird one, almost like they were laying down a gauntlet. I knew Stevo was a bit of an oddball, and he'd obviously got this idea for the most incongruous matchup of artists he could possibly find. I actually spoke to him and got the feeling he was looking to embarrass us, in a sense. But we agreed to do it, and from the word go it was obvious that we were the seen as the support band, and consequently were treated as such. There were issues with dressing rooms, our rider hadn't been adhered to in any way, shape, or form, and, to put it bluntly, we were treated like shit. And then we were kind of thrown to the lions in front of this black-dressed, pierced, wan-faced audience.

MARK CHUNG We had never heard of Showaddywaddy before we played with them. We had no idea who they were, and we were quite surprised when we saw them. Someone explained to us that it had some cultural reference, but we didn't really understand it. It was definitely a Stevo idea—he liked surprising people, and it fitted very much with his humour. Before gigs, I tended to find a quiet space to prepare and concentrate, which I did that night, so, no, I didn't see them.

DAVE BARTRAM We were definitely the underdogs, so subsequently, when we ran out onstage, we were full of purpose. We weren't going to be treated as second fiddle because we knew we were a decent live band, so we rose to the challenge and really kicked it out. It had the desired effect, and we proceeded to go down a storm. It was quite extraordinary to see that crowd reacting to it. The icing on the cake was, we watched Neubauten's performance—out of curiosity, more than anything—and they couldn't follow us. We literally blew them off the stage. I spoke to a few journalists afterward, and they were handing out the plaudits, saying they didn't expect us to be that good and all that sort of stuff. I used to take the *Melody Maker* on a weekly basis, and the headline of their review was 'England 4 Germany 2', in reference to the 1966 World Cup Final, which I thought was hilarious.

STEVO The Neubauten fans thoroughly enjoyed Showaddywaddy. Journalists like to pigeonhole people, don't they? 'Oh, well, if they're into this, they won't be into that.' But it's all entertainment. It worked well. When Neubauten entered the stage, it was more impactful when it was following 'Three Steps To Heaven'.

If Blixa and the disorganisers had hoped Showaddywaddy would be blitzed off stage they were sorely mistaken. A group of hardened professionals baptised in the blood of Brighton Top Rank will not be frightened away by the dialectic of the capital's post-modernists. Showaddywaddy played a gruelling 40 minutes and were received with deafeningly hypocritical cheers. But Showaddywaddy aren't intelligent enough to be two-faced. They left with a bitter diatribe against the event, its organisers and its audience who were still reeling from the embarrassment when Neubauten marched on unnoticed.

THE STUD BROTHERS, *Melody Maker*, September 19, 1987

DAVE BARTRAM No artist worth their salt likes to be treated badly, so I had a bit of a sound off about it. It might have sounded like a diatribe to some, but I was definitely hamming it up for effect. Still, it was an extraordinary night. Years later, *Time Out* listed it at number 56 in their list of '100 Greatest London Gigs Of All Time'!

MARK CHUNG *Funf Auf Der Nach Oben Offen Richterskala* was the one album where we actually rehearsed before recording. I think it's our weakest record, but we rented a rehearsal space for two weeks and actually prepared something for the studio. Obviously we knew that normally songs had structure, we just chose not to use it in our music. It was really more that we'd got a bit tired ourselves of doing everything without discernible song structures, and at some point we felt, *Why don't we try that?* And I know Blixa discovered structure with his lyrics, which kind of meant we needed to have structure in the music as well. But the main reason was, we wanted to do something different than in the past.

>>

IAN TREGONING When he was in New Cavendish Street, Stevo had an art gallery on the ground floor. There were some good bits in there—like the guy who did the melted soldiers for Test Dept [Malcolm Poynter], he was really good—but there was a lot *If You Can't Please Yourself*... kind of 'What the fuck is that?' stuff too. Anyway, a heavyweight art critic, I think it might have even been Brian Sewell, trashed the gallery on LBC Radio. So Stevo phoned them up saying, 'That's ridiculous, I demand a right to reply.' And so they agreed to have him as guest, and he had to get to the studio at 8am on a Sunday morning. Anyway, the night before, Stevo, Zeke, Matt, Paul Webb from Talk Talk, and I were around Matt's for one of our occasional boys' nights. We'd take a few bits and pieces but not get too hammered, just great banter, playing a bit of table football and staying up all night. And it was about 6am and Stevo goes, 'Right, who's up for some acid then?' And we were all, 'What? No, no, we're not gonna do any acid, Stevo!' And he pulled out a sheet of acid and woofed down four tabs of it. And we said, 'Stevo, aren't you supposed to be going on the radio in a couple of hours?' and was like, 'Yeah, yeah, this is getting me ready for it!' So anyway, he takes this acid and heads off, and we stayed at Matt's and tuned in.

MATT JOHNSON It was a roundtable discussion programme hosted by the broadcaster Gill Pyrah. There was Stevo; an environmentalist; art critic Brian Sewell, I believe; and another guest. Stevo was saying things like, 'They should fence off the rainforest! Put fences all around it!' And then, not unreasonably, somebody said, 'But who should do the fencing?' And Stevo replied, 'Fencing? What fencing?' He didn't know what he was saying as he was completely off his head. He then asked the other guests if they'd like to rape him! Completely rambling and incoherent. After a short break, Gill Pyrah said something like, 'Unfortunately, Stevo had to leave early.'

IAN TREGONING Stevo started out OK, but Sewell was soon shredding him, so Stevo really starts going off on one. And then, all of a sudden, you can hear footsteps in the background and the sound of chairs been dragged around as Stevo is bundled out of the studio, and the presenter cuts straight to the weather. We were all crying with laughter. But in a way, Stevo had a point, and that was you can't dismiss something just because you're unable to see where it's coming from. Of course, his motivation really wasn't really for the art, it was him sticking two fingers up to the establishment, which was a major part of what he used to do.

MATT JOHNSON I did have a cassette recording of that LBC show. I'd love to find it again. We used to sit around listening to it again and again, and we'd all be on the floor in hysterics and crying. It was so funny.

STEVO Sewell said to me, 'Stevo, your gallery is from the gutter and it will return to the gutter.' He bet me £500 that it would be closed within a year. I took that bet and he lost. He did honour it, though, and I directed the money to Battersea Dogs Home.

VAL DENHAM Around 1987, I had a solo exhibition of my paintings and photographs at the Discretely Bizzare Gallery. The show a was called *Masterpieces From Hell.** Most people really liked what I did, but I got a lousy review from a well-known London weekly listings magazine. I overreacted and wrote a letter to the magazine's art critic, telling her that she could basically go fuck herself. Stevo was furious with me—he said it was bad enough having to put up with Marc's over-the-top, volatile reactions to criticism, and now he had to contend with two out-of-control screaming divas.

HUW FEATHER I didn't see myself as an artist, so I never exhibited at Discretely Bizzare. Now I totally understand that I was a bit stupid not to take advantage of an opportunity like that, but back then I just didn't like blowing my own trumpet, I was much happier in the background.

Discretely Bizzare exhibited visual art that mirrored the temper of the record label from which it had developed. Its selection of artists and the nature of the art it showed were inclined toward an outsider sensibility—often violent and grotesque—in sympathy with the vogue for the 'abject' and 'transgressive' that was prevalent within London's avant-garde during the second half of the 1980s. Artists that showed there included Andy Dog (whose work appeared on sleeves for THE THE); Val Denham (sleeves for Marc Almond and others) and the sculptor Malcolm Poynter.

While Stevo's brave venture did not, ultimately, survive, it became an obscure but significant historical marker. It was, on the one hand, a premonition of the imminent rise to fashionability and economic power of contemporary visual art; on the other, an acknowledgment of the underground and sub-cultural avant-garde that emerged in the 1980s from punk and post punk and historically preceded the rise and rise of 'Young British Art'.

MICHAEL BRACEWELL, 'Early YBA Videos And Their Disobedient Prehistory', May 2019

---

* Val Denham's *Masterpieces From Hell* exhibition ran at Discretely Bizzare from October 8 to November 10, 1987. An interview with Denham filmed at the gallery, featuring comments from Marc Almond, can be found on YouTube.

TEST DEPT *A Good Night Out* was TD's final LP for Some Bizzare and fulfilled the band's contract with the label after an acrimonious split.* Without going into details, we went our different ways. We became more active politically which didn't sit too well in the mainstream music industry. The Long March continues!

CHRIS BOHN The fantastically generous and magnanimous 'You make the records you want to make' approach was brilliant for a while. But it became a different thing when none of the records recouped and nobody got paid. Mute would be the obvious comparison: a lot of great-sounding, nicely packaged records came out on Mute, and they weren't mean with their budgets, far from it. But they were a bit more careful about how they spent them, more realistic. Stevo soon turned from being this Santa Claus–like character into someone hiding from artists who wanted an audit. It just became a complete mess. He was like child entrepreneur figure, brilliant on one level and completely unrealistic on another. And a lot of people suffered as a consequence, Stevo included.

ROB COLLINS Then the money started running out. The deals that were done with the major labels should have been used to fund and market the records, but it ended up paying the company's overheads. And that's where it went wrong—the label couldn't honour its fiscal responsibilities. And the label never seemed to have any money in the bank—I always felt like, every week, I might not get paid. But I always got the little brown envelope with the cash, and sometimes a cheque, which I'd then run to the bank to cash. So, it didn't affect me directly, and I don't know if that meant Stevo took less, but he was very frivolous with money. Easy come, easy go.

STEVO Yes, there were financial issues, and I've got to be careful what I say here, but they didn't come from mismanagement of accounts, they came from the fact that Some Bizzare's needle time was being misdirected elsewhere.† I didn't find out about it until ten years later, and I'm still owed a load of money.

JANE ROLINK When we moved premises to New Cavendish Street, Stevo lived upstairs, and he was drinking too much and went off the boil.

---

* *A Good Night Out* (MOP 3) was released on Ministry Of Power/Some Bizzare in December 1987.
† 'Needle time', or neighbouring rights, are international performance royalties collected by the PPL.

ROB COLLINS I left when it was starting to go a bit weird. The Cabs had already gone, and Stevo needed to do a deal with someone to keep the label going. And that deal was going to be with Mute, and it very nearly happened.

DANIEL MILLER I was talking to Stevo a lot at that time, we were in touch constantly, and I'm sure it was talked about it, but I can't remember how far down the line it went. But there was definitely a discussion, although I don't recall there being a deal on the table as such.

ROB COLLINS Stevo felt I fucked him over because I went to Daniel and asked to start a label. And Daniel—who was already funding Blast First and Rhythm King—said yes.

I told Stevo I was leaving, and that Swans and Jim were coming with me, and he fucking lost his nut. Stevo couldn't do anything about Michael, but he just made it impossible for Jim.

J.G. THIRLWELL Yeah, that's absolutely correct. I was trapped and I was bitter, and I didn't record anything for about a year. And then we negotiated that I would do one more new album, *Thaw* (1988), and a compilation, *Sink* (1989). Is *Thaw* my angriest record? Probably. Are the two things connected? I think so.

ROB COLLINS Going to Mute was a big move for Michael musically. He'd always said to me to me that it wasn't simply about making this solid wall of noise—there was a lot more going on than that. He just didn't have the skills to do what he wanted to do at that time, and it took him a while to figure all that out. I think the essence of the band is sonically still the same, from the first EP to today. He's got it where he wants it now.

MICHAEL GIRA I ran into Stevo in New York a couple of times after we left Some Bizzare. He was really high-rolling in those days—he took me for a ride in his limo or something. But I don't recall any hostility about it. Like I said, I had respect for him from his origins, from where he came from.

ROB COLLINS Jane left and went to Rhythm King—she probably just got fed up with it all. I know I did, and I saw another opportunity. There was only so far I could go with Some Bizzare, with all the noise and chaos that was around it. To his credit, Stevo kept it going.

JANE ROLINK I felt I needed to move on, and I think the time was right. Things were not great there, and I did need to find my own feet. I went to work at Blast First with Big Black, then I moved to Rhythm King. But Some Bizarre was the place where I belonged. I just didn't feel like I fitted in other places. But how could you follow Some Bizarre? It was like family. We were so secure, it was lovely.

A condescending face over a soon to be dissolutioned security seeker.

Ø, from the sleeve of *If You Can't Please Yourself You Can't, Please Your Soul* (1985)

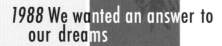

1988 We wanted an answer to our dreams

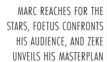

MARC REACHES FOR THE
STARS, FOETUS CONFRONTS
HIS AUDIENCE, AND ZEKE
UNVEILS HIS MASTERPLAN

MATT JOHNSON Stevo and I had pretty much parted company by the end of the *Infected* campaign, and he wasn't involved in *Mind Bomb* at all. It was a difficult time because I was very fond of him, but things, without going into too much detail, were getting completely out of control, so I started to distance myself. It was a very complicated situation, but drugs, paranoia, and general chaos all played a part. Later on, there were a few particularly difficult episodes, which eventually led to me making the decision to leave completely, but this is not something I have a desire to discuss publicly—or to hurt anyone's feelings with—so it will remain 'in the family', so to speak.

ZEKE MANYIKA I don't know whether both of them were trying to protect me, but I never found out what happened. I think the business side of it had just got so messy. Matt keeps on top of detail and takes that stuff seriously. And THE THE had become a big international act, and it couldn't be run it in the same haphazard way that Some Bizzare had when it started. The label was financed by all the acts but at different points, and Stevo wanted to keep it that way. But unless you have it tight contractually, you can't really do that, especially when some of the bands become so big [that] they have other obligations.

Stevo's behaviour had actually become a big problem, and the artists ended up having to manage Stevo. The number of times when people would call me in the middle of the night to go and rescue Stevo from a situation. It was like, *Hang on a minute, what's going on here?* I was used to it because we were friendly before I signed to Some Bizzare, so when I went with him for my own stuff, when we were filming in Africa, I knew I had to look after him, because he was in an environment that he didn't know.

LEE KAVANAGH I started working in the music industry when I was about eighteen, working for Clive Banks's plugging and publishing company, Multimedia, before moving to Derek Block Artists Agency. From there I went to Phonogram, where I was in the international department for many years. I knew of Stevo's reputation as this genius/crazy guy, and I knew Matt by his music. One day, I got a call out of the blue from Stevo and was invited to an interview, which Matt attended too. Stevo could never remember anyone's name, so he used to call everyone 'Rabbit Ears'. He was like, 'Awright, Rabbit Ears, do you want this job or what?', while Matt was much more professional and was asking me questions about my experience. It was almost like the roles were reversed, with Matt the serious manager interviewing me and Stevo the hinderance artist at his side. But you could see there was something about Stevo. He looked immaculate, wearing really fancy designer clothes with big, bold tweeds. I don't know what I was thinking, but I went back to Phonogram and just handed my notice in, and off I went to New Cavendish Street.

MARC ALMOND I don't remember how it happened or how long it took exactly, but Stevo phoned me up one day and told me he had done a deal with EMI Records. I signed on the dotted line, bemusedly smirked, and took the cheque. I once again had a strange sense of déjà vu. If my confidence was at an all-time low , Stevo made me feel much better by telling me that I was signed to EMI only because they were so keen on him; I was apparently just the by-product of a deal that enabled the company to work with the legendary Stevo.

LEE KAVANAGH I just didn't know what to expect with Stevo. He was fearless and there was a whiff of danger about him. He used to live upstairs from the office, and on a day when he had a really important meeting at EMI he came downstairs with no trousers on. And he left the office like that: with a jacket, shirt and tie, an Easter bonnet full of flowers (no idea where he got that from), brogues, a sarong, and walked up New Cavendish Street to EMI with his dog, Honour, in tow. Certain people got him, but you had to be very tolerant. Yet he would do all this crazy stuff then just say one brilliant thing and everyone would be on side again. Plus, the Artists on Some Bizzare were fantastic. Don't forget, he had this amazing product, so he could back up everything he was doing, as the music was so good. He had the ammunition.

STEVE SHERLOCK Stevo used to have some crazy ideas. He said to me once, 'I've got to go to EMI, and I want to walk in the office with you dressed as a court jester playing the flute behind me!' It didn't happen, but I guess that's why it's called Some Bizzare.

LEE KAVANAGH I'd been to see Marc play the year before at the Astoria, and I'd never seen a gig like it, he just had the audience in the palm of his hand. It was one of the best concerts I'd ever been to. So I was looking forward to working with him, but I was a bit nervous about how we would get along. I needn't have worried as we hit it off straight away, and we had a real laugh during all the long, tiring promotional tours we did around Europe and America.

ANNI HOGAN For the *Stars We Are* album, The Willing Sinners were reduced to Billy, Steve, and me and were renamed La Magia.* It was a lot of work, and again the sessions were quite angsty. Marc was under a lot of pressure from the new label and was on prescription drugs and kind of phased out. He was there some of the time but just sitting around reading magazines, while Billy and I were working 24/7 to make the record. We worked fantastically together, sitting opposite each other with two keyboards, just hammering things out.

I think personally I wrote some great tracks on *The Stars We Are*; it's very pop, but it's experimental pop, and a lot of different influences again. Billy's arrangements were brilliant, especially on the track Nico sang on, 'Your Kisses Burn'. His arrangement is as much the song as the vocals are, but he doesn't get a writing credit on it. But we were all over the show, I was in a complete mess, everybody had fallen out, nobody got on with anybody, it was tough, but through

* Marc Almond's first album for EMI, *The Stars We Are* (PCS 7324), was released on September 4, 1988, and reached no.41 on the album chart. The preceding single, 'Tears Run Rings', had reached no.26, his highest chart placing for three years.

all the darkness there was always a great creativity. And Marc's vocals are gorgeous on 'Only The Moment' and 'These Dreams are Yours'.

With each successive album, Marc Almond just gets better and better. Older and wiser, although not without his share of trials and tribulations, he religiously documents each shade, each mood and turns it into a rich carpet of luscious arrangements, sensitive but dynamic melodies and no-stone-unturned lyrics. These songs live a life of their own and all because the little chap with the heart that makes up two thirds of his height isn't afraid to put some of his very soul and essence into their making.

NANCY CULP, Q, August 1988

Although on this album he has mostly abandoned the hauntingly ornate chamber-rock orchestrations which made *Mother Fist And Her Five Daughters* one of last year's outstanding releases, and reverted instead to the simpler synth-pop themes of his youth, Marc Almond remains a maverick with a sharp eye for *outré* experience.

DAVID SINCLAIR, Vox, August 1988

LEE KAVANAGH Because I'd come from a major label, I had a fair idea how things should work, so when I'd speak to the record companies I could challenge them. When *The Stars We Are* came out, Marc started travelling and doing more promotion, and Stevo gave me a lot of freedom. I would always try and let him know what was happening, but he would just wave me away and say 'Carry on, old choops'.

ANNI HOGAN Stevo was always around, but Marc would be visibly antagonised when he was and just try to shut him up. Stevo has never been any different—he constantly talks nonsense and somehow managed to make a career out of it. He's just on another planet: Planet Stevo.

>>

J.G. THIRLWELL I increasingly felt the need to set up a studio that was my own place and where I could do pre-production. So I moved to a loft in Brooklyn, where I still live, right around the time that computers became accessible and at a

273

price point that was affordable. So, I got an Atari 1040 and an Akai S900 sampler and started work on material that turned into the Foetus Interruptus album *Thaw*, which I recorded in '87 and which then came out in '88.*

ROB COLLINS Jim has been in the same place in Brooklyn since the mid-80s. You have to phone him before you get there, and he throws the keys down and you go up in this industrial lift. That's what I loved about New York back then: people living in these places that you'd never ever think about, coming from grey Victorian London. Suddenly, you're walking into these lifts that are the size of your bedroom, clanking up and down inside this huge warehouse.

J.G. THIRLWELL It's crazy how much the price of sampling technology plummeted between *Nail* and *Thaw*. A Fairlight cost around £20,000 in 1985. The technology or the tools at hand have always influenced my music. And later on, as I got into using musical notation, I viewed that as a technology too, which was a whole different form of liberation. But once I was no longer shackled to going into an outside recording studio, I changed things up a lot and started exploring things that I'd never done before. And somehow the material did translate pretty well to a band setup, although it wasn't the intention. By that point I had done a lot of shows, so maybe I had started thinking in that mindset a bit, about things that would work live.

Thaw is more of the same because there's no one else out there so saucer-eyed, so blinkered, so raw to the world. And the world? Well, the world according to Clint is *one shitty place*. We're withered by convention, made puny by morality, rendered toothless by the law. It's an apparently godless, certainly godawful world and, if there *is* a God, He sits with idiotic pride on a throne made of human excrement and gold. He is vain, pompous and ultimately useless.

THE STUD BROTHERS, *Melody Maker*, September 1988

[*Thaw*] represents that feeling you get when you want to hit someone, but don't know who. It's that kind of pent-up frustration and violent futility that Foetus

---

* Under the new Foetus Interruptus moniker, J.G. Thirlwell released *Thaw* (WOMB FIP 5) in September 1988 on Some Bizzare. It would be his last album of new material for the label.

Interruptus bring out into the open for all the world to gasp at. Listen to this and ruin your karma.

JOHN FORTGANG, *Sounds*, September 24, 1988

J.G. THIRLWELL I didn't think that I could realise my music live, because it was such a studio creation, and so intricate. I had done a bunch of shows using backing tapes, but that had gone as far as I wanted to take it. When I did put a band together, the material from *Thaw* translated pretty well, and the older material kind of became something else altogether. There was a lot of crosspollination with Swans—Norman Westberg was in my band for many tours, and Algis Kizys and Ted Parsons, so there was a lot of swapping band members. I did it for several years, but there came a point where I felt like I was kind of steamrollering all of the nuance out of the recordings, which was being replaced by bludgeon and volume. Which was fine because the recordings had their own qualities, and the live thing brought something different to it. But there were times when I felt like I was doing a disservice to my music by playing it in that way.

Clouds of dry ice, strobes, portentous keyboard crashes, the whole rock theatre bit, as the band crash into a 90-mile-per-hour thrash metal storm. The slam-dancers up front, right on cue, go ape, and it's hell on earth.

TONY REED, *Melody Maker*, October 1, 1988

Clint Ruin moves further into the audience, and sings the Spanish words of 'Chingada' with a voice that could crush concrete. An arc of spit showers him. The change on Ruin's face is immediate. The mask of disdain dissolves into hatred beyond control. Clint jumps off stage, boots blaming and fists flashing, turning the offending gobber's nose into a bloody hot dog. The audience draws back, sensing you don't mess with Clint unless you really want to ruin your evening. Therein lies the gruesome reality of Foetus Interruptus. Some bands play with violence, some use its images like circus performers, but Clint Ruin is aggression personified on the platform of rock.

JACK BARRON, *NME*, October 1, 1988

J.G. THIRLWELL There was an incident at the Town & Country Club, and I ended up punching someone in the face. I didn't mind putting it out, but I didn't

275

particularly like it coming back at me. I don't know why crowds were like that in London at that time. And there were bomb threats in Holland for both Wiseblood and Foetus Interruptus shows.

>>

LEE KAVANAGH Sue Pocklington ran the gallery and did all the exhibitions. She knew what Stevo wanted and understood his ideas really well, so he left her alone to do it. I remember a Malcolm Poynter exhibition that did really well, and Philip Diggle, the Buzzcock's guitarist Steve Diggle's brother, his pictures sold really well. Helen Chadwick, Graeme Hughes, Tim Head, they all exhibited there. I remember Zeke bought Malcolm Poynter's head sculpture. We said to him, 'Zeke, it's our big exhibit, we're supposed to be showing it to the public,' and he said, 'No, my friend, I'm having it,' and walked out of the gallery with it under his arm!

ZEKE MANYIKA I loved Malcolm Poynter's stuff. It was really, really beautiful. I needed something artistic for my home studio in Knightsbridge—something to distract me when I hit a tough patch. It was this skull kind of head, and I combined it with this really interesting lighting by another of the Some Bizarre artists, and I just loved having it on my desk when was making music. I bought it and then carried it down New Cavendish Street under my arm. Stevo borrowed it for a Some Bizzare exhibition, and every time I wanted to get it back, he'd say, 'No, no, no, Perk, I need it for another exhibition in Berlin' or somewhere. And I thought, *It's fine, we're friends, it's safe*, but he never gave it back. It's probably worth a fortune now!

VAL DENHAM I don't think Stevo was predicting the YBAs or anything, even though Discretely Bizzare was a good year before all that. It was just another string to his bow, and it made him seem more intellectual, I suppose. Not that he was dim—he really wasn't. The thing about Stevo was he was interested in the outré, the avant-garde, the odd, the difficult, which is why he signed the bands he did. And it was the same with the gallery, so any artists that would offend the hoi polloi, genteel people, the Christians, he wanted to promote that.

>>

276

ZEKE MANYIKA Matt had split from his long-term girlfriend, Fiona, and was going through a hard time. I went to see him at his flat in Islington, to try and distract him. He had this new drum-machine sequencer out in the living room, and he'd been doing something with it. We were chatting, and he was getting quite distressed, so he left the room to have a few moments to himself. I just started programming the drum machine, and it triggered everything that Matt had been working on. He rushed back in saying, 'What's that?' I had written this anti-apartheid poem called 'Bible Belt', so Matt said we need to get that down, so he edited the poem to fit the rhythm, and that was that. It would have been easy for us to do a whole album, and fun, but it would've sounded like a THE THE record, and we decided that might be a bit be too much.

THE THE's *Infected* documented the degradation, depravation, and chilling reality of a 'decaying' Britain. In another time and space, on the other side of this world, all this seems nothing to the poverty-ridden repressive states portrayed in what seems logically and musically *Infected's* follow-up—the Matt Johnson-produced 'Bible Belt' by Zimbabwe-born Zeke Manyika.* 'They believe they are the chosen race/chosen by the colour of their face,' spits Zeke, angry, aggressive and convincing.

SARAH CHAMPION, *NME*, December 10, 1988

ZEKE MANYIKA Stevo and Andy Dog went to Zimbabwe for a holiday. My brother offered to drive them around, take them to Victoria Falls and Hwange game reserve. They were in the middle of the game reserve and a bull elephant appears in the road. So what does Stevo do? Hits the horn. My brother goes crazy, 'You don't do that to a bull elephant!' Apparently Stevo just laughed. But he was very respectful to my mum and dad and visited their house. My brother introduced him to my parents, and he puffed himself up and said, 'Hello! My name is Stevo, from Some Bizzare!'

LEE KAVANAGH Stevo loved to throw in a Latin term when negotiating with people. So one minute he'd be saying, 'You're pulling my fucking pants down' and

* Zeke Manyika's 'Bible Belt' (R 6187) was released on Parlophone in November 1988. Matt Johnson is credited as producer and remixer on a second twelve-inch version (12RX 6187), the sleeve of which features a striking painting by Andy 'Dog' Johnson.

then throw in, 'You bury my Fede'. He'd always have these little sayings and names he would call people, and it just broke the ice with everyone. It didn't matter if he was talking to the receptionist or talking to Maurice Oberstein, it was the same. He'd also buy Christmas presents for everybody. He was so generous, but he would buy the exact opposite of what he thought you wanted. So he'd go into EMI, and if you if you had a big beard, he'd buy you a shaving kit!

STEVE SHERLOCK I was walking through the West End on a job, in the late 80s, maybe early 90s. And this second or third floor window opens, and this bloke sticks his head out, rubbing his eyes, obviously just woken up. I look up, and it's Stevo. I called up to him, and he said, 'Awright? Come up!' But I didn't have the time, so I said I'd come back later and I never did. And that was the last time I saw him.

A statement from the management (no thank you why ltd): Three quarters of the conversations on earth are complaints. Don't complain, LIVE.

Ø, from the sleeve of B-Movie's 'Nowhere Girl' twelve-inch (1982)

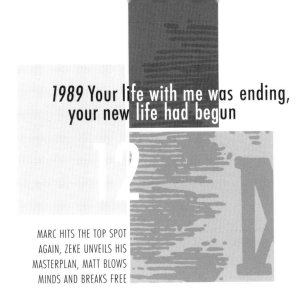

1989 Your life with me was ending, your new life had begun

12

MARC HITS THE TOP SPOT
AGAIN, ZEKE UNVEILS HIS
MASTERPLAN, MATT BLOWS
MINDS AND BREAKS FREE

STEVO If you put me in a corner, I'm going to fight. Whoever's closest is going to get hurt. It's a conscious decision to be one step ahead of people's expectations, for freedom's sake.

MARC ALMOND I was first told of ['Something's Gotten Hold Of My Heart'] charting while I was doing a showcase for a record-company conference in Germany. I was furious with Stevo for putting me up for this event, performing as light entertainment as record-company executives wined and dined. It was so demeaning. 'You've got to play along,' said Stevo. 'It's all part of the music business.' Was this Stevo the rebel, the anarchist? Not anymore. He'd become one of the boys; he was kissing ass more than any of us. He was the record-company friend—corporate Stevo. Maybe it *was* him the record companies wanted.

LEE KAVANAGH There was a lot of promotion for Marc's *The Stars We Are* album around the time of 'Something's Gotten Hold Of My Heart', especially when it went to no.1.* Some of the TV appearances, though . . . Marc would often go on these European music and entertainment shows on his own, without a band,

---

* The third single from *The Stars We Are* was Almond's cover of 'Something's Gotten Hold Of My Heart' (R 6201). In an inspired move, the song's original singer, Gene Pitney, was recruited to turn it into a duet. It reached no.1 on the UK chart on January 14, 1989, and stayed there for four weeks.

which would send producers into panic mode. Someone wearing headphones would always come out and say, 'The director's got an idea,' and we'd be like, 'Here we go.' And they'd bring on these props that had nothing to do with Marc or the song, things like a life-size plastic Venus de Milo, which Marc then had to perform with. Oh, the things they asked him to do.

ANNI HOGAN Rob [Collins] had started managing me, and Marc and Stevo didn't like that—they saw it as a threat. Rob had asked for half a point for me as the co-producer and co-writer on *The Stars We Are*, and they wouldn't give it to me. And that became a very difficult thing. Then, during the tour, the band was whinging about money, so I took it upon myself to try and get everybody better pay. And then everybody went behind my back, and it became a horrible mess. Marc got Jane to write a nasty letter to me, which I then responded to, and then another nasty letter came from Marc, and I ended up leaving. Although I was told that contractually I had to do some dates in Italy supporting The Cure, which was hell. Marc just wouldn't look at me, on or offstage. All my family lived in Rome, and we played the PalaEUR on my twenty-eighth birthday, and after the gig was just horrible.* Looking back, I think it was time for me to go. I wanted to do my own thing, but I never wanted to leave Marc. He didn't want me doing anything else but him. We've never spoken since, and he's kind of deleted me from as much of his story as possible. How weird is that?

FLOOD It's always a shame when it happens, but it's the nature of the beast. All artists are incredibly sensitive people, and they're put in these intense emotional situations. And there's always gonna be breaking a point. Everything is dysfunctional.

>>

MATT JOHNSON The thing is, if I get pressured to do something, I'll do the opposite. So, by this point, CBS had given up asking me to play live so that's when I thought, 'You know what, I'm going to put a band together and tour the world.' Around the same time, I was backstage at an Iggy Pop gig, and Johnny Marr, my old mate from years previously, was there, and we hadn't seen each other for ages, not since The Smiths became very successful. We both said, 'Oh, we should do

---

* The PalaEUR gig on June 9 was one of seven Italian shows Marc Almond and La Magia played with The Cure in 1989.

something together,' so I had that in the back of my mind when I started putting the team together for *Mind Bomb*.

WARNE LIVESEY Matt demanded a lot of himself and demanded a lot of the music, but he wasn't particularly demanding on people. Obviously, if you're trying to do a good job for somebody then you'll put pressure on yourself, but I never experienced Matt being 'difficult,' apart from being a constant piss-taker, and the pair of us weren't very good for each other on that front. I wouldn't say Matt was particularly more relaxed on *Mind Bomb*, but it's a different sort of record to *Infected*, with a different intent, but it wasn't intrinsically different in terms of the work process. Both of those records were up there in terms of the amount of time and energy I put into them, they're the two longest records I've ever worked on in terms of time of recording time. There were a few weeks off here and there, and a couple of points where I did another record when Matt was working with someone else, but I didn't even record all of the songs on either of those records, and still worked on them for a year each.

MATT JOHNSON I'd started writing and recording *Mind Bomb*, with Warne Livesey and Roli Mosimann, who were my co-producers on *Infected*. I decided to do the same with *Mind Bomb*, so do half with Warne co-producing and half with Roli co-producing. We'd already done 'Armageddon Days', which I played guitar on myself, and news came out that Johnny had left The Smiths, so I thought I'd give him a call. So I contacted him and he came around to my place and we sat up all night, chatting, and by the following morning he'd joined the band. I already had former ABC drummer Dave Palmer in place, who played on *Infected* and was at that time the best drummer in the country—he was incredible. Warne introduced me to James Eller, who'd been playing with Julian Cope. And then Johnny joined, and the four of us got together and there was such a fantastic chemistry. We got very, very close.

JOHNNY MARR When it was announced that I had joined Matt Johnson in THE THE, it was rather predictably met with negativity from some areas of the British music press. Matt was called upon to defend our collaboration and was denounced for having the audacity to harbour a fugitive from The Smiths. That we both maintained a belief in the mission of THE THE made the indie militia all the more suspicious, but the pettiness galvanised us. We were committed to what we were doing, and we thought that people who actually bought the records and paid to go into concerts might like what we were doing. And they did, and the album we made, called *Mind Bomb*, went into the Top 5 and shows sold out everywhere.

WARNE LIVESEY Matt's a mischief-maker, and we got ourselves into a bit of trouble a few times. We were working at AIR studios, about four stories above Oxford Street, and we'd asked the studio to take off the double-glazing panels in the control room so we could open them to get some fresh air. Matt was on this distilled water and grape diet, and I guess one day somebody must've a thrown grape out of a window, which of course we all thought was incredibly funny. This escalated over the following weeks to the point where we were ordering pounds of tomatoes from Berwick Street market and throwing them out of the window at people walking below, being careful to not actually hit them but close enough to give them a shock. One day, I misjudged it and actually did catch a woman who immediately looked up and saw us all ducking back into the studio. She was obviously quite well-to-do, as about half an hour later she turned up in reception with a lawyer. Luckily, the studio manager was pretty quick-thinking and sent one of the assistants up to replace the panels, so when she came into the room, the studio manager could say, 'Look, you can't even open these windows, let alone throw something out of them.' I think he blamed it on some kids breaking into the toilet and throwing stuff from there.

JOHNNY MARR When we recorded the album's opening track, 'Good Morning Beautiful', a story of a satellite addressing our planet and an exposition on humanity's self-destruction, we did it in the middle of the night, having been ingesting psychedelics for several days. When I plugged in my guitar, Matt approached me conspiratorially with saucer eyes and said, 'Can you make it sound like Jesus meeting the devil?' His request made total sense to me and I summoned up the appropriate response, which he followed by hollering demonically into an old blues mic, 'Who is it? Whose words have been twisted beyond recognition in order to build your planer Earth's religions? Who is it? Who could make your little armies of the left and your little armies of the right, light up your skies tonight?' It was stunning.

MATT JOHNSON Although we did have some guest musicians on *Mind Bomb*, like Wix on piano and organ—he had played accordion on 'This Is The Day'—and obviously Sinead O'Connor on 'Kingdom Of Rain', most of the album was just the four of us. I wanted to keep a strict band and have pretty much the same musicians playing on each track so the album could be toured. The spirit and the chemistry among the four of us was so strong, I knew that it shouldn't just be a studio thing and we should take it forward. Thinking back, it could well have been Johnny's suggestion go out on the road.

JOHNNY MARR Playing in THE THE, I was given the freedom to try anything and was encouraged to do things I'd not done before; fuzz sounds, industrial noises and radical echoes were all employed in the spirit of experimentation.

STEVE HOGARTH The *Mind Bomb* tour was scheduled for the summer of '89, and Matt was sounding out musicians for the band. I went over to see him at his place in Shoreditch, and we talked about it and he asked me if I would do it, and I said, 'Yes please.' Around the same time, Marillion got in touch looking for a singer, so I found myself in this really odd position of being offered a tour with undoubtedly the coolest band on the planet, and then getting another call from the least cool band on the planet. So that was a really peculiar decision to have to make. When I met the boys in Marillion, they were just really nice people and they said, 'You just do what you do, and we'll do what we do, and see what happens.' I wasn't asked to write in a certain way or sing in a certain way, it was offered to me as my own gig really. So, it was quite a tough one to turn down, and, you know, the rest is history. But to this day, I regret not having been able to do the *Mind Bomb* tour. It would have been great to be onstage with Matt, Johnny, Dave, and James—it would have been one hell of a band. And it would have been such a nice change for me to be at the back, out of the spotlight, just doing my thing. It would have been fantastic.

MATT JOHNSON Stevo had become more and more eccentric but also more and more destructive. For me personally, Stevo's peak was between *Soul Mining* and *Infected*—he could be amazing, incredibly persuasive, very passionate about who was representing. He would come up with outrageous ideas that other people simply wouldn't have, and then be very proactive in making them happen. And he could convince virtually any major label that these outrageous ideas were good ones, and that they should get behind them. So Stevo in his prime would have done a great job on *Mind Bomb*, but he wasn't in his prime anymore. And it was very painful, because he was a friend and someone I was very fond of and we had shared so many really memorable times together. But there was an increasing number of drugs around and, I suppose, they affected some people more than others. Once the negative feelings and paranoia set in, things started to deteriorate, the artists started leaving, and the downward cycle accelerated. It was incredibly sad and just became very toxic, very quickly.

WARNE LIVESEY I don't have any specific gripes about Stevo, but I never really connected with him as a person, either. I only met him two or three times over the whole period I was working with his artists, and he never came to the studio for anything I did for them. So, I wasn't party to anything going on with him and Matt, although for *Mind Bomb*, the record label negotiated my contract with my manager, rather than Stevo doing it, as had happened with *Infected*. So my contract was with CBS rather than Some Bizzare. Read into that what you will.

LEE KAVANAGH Matt's relationship with Stevo was difficult by the time of *Mind Bomb*'s release, so he took control. Stevo didn't understand it—he thought Matt was being disloyal and couldn't handle it at all. We held the album launch for *Mind Bomb* at the Crypt in Trafalgar Square, and Stevo just didn't turn up. I thought, *He'll get here soon*, but he never did, and it was a big deal for Matt—he felt let down.

STEVO Saying that my ears are good, because I can give you the music, is one thing, but marketing is just as important to me. You have to have an angle to pin things on; you have to find ways to get people to talk to create buzzes and get things working. Things don't just happen; you make them happen. So, after all the care and attention we put into marketing *Soul Mining* and *Infected*, whoever thought that putting a big bald head on a poster and sticking it all over London would help sell records obviously had a screw missing.*

* THE THE's third album, *Mind Bomb* (463319 1), was released by Epic on July 11, 1989, and reached no.4 on the UK album chart, Johnson's highest chart position at that point. It remains one of his biggest-selling records.

MATT JOHNSON Mal said Stevo acted as a prophylactic between the major labels and the artists, and he did. He was one of the last great British record industry eccentrics. Managers were supposed to be outrageous and colourful—the good ones, at least—and Stevo was the last of that breed. But even toward the end of the 1980s, it was becoming obvious that you couldn't behave that way anymore. Nowadays, you'd be out on your ear—in fact, you probably wouldn't even get in the building. You'd be cancelled or even arrested.

LEE KAVANAGH Stevo's relationship with Matt came to a sticky end soon after. Whenever Stevo suggested accompanying Matt on promotional trips, Matt would say, 'Oh, please don't.' Matt preferred to go on his own, but then Stevo decided to go along to Germany one time, and he just caused chaos.

MATT JOHNSON Stevo was a really important part of my career, and he's somebody I had a lot of fondness for. I've not seen him for a long time, because he's a difficult person to be around now, the paranoia and the bitterness set in long ago. Obviously, he sees things differently, but you have to be honest, you have *all* of the artists on one side of the argument and just him on the other side—who are you going to believe?

There were things that went on, which I would never say publicly, because I don't want to kick a person when they're down, but one by one he alienated all of the artists and just pushed everybody away. Marc stayed with him for a very long time—he was the most loyal out of all of us actually—and even he got to the point where he was at the end of his tether and couldn't cope with it anymore. So there's a tragic element to this really, because Stevo was somebody who was well liked and very popular, and a real friend to his artists at times, there was a lot of camaraderie amongst everyone.

LEE KAVANAGH Stevo ran things exactly as he saw them, but he did inspire everyone who was involved. I have a great memory of Mark and Blixa in the office for the release of Neubauten's *House Of Lies (Haus De Leuge)*, and Matt, Marc, and Zeke were there too, with Stevo on top form.*

---

* Einstürzende Neubauten's final album for Some Bizzare, *Haus Der Luge* (BART 333), was released on September 4, 1989, via Rough Trade.

STEVO I'm unreasonable. You can't talk reason to someone who's unreasonable. It's a waste of breath. They ended up going, 'Oh, it's Stevo, forget it.' I worked with EMI—not *for* EMI, with EMI—for two years, and I didn't raise my voice once. I didn't need to, which totally shocked them. They know beneath this there's a maniac, so they don't push their luck. And they *respect*. This business is made up about 80 per cent of people who admire anyone with artistic flair because they have none. It's full of people waiting to borrow, and then they all go shuffling off together. Well, fine. I'm shuffling off in the other direction.

>>

J.G. THIRLWELL The *Sink* compilation was the last thing I released on Some Bizzare.* As far as I was concerned, that chapter was closed, plus there was so much more that I wanted to do and try. I stopped changing the Foetus name and I started Steroid Maximus, which was kind of a life-changing thing for me. To do something so totally different musically, that wasn't perceived as a transgressive thing with lyrical content exploring the dark side of existence, just opened things up. With Steroid Maximus, it was purely the music that you inhabit and explore, and that was what I really needed at that time.

CHRIS BOHN Once Jim had cleaned up, he quickly moved on and started doing all these different amazing things, like Steroid Maximus, Manorexia, and his soundtrack work, while continuing to make great Foetus records. All really interesting, true Jim Thirlwell music that isn't a parody but rather a true reflection of the man. It was so great he managed to do that, to rescue himself and carry on with his original spirit shining through.

J.G. THIRLWELL It was definitely a journey, and I really am proud of those albums and the collaborations, but it was a weird time. I've reflected on it a bit, and I think I could have done more, to be honest. I was a bit of a slacker.

KEVIN FOAKES I found Jim's work absolutely fascinating and still do. Unlike more traditional musicians who'll write a song and then work up an arrangement,

---

* The *Sink* (WOMB INC 6) compilation was the final album J.G. Thirlwell put out on Some Bizzare. Released in October 1989, it contained previously available material and was credited to Foetus Inc.

286

he builds a sound world and then creates a song over the top. I understand the sampling aesthetic, because that's largely how I make my own music, and I love deconstructing his music to find out how he put it together and the choices he made. Over the years, as I've bought records to sample myself, I've found the stuff that he used for his music, loads of these easy listening records that he sampled for Steroid Maximus and Wiseblood's 'Pedal To The Metal'.

I'm not one of those 'it was all better back then' kinds of people, but of course two of my favourite Foetus albums are *Hole* and *Nail*, because they were the first ones I heard and they had a big impact, but I also find later albums like 2001's *Flow* just as interesting. He appeared on my *Search Engine* album, and I've remixed tracks for him, and occasionally help him out with graphic design.* He'll ask my opinion on a cover layout or to suggest a type face or something, and it's really nice to be involved on that level, especially as his record sleeves influenced me so much.

ZEKE MANYIKA Parlophone were going to sign me anyway, but Stevo had shown faith in 'Bible Belt', so I let him do all the dealings. And I wanted him to benefit from it. It was not a good atmosphere at Some Bizzare at the time. There were problems with all the big artists, many had left, and he was trying with a bunch of new bands. We had a good time doing *Mastercrime* and going to Zimbabwe and America to film, but it was very obvious it was a dead relationship artistically, and that was when he just disappeared basically.† I tried to reach him but he never got back to me, so I just didn't bother after a while.

LEE KAVANAGH Stevo had a knack of making you feel beholden to him, which, in the end, caused much resentment, I guess.

MARC ALMOND Stevo did sign some great licensing deals for me, with Phonogram, Virgin, EMI, WEA, and Mercury. Each one was a great experience for me and enabled me to work with some of the best people in the business. Fantastic A&R, marketing, and press departments, great producers, top studios, wonderful

* DJ Food's 2012 album *The Search Engine* (Ninja Tune ZENCD176X), not only features an appearance from J.G. Thirlwell on the track 'Prey' but also includes a re-recording of THE THE's 'Giant' with Matt Johnson on vocals.
† Zeke Manyika's *Mastercrime* (PCS 7330) was released through Parlophone on November 11, 1989. The latest Some Bizzare logo is on the back of the sleeve, and the CD inner features a sculpture by Malcolm Poynter.

musicians and arrangers, and I was lucky to make some classic and seminal records as a solo artist.

LEE KAVANAGH The *Jacques* album was a labour of love for Marc and was many years in the making.* The album was really well received with glowing reviews around Europe, especially Germany, where Marc played some fantastic shows. I remember one night when he'd finished the set, came offstage but the crowd would not leave so he came back on and played the whole set again. It was a special night that.

The piecing, aching poignancy of Scott Walker's voice was usually equal to the task of interpreting Brel's work. Almond's voice is a less dependable instrument altogether. Throughout this album it rarely succeeds in bringing these songs to the boil. At times, Almond sounds unnaturally detached, even matter of fact. Throughout *Jacques* there is little of the exuberance we might have expected. The kind of rousing intensity that Almond brought to Spector's 'A Woman's Story' on the *Tomb* EP. The kind of savage unrestraint on *Violent Silence*, his 1986 eulogy for Georges Bataille. Almond has been known to sing as if singing could change the world. But not here.

JONH WILDE, Melody Maker, December 1989

MARC ALMOND Listened to now, the album seems a very flawed and frustrating body of work. It could have been so much better, so much fuller and rounded, if I had taken time to record it properly, given it my full attention and worked in conjunction with a producer. Instead I snatched time when I could, recording it in dribs and drabs between other commitments. And it would have been better if I had deconstructed the songs, and recorded them with a more relaxed delivery instead of treating them so preciously—hey, if I'd just thought about it properly!

\>\>

Every year for the last ten years I go away for the whole of December. Zaire, Mozambique, Haiti, fifty-nine countries I've been to. I just go away and no one

* Marc Almond's *Jacques* (BREL 1) was released in December 1989. It was his first album to be issued independently by Some Bizzare.

288

knows where I am. I go away on my own. I don't drink. I swim, or I walk. I walked over 100 miles in Grenada—in four weeks, so I didn't kill myself. Sit-ups, aerobics, running up hills and no drink. So in January when I come back, everyone's screwed up because they've had too much Christmas pudding and got some threepences stuck in their throat, and I come back *shining*, ready to take on another year. Someone said to me, 'You're drinking now and you're going away in two weeks, why don't you stop drinking now and have a drink while you're there?' I said, 'No, you don't understand. When I go away I have to be totally and utterly wrecked, so every day I can feel myself getting better.' It's a psychological thing.

STEVO to Paul Sexton, *Select*, February 1991

MATT JOHNSON Stevo had been on Concorde once or twice, many years previously, and he was really proud of the fact. He had this expensive leather passport holder, which he carried around with him like a status symbol, and he'd leave the Concorde ticket stubs sticking out the top of it, even though they were quite old and dogeared. I used to ask him why he didn't just throw them away, and he'd say, 'They see these, Matt, and they *know*. They respect you.'

Accustom to inspiration, appreciate the history of the future.

Ø, from the booklet accompanying *Redefining The Prologue 1981–2006* (2006)

289

1990–95 Misery, complaints, self-pity, injustice

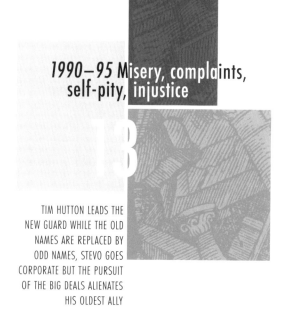

TIM HUTTON LEADS THE
NEW GUARD WHILE THE OLD
NAMES ARE REPLACED BY
ODD NAMES, STEVO GOES
CORPORATE BUT THE PURSUIT
OF THE BIG DEALS ALIENATES
HIS OLDEST ALLY

ZEKE MANYIKA I think Stevo lost his way, and although he had some good people around him, there was a different mood to the days of Jane and Rob. People like Lee and Mike were very efficient, and I don't think he could really work in that new kind of mode. He just didn't translate to the way the industry had changed.

MIKE HOLDSWORTH I was label manager at Rough Trade Distribution and looked after the Some Bizzare account, which basically entailed organising advances to them. Part of Stevo's world was an independent label, which had Swans, Neubauten, Coil, and Foetus, so we were the distributor. I think they had what was termed a PMD deal, which meant Rough Trade manufactured on their behalf, and then sold and distributed.

So, basically, Some Bizzare would deliver the parts to Rough Trade, and Rough Trade would produce the product and sell it, and Some Bizzare would get their monthly sales and then be accounted to. And sometimes they would ask for advances on their upcoming releases in order to fund other releases. By the stage I was working with Stevo, there weren't many new releases, mainly back catalogue. In 1990, Rough Trade Distribution was going through a collapse, so I took a voluntary redundancy before it actually finished, didn't do anything for six months, and then Stevo contacted me.

RICHARD NORRIS There's an enormous ego that characterises everything Stevo does. He kind of acts as if Some Bizzare was a band and he was the lead singer. And that does colour the working relationship with him, because it's very different from how you would normally work with a record company. And that kind of gets in the way a bit, but I don't think there's any malice in it. He's actually quite idealistic in terms of his views on art, and has done some incredible things with music, getting very left-of-centre people into the mainstream. And also, with his gallery, there were some really quite interesting things going on there too.

MIKE HOLDSWORTH The art gallery wasn't really functioning by the time I got there—it was just an empty space with the tube chairs and a few original artworks. On the first floor there were a couple of small offices, where me, Lee, and part-time accountant Janice worked, and Stevo lived upstairs on the second floor. There was the label side and the management side of Some Bizzare, and at that point, realistically, the management side, which was basically managing Marc, was taking up the bulk of Stevo's time. I guess I was the label manager; basically, Stevo asked me to run the label to keep it ticking over.

Rough Trade wanted me to do a retrospective Some Bizzare album, ten years of, and I said, 'No, I want to do a compilation of some new Some Bizzare artists,' which excites me. Some Bizzare has become almost its own pigeonhole, which is ironic, that's exactly what it was fighting against, so I've called the new compilation *Some Bizarre-ish*, with this Andy Johnson illustration of this person having a nervous breakdown. It's of all new artists and it's absolutely brilliant.*

STEVO to *Select*, February 1991

MIKE HOLDSWORTH Marc's Jacque Brel covers album was supposed to be the big record, which was going to put some funds back into the indie side of the label. But I guess the reissues were the main revenue stream at that time, another monthly bump into generating some sort of income through the label.

---

* Released in 1990 and distributed by Rough Trade, the third Some Bizzare compilation LP, *Ish* (SBZLP 003), featured tracks from new artists Stex, Vicious Circle, Agnes Bernelle, Tim Hutton, and Kandis King alongside established artists Zeke Manyika, Neubauten, Marc Almond, and Foetus. The cover was another Andy 'Dog' Johnson painting.

TIM HUTTON I'd been signed in the late 80s under the name The Neighbourhood and released an album, *A Certain Attitude*, on Parlophone. Money was sloshing around back then—they'd stuck us in Abbey Road for six months, which was really unproductive and was completely written off. Then my manager spent all my publishing on his massive cocaine habit, so he had to go. Luckily, my A&R guy was the lovely Clive Black, who wanted to keep me on for another album, and he put me in touch with Stevo. Obviously I'd heard of Some Bizzare, so when Stevo expressed an interest in what I was doing, I was quite flattered. I'd pretty much finished *The Conscious Kind*, and he was up for managing me, so he took it on. Parlophone had spent quite a lot of money already, but Stevo managed to get me out of the deal while keeping the album, which was pretty incredible really. He eventually put it out on Some Bizzare.*

MIKE HOLDSWORTH Stevo has a great energy, and he was a great salesman, he could pitch to anyone and get them excited about music, and that is a real talent. He had a real presence, too. And because of the success of Soft Cell and THE THE, he could pick up the phone and speak to the head of any record company in the world. Maybe his influence was diminishing at that point, but the people would still talk to him, because he had a track record which he could live on. But he was also mercurial, and you never knew which Stevo you were going to meet on any given day.

TIM HUTTON *Infected* was a big album for me, so Matt Johnson was one of the reasons I was interested in working with Some Bizzare. Although he'd not long left the label, he was still around peripherally. Marc Almond was still there, and Zeke was very much around. I thought it was a really good move at first, but I quickly realised Stevo was in full flight on the gear and drink, and being pretty mad. I had faith in him, though, because I realised he'd been like that for some time, and he'd still achieved quite a lot. Plus, I was really pleased to be out of my previous situation, and I felt that he was somebody who, despite his madness, had a really good track record. And, at that time, a lot of the really high-achieving managers were proper characters, so it was something to live up to on that level.

* Tim Hutton's *The Conscious Kind* (SBZ CD 005) was released on CD by Some Bizzare in 1991.

With a singular disregard for the machinations and limitations of the mainstream, Marc continues to doggedly pursue a perverse career path which has already spawned an LP of Jacque Brel songs this year and a welcome return to the *Top Of The Pops* studios with 'A Lover Spurned', one of ten songs included here. Dominated as ever by Almond's fetching semi-operatic warble of a voice, *Enchanted* is a torrid mix of torch song and sexually charged psychodrama, cloaked in grand melodramatic emotions. Toying with the conventions of a markedly European musical tradition, Almond dresses up these songs with gypsy violins, flamenco swirls and Gallic flourishes.

PAUL DAVIES, *Q*, August 1990

MARC ALMOND I look on *Enchanted* as my 'world' album. It's an exotic journey around the world and through it, a journey into myself. It certainly reflected the type of music I was listening to at the time. It is part Spanish, part Arabic, even part Turkish. There are Indian bhangra influences on the track 'Death's Diary', Middle Eastern influences on 'Orpheus In Red Velvet', Brazilian lambada on 'Carnival Of Life', Celtic flavourings on 'The Sea Still Sings', and Latin drama in 'A Lover Spurned'. The richly varied themes are encompassed in the cover picture, once again by Pierre et Gilles, who portrayed me as a sea-god swimming with a mermaid. It's my favourite album cover.

The more [Marc Almond] dabbles in matching his idols (the Brel-Piaf-Walker syndrome) the more we're reminded of their effortless greatness, in contrast to his *straining* greatness. Of course, another of the things that we love about Marc is how doggedly and wilfully he *strains*. But you do see the drawbacks it raises. Why listen to, say, a track from this new album when we could just bung 'The Sun Ain't Gonna Shine Anymore' on the turntable for the fifteen thousandth time?

CHRIS ROBERTS, *Melody Maker*, August 7, 1990

LEE KAVANAGH The release of *Enchanted* came with the usual European press tours to promote it.* Marc had a good relationship with Clive Black and Tris Penna, so there was good camaraderie with EMI around that time. It was a successful album for Marc, but how much involvement Stevo had with it, I'm not sure.

* *Enchanted* (PCS 7344) was released on Some Bizzare via Parlophone on June 9, 1990, and reached no.52 on the UK chart.

MARC ALMOND People ask me why I stayed with Stevo so long. Loyalty, stupidity, and an affection for him, I suppose. I remembered the person he was at the beginning, and there was still a lot of love for him in the music business. Deals were signed that ultimately didn't do me or his other artists any favours in the long term. And there were a few music business parasites that didn't always have Stevo or his artists' best interests at heart. But that's the story of the music business.

TIM HUTTON I grew up mainly in Africa, went to boarding school, and I ended up in London when I was nineteen, squatting and playing in bands that put records out on Crass's label. I'd also had my first kid and kind of settled down by the time I met Stevo, so I'd lived a bit. Being the sort of character he was, Stevo was fascinating to me. I was massively influenced by Prince and played and produced everything myself, so I guess I was kind of at odds with what Some Bizzare had put out in the previous decade. But Stevo was always looking forward, looking for the next thing. Just before we parted ways, he took on Bizarre Inc, so he always had one eye on the future.

What can we do to 'recapture what was' is the wrong way to look at it, things have changed in a fundamental way, and you have to address the changes. Look at the charts, the evidence is right in front of you. The people who are buying the dance singles are basically young. The albums are appealing to older buyers. The challenge for the industry is to find a way to break house or techno into the album market. With the right artist and the right company, it will happen.

STEVO to the *Los Angeles Times*, September 26, 1993

RICHARD NORRIS I met Dave through Genesis P-Orridge when we were both working on the *Jack The Tab* album. I'd gone to interview Gen for a magazine and brought him a load of psychedelic compilations that Bam Caruso, a reissue label I was working for, were putting out. Gen was telling me about this phrase he'd heard, 'acid house', and he was quite into the idea of making an album of it, without particularly knowing what it was. The idea of psychedelic dance music was quite appealing to me, so we went to a studio in Chiswick, and I brought along some people from Bam Caruso, and Gen brought along Dave, who I was quite in awe of and initially a bit timid with. Basically, the idea was to create a compilation album of made-up bands, so we could be anonymous. It was recorded very quickly, and the rule was every track had to be put down and mixed in an hour. Dave and I really got into it, and three or four of our tracks went on the album.

DAVE BALL I had a good vibe working with Richard on the *Jack The Tab* album and later that year he and I formed The Grid, the name suggested by his old friend Martin Callomon [who] had just got a job in A&R and offered us a deal on the newly formed East West label, a subsidiary of Warner Bros. Originally Gen was going to be in The Grid and I was signed as the producer, but it soon became clear Richard and I were a duo and Gen viewed the idea of working with a major label as a match made in corporate hell.

RICHARD NORRIS Around 1991, The Grid did a bunch of Soft Cell remixes, including 'What!', 'Tainted Love', 'Where The Heart Is'. We did them at Marcus Studios, which were run by a Swedish gentleman who was very keen to have Stevo's business. He had a bar in the studio—obviously not a great thing if you want to get some work done—and he was wining Stevo with Aquavit, which is the national spirit of Scandinavia. Stevo just grabbed the bottle and drank all of it, and ended up rolling around the floor, kicking his legs in the air, laughing his signature cackle. From that point on, we thought it probably best not ask him to the studio anymore, but he kept turning up. We'd pretend we'd gone out, but we could hear him downstairs at the reception, shouting, 'I know you're up there!' One time he brought his dog, Honour, with him and said, 'If she barks she likes it, and that means the track is finished.'

DAVE BALL Soft Cell enjoyed a lot of back catalogue chart success in 1991. Marc rerecorded the vocals for some of our hits, and I did additional synths and drum machine overdubs with producer Julian Mendelssohn at Sarm West studios in Basing Street. When freshly buffed album *Memorabilia—The Singles* was released, it reached no.8 in the UK charts. I personally prefer the original versions, as do Marc and most of our fans, but the two singles, 'Say Hello Wave Goodbye '91' and 'Tainted Love '91', reached no.38 and 5, respectively.

TIM HUTTON I got involved with Stex—I produced a load of tracks for him. He was another character. But there was a bit of old Some Bizzare spirit there—you know, the family thing—there was definitely that kind of vibe.

295

RICHARD NORRIS Stex was this larger-than-life character around West London who I used to bump into at Camelot Studios in Kensal Road. Cocaine may have been involved. He'd got this song—'Still Feel The Rain'—which I was never sure if he wrote or not, but Dave and I went to a studio in Kings Cross to record it. Stex brought a posse with him and some drugs, and Stevo had collared Johnny Marr to play on it too. It was an amazing session, because Johnny instantly came up with this riff that just couldn't be anyone else. There was loads of us in the control room, and at some point there were plates of cocaine being handed around both sides of the mixing desk. It was a pretty debauched session, and I was quite surprised the record turned out as good as it did.

JOHNNY MARR I was in a rehearsal room in London and Stex's manager—Stevo from Some Bizzare—dragged me into a session. He said, 'Play!' I stood on the studio floor and the riff was the first thing I thought of. Through the control room window, I could see all these people, dressed up, grooving around. It was like being in Sly & The Family Stone for the afternoon.

DAVE BALL I just remember there being *a lot* of white powder around. The session actually went really well, and Johnny was just fantastic. The way he plays guitar, well, you can't fault it, can you?

RICHARD NORRIS Before shooting the Stex video, Stevo took us all on a lurching pub crawl, picking up Johnny Marr on the way. It took us hours to get to the studio and Dave and I weren't even in the video, we'd just gone along for the ride. It was one of many, many Stevo pub crawls.

MIKE HOLDSWORTH 'Still Feel The Rain' was this really great, slightly clubby pop record, with a killer Johnny Marr riff, which really should've been a huge hit.* It almost got Radio One support, but it didn't quite cut through. Stex was a pretty good indicator of where Some Bizzare was in the early 90s: much more in that sort of world rather than the industrial rock of the 80s.

---

* Stex's 'Still Feel The Rain' (SBZ 12 002) was released by Some Bizzare on December 10, 1990, and reached no.63 on the UK chart. An album, *Spiritual Dance* (BZLP 004)—which included another track featuring Johnny Marr, 'If I Were You'—was released in 1992.

LEE KAVANAGH For artists like Agnes Bernelle, a great burlesque-style cabaret singer and quite an eccentric type herself, Some Bizarre was a perfect home.*

MARC ALMOND Having Stevo as a manager was a double-edged sword at times. I became a pawn in Stevo's games to secure more money from labels, mainly to support lifestyles that were beyond our means. I was often signed to deals that were financially too big for an artist like me, so when things didn't go as well commercially as hoped—which was more often than not—I was stuck in a deal with a record label that just didn't know what to do with me. All too often, marketing departments didn't know how to package or sell me, so albums like *Mother Fist* alienated me from the people I was supposed to be working with. I was then pressurised into doing TV shows and promo duties I felt uncomfortable with, and when I was inevitably dropped from the label, I ultimately blamed Stevo.

RICHARD NORRIS When Stevo was meeting Rob Dickens to sort out the deal with Marc and Warners, Dickens mentioned that Stevo's trousers were creased. So he added a Corby trouser press to the deal, and he specified it had to be their top of the range Centurion model. This became a bit of an in-joke, so for a *Top Of The Pops* appearance by The Grid, we got in touch with Corby to supply us with trouser presses, and they went for it. They even suggested we use one of their tie presses in place of a wah-wah pedal.

DAVE BALL I got a really nice surprise when I was asked if The Grid would do a remix for Marc's 'Waifs And Strays' single. Richard didn't mind, and I was delighted as it was the first collaboration of sorts since we disbanded Soft Cell. Everyone seemed to be happy with the end result, and I was very pleased because it felt like a door that had been shut for some time between Marc and me was now slightly ajar.

Marc asked us to co-write some tracks for his *Tenement Symphony* album. So we ended up writing three tracks together, 'My Hand Over My Heart', 'Meet

---

* Agnes Bernelle was a Berlin-born actress and singer who lived in England and Ireland. She first came into the orbit of Some Bizzare through Marc Almond, who recorded a duet with her, 'Kept Boy', for *The Stars We Are*. Almond convinced Stevo sign her, although the label boss drew the line at letting him produce the subsequent album. Almond did write one of the tracks on the album, 'It Was Me', with Billy McGee. The album, entitled *Mother The Wardrobe Is Full Of Infantryman* (AGI 7LP), was released by Some Bizzare in 1990. Sadly, Agnes Bernelle passed away in 1999.

Me In My Dream', and 'I Have Never Seen Your Face'. Richard programmed the drum loops, I played some synth parts, and Marc wrote the lyrics and vocal melodies.

MARC ALMOND The instant I walked in [to The Grid's studio] it was as if the last eight years of being apart had not happened. He was still the same old Dave, and it was great to see him again. In the time we were together we wrote three tracks—it was a return to a sparse, dark pop sound—the magic combination of Almond and Ball—and it invoked excitement about music in me once again.

RICHARD NORRIS The *Tenement Symphony* tracks that Dave and I worked on predate Trevor Horn's involvement. They were written and recorded, Marc had done his vocal, the whole lot, and then Trevor joined the project and our contract with Warners was null-and-void and our royalty rate reduced as we were no longer the producers. When we protested, Warners said, 'Well, sue us. It will cost you about £10,000, and that's probably all you're going to make on this record.' They were very upfront with their cowboy manners. I think we get a 'vocal production' credit on those records, and Trevor and the big guns came in and made it more orchestral, which is fair enough. He made a great record.

It's hard not to love Marc Almond. His extravagance, his operatic gestures, his sordid past, his guilt, his glitter—he's the sort of romantic for whom the adjective 'hopeless' was created. And even if part of it is affectation (he is after all, a born performer), his desire to make a big gaudy splash in the still waters of pop is, despite all odds, still thrilling. *Tenement Symphony* is a gorgeous piece of indulgence. The main point to remember, children, is that the opulence with which all this is staged doesn't undermine the feeling behind it—it's not an empty exercise in camp. 'All that glitters could be gold,' warbles Marc on 'Meet Me In My Dream'. In this case, it is.

CAREN MYERS, Melody Maker, October 14, 1991

Almond does the sensible thing and surrenders control to Trevor Horn. There's a snatch of The Grid, 'Jacky' bounds along like a frisky Alsatian pup, Horn and Bruce Woolley's 'What is Love?' showcases Almond's penchant for winsome melodrama, David MacWilliam's epic 'The Days Of Pearly Spencer' omits the distorted vocal chorus but Anne Dudley's orchestration and Almond's knowing panache see it through. Finally, 'My Hand Over My Heart' is like every good Marc Almond song thrust together—he sings his little heart out, Horn lets the song breath, there's a storming choir and the lyric is a corker. Unlike previous Almond albums, there's little dross to weigh *Tenement Symphony* down, like them however there are truly special songs. If this doesn't do it for him, we might all just as well go home.

JOHN AIZLEWOOD, *Q*, October 1991

LEE KAVANAGH When I was first away with Marc in America, it became apparent that if decisions needed to be made, we had to make them ourselves. For example, Marc was supposed to be having a big launch party in LA, and it was so badly organised—they'd even spelt his name wrong on the invite. So I called Stevo to get permission to pull out of it, but I couldn't get hold of him. And I soon realised he wasn't there for that sort of stuff.

MIKE HOLDSWORTH Maybe I was naïve, but there was a lot of stuff going on that I was oblivious to in hindsight. There was a fair amount of friction between Marc and Stevo, but they also had a great relationship. They'd worked together I don't know how long by that point, and they'd had some incredible experiences. And Stevo really cared for Marc and for his career. I was there when they brokered the deal with Warners and Rob Dickens for *Tenement Symphony*, which was a big production. Stevo was very active, talking with Warners about the release and the whole strategy around it. And I think that was quite a moment in Marc's career as well—he had some big singles off that album.[*]

MARC ALMOND On the whole, *Tenement Symphony* was a long way from my true direction at this time—I wanted a scratchy, sampled R&B, soul album with the producer John Coxon, and, as I have pointed out many times since in interviews, it was the album I felt most excluded from in the making. Trevor Horn would have had me phone in my performance if he could, and Rob Dickens believed the one thing spoiling his Marc Almond album was me. God knows how we must frustrate

---

[*] Marc Almond's first album for Warner Bros, *Tenement Symphony*, was released on October 14, 1991. It reached no.39 on the UK chart.

record companies—if they could just get rid of those annoying people called artists and be left to get on with it!

TIM HUTTON I was living in Shepherds Bush, and Stevo came around and said, 'Come on, I'm going to take you out to lunch.' So we went down the Goldhawk Road to a curry house that I used to go to quite a lot and had a massive meal. And then, at the end of it, he just looked to me, and said, 'Run!' And I was like, 'For fuck's sake, this is my local, you idiot!' But I didn't have any money, so I just had to follow him. Stuff like that, I really enjoy thinking back to with a chuckle.

RICHARD NORRIS In the 90s, Stevo wanted to start a society called the Face In The Food Club, which involved going getting dressed up in your finest clothes, going to a very posh restaurant, and then, halfway through the meal, at a given signal, pretending to die and drop your head straight into your food, whatever it was. I don't know how many members the club had, but Stevo was very keen. He also wanted to set up a travel company that went to extremely dangerous places and call it Holidays In Hell.

LEE KAVANAGH I think Stevo had probably been a millionaire two or three times over, and then lost it all.

MARC ALMOND Musicians were sending invoices into Some Bizzare and, unbeknown to me, there was no money to pay them. The pot, which at one time seemed to be bottomless, was empty and people, understandably, started to become disgruntled, walking out of sessions and refusing to work with us.

MIKE HOLDSWORTH I would say that Stevo did strive to pay artists, but I appreciate it may not have looked like that. I was party to various accountings and was aware of accounts being prepared and sent off to artists. People may have had to wait but there was money being paid, he wasn't actively not paying people. There may have been disputes over how *much*, and I know certain artists did feel extremely exercised, but when I met Michael Gira, when I met Jim Thirlwell, even when I met Mark Chung, if they were annoyed with Stevo they always seemed to realise that Some Bizzare had given them the platform to be where they where they were, musically.

MARK CHUNG Neubauten always catered to a very small part of society, but we had noticed there were certain people everywhere who appreciated what we were doing, and we were reaching those people globally. And, fairly quickly, we'd sold over 100,000 albums—a good part in Germany, but other territories too which soon added up. And that's really what triggered the conflict with Some Bizarre later, because at some point we knew we'd sold a lot of albums. Before, I'd always said to the band, 'Look, I know what Stevo has spent on studio costs and production, and it'll be unrecouped at this point so there's no need to get a statement from him.' But then, after three albums, we thought that we should get a statement.

STEVO Some Bizarre Limited did a historical audit on Neubauten, and I'm not exaggerating when I say it was about an inch and a half thick. It was a serious audit of the of the past accounts, which showed them to still be in a deficit.

MARK CHUNG We had a manager, but Blixa fired him, so I was handling the business side of Neubauten. Initially, I really appreciated what Stevo was doing for us, and I could see that he was taking financial risks. And also, on a personal level, we actually got along very well for many years, and I used to stay in this house when I was in London. But after the fourth album, we knew what the sales figures were and that some money must be coming in, so we needed to get an accounting. Also, as I was as the manager, the band were coming to me, asking, 'Why haven't we got a statement from Some Bizarre?' So, I tried to get one, and it took me a while to realise what a mess the whole thing was. There was no paper trail of anything, and there was nobody at the label who really did royalty accounting. It was the classic indie-label mistake, as I know now from working many other indie labels. Some Bizzare were very much focused on the creative and marketing, with the administration and royalty statements an afterthought. And if you don't get that sorted pretty early on, it's very difficult to sort out later.

At some point, after not getting any response from Some Bizarre, we hired lawyers to put a bit more pressure on them. And their lawyers wrote back and soon we were stuck in the English lawyer trap. It was chaos and it just deteriorated. To be fair, in a genuine attempt to get it resolved, Stevo audited himself, but the auditors wrote that essentially, they didn't have much to go on, and the end result was that they thought we'd almost recouped, but not quite. Which we didn't believe. So it went on and on, and while the band didn't deny that Stevo had been helpful to us, the expectation was, we should by now be getting statements, and we weren't getting them. So it really fell apart after that.

STEVO Every artist has a right to audit. They do not have a right to go around saying that someone is not paying royalties when the provisions are there to safeguard them. If they don't implement those provisions, then that's up to them. But running their mouths off saying they're not getting paid, well, that's just not on. We did an audit for Neubauten and we sent it over to them and they said, 'Oh, it's rubbish.' Great. So why did we bother? If they don't *want* to believe it, then they're not going to believe it, are they?

MARK CHUNG When we did the initial deal with Some Bizzare back in 1983, we had a big argument because Stevo wanted the publishing. And we knew enough to say, 'No, you're the label, we're not giving you the publishing.' And it went back and forth between us and Stevo and his lawyer at the time, John Kennedy. At some point, we agreed to compromise, which was to start a new publishing company, Dimehart Ltd, and we would put Neubauten's copyright with that, and have a 50/50 split on the publishing. Stevo also said, 'I'm getting sent loads of stuff that I can't put out on Some Bizzare, but I think it's commercial and could be successful. So I'll use Dimehart Ltd, and whenever I see something I'll put it through.' And Stevo and I agreed that I would deal with everything I brought in, and he would deal with everything he brought in, and Neubauten helped us cover the cost of the company.

Dimehart Ltd was a classic 50/50 company, which meant we both owned 50 percent of the shares and we were both managing directors, but it also meant we could cancel each other out on everything. When it was up and running, other artists asked us to do their publishing, including Swans and Diamanda Galas. So we published more, and they were all things that I brought into the company. Then it transpired that Stevo hadn't been paying mechanical royalties—to anyone, I think. So I went to the MCPS, because I thought they should be the ones to sort it out, and they told me that because Stevo was a managing director in both the label and the publishing company, they couldn't get involved as it was an internal conflict of interest. So we were stuck. So the dispute with Dimehart Ltd about mechanicals added to the ongoing dispute with Neubauten about royalties.

STEVO Michael Mann used Neubauten's *Armenia* on the soundtrack for *Heat*

(1995), and it really should have been the turning point in their career. The Hollywood doors should have flown open for them at that point. I don't know why they didn't. Maybe they complained about it too much.

KARL O'CONNOR All the bands airbrushing Stevo out of their histories need to remember how integral he was to their success. Even Mark Chung, who probably has a bigger axe to grind than most, has said as much. Of course, Stevo was a lunatic, but without him putting Neubauten in those big studios, I'm not sure those records would have sounded the way they did. And it was the same for Coil. I spent some time in Swan Yard with Coil in the early 90s, when they were trying to follow up *Love's Secret Domain*, and they were really stretching the hourly rate. I was there because my friend Mick Harris from Napalm Death was drumming on the sessions, and they were just sitting around. We get there in the morning, and Sleazy would just be reading GQ or something, and when Balance finally joined us, he was unfocused and distracted. It was an expensive studio, and I could see the clock running, and the only time it ever picked up was when Mick got really sweaty drumming and took his top off.

TIM HUTTON Certain things Stevo did, I don't think I'll ever forget. I was there when he threw the photocopying machine out of the office first-floor window, which was quite a thing. He was also barred from pretty much all the pubs in about a mile radius from the office. And he was running some sort of feud with the guys in the newsagents next door. One morning, we'd had an early meeting in a bar, and Stevo had had five Long Island iced teas before eleven o'clock. And he'd gone into the newsagents and started pelting the guys behind the counter with Cadbury's Creme Eggs. I've no idea why. It was probably quite painful if you get hit by one. But there was lots of stuff like that.

Anxiety can kill a man. When you're just pacing up and down waiting for something to happen, which is out of your control, it can destroy a man. I end up pacing up and down like a panther that needs to walk miles, but there's nowhere to walk, you keep facing a wall. So I have to get out of that situation and I find that London is very unhealthy. I don't particularly like hanging around the office so I have to get out, but where do you go? I don't go out to nightclubs and stuff. I'm in bed probably by eight . . .

STEVO to *Select*, February 1991

MARC ALMOND I never seemed to get a grip on what was happening with Stevo and Some Bizzare. No one seemed to be paying the bills, but I'd open a paper and see double-page stories about an engagement ring he was buying for his girlfriend worth half a million pounds. Nonsense, of course, but he was associating with unsavoury people, losing himself and alienating me further.

LEE KAVANAGH Toward the end the drinking became more frequent—he'd be falling down the stairs drunk and all this sort of thing, and you couldn't get any sense out of him. He'd get out on the window ledge shouting and hollering. We'd have to try and get him back in again and placate the police who turned up in full force. And Stevo's a big lad, it was a farcical situation.

One day, in his anger he picked up the full-sized floor photocopier and smashed it out of the window and it landed in the street. We were hiding under the desks not knowing what he was going to do next. I sat on the floor and thought, *Hmm, I'd better get of here pronto.* That was the last straw—I mean, who throws a photocopier out of a first-floor window? I wouldn't have believed it possible if I hadn't seen him do it with my own eyes. When I asked him why he did it he just glibly said that I was 'being negative' and it made him angry.

When I spoke to Matt the next day, he asked me if I would like work for him as his PA. I said yes straightaway, funnily enough. On my last day, Stevo was hiding outside, sweeping up the courtyard. He couldn't even look at me. He just didn't know what to do or say to me. I just shut the door behind me and that was that.

I live above the office, which is terrible. I'd rather have three Winnebagos, those big silver American cars, and make Some Bizarre mobile—instead of bands going on tour, it's like Some Bizarre on tour. If there's a problem with someone in Hamburg, just put your foot down and sort out. Bricks and mortar only restrict your freedom. There's nothing more frustrating than not seeing a tree.

STEVO to *Select*, February 1991

MIKE HOLDSWORTH As far as new Some Bizzare artists were concerned, Stevo would just play me some music or introduce me to an artist, but I didn't know where he was hearing this stuff. Bands like Echo City, who created these amazing soundscapes, were made up of people who'd known each other for a long time working in avant-garde music circles.

PAUL SHEARSMITH The original intention of Echo City was to get people to build their own instruments and play music as a community arts project. The first installation, called a sonic playground, was built on Weavers Field in Bethnal Green by Guy Evans, who was the drummer in Van der Graaff Generator; David Sawyer; Giles Leaman; and Giles Perring. That was about 1983, after which I became involved. Alongside the sonic playgrounds we started doing gigs, playing the instruments designed by David, and it developed to us appearing at festivals around Canada, America, and Europe, playing for people with disabilities and encouraging group musical participation. The instruments included Clangerphones, which were suspended aluminium chimes, and Batphones, which were tuned lengths of polyethylene tubing which you hit with a paddle. We'd build the sonic playgrounds and install the instruments for the community to engage with and make music. We also started recording some of the appearances and put them out through our own label.

NICK CASH I had played with Echo City and been involved in workshops and some gigs, although I was not a member.

PAUL SHEARSMITH I knew Stevo through Ian Tregoning, and he used to come down to our house. I liked him and we got on well. I once played him at squash and beat him 11–0, 11–0, 11–0. Anyway, I played Stevo some of the stuff Nick Cash and Giles Perring were doing as Unmen, as I thought he'd like it. He also listened to some of Echo City recordings and liked those, too, and offered to put out an album. For the cover, we used a photograph taken at a Singapore fringe festival we played at, showing a group of nuns playing one of our Batphones. We decided to call the album *The Sound Of Music*, because we were using sound to make music, plus we had the nuns on the front. We used the logo from the film hoping we would be sued, which would generate some publicity, but that never happened.*

IAN TREGONING Echo City were doing some really interesting stuff but they weren't really commercially minded. They were more involved with social work. I actually did a tour with them where I was playing drums. And out of that came Unmen, which was basically Giles Perring and Nick Cash, and I helped them

* Echo City's *The Sound Of Music* (SBZ CD 008) was released by Some Bizzare in 1992.

record some stuff at Blackwing Studios. And they met Stevo through me, although I had nothing to do with any of the deals.

NICK CASH Unmen came about after Giles came on tour with Fad Gadget. We got talking about a shared interest in film music, Morricone, John Barry, Lalo Shifren, et al. Soon after, we recorded a version of the Bond theme, but we concluded making our own music was more interesting and fulfilling. We borrowed producer Rico Conning's Akai S900 sampler and a Revox and started building tracks like audio collage, recording and sampling with the Akai and then editing on the quarter-inch tape with a blade. We didn't have a computer at that point.

MIKE HOLDSWORTH There was a release by Unmen and a couple of things from Foreheads In A Fishtank, but they didn't have the impact that the 80s Some Bizzare releases had.

RICHARD NORRIS Stevo's reasons for signing bands became increasingly less about the music. He worked with Bizarre Inc because of the similarity to Some Bizzare, and he picked up Foreheads In A Fishtank purely because he liked their name.*

NICK CASH Unmen had virtually an album's worth of material, so we approached Some Bizzare, Mute, and Warp. We just thought they were left field enough to be interested in what we were doing. Mike Holdsworth got back to us and said he really liked it and wanted to release it, but we needed a bit more music for an album. So we recorded another piece, 'The Unsleep', with Danny Arno, and that all became the *Love Under Water* album.† We didn't think too much about going with Some Bizzare—we had no idea where they were situated in terms of popularity at that time, though we were aware that Neubauten and Marc Almond were still with them. We didn't have much contact with Stevo. He wasn't involved.

TIM HUTTON *The Conscious Kind* came out in 1991, and the year after, Stevo got me an album deal with Sony. I made a whole album for fifty grand, and then he

---

* Foreheads In A Fishtank released two albums on Some Bizzare, both in 1992: *Buttocks* (SBZ CD 015) and *Yeah Baby Wow* (SBZ CD 017). A single, 'Haircut' (SBZ 12 014), was also issued the same year.
† Unmen's *The Unsleep* was released as a white-label promo (SBZ 12 013) and followed by an album, *Love Under Water* (SBZ CD 010), in 1992.

thought it would be a great idea if he spent more than that on a video for the first single, 'The Prophet'. So I did this video at Pinewood Studios with Bill Butt, who'd directed all the KLF videos, at vast expense. And then Stevo had this idea to launch the single—not the album, just the single—at the National Liberal Club in Whitehall. So, we had this massive launch, and then he had this campaign which involved these esoteric little stickers that had a picture of crown on them with the word 'thief'. I still don't really understand what it was all about—it was quite hard to keep up with his vision sometimes, but Stevo got really into it. There were all these little stickers around town, but they didn't have my name or the name of the single on it, so, of course, nobody knew what they were about, and the video got roundly ignored.*

MIKE HOLDSWORTH Stevo got Tim signed to a major, and they held quite large launch party at the National Liberal Club in Whitehall. But I can't remember if that record ever came out. Tim went on and signed another deal without Stevo a few years later with PIAS recordings.

TIM HUTTON Then, Stevo got barred from the Sony building for trying to strangle one of the legal department while he was in there working my record, so that didn't help. Not all the blame is with him—I shoulder some of it because, really, I allowed all this to go on, I should've put my foot down and said, 'This is ridiculous,' but I was kind of all at sea with it all. In the end, Sony didn't put the album out, and Stevo cut his losses and gave up, and that was the end of our relationship.

BEVERLEY GLICK I did interview Marc again—in the early 90s, when I was at *Vox*. I called him the Engelbert Humperdinck of the 90s, which he found quite funny. But years later, when I was at the *NME*, they asked me to go and review his gig at the Royal Albert Hall.† I broke my own rule and gave it a negative review—but unfortunately Marc thought it was the pinnacle of his career. And that's when he sent me a wreath. We didn't speak for a long time, and when his book came out I was really upset by what he said about me, especially as a couple of things were

---

* Tim Hutton's 'The Prophet' (THIEF 7) was released by Some Bizzare via Epic in 1992. It failed to chart.
† Marc Almond's *Twelve Years Of Tears* show was held at the Royal Albert Hall on September 30, 1992.

not true, and I didn't have any recourse.* But we did get back in touch again many years later, and he apologised.

Chartbusting star Marc Almond's record bosses have banned his album of gay pop songs—because they're too obscene. The gender-bender singer, who teamed up with rock wrinkly Gene Pitney for his no 1 single 'Something's Gotten Hold Of My Heart'—recorded the tracks years ago. Marc's lurid lyrics cover every kind of sexual perversion imaginable and are peppered with filthy four-letter words. But the former Soft Cell star's bosses at Some Bizzare records were horrified when they heard it and have refused to release it.

author unknown, *The Sun*, October 1993

In 1989 Marc Almond released *Jacques*, his album of Brel covers, and also recorded and subsequently aired live another dozen songs associated with his favourite milieu, the Rive Gauche. Remixed [as *Absinth*], these chansons are now unleashed on to a public keener than ever to wallow in Gallic unwholesomeness. Colourful arrangements of harmonium, celeste, accordion, strings and so forth meld agreeably with Almond's luvvy voice, which blooms in this exotic setting to an effect both entertaining and educational.

MAT SNOW, *Mojo*, October 1993

From the skittish, snarling, Eartha Kitt-ish 'Undress Me' to the heavy-lidded, savage torch song 'Incestuous Love', these are all songs of longing, sexual fantasy and desire. Most moving is Charles Aznavour's 'Yesterday When I Was Young', sung with Marc's distinctive sob in the voice. Sparing nothing on orchestration, this collection (recorded over the last ten years) goes far beyond camp to a world of genuinely wrought emotion.

LUCY O'BRIEN, *Vox*, October 1993

MARC ALMOND This whole period of European-styled music, which had included my Brel album, *Enchanted*, and *Absinth* was something I just had to get out of my system if I was to move on.† I know it would have been sensible (meaning more

---

* Almond's memoir, *Tainted Life*, was published in 1999 by Sidgwick & Jackson.
† Marc Almond's *Absinth—The French Album* (SBZLP 01) was released by Some Bizzare in October 1993.

commercial) to steer away from it . . . but I felt I had to be true to my heart. Many of my fans rate the Brel and *Absinth* albums as some of my best and truest work, but the music business frown, considering them to be tainted with the dreaded 'c' word—cabaret.

AMANDA HULL Working at Some Bizzare was my first job on leaving university. It was just Stevo, Mike, Janice, me, and Honour the dog. I saw Marc most days, but our conversations mainly existed of things like, 'Your cab is coming at 9am' and 'Can you come and meet Stevo next Tuesday?' Marc was polite but I was essentially the work experience, although I remember his tea order, 'Milk in first.'

Stevo was clever, funny, unpredictable, and a bit scary. I think the PA before me left because he threw a photocopier out of the window. I was twenty-two and enthusiastic, and worked for free in my summer holidays, and I think Stevo liked me. He used to call me 'Bunny Ears', or just 'Ears.' One day he asked me to go and plant a fake bomb under some record-company executive's car, but Mike said that wasn't a great idea.

MIKE HOLDSWORTH I was there for about two years, basically, then some ex-Rough Trade people started a company repping American labels in Europe and UK labels in America, and they asked me to join them. It seemed a much more stable environment at the time, so I left. I don't remember there being huge fuss—there wasn't any violence involved.

MARC ALMOND People had started to leave Some Bizzare: Jane Rollink, Mike Holdsworth, Lee Kavanagh, Rob Collins, to name a few. Some had lasted a while while others were only there briefly, but they all contributed and helped keep the ship afloat, even though it was full of holes. All were true music lovers and bought a knowledge and professionalism to the label, though, after a while, all found Stevo's unconventional ways of working a strain and moved on. Stevo was a maverick and a disrupter, but at times a cool, professional, old-school head was needed. As time went by, the company fell into debt, and Stevo's behaviour, once unconventional and truly refreshing in a staid music business, had become counterproductive. It seemed in the latter days as if Stevo was experiencing a continuous minor breakdown with the pressure of it all. The company was falling apart.

AMANDA HULL I really wish I'd kept a diary of my time at Some Bizzare, because every day was crazy. Stevo did all the Marc stuff, but I did quite a bit with Bizarre Inc and a band called Foreheads In A Fishtank. I loved 166 New Cavendish Street—it had an art gallery downstairs, and I can still remember the smell of all the vinyl in the basement. One of my jobs was to catalogue every demo, test pressing, and reel—all on a typewriter, no computers then—and I remember all the original tapes for early Soft Cell stuff had got a bit mouldy with damp, so I cleaned them all up and sorted them out. There was boxes and boxes of early merchandise, and the curtains in Stevo's flat were made from the backdrop material from the 'Torch' video—I remember thinking that was pretty cool.

The office moved to Mayfair in 1993.[*] I worked there too for a while, then went part-time, before they ran out of money to pay me. But I will always be thankful to Some Bizzare, as working there got me nearly every other job I did after. People used to say, 'If you can work for Stevo, you can work for anyone.'

Philanthropy for parasites.

Ø, from the sleeve of *If You Can't Please Yourself You Can't, Please Your Soul* (1985)

[*] Bourdon Street, Mayfair. The building was a converted convent, which fuelled a rumour that Stevo used the old confession booth to receive demo tapes from hopeful artists.

1996–99 I'm not the kind of person to hide when I can fight

DUBSTAR BURN BRIGHT,
MARC'S *FANTASTIC STAR*
BURNS OUT, AND CLEO WOOS
KOOT—ALL IN THE BEST
POSSIBLE TASTE, OF COURSE

STEVO When we were on Bourdon Street I bumped into Maurice Oberstein. Universal's head offices were around the corner, at the top of Berkeley Square. It was really early in the morning, and he was walking Charlie, his dog, and I had my Labrador with me, and we're both on our way to work. He said to me, 'Stevo, the thing with you is, you've got your head down and you're running at a brick wall. You need to tap yourself on the shoulder and tell yourself to go around the corner, because there's a door off the latch.' I think he was trying to tell me I was schizophrenic. But that was Maurice for you—he made me look completely sane.

MARC ALMOND The [new] album began with the title *Urban Velvet* and ended up being called *Fantastic Star*—a defiant, against-all-the odds, two-fingered gesture of a title that would become the final irony. The album of new and invigorating ideas that should have taken no more than a couple of months to record but which finally took three years, five producers, three A&R men, two record companies, countless months of recording and re-recording in five cities and three countries—of remixes, re-edits and re-re-re-recording—until every bit of freshness was squeezed out.

MIKE THORNE After the collapse of my creative relationships with THE THE and Soft Cell, which I attribute to Stevo's inappropriate management machinations, I'd resolved to have nothing to do with him or any of his acts again. But eleven years on, I thought that people could learn and should be given the benefit of the doubt. So, Stevo came over to my place in London and we talked pleasantly, if slightly guardedly, and I decided to let bygones be just that. I then met up with Marc, and the artistic fit was instant and close, and it was immediately obvious that we could do good things together.

We had been told to find a new sound, to get away from Marc's overused cabaret and synthi-pop sonic backdrops. This sounded very promising, adventurous, and exciting to both of us—a genuine licence. The new rhythm style was to be strong, simple guitars over a power-techno rhythm. There were already some demos that Marc had developed with Neal 'X' Whitmore,* and the pair of them came over to New York to start recording in August 1993, although Marc seemed to spend every other morning yelling at Stevo on the phone.

MARC ALMOND A few years earlier, while I was on a promo tour of the US with EMI for the *Enchanted* album, Stevo moved me to WEA. He then switched labels again in the middle of recording *Fantastic Star*, from WEA to Mercury. He was unconventional in his ways, to say the least, but for me it was stressful, and I sank deeper into drugs and drink and unprofessional behaviour.

STEVO I would say the lowest part of my relationship with Marc was the Warner Bros time. It was the height of his Halcion addiction.† It had been banned in the UK, so he was flying to America for a day to pick up a supply, and then flying straight back, on a regular basis. I was watching a documentary, I think *Panorama*, and it was about prescription drugs, and I thought, *God, this is someone I know.* So, I met with Marc and basically said, 'You're an addict, you're going to have to choose Halcion or Stevo.' And I let him use my management commission from the Warners deal for the rehab, which he finished. He was then going on TV telling people that he'd woken up one morning and just decided to get clean. And I was really pissed off, and I said to him, 'I'm really not happy that you didn't mention me.' So the next interview he did, he did say thanks to Stevo, and gave me some credit.

* Previously of Sigue Sigue Sputnik.
† Halcion is the brand name for Triazolam, a fast-acting benzodiazepine used for the treatment of insomnia and jetlag. It was banned in the UK in 1991.

MIKE THORNE Everybody at Mercury loved what we were doing and thought the album would be huge, but at some point, judging by incoming studio gossip, everyone in London was remixing or reworking this album. In the end it barely scratched the UK charts. '*The Idol*', which felt like a Top 3 single, barely staggered into the lower, also-ran sectors.

JANE ROLINK Marc and I remained close for quite a while. When I was a Rhythm King, I could get free records, and Marc's boyfriend was opening up a club called FF. He said to me, 'There's a slot, would you like to try and DJ?' and I was going out with a lad who helped me find my way around a deck, so I tried it and it worked. And then this whole Mrs Wood DJ persona came up, with a mop and a scarf on my head, and that was it. Marc did a vocal on one of my tracks and then said I couldn't release it, so it ended up on his *Fantastic Star* album instead, which was fine.*

For a leather-clad tattooed perv who's at such loggerheads with bourgeois morality, Marc Almond is actually a comforting and dependable English star. His interests in wholesome pop forms are undiminished, and jealousy, anger and pain remain grist to his mill just like they ever were. Though an acquired taste, like one of those Pierre et Gilles pics of him in a sailor suit, [*Fantastic Star*] is immaculate and super-artificial, all danger-filled saucy pop backing and vocal dramatics.

IAN HARRISON, Q, February 1996

Fantastic Star is more of the polished dance-pop he's been pushing for the past few years. And if you go in for Pet Shop Boys-ish neon melodica and even the occasional Neil Tennant-style vocal chat, then tracks like 'Out There', with beefed-up soulful backing diva extras, will thrill to order. Otherwise, his more theatrical crooning will make paperchains of your emotions on 'We Need Jealousy', Erasure-esque computer arrangements bubbling stroppily in the distance. Then there's the sheer rock cheek of 'The Idol (Parts 1 & 2 All Gods Fall)' with Almond self-mockingly attempting to fill Gary Glitter's camp-glam stack-heel boots to pleasingly Bolan-esque effect.

LAURA LEE DAVIES, Time Out, February 1996

---

* Marc Almond's *Fantastic Star* (528 659-2) was finally released on Some Bizzare via Mercury on February 19, 1996. It reached no.54 on the UK album chart.

"OK, so it's fair to say the first package of mixes received an average reaction from clubland and wasn't quite the instant hit Some Bizzare/Mercury were hoping for. Now we give you the mixes that should rectify that; None Eric/B-Flat/House of Usher & Da Clubheroes. No time to waste! Charts & reactions essential!

author unknown, promotional material for the 'Out There' single, January 30, 1996

MIKE THORNE *Fantastic Star* was marvellous to make to make, and I thought it was some of the best work Marc and I had done, separately or together. But when it got back to London it was remixed out of its tiny mind and the rest is history. It didn't go anywhere. I was so bemused by the rubbish going on in London, I just thought, *Next!* There's no point in dwelling on it.

MARC ALMOND In the spring of 1996, after the calamity that was *Fantastic Star*, Stevo and I parted ways. I'd probably stayed so long because my own life was falling apart, and I was too weak and co-dependant to break away, and Stevo and Some Bizzare were just another addiction. He had put me in some bad situations, even though he thought he had my best interests at heart. I was too naive and guided by the wrong advice to see beyond it. I didn't know what to do or where to go. I saw other managers and tried to find a way out, but I felt isolated and indebted to Stevo. I was addicted to drugs, and eventually Stevo saw to it that Warners paid for me to go into rehab. Ironically, it was that which opened my eyes and gave me the strength to leave him and Some Bizzare. But it was a tough entanglement to get loose from.

COLIN SCHAVERIEN I was looking for work in the music industry, so I got a copy of *Music Week* and sent my CV to 100 addresses in there and got two replies, one from a country & western label and one from Some Bizzare. I later found out the reason I got offered a job was because Stevo's bookkeeper had done my horoscope and star sign alignments and told him that I'd be an amazing addition to the company.

So, I was employed as kind of an A&R scout/day-to-day manager by Stevo, and we were based at 124 New Bond Street. But the reality was, my job was doing anything and everything.

MIKE HOLDSWORTH When I first joined Some Bizzare, Stevo was still partying quite hard. Then he got into a personal relationship with someone for quite a long time and was sober for that period.

STEVO I'd never seen *The Kenny Everett Video Show*, and I'd never heard of Cleo Rocos. I was just sitting in a Mauritian fish restaurant one day and saw her, walked up to her table, and got her telephone number. She always said the reason why she liked me was because I didn't know who she was. We were together for eight years. After we split, she went on *Celebrity Big Brother* and said that she'd only ever loved one man. And that was Kenny Everett. Nice, eh?

COLIN SCHAVERIEN On my first day in the office, I walked in, and Cleo Rocos was there in just in her underwear, trying to put on a straitjacket. She asked me to help her do up the fasteners on the back. When I asked her what she was doing, she told me she was going for an interview at Talk Radio and she wanted to show off the crazy, zany side of her character.

On my second day I got a call at around six o'clock, and it was Genesis from Psychic TV. He was asking after Stevo and chasing up unpaid royalties. When I told him he wasn't around, he proceeded to ritually curse the office down the phone. So those were my first two days at Some Bizzare, and it just got crazier after that. It was absolutely bonkers, working there.

ANDY WIGMORE I'd been working on *The Big Breakfast* and doing some radio presenting on what was then called London Radio but became LBC, as well as British Forces Radio. It was while doing that I met the lovely Cleo Rocos, who's an amazing lady. Cleo and I ended up doing an early morning breakfast show together, which was great fun. One day, she said, 'I've got to introduce you to a very close friend of mine,' and that was Stevo. We met in a restaurant called Rules in Covent Garden, and I instantly liked him. He was off-the-scale bonkers but charming with it, and the anecdotes that he would tell . . . I didn't know anything about him, but I knew about the bands he represented, and he had all these wonderful stories about the 80s and the people he met, what they did, and the clubs they went to. I thoroughly enjoyed his company. And after a while, he said, 'Look, I'm doing this band and I need a bit of bit of help, PR-wise, are you free?'

315

CHRIS WILKIE Our 1995 album *Disgraceful* was about to go gold, and we'd started to have Top 20 hits. But around the same time, we dismissed our original manager, so we were a bit of a rudderless ship. EMI were putting pressure on Food Records to put pressure on us to quickly appoint another manager, because this was a critical point in our trajectory. We saw every serious manager in the business—it was like a beauty parade or something. Then Andy Ross from Food asked us if we'd heard of Stevo, as apparently he was really keen. I was in primary school when Soft Cell first started having hits, and they were one of the bands that I liked most as a kid. And then, as I became a teenager, one of my all-time favourite bands was THE THE. I liked the inspirational quotes on the back of the record sleeves, and I thought Stevo must be a pretty spiritual guy. I'd read in the music press about his hijinks and shenanigans, and it seemed he was like a Robin Hood figure protecting the artists from these monolithic corporate institutions. So, I thought it was worth a shot, and also, at the very least, I wanted to meet him, because for me he was just as interesting as any artists I could think of.

ANDY WIGMORE We went to see Dubstar play, and they were great. Stevo didn't do things by halves, and when he went out, he dressed like he was going to meet the Queen. He was hugely flamboyant: three-piece suit, gold bling, slicked-back hair, polished shoes, so you can imagine him walking into a grungy West End music venue. I didn't know anything about the music business, and it was kind of a steep learning curve. I just started spending more and more time with him and was absolutely a hanger-on, but I had good press contacts, so I could handle that side of things. He would say, 'Let's go and meet so-and-so,' and it would be all these crazy, amazing people from the 80s: Marc Almond, Depeche Mode, Blancmange, all these icons. My impression was they all found Stevo slightly frustrating and they wanted to be annoyed with him, but they never could. The music business is completely dog-eat-dog, but he just had a way of navigating through it, which was to be tremendously charming all the time.

BILLY REEVES The *Some Bizarre Album* was a massive deal, and Stevo a very significant figure when I was a teenager, so when the offer came up, I was really keen to meet him. theaudience had been offered several record deals by this point, but Sophie [Ellis-Bextor, theaudience singer] couldn't do any of the label meetings because she was still doing her A-levels. Me being the former PR man

316

of a little record company, I was absolutely in my element. I was of the mind that theaudience didn't need a manager and that I could do it myself, although Alan Pell from Mercury, who we eventually signed with, thought we should be managed by Hall Or Nothing. He also mentioned that Stevo was interested and wanted to meet us. And before I had a chance to tell him we'd kind of made up our mind, he added, 'And he's bringing Cleo Rocos with him.' Now, as a man of certain age, I simply couldn't turn down an opportunity to meet Cleo Rocos.

CHRIS WILKIE When Stevo heard we were up for a meeting, he wanted to see us immediately. We were in Bridlington for a *Radio One Roadshow* appearance, so he asked to meet us at Leeds train station. It was convenient place for us to get back to the northeast afterward and him to go back down to London, but also he liked the fact there was a geographical connection with Soft Cell—he liked omens like that. Stevo wasn't afraid of thinking metaphysically, and he often saw things as signals from the universe. So, we met up, he was wearing a pinstripe suit, a Panama straw hat and carrying a cane—a real salad-days sort of look—and he really stood out at Leeds station, I can tell you. Anyway, he proceeded to enthuse about the group—he'd obviously done his homework, and he knew the music pretty well. He identified me straightaway as the person who was interested in him, and he liked the fact that I was conscious of his legacy.

BILLY REEVES It was explained to Stevo that Sophie wouldn't be able to come, although it would have been great for her and been really good fun, and he was fine with that. So we met in this really quite posh vegetarian restaurant in London somewhere, and the whole afternoon was brilliant. Cleo looked exactly the same as she did in the 80s, and Stevo was wearing an outfit which can only be described as *Brideshead Revisited*—cream flannels, white pumps, a collarless shirt, and a cricket tank top. The top had two holes in it and the trousers had a stain down them, so he looked like a guy who was either on his uppers and those were the best clothes he could put on, or he just didn't give a shit, and I had no idea which it was.

I told him exactly where we were at that point, and also that I was getting leaned on by Mercury to go with Hall Or Nothing. He didn't put any heat on me, he just made his pitch—you know, 'We'd like to manage you, we've got contacts outside the UK, we can sort out North America,' and so on. He'd obviously really listened to the music and knew what he was talking about. Also, he was the first person that had been really honest about Sophie. Other industry people had been flattering me about my songwriting and trying to play me at my own game, but he knew Sophie was 99.9 percent why people would be interested in theaudience, and he was totally right. I would argue that Sophie Ellis-Bextor is the only genuine household name to have come out of that whole Britpop scene. And he saw that.

CHRIS WILKIE After the meeting at Leeds station, I'd gone back to my parents' house in Gateshead, and that evening I got call from Stevo—no idea how he got my parents' number—and he was keen to expedite things as swiftly as possible. I told him I'd not had a chance to talk to the rest of the group yet, and he said, 'OK, talk to them, and I'll call you back tomorrow.' He calls the next day at 8am. He wanted to impress upon me how he was in the prime of his managerial career and offered to give me Matt Johnson and Marc Almond's phone numbers so I could call them for verification of his credentials. Anyway, he wanted to come up to Newcastle and meet us for Sunday lunch, and this time he was going to bring his girlfriend, Cleo Rocos. *The Kenny Everett Video Show* was essential viewing when I was a kid, not least because of Cleo. It was also a great for music—my first memory of David Bowie was on that show.

I got the other members of the band on board, and we met up at the Gosforth Park Hotel, which was where all the bands used to gather when they were on *The Tube*. Everybody got along really well—Sarah and Cleo especially—but what clinched it for us was our first manager had served us a high court writ, and we'd made a counterclaim, although we were very worried about the potential outcome. And Stevo said, 'Look, I can remove this Sword of Damocles from over your head, just let me take care of it.' And, beyond that, he was pretty confident about renegotiating our contract so we got more money if EMI took up the option for a second album, which in light of *Disgraceful*'s success was pretty much guaranteed. So we appointed our lawyer to start cooperating with him, and we all thought, *Let's see how it goes.*

BILLY REEVES When Stevo went to the loo, Cleo leaned in and said, 'You know, Stevo and I live together, but we're not an item.' I hadn't asked about this—she just seemed very keen to tell me. Then Stevo came back, paid for the lunch, and we said our goodbyes. It was a very jolly afternoon. Stevo wasn't anywhere near as mad as Alan Pell had made out, and I thought he and Cleo were just classic English eccentrics.

ANDY WIGMORE I never got to the bottom of Cleo and Stevo's relationship, but they were very close. And I know they absolutely adored each other. They were like man and wife and they bickered in the most funny, affectionate way. I liked them immensely as a couple and was very fond of them.

CHRIS WILKIE By the summer 1996, we were headlining the *NME* tent at the Reading Festival, so that was a big flashpoint for us, and Stevo was there for that. Andy Ross did express reservations about having such a wildcard at the helm at such a pivotal moment, but we were all getting along. The first time I started to notice that things weren't going to be that straightforward was the EMI conference a month later, at the Birmingham Metropole. The entire hotel had been booked out, some of the artists were performing, and the whole workforce was there for a three-day jolly. Stevo had been in the US, taking care of our North American deal, and he said to us, 'I've got a meeting in Clive Black's suite, you should all come along.'

We all went up there and Clive Black opens the door wearing an undersized ladies' bathrobe and is soaking wet, as he's obviously just got out of the shower, but he lets us in, and Andy Ross is there. Then Tony Harlow, who at the time was the head of marketing at EMI, comes in, and they and Stevo all start shouting at each other. First of all because apparently it's a real breach of protocol to bring the artist to such meetings, and secondly there had been a lot of grievances which we hadn't been aware about what EMI perceived as Stevo's insane publicity stunts and suggestions for promotional activities. The one that had really offended the big boys at EMI was his plan to celebrate *Disgraceful* going gold with an event at Selfridges. Stevo would be dressed as Santa Claus with the gold discs in his sack, and Cleo would of course be Mrs Claus. The real problem was, he wanted Clive, Andy, and Tony to be dressed as elves in green tights and curly pointy shoes, and when Stevo was handing out the discs, they would jump up and down, clapping their hands excitedly like his little helpers. He'd actually walked them through this plan, and they were so offended by the way he wanted to portray them, I don't think the relationship recovered.

319

BILLY REEVES theaudience's next gig was at the Camden Falcon, which was the final one we did before we signed to Mercury. The whole of the music industry was there, *man*, including Nicky and James from Manic Street Preachers, one of the biggest bands in the country at the time, God bless 'em. And Stevo and Cleo were there too, and she was absolutely brilliant. People were constantly going up to her, including all my overexcited mates, and she was just fantastic.

RICHARD NORRIS Stevo was very proud of his tailoring. He lived in West London for a bit, and I remember him taking me into his bedroom, where he had forty or fifty suits lined up. He was certainly living the life of a kind of bespoke-tailored gentleman.

COLIN SCHAVERIEN When people found out I was working at Some Bizzare, the common response was, 'Stevo is an absolute lunatic, how can you work with him?' He was definitely a big character, and labels would certainly know when he was coming in as he'd dress up in tweed three-piece suits and handmade shoes. He'd also had help with elocution in order to come across like a refined country gent, and a lot of that came from Cleo.

ANDY WIGMORE His office, my God, it was bonkers. It was on New Bond Street, right at the top. He said, 'I've moved into a new office, come and have a look at my den.' And it was like a Roman emperor's chamber. Statues and greenery everywhere, the biggest plants you've ever seen. It felt like walking off the street and into a jungle. It was really over-the-top but it was weirdly classy, which was his personality, I suppose.

CHRIS WILKIE The Some Bizzare offices at the time were surrounded by jewellers and boutique clothing stores, very expensive premises. There was a large informal meeting room, which led to the window where you could look out onto New Bond Street, and there were pieces of art all around the place, like Helen Chadwick's *Train Of Thought*, which was a section of a tube train. There was also a special office, which was for important meetings, where only Stevo could sit at the desk, and there was room for just a couple of other people. In there was also a real, working fountain, very big and encrusted with gemstones and a plaque at the bottom saying, 'Be careful what you wish for.' And it was filled with free-flowing

Dom Perignon champagne—probably nonvintage, I imagine. The idea was that when you got to a celebratory point of a meeting, you could casually fill your glass for a toast. Of course, the champagne was inevitably flat because it had been through the system so many times. We used to think it was so over-the-top that it was hilarious, until we realised who was paying for it.

COLIN SCHAVERIEN There was literally no one in the office apart from myself, a bookkeeper who came in once a month, and Stevo, so I was tasked with doing pretty much everything. In terms of the company structure, the label was fairly defunct by that point. So I was tasked with repackaging and repressing a lot of the catalogue by Neubauten, Swans, Foetus, Psychic TV, and Marc Almond, which was part of a new deal Stevo had with Pinnacle, to essentially generate some revenue as he was experiencing some financial issues. He was living just across from the office, by the American Embassy, and spending not insignificant amounts on Cleo and her mum, I think.

MARK CHUNG Then the weirdest thing happened. I'd been managing director of the German branch of Play It Again Sam, and in 1996 I'd been headhunted by Sony to take the Senior Vice President role in London. So, we moved to London to a flat on Upper Brook Street, number 3, so I could walk to work. Then, one morning, I step out, close the outside door, and I can see from the corner of my eye, somebody standing on the left closing the door for number 4. And it's fucking Stevo. I mean, how can this be? How big is London, and I rent a flat right next door to Stevo. What's the likelihood of that?

So, we walked into Grosvenor Square together, and I said to him, 'I think life is telling us something here, Stevo. Why are we having these lawyers talk to each other costing us a fortune? Let's resolve our shit.' And I said my problem is, I don't want to be involved with a publishing company that doesn't pay the writers, and because you're not paying mechanicals, I can't pay the writers. So, Swans and Coil weren't getting mechanicals for their records and that is shit. And he was going, 'But I feel I should have a share of the publishing company.' He never brought a song into the publishing company, which was fine—it was there for him and I would have honoured it—but he never bought anything to it. So, I said, 'Look, you keep all the publisher's share for the next five years and just pay the 85 percent mechanicals (all our deals with writers were 85/15 splits). I'll pay that through to

321

the writers, and you keep the 15 percent, and you will see it's not actually a lot of money, and then we don't have to argue about it.' So we shook hands on that in front of the American Embassy on Grosvenor Square, and I thought, *What an amazing thing to happen and in a way quite magical.* Then he called me next day, and that was when I really lost my faith in him.

COLIN SCHAVERIEN A big part of my job was dealing with the fallout from the re-pressing of the back catalogue, particularly with Neubauten, as contractually there were definitely grey areas. Mark Chung was very persistent and angry about what he saw as Stevo's lack of legal standing in terms of the exploitation of those records.

MARK CHUNG Stevo called me at Sony and said, 'Yeah, Mark, I've been thinking, you seemed so keen to get rid of me yesterday. Why don't you just give me all the shares of the publishing company and I'll be gone.' But then he went on to say that there was a conflict of interest with Dimehart, because we were shareholders and managing directors together. By suing Some Bizzare over the Neubauten royalties I wasn't acting in the interests of our publishing company, and that's not gonna look good for me, and that he could create a lot of negative PR, etc., which would not be helpful to my position at Sony. He was basically trying to blackmail me, threatening to tell people I hadn't honoured my duties as a managing director of the publishing company, which was bullshit anyway. I was really pissed off, and said, 'You're a fucking asshole. This is the last time we speak, never, ever call me again. If we need to do business there are lawyers and accountants.' And I've never taken a call from him since. I was disappointed because I remembered quite fondly that we actually had got on well, and then we had this magical moment and found a deal which I thought was pretty fair and addressed the entire publishing issue. I actually didn't need the money from the publishing company, but I was absolutely not going to hand anything over because of what I perceived as blackmail.

CHRIS WILKIE As time went on, the impression I was getting from the label was that Stevo was a problem. He created trouble where there wasn't any, and he just didn't do things in a sufficiently business-like and salient way. Also, most of his ideas just seemed to be a bit too . . . silly, for want of a better word. But he did start to take on some extra staff at Some Bizzare, which really helped with the business side of things, particularly his second-in-command, Colin. Their influence started to bring things under control, and at that point Stevo became more like a figurehead.

COLIN SCHAVERIEN On the management side, I kind of got thrown straight into the deep end. I was looking after Dubstar, as Stevo was pretty hands off with them, and Messiah, who had a deal with American Recordings, Rick Rubin's label, but there had been a big fallout there. Bizarre Inc, who were signed to Mercury, were still in the frame, although it was coming toward the tail end of that campaign, which hadn't really connected. And then I was tasked with trying to bring in new bands and new artists into the management side.

CHRIS WILKIE On our first trip to New York, Cleo was with us, and she wanted to light a candle for Kenny Everett at St John The Divine cathedral. After that poignant moment, Stevo decided to show us the 'real' New York. We all got a taxi up to Washington Heights, which at that point was pre-gentrification and in the middle of a crack-cocaine crisis. We managed to find the only Irish bar in this predominantly Dominican area, which was just filled with reprobates. We then headed on to Harlem, where we were threatened and hassled for money. Then we got another taxi, and for some reason Stevo sat up front and started to threaten the driver, telling him he's got a gun. The driver just freaks out, pulls over, and throws us out in the middle of Alphabet City. So, we're now wandering around in a daze and people are throwing syringes at us, probably trying to knock the really expensive hats Stevo and Cleo are wearing off their heads. I couldn't get back to the hotel fast enough. I was absolutely terrified.

COLIN SCHAVERIEN Stevo's relationship with Marc had literally just ended when I joined, so I did deal with some of the termination, in terms of having sight of faxes coming in from lawyers. But, ultimately, it was definitely the end of an era, and I think Stevo was a bit rudderless. He spent very little time in the office during that that period—he'd pop in, give a bit of direction, and then go again. Ultimately, for me, it was probably the best education I could have, because I was having to learn about everything—dealing with labels, sorting out tours, arranging international distribution. I was flying to LA with Dubstar; having meetings with A&M, who signed them over there; accompanying them on video shoots; just doing everything in terms of looking after a popular band. It was great for me, because I had to learn everything on my feet.

CHRIS WILKIE Part of the reason so many people wanted to manage Dubstar was, when EMI picked up the option for a second album, whoever got the management gig was going to be able to commission 20 percent of that deal straightaway, pretty much without having to do a thing. And, at that time, Stevo was very interested in 'now money', as I think he'd been having financial problems, which working with us managed to solve, to a certain extent. And, because of this, his reputation was in a state of recovery, so he was able to engage with the industry from a stronger position than he had for a little while.

ANDY WIGMORE One day, Stevo said to me, 'I'm doing this deal with EMI, and I want you to deliver my comments on the contract.' He'd bought a really ornate messenger's tube from an antiques shop for about five grand, and he put this rolled-up contract with his comments on in big black pen into it, and told me to take it to Clive Black at EMI. I was quite naive and didn't realise that I couldn't just wander in there and see the MD of a major record label, but after much persuading the secretary called him, and down he came. I gave him the messenger's tube and he sat down, opened it, and started giggling. He then ripped up the contract, stuffed it back in the tube, and said, 'Tell Stevo to fuck off!'

When I got back to Bond Street, Stevo was already laughing, saying, 'I knew he'd do that! Now let's do it properly.' So we went back over to EMI, walked straight past reception up to Black's office, where Stevo launched into an expletive-filled speech, basically telling Black, who was in stitches, why he was going to sign the contract. The deal done, Stevo celebrated by having a cup of tea. Not quite the rock'n'roll response I was expecting, but, it transpired, that was his favourite drink.

COLIN SCHAVERIEN At the start of 1997, Stevo was definitely in a state of flux. Losing Marc, and coming out of an incredibly successful period, and not being able to replicate it, weighed heavily on him, I think. He'd started flirting with the tabloids—Max Clifford was two doors down on Bond Street, and there had been conversations about planting stories for Cleo in the press, and I think he was he was trying to work out what his role was. And he was fairly desperate in terms of trying to bring money into the company, either through re-pressing the catalogue or going out there and trying to find new management clients. I just think he was a bit lost, really, but, ultimately, he burned quite a few bridges in the industry historically, and there weren't that many doors open.

>>

ANDY JONES Koot had been together as a band for about five, six years before we got a record deal. We were all living together in a house down in Canterbury, and we were friends with Morcheeba. They took us under their wing a bit, and we did some demos with them, and then we started getting a buzz on our own. We moved to southeast London and gradually started contacting record companies. We used to rehearse at a studio in New Cross, and we got pretty much every major label to come down and watch us—we used to line them up in slots. It wasn't like we had any fan base or were getting any press—they were coming down based purely on these vibey demos we were sending out.

One of the people that came down was Eddie Pillar from Acid Jazz—he actually drove his scooter into the rehearsal studio. Eddie loved what we were doing offered us a record deal with Acid Jazz. With publishing it was about forty grand, but as there were six of us in the band, with four of us actually signed, that wasn't going to go far. So, we thought, *We need a manager*, and we were introduced to Colin, who suggested Stevo. He wanted to see the heads of agreement from Acid Jazz, which we felt a bit bad about because we knew any manager we got would want to renegotiate the deal. Anyway, we got the heads of agreement, and then Stevo goes into Svengali-mode and calls us in for a meeting.

ANDY WIGMORE I worked with Stevo for less than a year, but it was pretty intense. We met for breakfast nearly every day and had meetings at places like Giovanni's and Joe Allen's in Covent Garden, all these 90s hang-outs, and people would greet him like a long-lost friend. He was incredibly generous, and if he had money, everyone shared. I'm sure he lived hand-to-mouth, but that was just his nature. His wonderful dog, Honour, was his best friend, and she went everywhere with him, no matter where it was.

Stevo could be the most flamboyant, amazing creature, but at the same time was unbelievably street smart and could really read people. I'm sure there're lots of people that didn't like him, but he was a smiling knife, and he would punch them with charm. He said, 'Don't believe anything you hear, and only 50 percent of what you see.' I didn't know what he meant back then, but I do now.

COLIN SCHAVERIEN Stevo was spending an awful lot of time just looking after Cleo and her mum, and, for whatever reason, Cleo was definitely on his coattails a lot. She wouldn't allow him to drink, and he was exercising a bit. There were still excesses, but things like sending teddy bears to meetings and asking for sweets as part of a deal, all of that had stopped, because the walls had closed in, in terms of the business evolving. There wasn't the freedom to go and do things like that anymore. He was still very good at winding up the industry—especially at the top end, the president/MD level—and he still had a lot of contact with people like Howard Berman, Rob Dickens, Clive Black. He was close to those guys, but there was also an underlying feeling that he'd put too many noses out of joint.

CHRIS WILKIE On the second trip to New York, which Cleo did not accompany us on, Stevo was a different prospect. On the first night, he arranged to meet us at the New York Athletic Club, overlooking Central Park. I noticed that he was smoking a cigarette, which I'd never seen before. Then I realised he was drinking vodka, which was weird, because I was told he was very resolute about not drinking. So he said to us, 'Oh, there's a place I know that I think you're gonna find really interesting,' and we got a cab downtown. We eventually got to the place and there's this turnstile arrangement to get in, past which I walk into this room, and it's like a Roman orgy. It was filled with predominantly naked or half-naked people in various stages of coitus. It looked like people who just finished work and rocked up and started undressing. I'm trying to find Stevo, but I can't see him for all the naked bodies. We stuck around for about sixty seconds and then left. I've no idea why he took us there. I think he was just trying to shock us. What was abundantly clear from that second New York trip was how much of a civilising element Cleo was—she made dealing with Stevo much easier in lots of ways.

ANDY JONES So we got ushered into the New Bond Street office, and my abiding memory of first meeting Stevo was him wearing a full safari suit and sitting under a straw parasol, set up basically like he was on holiday on a beach. He gave us the spiel, reeling off names—Moira Bellas, Rob Dickens, Seymore Stein, etc. And then he goes, and this is a classic play, 'I've just got to go off and make a call, you stay here and have a little chat with my girlfriend.' So, he leaves the room and in walks Cleo Rocos. We're playing it cool, but as children of the 1980s, internally our jaws are dropping. And she's cooing, 'Hi boys, Stevo has been saying such great things about your music. I heard it too and it's amazing.' And we just didn't know what to do with ourselves. We were well aware that she was softening us up something chronic, but we all left the meeting of the mind that while Stevo may be really eccentric, he also really knew his stuff. So we just threw the dice in the air thinking, *What's the worst that can happen?*

COLIN SCHAVERIEN We were speaking to the then-editor of *Kerrang!*, Phil Alexander, and we ran competition with him, out of which emerged Tampasm. We ended up signing them to Alan Pell at Mercury for a two-single deal, but they never went beyond that.*

ANDY JONES I'm sure Stevo liked Koot, and I could see he was really into the music, but the fact of the matter was, at that point he needed a band with which he could get a huge deal. So, as far as Koot fitting in with what Some Bizzare had done before, I guess if you look at Dubstar and Bizarre Inc there was a lineage of more soulful pop there, but I think the main thing was he needed a band who could bring some much-needed money into the firm. We didn't know that at the time—we thought he loved us, and I still think he probably did like music, but there was a practicality involved, for sure.

COLIN SCHAVERIEN It's really hard to say if he still cared about the music, because from what I could gather it was more about keeping the wolves from the door, in terms of the finances. There was a lot of trying to get money in, and a lot of trying to work out how to get that money in. And, as we all know, when you're chasing money, it never comes. It's when you're walking really slowly that things come to you. And I think he was running very fast, trying to get deals done.

---

* All-girl rock band Tampasm released two singles for Some Bizzare via Mercury in 1997: 'Darling Self Destruct' (MER 489) and 'This Is Carnage' (MERX 495).

ANDY JONES I'm sure the Koot deal was probably the biggest deal he had at that at that point. It was one of those ridiculous feeding-frenzy things that happened before Napster put a stop to all that.

CHRIS WILKIE The second Dubstar album, *Goodbye*, hadn't done quite as well as the first one, and in early 1998 we had our first formal meeting with the new managing director at EMI, Neil Ferris. He liked the band and wanted us to take our time and not rush into doing the third album. He suggested we go away somewhere really peaceful, which is how we ended up in this mill in Oxfordshire, owned by the family of Roger Hodgson from Supertramp. The idea was we would get our heads together at this place, but then Stevo turned up, unexpectedly. He had Honour with him, and the first thing I noticed was he'd bleached his hair pure white, and it was greased back. He was wearing a beautifully tailored tweed suit and spats. I'd never seen a person wearing spats in real life before—he looked like Toad Of Toad Hall. He seemed a bit dishevelled, and it transpired that he hadn't been to sleep that night. When he took off his jacket, the back of his white shirt was soaked in blood. He just says, 'Ah, yeah, I got stabbed last night.' He'd been in South London at a gig, got into an altercation outside the venue and been stabbed, and over the course of the night had somehow made his way to this remote place in the middle of Oxfordshire. So we get his shirt off, and it's a significant wound that requires medical attention. But Stevo said, 'Fuck that, let's go to the pub.'

STEVO You have to be prepared to be knifed and headbutted. You have to be prepared to go into the armpits of society to find great music. The best music comes from anger, from paranoia. It's the way out of a situation. I've found unemployable reprobates and given them a tax liability. As I have proven, you don't need an education to be in the music business.

CHRIS WILKIE So Stevo, Sarah, me, and Honour go to the pub. Stevo was drinking heavily, and then he told us that he and Cleo have split up. Now, this was a loaded comment, because given the state he arrived in and the obvious calming influence that Cleo had on him, I started to fear for the future. By the time we got back to the mill, it was dark, and we couldn't find the keys. All of a sudden, there's a smashing sound—Stevo had got impatient and punched one of the front

328

windows in. The band went to their rooms and Stevo fell asleep on the couch downstairs. I'm woken up at the crack of dawn by Stevo, hair now in spikes, bouncing up and down on my bed, laughing maniacally, while Honour runs around the room, barking. He looked like a demonic sun god or something and absolutely terrified me. Anyway, he gets off of me, smooths his hair down, and says he and Honour are going back to London. I offered to organise a car for him, but he says, 'Nah, I'll hail a cab.' When I questioned him on the unlikelihood of this, he just said, 'I'll be fine, I'm very resourceful,' and leaves. And I didn't see him again for over five years.

ANDY JONES So then Koot were swept up in this whirlwind. It was just crazy. Stevo put on a couple of gigs at the Water Rats in London, Paul Godfrey from Morcheeba was DJing, and every major record label was there. Paul introduced us as the best band in the world and tells everyone to 'get your fucking chequebooks out!' It was proper late-90s, completely over-the-top music-industry madness, everyone thinking they were gonna sell CDs forever. We did another two gigs, and then a bidding war breaks out. Stevo told us, 'I've got an offer of £120,000 from London Records,' and we were like, 'Whaaat!?' And the money just started going up and up and up and up. Then Warners came in with an offer of £150,000 and a five-album deal.

COLIN SCHAVERIEN I bought in Koot, and there was essentially a bidding war, and they ended up signing with Rob Dickens at Warners. It was quite a funny story because I went in with Stevo, to see Rob and Moira Bellas, who was the MD at the time. Rob was pretty direct and just said, 'How much do you want?' And Stevo said, in his rather brash, abrupt way, 'I want eighty grand,' and Rob put out his hand and said, 'Done.' Then Stevo said, 'You do understand that eighty grand is for me, that's my tax bill. The band is extra.' And I think he ended up getting it, but, ultimately, that was why we parted ways, because we had an agreement that anything that I bought in, I'd get compensated for. Also, there was so much stuff going on in terms of the underlying karma within Some Bizzare that I just thought it better if I set up my own company, which I did, with Simon Napier Bell.

ANDY PETTITT You need to have a certain constitution to work with Stevo. It's a multifaceted job—part personal assistant, part babysitter, part label manager, part legal consultant. But getting the job was pretty traditional in some ways, as it was through an advert in *NME*. I didn't know much about Some Bizzare at that point, but it seemed vaguely intriguing. I'd actually just finished the quick crossword in the *Guardian* when I saw the ad, so I faxed it to Stevo with my phone number at the top. He phoned me up, I went over, and I had what passed for an interview. He showed me a couple of videos, including a Koot one, which they'd just filmed in Atlanta—he was very proud of that—and then he proceeded to tell me about the girl who'd just been in before me, and he made it very clear she had certain assets that I did not possess. He then tried to get me to stand in the middle of Trafalgar Square with birdseed all over me, which he considered as some kind of induction and found hilarious. And then we went and had a few drinks. He phoned me up a couple of days later, didn't say I'd got the job but asked me to meet him in Notting Hill on Thursday. I thought it must be for some kind of trial shift, but I was thinking in far too formal terms, employment wise. I got there to find I was helping him move house.

ANDY JONES What most people don't realise is, when a major label signs a band for five albums, it's not necessarily a great thing, as those albums are options. So, the band is tied to the label and can't go anywhere else, but the label doesn't have to put those albums out. What Stevo did, which was really clever and quite unusual, was sign for five albums, but with two albums firm. Which meant they had to release a second album, even if the first one tanked. What it also meant was, whatever happened, he had a bunch more money coming in to commission, because to make our second album, Warners would have to give us a quarter of a million quid. So, the total sum for signing with Warner Music was £400,000, and then we signed a publishing deal with Warner Chappell for another £200,000. And we had a recording budget for the first album, which, after we'd been bounced from super producer to super producer, was touching on 375 grand. It was a crazy, crazy period. And Stevo is, of course, commissioning all these deals, and I assume that's what kept Some Bizzare afloat. I think inadvertently we upset a lot of people who had been very supportive, just through Stevo being so hardcore when it came to getting us this deal. But, really, Koot were just passengers on a train that Stevo was driving, and he was determined to get as much money as possible.

ANDY PETTITT It took me about a week to work out whether I was working for him or not. Eventually I started at Denmark Street, which was where the Some Bizzare offices had recently moved to, and the only other person there was a kid who'd done the commercial music degree at Westminster Uni and was there on work experience—*experience* being the operative word. I got the impression he was desperate for someone to take Stevo off his hands. Which I obviously did, as once he'd gone it was just me and Stevo for five years.

CHRIS WILKIE When we did the management agreement, Stevo proposed—to inspire confidence, I suppose—that by the time we picked up the option to commence a third album, if we hadn't doubled the units sold for *Disgraceful* with the second album, *Goodbye*, then we could walk away. I didn't have any issues with Stevo—I basically liked him, and I still do—but he created a lot of problems with EMI, which affected our relationship with the label. He'd started to become increasingly erratic and, with Cleo not around, without her literal sobering influence, I couldn't see in good conscience how we could go on. There were no hard feelings, but that was kind of the end of that.

ANDY PETTITT By the time I'd started, he'd split from Cleo and was fully back on the sauce, and we ended up being barred from every pub in Soho, except for the Crown & Two Chairman on Dean Street. One of the main reasons was, he always carried a CD of new Some Bizzare stuff in his pocket, and after a couple of pints he would insist the pub put it on. Some of them would go along with it and some of them wouldn't. Either way, it ended up with us getting barred.

Another time, he was winding up a bunch of squaddies by shouting across a bar at them. They were big guys, but he kept doing it until one of them came over and said, 'Look, if your mate doesn't stop, he's gonna get filled in.' So I was trying to get him to leave, and he was like, 'No, no, I'm fine, I'm fine.' And then he gets up to go to the toilet, and as he walks past the squaddies he leans in and says something, and they all just jumped on him.

It was like a saloon fight, I was trying to get him out . . . honestly, he was an absolute liability.

STEVO Andy's uncle is Michael Gambon. People don't fuck with you when you employ Dumbledor's nephew. He'll get his uncle to turn them into a frog or something.

CHRIS WILKIE I was nervous to be around Stevo at times, and there were obviously situations where things could have become dangerous, but I never got the impression that he was an unkind person, or that there was any malice aforethought on his part. It was more his inability to control himself, and, once he started to find something funny, there was never a point where he could start to rein it back in.

ANDY PETTITT Stevo is the worst person with money I've ever met in my life. He moved from Notting Hill to Buckingham Street, which is adjacent to Villiers Street, behind the Strand. At this point, I had no idea about his finances, I just thought, *Blimey, this guy's clearly doing OK. An office in Tottenham Court Road and living in a big old house in the West End.* He had a lot of really expensive, nice clothes—I probably carried most of them into a removal van on the first day I worked for him. A lot of them were far too big for him because he lost a lot of weight when he split up with Cleo. And he loved seersucker suits and co-correspondent shoes. But then I started to see what money was coming in, and what was in his bank account—both derisory amounts. He just continued to live in a way that was completely unrelated to the amount of money he was making, and I just could not believe it. What he should have been doing was downsizing and making his business more viable, because the rent for the house and the office, plus his other liabilities, was just completely unsustainable.

STEVO You have to have faith that things will come together, that they're gonna drop into place the way they're supposed to. And you will create great things if you have that belief.

With danger comes pleasure.
Ø, from the sleeve of *If You Can't Please Yourself You Can't, Please Your Soul* (1985)

2000–22 All my exotic gestures no longer in demand

15

KOOT CRASH, COIL CURSE,
SOFT CELL RETURN, AND
STEVO FINDS HIS HAPPY
PLACE ON MYSPACE

STEVO I always try to be aware of people's expectations. When I was a kid, I was taught how to play chess, and part of that was learning how to think for the other side. To realise there are repercussions for every move; if you do this, something is going to happen. I knew this from a very young age. So, on an artistic level, to be aware of the other side's expectations, that your move is going to have repercussions, and to be one step ahead, is very important.

ANDY PETTITT As well as Koot, Stevo was managing a band called Lorien, who Rob Dickens had signed to his Sony boutique label, Instant Karma. Giles Martin was the A&R guy for them before he became custodian to all things Beatles-related. Stevo was looking after a solo artist called Kai Motta, too. He would tell me that he was actively looking for new artists, but he wasn't a huge gig-goer—if something took his interests, he'd go, but part of his problem at that time was he wasn't particularly plugged in to any scene, for want of a better word. He wasn't great at picking up on buzzes around unsigned bands, but he would still receive an incredible amount of demo tapes and CDs. So, on the occasions when we weren't fighting legal battles, we'd whack some of them on and see if anything took our fancy. Sometimes a lawyer would give him a tip off and he'd investigate things that way, but I wouldn't say he had his ear to the ground in the most intense and organic way. This, to me, was a massive problem.

KAI MOTTA I started listening to hip-hop when I was about twelve, things like Doug E. Fresh & The Get Fresh Crew's 'The Show', stuff like that. At the same time, my mum and dad were straight out of the 60s—Bob Dylan, the Grateful Dead, Jack Kerouac—so it was a pretty good upbringing. I got into playing the guitar and became a bad Dylan impersonator for a while, as most people do. And then I started rapping over the top, just blending the two influences. I was lucky enough to be surrounded by some phenomenal musicians of different ages, influences, and styles, and my plan was to just rap and play my guitar while the other guys did their thing. In my head, it was like Public Enemy meets Dylan. You wouldn't have thought if you heard it, but that's what I was aiming for.

POLLY BIRKBECK The PR company I worked for were approached by Warners to represent Koot. They were a really good band—great musicians and interesting production—but they didn't really fit anywhere, genre-wise. It was that time after Britpop, and it was looking like they were going to be lumped in with Stereophonics and Toploader, even though they were more soulful and rootsy. I just remember meetings where Stevo would turn up with his Labrador and stand up to pontificate in his eccentric way. He brought in big cakes, too. It was all very old-school, and he could be quite funny, but I used to think his way of doing things was really not going to help the band. But it wasn't my place to say anything.

STEVO Sony got their own version of Koot—Toploader—and they put out 'Dancing In The Moonlight', which was really similar, and that took the wind out of it completely. Ruined it. The Koot record took too long. In hindsight, we should have just put it out independently.

ANDY JONES We were given all the resources we'd ever need to be a successful band, but sometimes the zeitgeist just isn't there, and sometimes the songs aren't there either. We had some pretty good songs, but not half a million pounds worth of good songs, and the expectations were high because Warners had thrown a load of money at us.

So, we produced the record, and on the day we delivered it to WEA, Moira Bellas was still running the company, and don't forget she was the one who put the money behind Koot. The album was accepted, mastered, A&R'd, etc ... and as the final version was readied, Moira Bellas left the company. Everything stopped

334

for six months, then we were called in to speak to the new MD, a guy called John Reid. He basically sat us down and said, 'So, what do you think of the record you've made?' And one of the band members—not me, I hasten to add—just said, 'To be honest with you, I'm really over it.' Which was fair enough, as we had a batch of new material we'd been working on for the past six months. Warners then decided to cut their losses, but remember Stevo had signed us for two albums firm, so we left the label but they still had to pay us a quarter of a million quid for the second album. Which we got straight to work on.

ANDY PETTITT Stevo would often talk about Daniel Miller because, the way he saw it, he was instrumental in creating Mute. He'd always say he passed Depeche Mode to Daniel so he could take on Soft Cell. But Daniel was much more effective at moving Mute on through the 90s and beyond than Stevo was with Some Bizzare. Stevo's type of modus operandi only works if you've got something amazing, but once your product is not quite at that level, the eccentricities become a real issue.

KAI MOTTA Stevo wasn't on my radar at all—I had no idea who he was. Some A&R guy put us in touch, and I went to meet him. I thought he was all right, fucking hard bloke, but at the same time I kind of liked him. Obviously, he wanted to make money—I wouldn't say it was his main goal, but he definitely wanted a return on his investment. Although he did want to work with stuff that was different, which I really admired him for. He was right behind everything I wanted to do, didn't want me to change anything. So I went straight to a studio with the band and recorded thirty songs. I was really into the idea of doing things in a single take—you play, and if you fuck up it stays on the record—I don't think the others were necessarily ready to record like that, but that was how I wanted it. And it was a great time.

I was twenty-four, twenty-five, so quite old as far as the music industry was concerned, but I had a bit of a following around London. We played that Hope & Anchor, Water Rats, Dublin Castle circuit, and I was doing open mics every night of the week. I was just playing and playing and playing. I'd had a bit of interest here and there, but nothing that was leading to a deal. Then Stevo got involved, and the head of Sony, Columbia, and Warners were all at the next gig. He signed me up with an agent and got all the right people in place. He was incredibly well connected.

ANDY PETTITT What Stevo should have been doing was re-establishing the identity of Some Bizzare as a musical force. The finances would have then taken care of themselves, because the label had a coherent vision. We were coming out of Britpop, and bands like Radiohead were massive, and the electronic music scene was quite underground. So, there were opportunities for him reconnect Some Bizzare to electronic music, and be the go-to-guy for that genre. But instead, he was trying to pick up artists that he could licence on to bigger labels in order to get some money in, because quite frankly it was a hand-to-mouth existence at that point. Which is why Some Bizzare ended up with all these disparate acts, from Kai Motta's kind of folky rap stuff to Koot's swampy rock. There was no tangible identity, and I think that was an issue for him, for sure.

KAI MOTTA I think he connected with the attitude in what I did, with the polemical side of it. I had a song based on *First They Came* by Pastor Martin Niemöller, and he really liked that and said he knew loads of people that would be into it, and I thought, *OK, this is a good sign.* I signed the management deal as a band, not a solo artist, and, to celebrate, Stevo took me to several strip clubs, which was all right. He chose all the songs for the album, too, which I thought was fair enough—he was paying for it, after all.*

POLLY BIRKBECK Koot ended up a bit of a flash in the pan. It just didn't happen for them, which was a shame as they were good. And, despite everything, you couldn't not like Stevo—unless you worked at the label, then he probably drove you mad. The word 'maverick' gets thrown around a lot, but as far as someone who had their own way of doing things, Stevo definitely had that. Sometimes it worked, sometimes it didn't. And, as the years went on, it definitely didn't work for him.

ANDY JONES The reviews for our debut album, *Skyjacked*, were pretty good, and we arranged an album launch gig at the Camden Palace, on a Feet First club night, which pretty much guaranteed a full house.† Now, the artwork for *Skyjacked* is a kid's drawing of a plane, and the flyer for the Camden Palace gig had that plane smashing through a stack of Koot logos. A pretty harmless image, but

* Kai Motta's *Picture That* (SBZ 038 CD) was released on enhanced CD by Some Bizzare on May 14, 2001.
† Koot's album *Skyjacked* (SBZ CD 040) was released by Some Bizzare on September 10, 2001. It contained some of the tracks from the unreleased 1999 Warners album and six newly recorded, self-produced tracks.

unfortunately the date of the gig was September 11, 2001. It could almost have been one of Stevo's mad schemes. We still played the gig, but the venue was empty, as everyone was at home either glued to their televisions or too afraid to go out.

That ended up being Koot's last gig, but to this day we all still work with each other in various forms. There wasn't really an ending with Stevo, either. All that happened was, we moved out of our studio and started doing other stuff, and there was no real need for Stevo to contact us anymore. We're probably still signed to Some Bizarre! But, you know what, Stevo kept every promise that he made us on that first day we met him. He got us a massive record deal, and we got to work with some amazing people. It wasn't his job to write the songs and get us hits—that was down to us. Did his abrasive personality and communication issues help when things got hard with the label later? Probably not, but the bottom line was, a band can't sign a deal for the best part of three-quarters of a million quid and then not deliver the goods. It was a simple as that.

KAI MOTTA I knew Koot quite well—nice blokes—but they had a pretty hard time. Warner's pumped a massive amount of money into them but never let them release anything. Stevo put their album out himself, too.

ANDY JONES The Droidz track that was on *I'd Rather Shout . . .* was basically Koot.* There was a computer programme you could get where you could type in words phonetically, literally every syllable and spaces, and then add notes, and you'd get a kind of vocoder effect. We were using it occasionally on Koot records, and we had these two songs which we were into but our singer Graeme didn't want to sing, so we took his vocal off and got the computer to sing them instead. And Stevo jumped on it and said, 'Oh, you've got to do this, you can have a whole offshoot band,' so we called it The Droidz. To be honest, it was fairly prosaic.

KAI MOTTA From a success point a view, I didn't get that far, but I got a lot further than I would have if I hadn't worked with Stevo. He took me on, put his own

---

* The fourth Some Bizzare compilation album, *I'd Rather Shout At A Returning Echo Than Kid That Someone's Listening* (SBZ 042 CD), was released on September 24, 2001. Featuring tracks from Koot, Egil, Lorien, Kai Motta, Sandoz, The Droidz, and Richard H. Kirk in his Orchestra Terrestrial guise, the main draw was a new track from the reformed Soft Cell. 'God Shaped Hole' was a strong return, and Almond and Ball would later express regret at putting it on this album instead of one of their own.

money down, and put the album out himself. It got reviewed across the board, mostly favourably, but eventually the rest of the band wanted to get on with other things. So, I went to Stevo and asked to be released from the contract. Because there hadn't been any bites, he was like, 'Yeah, all right.'

>>

ANDY PETTITT Stevo and Matt's relationship was non-existent by that point. There were kind of vague dealings relating to a proposed DVD release of *Infected*. In Stevo's mind, he always felt a lot of the visual aspect of THE THE came from him. He felt that the *Infected* film was basically his baby—that he was responsible for it being made. I wouldn't say that he was resentful of Matt, just frustrated that Matt wouldn't engage with him.

STEVO It has nothing whatsoever to do with money, it's to do with politics. You don't do a record and a film, at the height of AIDS and HIV—a record and a film that references safe sex and has a good message—and then basically make it unavailable. That's what Kubrick did with *A Clockwork Orange*, and Matt has done the same with *Infected*. We made an amazing film, an incredible film, that is still relevant now, and you can only get it on a dodgy old VHS.

This next track is from *Horse Rotorvator*, which we consider stolen property, along with *Scatology*. We want the stolen property returned by the man who stole it, Stevo Pearce. Until he returns it, it's cursed.
GEOFF RUSHTON/JOHN BALANCE, Royal Festival Hall, London, September 19, 2000

ANDY PETTITT I never met or spoke to either of Coil, but there was correspondence from them that Stevo found quite unsettling, and not in a business sense. They were handwritten, vaguely threatening letters, which were laced with occultist qualities, which gave Stevo the willies, not to put too fine a point on it. They were the only band he was wary of, and Stevo left them alone, because he didn't want to poke the bear.

We have no news over Nothing releasing *Horse Rotorvator* and *Scatology* because we gave them it about five years ago and had it legally able to be released in the US, but Nothing's lawyers were unhappy with a slightly less than watertight legal

338

situation so didn't go ahead. Since then, that fucking arsehole Stevo Pearce has reared his very unpleasant head again and asked Nothing for more money and generally thrown a spanner in the works. He originally gave Coil permission to give it to Nothing as part of a half-hearted attempt to be nice to us and make some amends, including financial for the terrible way he has continued to treat us over the fate of these two records. Actually he wasn't trying to be nice he was trying to cover his ASS for some early crap he tried to pull off. Since then he has re-issued the CDs in the UK without our permission in the mistaken belief that he holds sole copyright on these two titles and has not paid us royalties to date. He even refuses to supply us with copies of our own records repeatedly ignoring requests for promotional/complimentary copies!

I repeat again that these two titles issued by Some Bizzare are cursed by me, John Balance. Do not buy them!!!! They are subject to complex BINDRUNES which tie Stevo up into his own hell with each subsequent purchase. This will only end when he signs over the rights to both titles to Coil without attachments.

GEOFF RUSHTON/JOHN BALANCE, Coil mailing list, July 1999

ROB COLLINS Some Bizzare did two albums with Coil, so at some point everything was OK and everyone was happy. I didn't even think about what the deal was at the time, I just assumed it would be dealt with by Stevo and Sleazy. But I think the band were probably in the right and that they were owed money.

STEVO I've never been sued by an artist, a publisher, or a record company and I've never sued an artist, a publisher, or a record company. Unfortunately, that could be classed as an act of weakness. I met these Coil fans in a club, and they went mental. This guy was going to kill me because he'd read this Coil book that said they'd never signed a contract with Some Bizzare. I don't know what's in my filling cabinets, it must be Scotch mist. They certainly have signed contracts.

Stevø has recently written to me saying he had recorded the 'death threats' left by me on his office answer-machine in the middle of the night. I have NEVER threatened him in this way. I HAVE cursed him on his answer machine, that way I was able to create an actual artifact, a magnetic tape HEX which is better than having just ranted or intoned it down the telephone to him in person. And the nature of the curse is that he will have problems and confusion until he gives us the money he owes us and releases the rights to these two albums back to Coil and Threshold House properly and legally and forever. The curse is genuine. It is a curse and a spell designed to retrieve STOLEN property, i.e., our artistic legacy and part of our LOST financial security.

GEOFF RUSHTON/JOHN BALANCE, Coil mailing list, June 2001

STEVO Somebody stole the Some Bizzare sign from Denmark Street, unscrewed it from the wall. Rushton phoned up the day after, saying, 'Hmm, I wonder where your sign went?' Which kind of implied that he knew all about it. He'd also phone up at 3am and leave slurry satanic curses on my answering machine. The thing that concerned me was the confidence he had that I was going to be destroyed and that my record label would fail. That wasn't magic—he obviously had some industry backing that was so powerful they could actually put me out the game.

MARC ALMOND It is probably to Stevo's advantage that some of the artists are no longer with us—Sleazy, Geoff, Genesis—as I'm sure they would be most vocal about their dealings with him.

ANDY PETTITT The dispute that really got his goat was the one with Neubauten, because they decided to put the albums they'd made on Some Bizzare out themselves. They still had the German masters, so they pressed the albums up and released them on their own Potomak Records. I came to understand that their argument was they weren't getting paid royalties by Stevo, so they took it upon themselves to reclaim their intellectual property. Of course, Stevo had other views on that and reserved most of his ire for Mark Chung. He found it incongruous that a person who he considered to be undertaking fraudulent activities—which is how he characterised Neubauten pressing their own albums—was working for Sony.

MARK CHUNG Under German law, if the label isn't paying royalties for three, four years, and obviously you can prove that to a court, then the contract will swiftly be invalidated. That's not what happens under British law. Rights assignment remains in force regardless of the breach of the obligation to issue royalty statements—essentially until you've had a final court ruling on the entire matter. And this can take years and years of very expensive legal and court action. And that's where the resentment comes from with Neubauten. Because obviously the band at some point said, 'Well, he's not paying us, fine. We want the rights back and we'll put all the records out ourselves.' But they couldn't get the rights back, and at some point Neubauten just released the albums themselves, because they had the masters and they put it out in Germany. And then there were two versions of the albums out there, the Some Bizarre one and the Neubauten one, and then Blixa would say, 'Don't buy that one, buy our one.'

It worked fine in the offline world, actually, because Stevo was not that well organised, but it became a problem online because he'd get just somebody to write to Apple, Spotify, etc., send in a scan of the rights assignment, and make them take it down. It would take thousands of pounds to take this case to court and maybe Neubauten should do that, but I left the band in '94 and stopped managing them then as well, so it's up to their current managers to decide. But I imagine they've come to the same conclusion: how much money is actually in Some Bizarre now? Probably very little. So the best thing they can do is get their rights back. Maybe somebody will do it one day.

STEVO The reality is, the last deal I signed was with Plastic Head in 2008, and the correspondence I have from interGROOVE, who were a small electronic music label in Germany, has all four Neubauten albums listed on Phononet GmbH registrations as interGROOVE/Some Bizarre. Meaning interGROOVE were the distributor, and Some Bizarre the copyright holder. And it says, 'Have a nice day.' In other words, as far as the Germans are concerned, we've gone through their process and won the battle. The bootleggers—Potomak Records—went through the same process and didn't satisfy the German authorities that they own the rights to those four Neubauten albums. They lost the battle. I received the thumbs up saying that what can be retailed in Germany has to be recognised as Some Bizarre, not Potomak. Then Plastic Head refused to go through with the deal, saying if they proceed, it will affect their ability to get more labels from Germany. In other words, they didn't want to upset Mark Chung. We'd already pressed up the product—all I needed Plastic Head to do was to ship it to retail in Germany, but they refused, so I had no choice but to terminate. That was the beginning of the end of Some Bizarre being able to trade.

CHRIS BOHN I'd say people didn't actually get ripped off, rather they never got what they thought was owed to them. Some of the Some Bizzare records cost a fortune, and even though many of them sold extremely well, who knows when they recouped the costs.

ANDY PETTITT Working with Stevo, I got to see both sides of him, and there was never any malice with him, really, it was just rampant egomania. He always intended to have good relationships with his artists, but unfortunately, he wasn't very efficient when it came to matters of business, and that was what was behind a lot of the disputes. I learned so much about contract law from going through the archive of labyrinthine contractual disputes he was having with various legacy artists. Stevo would dictate these letters to me, and then I'd have to turn them into English.

MARK CHUNG Stevo has always been somebody who's operated on opportunistic instincts, and maybe he thought he could get more out of me at that time. He used to love Luke Rhinehart's *The Dice Man*, and he would make decisions based on how the dice fell and stuff like that. So, if I put it into that line of things, I can go, 'OK, that's just Stevo,' but that doesn't mean I have to talk to him anymore. But that is just my personal disillusionment with him. It was a pity because I did think he did some really important and good work, and I was proud to be involved with Some Bizzare, and a lot of things that came from that were good. Although I still don't think Neubauten have had a statement. But what went wrong at the end of the day was the non-payment of artists, but I don't really think that was intentional or fraud or anything like that, it was just a total inability to deal with the business side of things.

STEVO If you get a reputation, like me, where you're not prepared to sue anyone, then everyone is going to take advantage of you. If you're not prepared to be litigious, then you shouldn't be in this business. I am not litigious. I don't want to be fighting law lawsuits all the time. I find the whole thing repulsive.

ANDY PETTITT Once Stevo got an inkling that something was brewing with a Soft Cell reunion, he reached out to Dave. Obviously, Langey [Mark Langthorne] was looking after Marc and had been doing so for some years. I think there was a bit of uncertainty on Dave's part, as he hadn't been in contact with Marc for a while, so having Stevo in his corner made him feel more comfortable. Everyone recognised Stevo was intrinsic to Soft Cell, like it or not, and regardless of what they both went on to do in their solo iterations, he was a significant part. So, the management side of it was Langey and Stevo working things out, while Dave and Marc, although on good terms, would travel separately, had different preferences for where they wanted to stay, etc. It wasn't a *let's get the band back together!* kind of thing, it was a pretty hard-headed decision on their part, in terms of their reasons for doing it.

DAVE BALL Soft Cell had been invited to launch a new music venue called Ocean in Hackney, East London.* I remember Marc and I are waiting very nervously in the wings; we hadn't played in front of an audience together for seventeen years, and we were going to debut some new songs. The place was filled with two thousand fans going mad on both nights. I say two thousand although believe this venue had what's known as rubber walls (i.e., the promoter printed a few hundred extra tickets that didn't go through the books).

When we kicked off with 'Memorabilia', the place went ballistic. I think a lot of the older fans couldn't quite believe we were back onstage together again. In fact, neither could we.

ANDY PETTITT Once the reunion had been announced, the BBC wanted to include Soft Cell in their *Young Guns* documentary series. It was Stevo's idea to film all his segments in a cell in Charing Cross police station, wearing an arrowed prisoner's suit. The producer's must have thought he was mad—not an uncommon reaction to Stevo's demands—but they sorted it out for him. Before he did it, he said, 'I want to look good in this, so you and me are gonna go hiking.' And we ended up hiking along Offa's Dyke on the Welsh border for three days. We stayed at this bed and breakfast, then went hiking across the mountains. And we were still up there at 8pm, without water or food, just two B&H, which we couldn't light because it was so windy. We almost had to call Mountain Rescue—it was absolutely terrifying.

Pretty much the first gig on the Soft Cell comeback tour was a party at the Cannes Film Festival. It should have been a great trip, and it was, until Stevo

---

* Soft Cell's Ocean shows took place on March 16–17, 2001. They were the duo's first shows for seventeen years.

drunkenly bet Dave he could swim to an island, which appeared to be about ten miles away on the horizon.

DAVE BALL We were all in Stevo's room, and he said, 'I'm going to swim to that island.' I said, 'You won't make it, it's further away than it appears.' But Stevo got his swimming trunks on and disappeared, so we just tucked into his mini bar. Then Andy came into the room and asked if we'd seen Stevo, and I said, 'Yeah come over to the window,' and pointed at a little dot out in the sea. And Andy said, 'You're fucking joking.' He could've drowned—there was a minute where we lost sight of him and thought that was it. There was a regatta going on, and yachts were sailing up to him to see if he needed help, and he refused to get out of the water. Eventually the Coast Guard were called, and they dragged him onto the boat and brought him back to shore. It was quite something. Stevo generally behaved worse than the band.

ANDY PETTITT The hotel wasn't happy, and we were all summoned to the lobby— Stevo, Marc, Dave, Langey, and me. Stevo, who was wrapped in a towel, was shivering, and pointing to Dave saying through his chattering teeth, 'Don't think you won that fucking bet!' The hotel cleared all our mini bars, and none of us were allowed a drink onsite for the remainder of the time we were there.

KAI MOTTA In the early 2000s, the music industry was on the cusp of becoming entirely run by accountants rather than the larger-than-life characters like Stevo. Suddenly, the industry changed, and it became this bland world with *Britain's Got Talent* and *X-Factor*, and super-quick profit became the ultimate goal. And that kind of destroyed people like Stevo who wanted to do something different. Of course, he had his own way of doing certain things, which I may not have agreed with, but music is certainly a lot fucking duller, in my opinion, without people like him around.

ANDY PETTITT Dave wouldn't fly anywhere, so I had to accompany him on trains around Europe. Soft Cell been booked on the NBC *Today Show* to do this massive American TV appearance, and Dave said he'd only go if they put him on Concorde, fully expecting that they'd say no. But they agreed, and I then had to spend two days trying to get him to take the ticket because he refused to accept it.

344

MARC ALMOND Dave and I contractually had to involve Stevo in the *Cruelty Without Beauty* campaign because he part-owned so much of the Soft Cell catalogue.* I had my own management by then, so he was really only acting for Dave. I was unhappy about it, but I hoped that it would be a different Stevo from the past, and in many ways he was, for a while at least.

ANDY PETTITT Stevo was instrumental in getting Cooking Vinyl to work with Soft Cell.

STEVO When I did the Cooking Vinyl deal, on the day of execution, right at the last minute, they suddenly said, 'Oh, and we want a live album, too.' Which was an old Stevo tactic.

ROB COLLINS I was at Cooking Vinyl by this point, and when we did the Soft Cell record, Stevo was managing Dave and involved with promotion. He was all right, you know. I mean, he was still Stevo, and a lot of other people in company who didn't know him found him difficult, rude. I didn't bring the deal in, but I remember being like, *Are you sure?* Yes, they were a name, but names don't often continue selling records after being away for so long. And I was right. It was assumed there'd be a lot more interest from the media in general for a new Soft Cell album, but there wasn't.

DAVE BALL I was still legally obliged to Stevo as a manager when we did *Cruelty Without Beauty*. The general consensus was that we should have made 'The Night' the first single and come back with another Northern soul cover. But we'd spent the video budget on 'Monoculture', which I still think is a great track. It was worth it just to see Stevo in a clown outfit. What we didn't tell him was the clown face makeup was based on the serial killer John Wayne Gacy. Stevo had no idea, which made it even funnier—that tickled our sick sense of humour. But *Cruelty Without Beauty* wasn't really promoted very well, which was a shame, because there were some good songs on there.

---

* Soft Cell's comeback album, their first since 1984's *This Last Night In Sodom*, was *Cruelty Without Beauty* (COOK CD245), released by Cooking Vinyl on October 8, 2002. The band embarked on another tour to promote the album, which resulted in the release of a live album, *Live* (COOK CD267), in 2003.

ANDY PETTITT The Soft Cell album probably wasn't their strongest work, but it was product, and it sold the tour, which went reasonably well in terms of tickets sold and what have you. I don't think it was ever going to be anything other than a one-album situation. They're just so different—I can't think of two more dissimilar people than Marc and Dave, in lifestyle and their views on life. And the reunion was a commercial situation that suited everybody's particular interests at that particular time. That's just what it was.

MARC ALMOND We got though the project, but it was seventeen years before Dave and I made another record.

STEVO I got involved to help them out, they asked me and I said yes. There was a US tour—Dave Ball is sitting on a boat because he's got aerophobia and is scared to fly. He's halfway to Canada, and all of a sudden the tour is cancelled. That tells you everything you need to know about the Soft Cell reunion.

KARL O'CONNOR Soft Cell were on an amazing trajectory when they split, and their timing couldn't have been worse, because if they'd just kept it going for a little longer, they would have ended up where The Cure or Depeche Mode or New Order got to in the US. They would have been seen as one of those great alternative British college-radio kind of bands. But then again, it's kind of brilliant that they didn't. Obviously, they came back, but everything Marc Almond and Dave Ball have put out as Soft Cell since *This Last Night In Sodom* just doesn't hit the mark for me. The working environment had changed, and the dysfunctional family they were part of no longer existed. For me, not being on Some Bizzare made a huge difference to the music they made.

ANDY PETTITT I'm afraid a lot of Stevo's issues around this time, whether it be Soft Cell or any of the other bands, stemmed from the fact the music just wasn't quite strong enough. There was precious little money coming in from the back catalogue at that time—he needed to repackage it and re-promote it. He also needed to aggressively stake his claim for a certain piece of musical territory, and then maybe that would have plugged him into a new scene with some new artists. But, for whatever reason, he was never really able to do that. I just don't

346

think that he had his head in that world anymore, which was unfortunate.

KAI MOTTA Stevo is a tough bloke, although I always felt there was bit of a shield up. I moved to Brighton and did a gig down there, which he came along to. It was a really good gig, and he stayed at my place afterward. Anyway, I got up next morning and he'd already got up, done all the washing up and tidied the place. And it was moments like that where you saw who this person really was.

ANDY PETTITT Everything is an opportunity for Stevo—he sees everything as a potential megaphone to broadcast whatever his agenda is on that day. Getting him to answer a straight question without multiple digressions and conspiracies is impossible.

KAI MOTTA I felt for Andy, because working for Stevo is not easy. Andy was quite a fragile bloke, and Stevo could be a bit of a fucking monster. And he worked for Stevo for quite a while, and sometimes he'd say things to Andy and I'd think, *I'd never let anyone fucking talk to me like that.* And then suddenly, Andy had this album come out, and I thought, *Fair play.* He took loads of shit from this guy, but he'd hung in there, learnt all he could about the music industry, and then put his own stuff out. And it was pretty good, too.

ANDY PETTITT Stevo finally caved in to the inevitable and accepted he had to give up the office in Denmark Street. I was living in Battersea, South West London, so when he said he was moving the office to his home in Highgate, North London, there was no way I was going to travel all that way to sit in his flat every day. I was frankly burned out as hell, and there wasn't a huge amount going on for him music-wise at that point either. Plus, my own music was starting to get somewhere. I'd formed Shortwave Set from the friendships I'd developed while working at Some Bizzare—Dave Farrell was in Koot, and I'd heard Ulrika Bjorsne on a demo that had been sent into the office. We picked up a manager and got a single deal, and off the back of that were offered an album deal with Independiente at the end of 2004. Were we tempted to work with Stevo on Shortwave Set? Absolutely no chance.

PETER ASHWORTH I have a real loyalty to Some Bizzare. It means a lot to me. I'm sad that for some people Stevo became impossible to work with. When he moved to Hampstead, he ended up about ten doors down from me, and we started to socialise a bit more. Going out for a quick drink at the local meant that you were probably going to get back home twelve hours later.

ANDY PETTITT Stevo and Dave didn't fall out over the whole Soft Cell reunion, which was, to me, a small triumph. Stevo was keen to be involved with what Dave did after that, and Dave was vaguely amenable. There was talk about there being another Grid record, and that obviously did happen, but after I'd left.

DAVE BALL I was the only person from the original Some Bizzare period who still spoke to Stevo. *The Bedsit Tapes* and *Demo Non-Stop* were taken from my old cassettes that had been gathering dust for years.* They got remastered and tidied up, but they were for the extreme collector, really—strictly lo-fi but nice for the completist. It was appropriate to release them on Some Bizzare, as it seemed to have become a dusty catalogue label, mostly trading on past glories.

The Horse Hospital is proud to present Redefining The Prologue: an exhibition featuring original cover artwork, paintings, sculptures and a programme of screenings and music from the legendary eighties record label Some Bizzare. The exhibition will include sculptures by Malcolm Poynter and Helen Chadwick, paintings by Andy Dog, Philip Diggle, Val Denham, Graeme Hughes and Bob Robinson, signed album artwork, a comprehensive collection of original chromalin proofs, and limited edition prints, in addition to a rotating programme of music and weekly film screenings of material from artists such as Soft Cell, THE THE, Cabaret Voltaire, Einsturzende Neubauten and Test Dept.

author unknown, programme notes for the *Redefining The Prologue* exhibition

STEVO Universal wanted a compilation for the twenty-fifth anniversary of the *Some Bizzare Album*, but I didn't want to do a retrospective, so half of it was old stuff and half of it was current Some Bizzare artists. The guy who did the artwork for

---

* Soft Cell's *The Bedsit Tapes* (SBZ046) was released by Some Bizzare on July 25, 2005. Containing demos of the songs that made up the band's early set, recorded between 1978 and 1980, it includes their cover of Black Sabbath's 'Paranoid'. *Demo Non-Stop* (SBZ059) was released on November 13, 2006, and contains rudimentary versions of songs that would go on to appear on the band's early releases on Some Bizzare.

all the new Soft Cell releases, Allon Kaye, knew someone at the Horse Hospital in Bloomsbury, and they came up with the idea about doing an exhibition at the same time. It was all artwork from the gallery. I ended up having to give a load of it to my accountant when I left him to offset outstanding fees.*

ZEKE MANYIKA My wife and I bumped into Stevo at the Some Bizzare exhibition at the Horse Hospital, and he was very rude, very defensive. He made a presumption and assumed I knew everything that was going on between him and Matt. But I knew nothing. So that was a bit hurtful, and was why it took me a long time to go and see him, when he tried to get back in touch. He was trying to do something with *Mastercrime*—someone had approached him to reissue it. I thought it might have been his way of trying to apologise, but he was seriously paranoid when I eventually saw him.

KARL O'CONNOR British Murder Boys did a Seed Records night at the Coronet in Elephant & Castle [October 21, 2006] and The Grid were on the bill. I was coming in and I saw a guy having a tear-up with the bouncers. It was Stevo, who I'd never met before, and he was winding these guys up and about to get chinned. I knew the bouncers, so I stepped in and said, 'It's OK, mate, he's The Grid's manager.' And Stevo just looked at me and went, 'Who are you?' And just walked straight past me, 'Whatever!' It was the most perfect way that I could have ever met him. He was a total cock and brilliant with it. I was so happy.

LARA PADDOCK My involvement with Some Bizzare was happenchance, really. I was working in New York for a latex clothing designer, and I'd set up a MySpace profile. Through my job, I was into the fetish scene, although I didn't have any latex pictures up, so I'm not quite sure what made me stand out to Stevo. Anyway, we started chatting on MySpace, I'd obviously heard of Soft Cell, but I didn't know

* The *Redefining The Prologue* exhibition was held at the Horse Hospital from October 7 to November 4, 2006. A fifth Some Bizzare compilation, also entitled *Redefining The Prologue* (1707688), was released to coincide with it and featured a mix of 'heritage acts' and newer artists such as Monkey Farm Frankenstein, Meka, Mainstream Distortion, The Dark Poets, and ZGA. It was notable for featuring Depeche Mode's original version of 'Photographic', the first time the band had appeared on a Some Bizzare release for twenty-five years. The same year also saw releases on Some Bizzare by Monkey Farm Frankenstein (*Twitch The Def Nerve*, SBZ051), Meka (*High Heel Shoes*, SBZ048), and Mainstream Distortion (*Bully*, SBZ049), all on CD.

349

any of Stevo's background history. Stevo said he was going relaunch the label for the digital age, and did I want to work with him. I've always been a huge music fan, but I'd never worked in the industry. And the next thing I know I've decided to go out to London to work for this record label. I just took a big dive off the cliff and thought all these amazing things were going to happen. I'm still not quite sure if it was a great rock'n'roll experience or just a nightmare.

RICHARD NORRIS You did see many sides to Stevo when you worked with him. He could be quite kind and thoughtful at times, but that was with his artists, who he was very loyal to. But within major record company walls that wasn't the case. The music business has continued to evolve, and it's a completely different game now. So, the of idea of these characters making a show as you're going into the record company or doing pranks that involve the MDs and CEOs, that's gone. I don't think it's in Stevo's nature to calm down, though, and I don't think anyone who knows him would want him to either. Apart from those who have to deal with him on a day-to-day basis, of course.

LARA PADDOCK I'm not sure if I was so keen for a change that I didn't ask enough questions, or if Stevo deliberately didn't give me all the details, but I landed in London, got off the plane, took a taxi up to Highgate, and walked into this council flat, which was his office and his home. And that was where we both worked and lived. Stevo in the living room and sleeping on the couch, and me from the bedroom working on my own computer. It was not at all what I expected.

HUW WILLIAMS I was working with a production team in London and had done various remixes for people like Martina Topley Bird. My wife Nathalie, Risqué's singer, was writing novels and poetry after working for years in neurosciences. We had just moved to Barcelona and had started the band, for fun initially, but our first single, 'Do You Believe In Heaven', picked up a lot of interest. We were heavily influenced by John Carpenter and various post-punk and new wave acts, including Some Bizarre bands like Cabaret Voltaire and Soft Cell, and electroclash acts like Felix Da Housecat and Fischerspooner.

LARA PADDOCK By the time I arrived in 2007, almost all the music for the new *Some Bizzare Double Album* compilation had been selected. Most of the music had been sourced via MySpace, which at the time was pretty cutting-edge. So, on that very first day, I took a nap and then we went right off to a studio to decide how long the spaces between each song on the album should be. Which was a really cool thing, but pretty surreal. And from there on I just tried to hold on to my hat as Stevo pretty much threw me into everything. I had a lot of responsibilities and had to learn on the way. He was trying to get everything ready for iTunes, and a big part of my job was to go through the entire Some Bizzare back catalogue and input all the necessary information for digital distribution. And it was a big job, which as far as I know was never really accomplished.

HUW WILLIAMS We got involved in MySpace quite early on, and it was such a great time. We met so many people through it, and we toured the world due to it. It was also how we were introduced to Stevo. We were already big fans of his 80s bands, in particular Depeche Mode and Psychic TV, and I also liked Bizarre Inc and The Grid from his 90s bands. As for his reputation, we had music-writer friends who told us stories, so we knew all the teddy bear and Trafalgar Square lion stories. We loved it!

RICHARD NORRIS Stevo came down to visit me in Lewes because he wanted me to sign off on a Grid compilation he was trying to put together. I was careful not to take him into any pubs that I thought I might want to go back to, because he's notorious for getting banned from public places. There was one Soho pub that he got banned from before even managing to order a drink, which is quite something. I still have a definite soft spot for Stevo, but if there's a few days of relentless madness, you need to take a break from it.

DAVE BALL The Grid didn't have a label at the time, so Richard and I thought we'd do Stevo a favour and let him put out our comeback album, *Doppelgänger*, on Some Bizzare. I don't think we saw any money from it.[*]

RICHARD NORRIS Dave's relationship with Stevo is very long suffering, but Dave is a very, very loyal person—he was probably the last of the original artists to still work with him. We were both a bit wary of putting *Doppelgänger* out on Some Bizzare, but it was all fine. It was a small deal, and the album didn't do particularly

---

[*] The Grid's *Doppelgänger* (SBZ093CD) was release on Some Bizzare on March 24, 2008. It didn't chart.

well, but we only licenced it to him. Unfortunately, he then tried to licence it to other people, so once again we were back into that.

DAVE BALL It's a typical Stevo tactic, and that's what let's him down. He's always trying to do these little dodgy deals, and when people catch him out it takes away any trust. I didn't want to waste any more time listening to a manger who gets stoned all the time and talks shite. That's not what I wanted any more. I realised I needed a proper manager who would get the work done.

LARA PADDOCK They were still putting out quite a few albums.* Because I'd never been to London before, he was taking me out and showing me the town. But a couple of weeks in, I realised there wasn't any money, and no one was getting paid. So I put a stop to all the going out, and I pretty much became a shut-in. It was all work and no play because I didn't feel comfortable with him spending money that didn't seem to belong to him.

PEDRO GRANJA DE CARVALHO When I was around sixteen years old, here in Portugal there was a great radio program called *Som Da Frente* made by António Sérgio. It ran from 1982 until 1993, and it was my musical education, along with the Portuguese journal *Blitz* at more or less the same time. So, at a very young age, I loved Cabaret Voltaire, THE THE, Test Department, Einstürzende Neubauten, Soft Cell, Swans, Depeche Mode, etc. At that time I was not paying any attention to who was releasing this music, it was just the art I was interested in, which I thought was from another world. I never thought of making music myself, I just considered myself privileged to know that sound. So, my first contact with Some Bizzare was bizarre—I loved the sound and identified myself with it without knowing where it came from.

LARA PADDOCK I think, overall, Stevo liked the music on the new *Some Bizzare Double Album*, but I do remember one night when we were working on the running order, and him saying, 'Oh God, what drugs was I taking when I signed this?' Of course, I think he was half joking, and perhaps there was a little marijuana

---

* Some Bizzare still had a pretty busy release schedule for most of 2008, including *Scanners* by Kontour (SBZ081CD), released on February 4, and *Who Has Stolen The Air?* by ZGA-FIGS (SBZ076CD), released on March 31.

involved that night, but the fact is that there were thirty-four artists on the album, which is a lot, and a couple of the tracks were super heavy and intense, so whether he was passionate about every single one of them, I couldn't say. I am a fan of many of the earlier Some Bizzare releases, and even though some of the tracks on the new album weren't really my thing, all the artists I worked with were really great people that had put their faith in Stevo and the label.

PEDRO GRANJA DE CARVALHO I'd had some success making music in Portugal with my friend Carlos Matos under the name Ode Filipica, but in the 90s I had to stop and earn money. I carried on with my art, painting and making noises, in my free time. I need to be creative, and my philosophy is to be like a child, free to make things to liberate me and transcend this reality. I started putting my music up on MySpace under the Pedro INF name. People laugh about MySpace now, but it was great for making music friends and to reach potential fans. Even now I cannot understand why MySpace was destroyed with stupid layout changes. Anyway, it was on MySpace that Stevo contacted me. I received a message from him saying he wants to release my music. I thought he wanted a track for a compilation, but no, he wants me to a Some Bizarre artist.* So I do some research and find that Stevo is the person who discovered and released the music by all my beloved bands in the 80s. I couldn't believe it—I rushed to my record collection, and there I saw the Some Bizarre logo everywhere.

KARL O'CONNOR Time moves on, and the main problem with electronic music, particularly the cutting-edge stuff from the 80s, was that it dated so quickly. And post-acid house, singing over electronics just became redundant, it seemed so old-fashioned. It came around again, but if that's what you were known for then, it was difficult to plant your foot in separate decades. Hardly any of those electronic artists managed to do it—in fact, Richard H. Kirk was the only one. Saying that, Some Bizzare did completely lose it in the 00s. Those later compilation albums, especially the MySpace one, were just so bad.

LARA PADDOCK Every band on the new compilation had a paper contract that needed to be signed. Once we'd managed to get all the signatures, we took them

---

* Pedro INF's first album for Some Bizzare was *Pedro INF* (SBZ079CD), released on July 18, 2008.

to the lawyer's office, and then afterward Stevo insisted that we stopped for a drink to celebrate. We drank a bunch of Laphroaig and he left the briefcase, with the contracts in, on the bus. Because it was London and not New York, somebody turned the briefcase in, and he was able to recover it, but, you know, he did not have his shit together. And that's most likely one of the big reasons why this great opportunity to get everything out there digitally, to promote the new album and get Some Bizarre back in the spotlight, just totally fell to pieces.

STEVO Why did I put Mute acts—The Normal and Fad Gadget—on the reissue of the first Some Bizzare album? I was doing Daniel a favour.*

LARA PADDOCK The *Some Bizzare Double Album* came out and just disappeared, which was a shame as it was such a cool concept, gathering all these unknown artists from MySpace.† People forget that it was the first big social media outpost, and in my mind it was really cutting-edge and cool to give a voice to artists who didn't have a means to get signed or have enough songs for an album. It wasn't that different to the original Some Bizzare album, with Depeche Mode, Soft Cell, and THE THE. But because Stevo was so focused on trying to get the back catalogue digitised so he could settle the disputes with his artists, the album just kind of fell through the cracks. I mean, I'm surprised that a physical album actually came out.

STEVO Apart from a couple of tracks, I put the *Some Bizzare Double Album* together completely from MySpace. We got a good review from Phil Alexander in *Kerrang!*—we got a nine out of ten.

HUW WILLIAMS After chatting on MySpace, Stevo said he would 'kill' for our album. As it was our debut, we took that as a good sign, maybe we were a bit naive. Everything was done over MySpace or email, and we collaborated with some of the other bands featured on the new Some Bizzare compilation. The Dark Poets were very encouraging, and we also worked with Crackdown. Stevo ran the label from

---

* The original *Some Bizzare Album* (SBZ101CD) was reissued at some point in 2008, with additional tracks by The Normal, The Residents, and Fad Gadget, perhaps to better reflect Stevo's DJ sets at the time.

† The *Some Bizzare Double Album* (SBZ099CD) was released on CD on July 28, 2008. It featured thirty-four artists, including The Grid, Risqué, Pedro INF, and The Dark Poets.

his flat in London, which was opposite a graveyard, apparently. There were a couple of times when we spoke on the phone and he seemed to be relieving himself in the sink. He was a funny guy. We only met him once, when we played live at Skin Two's Rubber Ball in London. Stevo and Lara met us there, and he gave Nathalie a box of chocolates. Lara ended up appearing onstage with us at a gig in Greece, as a submissive to a dominatrix called Dante Posh. It was an interesting show.

LARA PADDOCK Risqué were playing this big latex party in London, and I bumped into a friend from the New York fetish scene who was a pro-domme. Hugh and Natalie said, 'Oh, we have this gig in Greece at this porn festival. Will you come and be part of the performance?' So my friend and I went along to add a layer of kink to Risqué's show. But it was a pretty hardcore scene out there, and it we were all a little bit over our heads.

HUW WILLIAMS *Tie Me Up, Tie Me Down* was recorded and produced partly in Barcelona, and then we moved to the South of France, where it was finished. Stevo was credited as executive producer, and he paid for the album to be mastered at the Exchange in London. He also paid for a publicist, which cost a couple of grand, although I hit up lots of magazines myself. We also went to Paris to shoot a video with the photographer Paul Von Borax. Stevo was supposed to be involved with that but wasn't in the end, which was something we got quite upset about.

LARA PADDOCK A lot of people seemed to be very upset with him, for royalties not being paid or money not being dispersed as the artists thought it should be. There was a lot of screaming and yelling from his 'office'. He told me tales of having fabulous properties and so many credit cards he could cover a wall with them. He told me he was letting everyone crash at these properties like some sort of like communal house, and I think he thought that was acceptable payment for the artists. It sounded like he was just throwing cash around, like oodles of money, but maybe, because he was so young and inexperienced at the time, he didn't understand he was supposed to disperse that cash. He kept trying to get Marc Almond to meet with me, but of course that wasn't happening, as Marc didn't want anything to do with him. We did go out for drinks with Dave Ball one night because his girlfriend had a track on the compilation and we needed her to sign the contract.

HUW WILLIAMS Stevo asked us to remix a Marc Almond track, which we did, but there ended up being huge arguments over email between Marc, his manager, and Stevo, which we were caught in the middle of. Also, we had gigs booked around the album release, and it was delayed, so we were playing live with nothing to promote.* So we thought we'd step back after that. We have mixed feelings about our involvement with Some Bizzare. We were proud to be part of the legend but at the same time happy to be away from it.

PEDRO GRANJA DE CARVALHO My music is free, avant-garde, reality cracking, Dada-esque, and full of love. I produce music like I am producing a painting—the goal is not to remember how it was done but laugh like crazy when I am doing it, out of my mind and time traveling. I make music and painting to satisfy myself, not the world. Art does not need humans to exist—a stone, tree, the rain are all art. Art is for cosmic harmony, art is everything by itself.

DAVE BALL I had no idea where he was finding all these new acts for the label—they were probably things he'd signed for 10p or something. But he was definitely pushing them on us for the Soft Cell *Heat: The Remixes* project.† Mark Langthorne and I were saying that he had to get some big names on there—you couldn't just have the remixes done by acts no one had ever heard of. So we approached people like Pet Shop Boys and Scissor Sisters. They all said yes, but the problem was they wanted quite a lot of money, and Stevo was trying to do everything on a shoestring. Which is why he was using acts like Dark Poets and Monkey Farm Frankenstein, trying to promote their names while doing the album on a budget. And the end result is exactly that—it sounds like a not-very-well-thought-out, bargain-bin remix album. It was nowhere near as ground-breaking as *Non-Stop Ecstatic Dancing*.

LARA PADDOCK I'm quite eccentric and I've worked with other eccentric people, but Stevo was a very challenging person. I think in a lot of ways his heart was in the right place, but it was also twisted. He definitely got off on negative energy.

* Risqué's debut album, *Tie Me Up, Tie Me Down* (SBZCD092), was finally released by Some Bizzare in 2009.
† On September 15, 2008, Mercury issued *Heat: The Remixes* (5311758) and on the same day reissued *Non Stop Erotic Cabaret* as a deluxe-edition CD (5303216). The reissue included all the original twelve-inch singles and B-sides recorded with Mike Thorne. The difference between the old and new versions was stark.

He could be funny and generous but also a little bit frightening, too. In the end it was just too much to manage, so I ended up returning to New York and getting my old job back. I tried my best to help him and the label, so I hope I left only positive thoughts and put out some good energy.

STEVO Some Bizzare attracts new artists because they love the history of the label, but we don't get any help from the industry. Everyone's helping Mute Records—in 2011, they did a whole bloody Mute festival at the Roundhouse. If I make a move on something, Daniel is running behind me trying to sign it up. It's like I'm working for Daniel and Mute, not Some Bizzare! What I'm saying is, all the Mute bands go on tour together, and work on each other's records and support each other, which is how Some Bizzare used to be. So why will they do that for Daniel and not Stevo?

FLOOD Both Daniel and Stevo are incredible individuals, but I think the biggest difference between them would be that there was always a level of stability with Daniel. Particularly because he produced a lot of the bands—Nick Cave and Erasure were pretty much the only people in the early days where Daniel wasn't involved in the production. Most of the other bands that I worked with on Mute, Daniel was running the show. There's a different way that the bands respond to that. And I think also, with Depeche being so consistently successful and Mute also having Yazoo, and then Erasure, and also Nick and Swans, all major bases were covered. Whereas Soft Cell were done by 1984, and for Stevo, once they'd fragmented, he didn't really have anybody else of that stature to fill that commercial space.

STEVO People from outside the UK who are into music and who are fans of Some Bizzare must wonder what's going on. You can't get the records, there are bootlegs flying around all over the place, there's all this animosity between the label and the bands. If you were from South Africa, Israel, Australia, Brazil, or wherever, they must think what's going on in England with Some Bizzare, why don't they like Stevo, what's he done? It must be so strange for someone that's into the label overseas and looking at how it's being administrated here.

PEDRO GRANJA DE CARVALHO I do not make art for money, and I know Stevo does what he does for love. I hope he gets money off it, but my personal opinion is

357

that he releases me for love not for money.* I love Stevo and his spirit. I understand his cosmic power.

STEVO I've not been releasing music because I've been working on my painting. I paint most days, and when I'm not painting I'm walking, all around the country. I've also written a script for a short movie, and I've been working on my own books, which have been taking up most of my time, but they'll be going on presale soon. It's all going to come together. And obviously, moving forward, I'll be rereleasing all the classic Some Bizzare titles, plus also new material from new artists. And that's what excites me the most. The new Some Bizarre website, which is in development, is going to be like no other. It'll be a show-the-rest-of-the-music-industry-how-to-sell-records website. It's artist-friendly and visually stimulating, and I'm really excited about it.

Scheduling records will take some time to get right from marketing point of view, to make sure these classic records have their best shot in the current marketplace. People have been waiting so long, we might as well take our time and do a good job and pin the release dates on the right day. I'm still excited about music and working with great artists, both old and new. Whenever people have asked me what my favourite Some Bizzare record is, I have always given the same answer: it's the one I haven't produced yet.

A person that gives you a false smile is the enemy 'A false smile is a lie'
And the people who use it to climb the bureaucratic ladder—hard luck.

Ø, from the sleeve of Marc & The Mambas' *Torment And Toreros* LP (1983)

* Pedro INF's second album for Some Bizzare, *Azphonix* (SBZCD115), was released in February 2010. The following month, Satanpornocultshop released their album *Arkhaiomelisidonophunikheratos* (SBZCD116) on the label. Its glitchy, sample-heavy electronica is most notable for being the last album to date to be released on Some Bizzare.

358

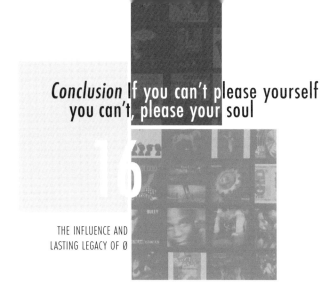

Conclusion If you can't please yourself you can't, please your soul

THE INFLUENCE AND
LASTING LEGACY OF Ø

STEVO Some Bizzare and Stevo are not included in the music industry, we are excluded. With all the wonderful music that we produced, there should be an arts programme about Some Bizzare. It should be up on a pedestal. Where's our BBC Four documentary? People have had awards for their contribution to music—Marc Almond has an OBE. Why haven't I got an OBE? There's a massive conspiracy here.

ANDY PETTITT Stevo is absolutely unique, he really is, with all the good and bad that goes along with that. He's an incredible guy and taught me a lot, some of which was what *not* to do rather than what you should do. But he really was one of one of the most amazing people I've ever worked with in my life. He took the royalties that he made from Soft Cell—this huge, huge success at a very young age—and rather than do sensible things with that money, he invested it in the most uncompromising, uncommercial, confrontational music. He wasn't going after another 'Tainted Love'—he didn't just want to replicate that—he put his resources and his efforts into some really underground and interesting music, and you've got to respect that. You know that George Bernard Shaw quote, 'The reasonable man adapts himself to the world; the unreasonable one persists in trying to adapt the world to himself. Therefore, all progress depends on the unreasonable man'? Well, that's Stevo.

ANDY JONES When we worked with Stevo, the music industry was a completely different world from the one he knew in the 80s. We let him do this big deal, which was great for him, but in retrospect it wasn't really great for the band. You can't be taking that sort of money, doing the sort of music we were doing, and expect the record label to be happy when it doesn't connect with the mainstream. Saying that, the thing I love about the Stevos of the world is that, however many things they clumsily get wrong along the way, the bottom line is they're music enthusiasts who are sticking their neck out in a business where you'd be better off betting on a horse. If you wanted to run a successful business and make money, you just wouldn't put your money on a bunch of guys sitting in their bedrooms trying to write songs. So, to me, I always feel that however flawed these people are, there's an element of, *Well, at least they're giving it a go.* Because you have to be crazy to want to.

CHRIS WILKIE We really can't complain—I'd read *Starmakers & Svengalis*, so I knew about Stevo's past, and we went into it with our eyes open. And he accomplished a lot of the things that he said he would, like sorting out our legal problems and arranging a North American deal, for instance. The Some Bizzare story is one of licencing in many ways, and he really is very good at doing deals. For sure, he put people's noses out of joint at EMI, but I think all the other problems we had after weren't anything to do with Stevo—they were to do with us, the band. In the end, we got what we really wanted out of it all: some pretty unbelievable anecdotes.

ANDY WIGMORE Stevo is a very special man, just completely off the charts, really flamboyant but also really pioneering in so many ways. He did so many crazy things and was an enthusiast. I always felt anything was possible when I was with him. It's only now, with hindsight, that I look back and think how incredible it was to be part of what he created, if only for a short time.

COLIN SCHAVERIEN The industry has become fairly unopinionated, when it should be very opinionated. It's become quite vanilla, both in terms of musical output and the type of people working in the industry. It's missing the mavericks, and I think Stevo was a proper maverick. Of course, he and I had a financial fallout, but I still think really fondly of him, and if I could see him, I would thank him for the education. But as far as him working in the industry now, I don't think it wants or allows people who are so clearly outspoken and slightly on the edge to be part of it anymore. And that's a shame.

TIM HUTTON I've got fairly benign feelings toward Stevo, as my time with Some Bizzare was a huge learning experience. My previous situation, where I ended up trusting this guy with basically all my money, my publishing, everything, was really foolish and very naive of me. I'd just had a baby and suddenly realised I was sixty-five grand down and completely broke, so that was a that was a tough time, which Stevo got me out of. He brought the best out of me, in a lot of ways, in terms of being a more well-rounded person. I was a little bit held back before that, so it was educational on that level.

MIKE HOLDSWORTH Independent music in those days was the Wild West. There were no rules. Everything is very well organised for the bigger indies now—it's an industry—but back in the 80s, when Rough Trade, Factory, Mute, Some Bizzare, all those labels were starting out, there was no pattern of how to do stuff. Everything's very structured now, which is great, and in many ways it's better for artists and musicians. But having that sort of open frontier, and creating your own rules, was very exciting and creative. People had a lot of fun. Characters with eccentricities were championed and appreciated, and it was those mavericks that made waves. Stevo was one of them—he was a maverick, and he certainly made waves.

RICHARD NORRIS The interesting thing about Some Bizarre is that it promoted some quite extreme positions and some quite hardcore, authentic art statements, but did it within the commercial, pop mainstream, and that's a really difficult thing to do. And I don't think many people have managed to do it since. Maybe the KLF a little bit, but they had an element of humour, which gave the music the element of novelty. But, with Some Bizzare, there were statements of intent that Stevo stuck with when he really didn't need to. After 'Tainted Love', I'm sure he could have signed completely different acts and had even greater success, but he chose not to. So, if it was all about the money, he could have done it very, very differently.

LEE KAVANAGH Everyone who worked in the music industry at that time has a Stevo story—even the people who never met him. But I learned so much from

Some Bizzare because the gems that Stevo used to come out with and the ideas that he used to have were absolutely out of this world. And when everybody was on board with him, it was a little bit of genius.

KEVIN FOAKES I think something like Some Bizzare could happen again, just not in pop music. It could happen in the independent sector, and there have been mavericks like Stevo—well, maybe not exactly like Stevo—who've got superb A&R skills and a personality to match, and once they've got a bit of money under their belt, they run with it. Most of the time, they burn bright and burn out. The last example of that I can think of is James Lavelle and Mo Wax. He didn't have a no.1 with this first thing, like Some Bizarre, but once he got the ball rolling and had people like DJ Shadow, Dr Octagon, and Money Mark, he just assembled a ridiculous empire, pretty much solely built around his own tastes. And that incorporated art, fashion, and film, as well as music. Lavelle also lost his shirt on the way, burnt bridges, and carried on by himself. Maybe not in the same sphere, but Wiley, who basically started the whole grime scene, had no.1 singles, did major label deals, put things out independently, and sold records out the back of his car. He also had very public meltdowns, pissed people off, and damaged his career on social media. So, you can definitely draw some parallels there.

WARNE LIVESEY Career-wise, the records I did for Some Bizzare were very important to me. From an experience point of view, the work I did with Jim, although demanding, was good grounding in terms of getting the most out of a small studio with a limited amount of equipment. Conversely, working with Matt, with everything and anything at our disposal, taught me how important maintaining an identity and keeping something gritty at the core is, when working on a much bigger canvas. Most artists who want to work with me more often than not will cite *Infected* or *Mind Bomb* as the reason. Plus, *Infected* was the first major label record I co-produced, so that was that was a real turning point. I wasn't getting any offers as a producer before that record. Then, after it came out, it went crazy.

MICHAEL GIRA Stevo can be a dick, so it's best not to talk too specifically. What I will say is, I liked Stevo a lot because he came from this proletarian background. And I met his dad, who I believe was a mason or a plasterer, and that was the kind of work I had been doing. So I felt some kind of affinity with Stevo, coming from a background like that and then turning it around and becoming who he became, through sheer force of imagination and will. But then later, Stevo became kind of something else, so that's enough said.

TEST DEPT We have to recognise Stevo for his musical passion and maverick tenacity manging bigger label partnerships. His approach was to penetrate the mainstream and use the majors to distribute his anarchic philosophy as widely as possible. The true joy of our time with Some Bizzare was having Jane Rolink looking after us and making sense of our chaotic lives, as well as Marc Almond, THE THE, and Jim Thirlwell. Unfortunately, echoing the experiences of many SB artists, our long-term relationship with the label fractured after it became clear that matters were not as they should be concerning deals, royalties, and payments.

ANDREAS MCELLIGOTT I wasn't particularly into the music but I admired Some Bizzare—they were mavericks, especially Stevo. He was not your typical music industry sort of person; he wasn't afraid to take risks. He virtually gave 'Tainted Love' to Phonogram because he knew it was gonna be massive, he had total faith in it. And his reasoning was, *When they want the album, that's when I'll sting them.* And that's exactly what he did. He was just a wideboy from Essex in many ways, but Some Bizzare was seen as visionary at that time—they were an important label.

PAUL 'BEE' HAMPSHIRE It was a real formative, seminal time. It was just so rich with light and dark. We were uncovering all this stuff that had been lost in culture, like the Process Church Of The Final Judgement, while discovering new things as well, like ecstasy. We felt like we were explorers.

ALAURA O'DELL Some Bizzare was a small label, but even now, I'm in the grocery store and every other day they're playing 'Tainted Love'. I'm like, *Really? Still?* But it was an interesting period, and so much innovative art was born out of it. Not just the musicians but filmmakers and artists like John Mabury and Derek Jarman. I think we have to give Stevo credit because he was really good at rustling up publicity, and he was a go-getter. Whatever I might think of him personally, he didn't do anything directly bad to me. He was just so brash, but that was his personality. I guess that's what makes us all special in the end, that we are all unique.

STEVE SHERLOCK My view on Stevo these days is if you accepted his help, and he took you from playing the local pubs and put you on a world stage, it all comes with strings. But at the time, not honouring an agreement hurt. He is absolutely what he is, and he is obviously good at it. He always looked after his revenue stream, and if came between his artists and his own interests, well, it's obvious what came first.

ZEKE MANYIKA Stevo was a remarkable young man. A dyslexic working-class boy whose life could easily have floundered without making much of a mark, given the low expectations his background would normally elicit. What a waste that would have been—it makes you wonder how many are hindered by society's prejudices. I think maybe too much happened to him too quickly, as he was very young. But he had a good heart, great ears, and I for one am prepared to overlook the occasional awful behaviour because he was often a very good friend indeed.

IAN TREGONING There's a deep affection for Stevo, despite the fact he fucked up a lot of things very badly. You know, having a night out with Stevo in the 80s and 90s was just fantastic. He was great fun and just ridiculous, you'd end up aching with laughter. But there were a few things that happened, and I thought, *I just don't need that in my life*. There were a lot of opportunities for him to make good, and he didn't. And on balance, I think people decided just to cut him loose.

FLOOD Stevo was a showman, but you never really knew what was going on with him. He was always really on it, but it was that random element that got everybody to do things for him. He did eventually piss people off, and there were a few bands where his behaviour started to wear very thin. But he is so important, and Some Bizarre is an integral part of the music business.

KARL O'CONNOR What I loved about Some Bizzare was the friction between this working-class bloke and some of the greatest artists of a generation. And the music that friction produced hasn't been surpassed. No new band has made a record as good as *Cop*. No single solo artist has made an album as innovative as *Hole*. There's nobody else who can do what Matt Johnson does. And that's not just me saying, 'Oh, kids can't make music like they used to'—it's not as basic as that. It's the intensity that doesn't exist anymore, and that's hard to generate unless it's coming from a genuine place. And that's ultimately what Some Bizarre was about: intensity, which is why its brilliance was so short-lived. And I find that really inspiring, still, and everything that happened with Some Bizarre in the 80s still resonates with me now, in the way I approach my own art and run my own label. It's all about encouraging chaos and taking risks.

JANE ROLINK We didn't fit in then and we still don't fit in now. I've never fitted in anywhere except Some Bizzare. People who were different could all come together and just be who they were, be free. It was brilliant.

RUSTY EGAN I'm really close friends with a very, very, very wealthy and successful music-industry bloke, the man who signed Soft Cell. And I was around his house the other day—sorry, one of his houses—and he said, 'Is Stevo OK, can I do anything for him?' But what can anyone do? If you gave him a load of money, he'd probably set fire to it.

PETER ASHWORTH Stevo was seriously important—his madness and wild risk-taking allowed others to create. He was a great motivator and a catalyst, and without him the scene would not have been the same. The trouble is, he didn't know when to stop. I find it very interesting that some of those who have had the greatest success seem to be attacking him most, and I'm thinking, *Where's the generosity of spirit, guys?* I find it extraordinary that people who have done incredibly well financially and still have a creative world to play in forty years after he started Some Bizzare, are moaning about him.

STEVE PARRY A few years ago, Stevo had got together with some distributor and wanted to re-release the *Some Bizzare Album*. He sent me the contract and it was still the magic figure of eight grand. He'd also mistakenly sent me THE THE's contract. These are the adventures of Stevo—it's like a bloody *Carry On* film.

NEIL ARTHUR Stephen and I met up with Stevo on the South Bank around 2008. There was a reissue of the original album, so he got in touch. It wasn't a very long meeting, and he went on about a lot of stuff, and I just shut off after a while, like I used to. It was nice to see him, though, and at least he'd stopped wearing his Star Trek outfit.

STEVE HOVINGTON As a band, we didn't have a particularly professional approach, and neither did Stevo. His style of management in the early days was, if he didn't like something then he would throw things, particularly at the record label—poor old Roger Aimes. I'm painting a picture of some kind of hooligan here, but Stevo obviously had a very engaging side to him, and we liked him. He'd had quite a hard upbringing, but he was a decent guy.

BEVERLEY GLICK The thing about Stevo is, if you gave him the time of day, then he was super loyal, and kind of still is. He occasionally sends me very sweet, slightly weird messages. I think it's a bit sad that so many people he worked with over the years don't want to work with him now. I mean, I get it, but it's still quite sad. He did have his own brilliance, and some of the things that those artists achieved, I don't know if they would have got so far without Stevo behind them. He's clearly become a bit more eccentric as he's got older, so I can't imagine the record companies of the twenty-first century allowing him to manipulate them in the same way as he used to—they just wouldn't have it. There might also be a bit of score-settling there too, I suppose. But I've still got a soft spot for Stevo, and I always did. We had a lot of fun and adventures together.

ROB COLLINS I think there was a moment when Stevo could have taken over the world, with the acts that he was working with, and his ability to find things and drop them into the right place for them to be successful was pretty good. But it lasted fifteen minutes. I don't know whether success went to his head, but there was a lot riding on him. He was almost as much a celebrity as the artists were at the time. But I think he falls in love with music too easily and lost his Midas touch pretty quickly. But any label that sets itself up to do their own thing and stick two fingers up to the establishment is following in the footsteps of Some Bizarre. We were never that commercially astute, it was all about the 'wow' moment, the art and the confrontation. We felt like a little gang against the world and wanted to educate and inform people about these amazing artists. I'm sure hindsight shows we were deluded, but some really great music came out of it, and it probably does need to be reassessed in a in a wider context.

MARK CHUNG Even though I was the bass player in Neubauten, I was also the manager, so I had more to do with Stevo than the rest of the band. I imagine they all probably hate him, and Blixa hates him the most although understands him the least. Obviously, I can see why they, and so many other bands, are pissed off, because it's really annoying not to have control over your repertoire. But the second best thing would be to have a partner that you can work with and do things together, but that is not the case with Stevo either. However, I would also say that if it hadn't had been for Some Bizarre, none of us would have gone where we went, because we couldn't have made the recordings we made at that time, we just didn't have the money.

I do think in those first six years, it was good, and it definitely benefitted the band, while at the same time being financially detrimental. So it was both things, which on reflection is quite suitable, actually. Stevo made things possible and impossible, all at the same time.

ANNI HOGAN Some Bizarre was just like, *Wow. Wow!*

JOSE WARDEN I went to one of Soft Cell's Hammersmith shows in 2021, and Brian went to the show in Leeds. It was, I have to say, the best show that I have ever seen them do. It is actually really nice going to see them live now and just being able to dance to 'Memorabilia', which is my absolute favourite song of theirs, and not having to think about backing vocals. I remember that night thinking that 'Tainted Love' wasn't actually a bad song after all—I heard it so many times in the early days that it nearly drove me to fucking madness.

HUW FEATHER Some Bizzare was its own thing. It was fascinating. It was disastrous. It was chaotic. It was the most brilliant thing in the world.

DANIEL MILLER Although we had similar musical tastes, I think we had very different approaches to working with artists. There was a lot of—shall we say—chaos around the music industry at that time, and I felt a sense of responsibility to not to get involved in that chaos. I'm not saying that Stevo did, but we're different people with very different personalities. I think the fact that Some Bizzare was originally through a major label, and then wasn't, and the loss of that kind of funding, could have been a factor. He did release some really great music, but really great music doesn't always sell, as I know only too well. But his vision, and the fearlessness to pursue that vision, is Some Bizzare and Stevo's legacy. And that fearlessness got him into scrapes, but he did an enormous amount for the kind of music that we were both interested in.

DAVE BALL The initial few years were great. It was mental, and we were all really busy, and we had a ball. And then egos got in the way, and I think Stevo thought he was like God's gift at that point. Because he'd signed Soft Cell and THE THE, and discovered Depeche Mode and Blancmange, and put together the *Some Bizzare Album*, which was genius for a seventeen-year-old. He should have been the busiest A&R man in the world after that. But there you are.

MARC ALMOND I have a lot to thank Stevo and Some Bizzare for. I had two no.1 records with them, and it gave me opportunities that enabled me to be the artist I am today. I'm grateful for the people I met at the label, for the artists I worked with and who I became friends with.

Being with Some Bizarre at its peak were some of the best times of my creative life. Stevo was truly a maverick, a real original, a one-off. He was like the great character managers of the 60s and 70s that you would read about, and the people in the business loved him for it.

STEPHEN 'MAL' MALLINDER What underpinned it all with Stevo was money. He has a withering respect for money, which can be a healthy thing unless the money is someone else's. But Stevo was all about 'the deal'. He related more to the artists than he did to the industry. He regarded major labels as corporations to be exploited, and success for him was being able to do a deal that made him feel he'd won. Hence, he became incredibly combative, because he saw labels as people who were at trying to outfox him. He was just interested in arm-wrestling record labels and getting money out of them. But most of all, Stevo saw himself as an artist, and I think he was a frustrated musician in some ways.

J.G. THIRLWELL I would say it's for historians to decide why Some Bizzare didn't have the same trajectory as Mute—probably enough time has passed for someone to figure it out. It's an apt comparison, but Mute developed in one way and Some Bizzare in another. Stevo was very erratic, and I think he alienated a lot of people with his flamboyant stunts and behaviour. I think a lot of the artists didn't really want that to be their calling card. I'm grateful to have been able to make *Hole* and

Nail, and they were very successful, but I don't really have any comment about why what happened, happened. But it just seemed to just stop dead. I think there weren't great A&R decisions after that initial success.

MATT JOHNSON There was a period in the mid 1980s when Some Bizzare was the most exciting independent record label in the world. Stevo had an instinct for signing the right artists at the right time and was very good at marketing them. He was always open to meeting new people and creating fresh networks. It was a very fertile period, very sociable and exciting. In all honesty there wasn't a labelmate on Some Bizzare I didn't like and respect. Obviously I was closer to some than others—Jim is still one of my closest friends today—but I enjoyed the company of all of them: Marc and Dave, Sleazy and Geoff, Mal and Richard, Genesis, Mike Gira, Zeke, Marc Chung, Mufti and Blixa, the guys from Test Dept. and all the others.

The sad thing is that although Stevo knew how to build something he just didn't know how to maintain or sustain it. He was someone who saw the big picture rather than bother with all the little details. But the devil is in the detail. Stevo had a clear and creative vision of where he wanted to take Some Bizzare, but he just couldn't back it up with the day-to-day efficiency that is essential to longevity. What he desperately needed was a trustworthy business partner who could administer Some Bizzare effectively and ensure everyone got paid on time and paid in full. He also desperately needed a loving partner in his personal life who could have helped protect him from the demons that would eventually engulf him.

MARC ALMOND It was a strange symbiosis—I often think that if I was Stevo's Elvis, then he was definitely my Colonel Tom Parker. I'm not sure if that's a good thing or not, but despite everything I wish him well. He's an architect of his own misfortunes, but then again so are we all.

STEVO I made up the quote, 'With every kick in the face, and every hurdle you pass, the rewards get greater.' Well, all the kicks to the face that I've had, and all the barriers that I've needed a pass, have all been put in place by my own administration. All the all the pain and all the agony is because the music industry is back-to-front. The accountants are running the show based on speculation, when the people who create the assets should be in charge. I mean, the real value of anything creative is not what's on the year end accounts.

Your true value is, if you lost everything tomorrow, and you had nothing, what could you get the following day? Meaning, if I lost Some Bizarre, I will have lost everything. But the following day, I'll still be Stevo—and that's the most important thing.

"Conform to deform.

Ø, from the sleeve of *Redefining The Prologue 1981–2006* (2006)

NOTES AND
SOURCES

All interviews conducted by the author between 2020 and 2022, unless otherwise stated below. Permission has been sought where possible.

01 PRE-1980: REDEFINING THE PROLOGUE

10 *I was a very difficult child* . . . Paul Sexton, 'The Bizzare Adventures Of Stevo', *Select*, February 1991

17 *Marc had heard my strange electronic bleeps* . . . Dave Ball, *Electronic Boy: My Life In And Out Of Soft Cell* (Omnibus Press, 2020)

02 1980: THE TAPE IS YOUR VOICE

26 *They called it the Futurist Chart, not me* . . . Pierre Perrone, 'Stevo: Bizzare After All These Years', *Independent*, October 27, 2006

41 *We did a gig with Fad Gadget* . . . Jonathan Miller, *Stripped: The True Story Of Depeche Mode* (Omnibus Press, 2003)

03 1981: DANCING, LAUGHING, DRINKING, LOVING

55 *We couldn't decide on what to release* . . . Dave Ball, *Electronic Boy*

67 *It was incredible. I had to have this record* . . . *Young Guns Go For It*, 'Soft Cell' episode, BBC Two, June 2000

67 *He came to my office and said to me* . . . *Young Guns Go For It*

67 *I think that he the deal just to get me out of the room* . . . *Young Guns Go For It*

70 *Expect the unexpected with Stevo* . . . *Young Guns Go For It*

74 *The whole Non Stop Erotic Cabaret album* . . . *Young Guns Go For It*

76 *Walking down Soho, you'd hear Seedy Films* . . . *Young Guns Go For It*

04 1982: I'M LOST AGAIN AND I'M ON THE RUN

82 *We recorded 'Torch' in New York* . . . Marc Almond, *Tainted Life: The Autobiography* (Sidgwick & Jackson, 1999)

83 *Cindy came over to England for the video* . . . Marc Almond, *Tainted Life*

198 *Bursting with inspiration, I began to think* . . . Marc Almond, *Tainted Life*

200 *Eventually the album was completed* . . . Marc Almond, *Tainted Life*

08 1985: BUT PEOPLE THEY DON'T REALLY LISTEN

212 *Scatology was the way we wanted it* . . . Maurizio Pustianaz, *Maelzel* fanzine, 1986

214 *'Tainted Love' was the most successful song* . . . Tim Stark, *EB Metronom Musikmagazin*, 1987

214 *We did 'Tainted Love' because it's a good song* . . . Geoff Rushton to Tom Vague, 1985

214 *We grew up during the end of the Labour government* . . . Graham Cunnington, Angus Farquhar, and Paul Jamrozy, *Test Dept: Total State Machine* (PC Press, 2015)

223 *There's only one thing that we did* . . . Geoff Rushton to Tom Vague, 1985

228 *Somebody had the bright idea that I should* . . . Marc Almond, *Tainted Life*

09 1986: I'VE FLOWN AROUND THE WORLD STANDING ON THE WING OF A JET

235 *The whole foray into industrial dance music* . . . Nick Soulsby, *Swans: Sacrifice & Transcendence* (Jawbone Press, 2018)

241 *The Horse Rotorvator was this vision I'd had* . . . David Keenan, 'Coil Interview Transcript—Threshold House, 21/7/98 15:00–17:00', Brainwashed.com

241 *Everyone says [Horse Rotorvator] is our best album* . . . David Keenan, 'Coil Interview Transcript—Threshold House, 21/7/98 15:00–17:00'

247 *I wasn't involved until quite late in the project* . . . Peter 'Sleazy' Christopherson to Suki, 1987

247 *Matt had gone from being* . . . Jake Bickerton(director), *The The—Infected: The Movie (A Short Documentary)* (2017)

248 *Going all that way with camera crews and people* . . . Peter 'Sleazy' Christopherson to Suki

249 *The skill is to is to exploit situations* . . . Peter 'Sleazy' Christopherson to Suki

249 *We decided to shoot 'Out Of The Blue'* . . . Jake Bickerton(director), *The The—Infected: The Movie (A Short Documentary)*

250 *I didn't go [on the shoots]* . . . Andy 'Dog' Johnson to Suki

250 *For 'Twilight Of A Champion', we went* . . . Jake Bickerton(director), *The The—Infected: The Movie (A Short Documentary)*

14 1996–99: I'M NOT THE KIND OF PERSON TO HIDE WHEN I CAN FIGHT

311 *The album began with the title* . . . Marc Almond, *Tainted Life*

328 *You have to be prepared to be knifed* . . . Pierre Perrone, 'Stevo: Bizzare After All These Years'

15 2000–22: ALL MY EXOTIC GESTURES NO LONGER IN DEMAND

339 *I've never been sued by an artist* . . . Pierre Perrone, 'Stevo: Bizzare After All These Years'

343 *Soft Cell had been invited to launch a new* . . . Dave Ball, *Electronic Boy*

16 CONCLUSION: IF YOU CAN'T PLEASE YOURSELF YOU CAN'T, PLEASE YOUR SOUL

363 *We have to recognise Stevo for his musical passion* . . . Graham Cunnington, Angus Farquhar, and Paul Jamrozy, *Test Dept*

ACKNOWLEDGEMENTS

Hannah, Theo, and Sam, for your love and patience; Mum, Dad, Charlotte, Owen, and Russell for your support over the years; Brian and Mark (The Brothers Of Mercy) for being there then, and for still being here now; Grant, Liam, Mikey, and Simon (The Post-Punk Dads' Listening Club)—I'll stop banging on about it now; Tom Seabrook for having faith in the book and, like all the best editors, making it better; Karl O'Connor for the encouragement as well as the soundtrack; Peter Ashworth for the pictures and generosity of spirit; Clive Coward and Simon Dell for access to their archives; Nick Soulsby and Tom Vague for the Coil quotes; and Chris Smith, Gillian Glover, Fiona Glyn-Jones, Mark Langthorne, Jessica Lord, Steve Malins, and Zoe Miller for the interviews. Finally, thanks to Ø, without whom . . .